"Bascomb blends the material into a narrative that sounds like a Jason Bourne movie, as operatives track, find, and then capture their man."
— *Philadelphia Inquirer*

"Gripping." — *Economist*

"[Bascomb] uses anecdotes and you-are-there details to create scenes of occasional humor, suspense, and horror . . . One finishes reading *Hunting Eichmann* with a sense justice was served and that the good guys won." — *Pittsburgh Post-Gazette*

"Fast-paced and suspenseful." — *Oregonian*

"Groundbreaking . . . *Hunting Eichmann* provides an expansive view into the personalities of the hunted and hunters." — *Jerusalem Post*

"Stunning." — *U.S. News & World Report*

"Israel's capture of Nazi war criminal Adolf Eichmann has become the stuff of legend . . . Neal Bascomb's account sheds some new light on the 1960 arrest." — *New York Post*

"Chilling, authoritative, and timely . . . An exhaustive, well-researched volume that supersedes prior accounts." — *Washington Times*

"An exciting thriller that grips the reader's interest until the very last page . . . an impressive achievement." — *Jewish Advocate*

"Admirably researched and relentlessly paced, *Hunting Eichmann* brings us closer to the manhunt for the Holocaust's architect than we've ever come before."
— Stephan Talty, author of *Empire of Blue Water*

HUNTING EICHMANN

BOOKS BY NEAL BASCOMB

*Higher: A Historic Race to the Sky
and the Making of a City*

*The Perfect Mile:
Three Athletes, One Goal, and Less Than
Four Minutes to Achieve It*

*Red Mutiny: Eleven Fateful
Days on the Battleship* Potemkin

*Hunting Eichmann: How a Band of
Survivors and a Young Spy Agency Chased
Down the World's Most Notorious Nazi*

HUNTING EICHMANN

HOW A BAND OF SURVIVORS
AND A YOUNG SPY AGENCY
CHASED DOWN THE WORLD'S
MOST NOTORIOUS NAZI

Neal Bascomb

MARINER BOOKS
HOUGHTON MIFFLIN HARCOURT
BOSTON ■ NEW YORK

First Mariner Books edition 2010

Copyright © 2009 by Neal Bascomb

www.hmhbooks.com

Library of Congress Cataloging-in-Publication Data
Bascomb, Neal.
Hunting Eichmann : how a band of survivors and
a young spy agency chased down the world's
most notorious Nazi / Neal Bascomb.
p. cm.
ISBN 978-0-618-85867-5
1. Eichmann, Adolf, 1906–1962. 2. War criminals —
Germany — Biography. 3. Fugitives from justice — Argentina
— Biography. 4. Secret service — Israel. I. Title.
DD247.E5B37 2009
943.086092 — dc22   2008035757

ISBN 978-0-547-24802-8 (pbk.)

Book design by Melissa Lotfy

Diagram by Michael Prendergast

Printed in the United States of America

DOC 10 9 8 7 6 5 4 3 2 1

Justice should not only be done, but should manifestly and undoubtedly be seen to be done.

—Lord Chief Justice Gordon Hewart, 1924

. . . And you have come, our precious enemy,
Forsaken creature, man ringed by death.
What can you say now, before our assembly?

—Primo Levi, "For Adolf Eichmann," 1960

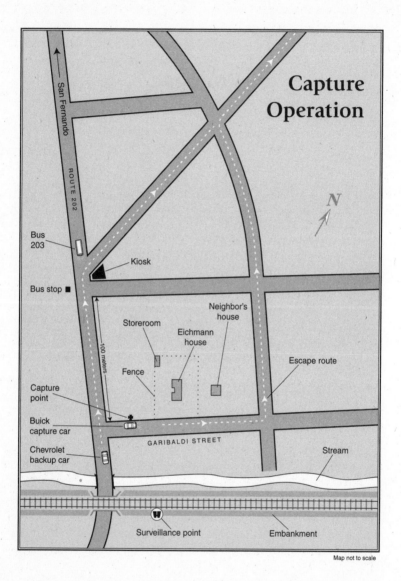

Capture Operation

San Fernando

ROUTE 202

Bus 203

Kiosk

Bus stop ■

100 meters

Storeroom

Neighbor's house

Eichmann house

Fence

Escape route

Capture point

Buick capture car

Chevrolet backup car

GARIBALDI STREET

Stream

Surveillance point

Embankment

N

Map not to scale

Prologue

THE MAN FROM BUS 203 WAS LATE.

For three weeks now the team tracking him had watched their target return from work to his small brick bunker of a house on Garibaldi Street. Every night was the same: At 7:40 P.M., bus 203 stopped at the kiosk on the narrow highway 110 yards from the corner of Garibaldi Street; the man exited the bus; another passenger, a woman, also exited at the same stop. They separated. Sometimes the man stopped at the kiosk for a pack of cigarettes, but this never took more than a minute. Then he crossed the street and walked toward his house. If a car approached, he turned on his flashlight — one end red, the other white — to signal his presence. When he reached his property, he circled the house once before entering, as if checking that all was secure. Inside, he greeted his wife and young son, lit a few additional kerosene lamps, and then sat down for dinner. He was a man of precise routines and schedules. His predictability made him vulnerable.

But on this night, Wednesday, May 11, 1960, 7:40 passed, and neither bus 203 nor the man was in sight. The team waited in two cars. One black Chevrolet sedan was parked on the edge of Route 202, facing toward the bus stop. Once the man showed, if he showed, the driver in the backup car would flick on his headlights to blind him before he turned left toward his house. The capture car, a black Buick limousine, was stationed on Garibaldi Street between the highway and the man's home. The driver, in a chauffeur's uniform, had popped the hood to give the impression that the limousine had broken down. Two other men stood outside the car in the cold, windy night, pretending to fiddle with the engine. These two were the strongmen, tasked with grabbing the target and getting him into the car — as quietly and quickly as possible.

At 7:44, a bus finally approached on Route 202, but it drove straight past the kiosk. The team could only wait so long in this isolated neighborhood on the northern outskirts of Buenos Aires, Argentina, without attracting too much attention. There was only a scattering of houses on the flat, nearly treeless plain. Cars foreign to the neighborhood stood out.

The team leader, hidden in the limousine's back seat, insisted that they stay despite the risks. There was no argument from the team. Not now, not at this critical hour. The man must not be allowed to elude capture.

Exactly fifteen years previously, in the last days of the Third Reich, SS lieutenant colonel Adolf Eichmann, chief of Department IVB_4 of the Reich Security Main Office and the operational manager of the Nazi genocide, had escaped into the Austrian Alps. He had been listed as killed in action by the woman who now impatiently waited for her husband's return from work. He had been sought by Allied investigators and independent Nazi-hunters such as Simon Wiesenthal. He had reportedly been executed by Jewish avengers. He had been rumored to be living in West Germany, England, Kuwait, the United States, and even Israel. His trail had gone from hot to cold to hot again.

He had been so successful at hiding his identity that the Mossad agents now in position on Garibaldi Street were still not 100 percent certain that the man they had come to capture was actually Eichmann. A contingency plan, one of many, was in place if it turned out not to be him. Nonetheless, they were sufficiently convinced to stage a dangerous operation on foreign soil involving more than ten agents, including the head of the Israeli secret service himself. They had read Eichmann's file and been thoroughly briefed on his role in the mass murder of Jews. They were professionals, but it was impossible for them to be impartial about this mission. Since arriving in Argentina, one agent kept seeing the faces of the members of his family who had been killed in the Holocaust.

They could wait a few more minutes for bus 203.

At 8:05, the team saw another faint halo of light in the distance. Moments later, the bus's headlights shone brightly down the highway, piercing the darkness. Brakes screeched, the bus door clattered open, and the two passengers stepped down onto the street. As the bus pulled away, the woman turned off to the left, moving away from the man. The man headed for Garibaldi Street, bent forward in the wind. His hands were stuffed into his coat. Thunder cracked in the distance, warning of a storm. It was time for Adolf Eichmann to answer for what he had done.

1

OUTSIDE MAUTHAUSEN, a concentration camp built beside a granite quarry on the northern edge of the Danube River in upper Austria, Obersturmbannführer Adolf Eichmann stood at the head of a long column of 140 command cars and trucks. It was noon on Sunday, March 19, 1944, and he was thirty-eight years old to the day.

Dressed in his pale gray SS uniform, he looked to be a man with the sympathies and humor of a piece of granite. He had fine, dark blond hair, narrow lips, a long nose, and grayish blue eyes. His skull turned sharply inward at his temples, a feature only accentuated by the peaked cap now drawn over his head. Of medium height, he held his trim frame slightly forward, as if he was a tracker on a fresh trail. As he watched his men prepare to move out, the left corner of his mouth twitched unconsciously, drawing his face into a temporary scowl.

The convoy carrying more than five hundred members of the SS was ready. Down the line of vehicles, engines rumbled to life, and black exhaust spewed out across the road. Eichmann climbed into his Mercedes staff car and signaled for the motorcycle troops leading the column to advance toward Budapest, following the trail blazed by the First Panzer Division.

Twelve hours before, eleven Wehrmacht divisions had stormed across the Hungarian border while paratroopers had dropped into the historic capital city to seize strategic government buildings and positions. Adolf Hitler had ordered the occupation of the country to prevent the Axis partner from pursuing an armistice with the Allies now that the Red Army was advancing from the east.

As the column of vehicles sped away from Mauthausen, Eichmann expected that in a few months, this camp and its satellites would be filled with more Jewish slave laborers to work in the quarries and surrounding munitions, steel, and airplane factories. "Send down the Master in person," Reichsführer-SS Heinrich Himmler had ordered, referring to Eichmann in his instructions to comb Hungary from east to west of its Jews. Those who were physically fit were to be delivered to labor camps for "destruction through work"; those who were not were to be exterminated immediately. Eichmann's mission was a secondary, but critical, one in the invasion of Hungary. He inflated with pride at the confidence Himmler had shown in him by charging him to oversee the operation personally. Eichmann would stop at nothing to live up to his new moniker, "the Master." He gathered all of his senior, most effective officers from across Europe to aid in his efforts.

With the German army already encircling Budapest, the SS column met little resistance and made easy progress into Hungary. Along the 250-mile route to the capital, Eichmann's staff felt confident enough to take a break and gather around him to toast his birthday with a bottle of rum. Besides this stop and two for refueling, Eichmann had nothing to do on the journey but chain-smoke and further consider his strategy to eliminate 725,000 Jews from Hungary as rapidly as possible, without any uprisings (as had happened in Poland) or mass escapes (as in Denmark). Those two operations colored his thoughts as the mile-long convoy advanced down the road with a thunderous roar.

In devising his plan for Hungary over the past weeks, Eichmann had been able to draw on his eight years of experience overseeing Jewish affairs for the SS. As chief of Department IVB_4, he was responsible for executing Hitler's policy to annihilate the Jews. Eichmann ran his office as if he was the division head of an international conglomerate. He set ambitious targets; he recruited and delegated to effective subordinates; he traveled frequently to keep tabs on their progress; he studied what worked and failed and adjusted accordingly; he made sure to account to his bosses in charts and figures how effective he had been. His position required navigating frequent policy changes, legal restrictions, and turf wars. And although he wore a uniform, he measured success not in battles won but instead in schedules met, quotas filled, efficiencies realized, guidelines followed, and units moved. Operations he had managed in Austria, Germany, France, Italy, the Netherlands, Belgium, Denmark, Slovakia, Romania, and Poland had revealed to him the best methods to realize this success. Now he intended to bring these to Hungary.

The first stage of his plan focused on isolating the Jews. Orders would be issued to require the wearing of the Yellow Star, to prohibit travel and the use of phones and radios, and to ban Jews from the civil service and scores of other professions. He had more than a hundred such measures aimed at identifying and removing the Jews from Hungarian society. The next stage would secure their wealth for the Third Reich's coffers. Bank accounts would be frozen. Factories and businesses owned by Jews would be expropriated and the assets of every single individual plundered, down even to their ration cards. Next came ghettoization, uprooting Jews from their homes and concentrating them together until the final, fourth stage could be effected: deportation to the camps. Once they arrived there, another SS department was responsible for their fate.

To prevent any escapes or uprisings, Eichmann intended to launch a campaign of deception in all four stages. He planned on meeting face-to-face with Jewish leaders to reassure them that the measures restricting their community were only temporary necessities of war. As long as these leaders, organized in a council, saw to their implementation, he would promise that no harm would come to their community. Bribes would be taken from the Jews on the promise of better treatment, a move that not only extorted more Jewish wealth but also gave the impression that individuals could be saved if they met German demands. Eichmann also thought it best to initiate stages three and four in the most remote districts, leaving Budapest, where there was the greatest chance of an organized resistance, until last. Even when the Jews were forced onto the trains, they were to be told that they were being relocated for their own safety or to supply labor for Germany. These deceptions might be seen for what they were, but they would buy enough time and acquiescence that brute force could do the rest.

For all these plans, Eichmann knew he needed the assistance and manpower of the Hungarian authorities. Given his limited staff of 150, winning their cooperation was going to be his first order of business once he arrived in Budapest. Otherwise, his shipment schedules for Auschwitz, Mauthausen, and other camps would run late.

When they reached Budapest, the German army was in the midst of taking positions throughout the streets while squadrons of fighter planes with black crosses on their wings buzzed low over the Danube. Gestapo agents fanned out across the city to arrest prominent Hungarians who might resist the occupation. There were hundreds of Jews on their lists. Eichmann established his command at the grand Hotel Majestic, which stood on a forested hill west of the old city of Buda. Sentry posts and three rings of barbed wire were placed around the hotel, while guards with German shepherds were brought in to patrol the grounds.

Fearing assassination by Jewish partisans and Allied commandos, Eichmann was very careful with his security. He preferred to remain in the background, exercising his authority through his subordinates, and he rarely allowed his photograph to be taken. As a precaution, he always carried with him in his staff car an arsenal of submachine guns and grenades.

In his new headquarters, the Master spent the first of many sleepless nights putting together all the elements of the machine that would, stage by stage, systematically exploit and then remove every single Jew in Hungary. In his mind, they were the enemies of the Reich, and like a cancer, they needed to be rooted out and destroyed.

At the crack of dawn on April 15, the last day of Passover, this machine came to the door of the family of Zeev Sapir. Zeev was twenty years old and lived with his parents and five younger siblings in the village of Dobradovo, located ten miles outside Munkács, a city in the mountainous Carpatho-Ruthenia district of northeastern Hungary.

Gendarmes roused the family and ordered them to pack. They could bring food, clothes, and bedding, but no more than fifty kilograms per person. The few valuable family heirlooms they owned were confiscated before they were driven into the streets. Gendarmes then bullied and whipped the community of 103 people to Munkács on foot. The very young and old were carried in horse-drawn hay carts.

In the month since the Germans had occupied Hungary, Sapir had endured with dignity the many strictures placed on the Jews. There had always been anti-Jewish fervor among the people of Carpatho-Ruthenia. Born into a strongly Orthodox family, Sapir grew up being called "Jew-boy" by other children and had lived through the various regimes that had controlled his corner of the world during his short life. Whether Czech, Hungarian, or Ukrainian, they had all oppressed his people. The Hungarians had taken his elder brother away to a forced labor camp a few years before. At first the Germans proved no worse. Zeev wore his Star of David along with the rest of his community. He maneuvered around the curfews and travel restrictions to continue his black-market trade in flour that supported his family. The other measures imposed by the new government, such as press restrictions, job expulsions, prohibitions from public places, and seizures of Jewish property, among many others, had not had much immediate effect on the poor, rural village that was his home.

Now, however, he was scared. His family reached Munkács in the evening, exhausted from carrying their baggage during the long march. The streets were packed with men, women, and children, all moving in the same direction. They arrived at the brickyards of a former brick factory, their new home. Over the next several days, 14,000 Jews from the city and surrounding regions were crammed into the ghetto. They were told that they had been removed from the "military operational zone" to protect them from the advancing Russians.

The news was no comfort to Sapir, whose family lived in a makeshift hut with little food other than spoonfuls of potato soup served from bathtubs. There was even less water, the ghetto having access to only two water faucets. As the days and nights passed, the crying of children from hunger and thirst almost became too much for Sapir. Then came the torrential rains. Exposed under the open sky, there was no escaping the downpour that turned the brickyards into a mud pit and fostered an epidemic of typhoid and pneumonia. Somehow Sapir, his parents, and his four younger brothers (ages fifteen, eleven, six, and three) and sister (age eight) avoided getting sick.

By day, the Hungarian gendarmes played their cruel games, forcing work gangs to transfer piles of bricks from one end of the ghetto to the other for no reason other than to exercise their power.

By his third week in the ghetto, Sapir had no idea how long they were to stay there or where they would be sent afterward. One ventured such questions at the risk of a severe beating. Sapir read in a local newspaper he was passed that a high-ranking SS officer would soon inspect their ghetto. Perhaps this German officer, whose name was Eichmann, would provide an answer.

On Eichmann's arrival, the entire population of the ghetto was ordered to gather in a semicircle in the main yard. Surrounded by an entourage of thirty Hungarian and SS officers, Eichmann strode into the yard wearing square riding pants and black boots and cap. In a strong, clear voice, he announced to the prisoners: "Jews: You have nothing to worry about. We want only the best for you. You'll leave here shortly and be sent to very fine places indeed. You will work there, your wives will stay at home, and your children will go to school. You will have wonderful lives." Sapir had no choice other than to believe him.

Soon after Eichmann's visit, on May 22, the trains arrived on the tracks that led to the former brick factory. Brandishing whips, blackjacks, and Tommy guns, guards forced them from the ghetto to the train tracks. Every last man, woman, and child was stripped, their clothes and few belongings searched for any remaining valuables. Those who hesitated to follow orders were beaten miserably. The terror and confusion were profound.

A guard shredded Sapir's personal documents and then returned his clothes. After dressing, he stayed with his family and the others from his village as they were hustled into a cattle car. All 103 Jews from his village were crammed into a single car that would have fit 8 cows. They were provided with a bucket of water and an empty bucket for a toilet. The guards slammed the door shut, casting them into darkness, and then padlocked the door.

The train rattled to a start. Nobody knew where they were headed. As the train passed small railway stations along the way, someone attempted to read the platform signs to get some idea of their direction, but it was too difficult to see through the car's single small window, which was strung with barbed wire to prevent escape. By the end of the first day, the heat, stench, hunger, and thirst became unbearable. Sapir's young siblings wept for water and something to eat; his mother soothed them with whispers of "Go to sleep, my child." Sapir stood most of the time. There was little room to sit, and what room there was, was reserved for the weakest. Villagers of all ages fainted from exhaustion; several died from suffocation. At one point, the train stopped. The door was opened, and the guard asked if they wanted any water. Sapir scrambled out to fill the bucket at the station. Just as he came back, the guard knocked the bucket brimming with water from his hands. They would have to do without.

Four days after leaving Munkács, the train came to a screeching stop. It was late at night, and when the cattle car door crashed open, the surrounding searchlights burned the passengers' eyes. SS guards shouted, "Out! Get out! Quick!" Dogs barked as the Jews poured from the train, emaciated copies of their former selves. A shop owner from Sapir's village turned back toward the car: he had left behind his prayer shawl. A man in a striped uniform, who was carrying away their baggage, pointed toward a chimney belching smoke. "What do you need your prayer shawl for? You'll soon be in there."

At that moment, Sapir caught the stink of burning flesh. He now understood what awaited them in this place called Auschwitz. An SS officer divided the arrivals into two lines with a flick of his hand or a sharply spoken "Left" or "Right." When Sapir and his family reached the officer, Sapir was directed to the left, his parents and siblings to the right. He struggled to stay with them but was beaten by the guards. Sapir never saw his family again. As he was led down a dusty road bordered by a barbed-wire fence, his battle for survival had only just begun.

Six weeks later, at 8:30 on the morning of Sunday, July 2, 1944, air raid sirens rang throughout Budapest, the Queen of the Danube.

Soon after, the first of 750 Allied heavy bombers led by the U.S. Fifteenth Air Force released their explosives onto the city. Antiaircraft guns and German fighter planes attempted to thwart the surprise attack, but they were overwhelmed by wave after wave of bombers and their escorts. Eichmann hunkered down in his two-story hilltop villa, formerly owned by a Jewish industrialist, as Budapest was set ablaze. Four hours later, the last of the bombers disappeared on the horizon. Columns of smoke rose throughout Budapest. The saturated bombing flattened whole neighborhoods. Refineries, factories, fuel storage tanks, railway yards, and scores of other sites were destroyed. Thousands of civilians died.

Emerging unscathed from his villa, Eichmann saw Allied leaflets drifting down from the sky and landing on his lawn. The enemy propaganda revealed how the Soviets were pushing east through Romania, while in the west, the Allies had landed in France and Italy and were driving toward Germany. The Third Reich was facing defeat, the leaflets promised, and all resistance should be stopped. Further, President Franklin Roosevelt had declared that the persecution of Hungarian Jews and other minorities was being followed with "extreme gravity" and must be halted. Those responsible would be hunted down and punished. Neither an Allied bombing nor a threat by an American president nor even Hitler himself was going to divert Eichmann from completing his masterpiece, the destruction of Hungarian Jewry, which had begun in earnest with the deportations from Munkács.

Eichmann left his villa to assess any damage to his headquarters at the Hotel Majestic. His achievements to date were fresh in his mind. By the first week of July, the plan that he had crafted had shown itself to be monumentally effective. Five of the six operational zones where Jews were slated for deportation, totaling 437,402 "units," had been cleared by the Hungarian authorities, who had proved to be more than willing accomplices in his designs. Every day, an average of four trains carrying a load of 3,500 were received at Auschwitz-Birkenau. Only 10 percent of arrivals were deemed fit enough for the labor camps. The balance earned "special treatment" in the gas chambers. Eichmann's early coordination with the camp's commandant, Rudolf

Höss, ensured that the extermination camp was ready for the numbers to be processed. The staff had been increased, the ramps expanded, a new three-track railway system built, and the crematoriums updated.

Only the Jews of Budapest remained in Hungary. They had already been relocated into designated houses marked with a yellow star, and a curfew prohibited them from leaving these abodes except between 2:00 and 5:00 P.M. Police and gendarmes from the outlying provinces were in place to assist in the upcoming deportation, and the trains were being scheduled.

Still, there were forces gathering against Eichmann's plans, and with the Allied advance on both fronts and now the attack on Budapest, these forces had some teeth. Over the past few weeks, international protests — from Roosevelt to Pope Pius XII to the king of Sweden — had urged Admiral Miklós Horthy, the regent of Hungary (whom Hitler had kept in a figurehead position), to end the actions against the Jews. Horthy was receptive to these calls, not only because of what he had recently learned about the extermination camps from a report by two Auschwitz escapees but also because of the recent coup attempt by Hungarian state secretary László Baky, a key ally of Eichmann's in the Interior Ministry. Five days after the Allied bombing, on July 7, Horthy suspended the deportations and dismissed Baky and his cronies from their positions.

Incensed at the interruption, Eichmann nonetheless ordered his deputies to send 7,500 Jews held in a brick factory north of the city to Auschwitz. He met no resistance. A week later, he attempted the same with 1,500 Jews at the internment camp Kistarcsa, eleven miles outside Budapest. After the city's Jewish Council learned of the train's departure, they convinced Horthy to halt it en route to the extermination camp and return to Kistarcsa. Berlin had yet to respond to Horthy's suspension of the deportations, but Eichmann did not care. He was not about to allow the regent to block his plans. On July 19, he summoned the Jewish Council to his office. While one of his underlings kept the members of the council occupied, Eichmann sent SS troops to Kistarcsa and brutally forced the Jews back onto the train. Only when it crossed the border into Poland did Eichmann release the council.

That same week, Hitler weighed in on the conflict with Horthy. Wanting to keep him in alliance with Germany, Hitler offered to allow 40,000 Budapest Jews to immigrate to Palestine, but the rest were to be deported to the camps as planned. This did not please Eichmann, who did not want one single Jew to escape his hands. He strode into the office of the German plenipotentiary in Hungary.

"Under no circumstances does the SS Reichsführer Himmler agree to the immigration of Hungarian Jews to Palestine," Eichmann raged. "The Jews in question are without exception important biological material, many of them veteran Zionists, whose emigration is most undesirable. I will submit the matter to the SS Reichsführer and, if necessary, seek a new decision from the Führer."

The plenipotentiary and Berlin were unmoved. With the war going poorly for Germany, many in the Reich leadership, including Himmler, viewed the Jews as much-needed bargaining chips. Eichmann thought this was weakness, even though he was worried about his own future, admitting to an SS colleague that he feared that his name would top the war criminal lists announced by the Allies because of the unusually public role he was playing in Hungary.

In August, when the Russians conquered Romania, Himmler shelved the plans for the deportations completely. Eichmann was ordered to disband his unit in Hungary, but still he did not relent. Except for a short mission to Romania, he lingered in Budapest for the next two months, waiting for his chance to return to his plans.

He rode horses and took his all-terrain vehicle out to the countryside. He spent long weekends at a castle owned by one of his Hungarian counterparts or stayed at his two-story villa, with its lavish gardens and retinue of servants. He dined at fashionable Budapest restaurants and drank himself into a stupor at cabarets. With his wife and three sons in Prague, he kept two steady mistresses, one a rich, thirty-year-old divorcée, the other a Hungarian count's consort. Eichmann had enjoyed some of these pursuits since first coming to Budapest, but now he had more time than ever to indulge in them. Even so, he was increasingly edgy at the progress of the war. He smoked heavily and often barked at his underlings for no reason.

In late October, with the Russians driving only a hundred miles from Budapest and Horthy recently deposed as regent, Eichmann made one last bid to finish what he had started in Hungary. "You see, I'm back again," he declared to the capital's Jewish leaders. He secured permission from the German plenipotentiary to send 50,000 Jews to labor camps in Austria. The fact that there were no available trains to take them on the 125-mile journey, because of Allied bombing raids, did not deter him. As winter settled in, he sent the first 27,000 Jews, including children and the infirm, on a forced march. With few provisions and no shelter, scores began falling behind within a few days. They were either shot or left to die in roadside ditches. Even the Auschwitz commandant Höss, who witnessed the scene while driving between Budapest and Vienna, balked at the conditions the Jews endured. It was intended slaughter, something that Himmler had decreed must stop. When Eichmann was ordered by a superior officer to cease the march, he ignored the order. At last, in early December, Himmler summoned Eichmann to his headquarters in the Black Forest. Before they met, Eichmann cleaned his nicotine-stained fingers with a pumice stone and lemon, knowing well the Reichsführer-SS's aversion to cigarettes.

"If until now you have exterminated Jews," Himmler said in a tone laced with anger, "from now on, I order you, as I do now, you must be a fosterer of Jews . . . If you are not able to do that, you must tell me so!"

"Yes, Reichsführer," Eichmann answered, knowing that any other answer or action on his part was suicide.

On a late December morning in 1944, the winter wind cut through a wooden hut at Jaworzno, an Auschwitz satellite camp. On his bunk, Zeev Sapir shivered constantly. He had swapped his extra shirt for a loaf of bread, and his scant remaining clothes hung loosely on his emaciated body.

At 4:30 A.M., a siren sounded. Sapir jumped out of bed to avoid the rain of blows he would endure if he delayed. He hurried outside with the hundred other prisoners from his hut, exposed now to the bitter wind and the cold as they awaited roll call. Then he began his twelve-hour shift at the Dachsgrube coal mines. He was required to fill forty-five wagons of coal per shift or receive twenty-five lashes. This would have been difficult if he had been in the best of health, but after a breakfast of only one cup of coffee and one-sixteenth portion of a loaf of bread, every shift was a Herculean effort. Sapir often fell short.

That evening, when Sapir returned to the camp, exhausted and with his skin coated with coal dust, he and the other 3,000 prisoners were ordered to start walking. The Red Army was advancing into Poland, the SS guards told them. Sapir did not much care. He was told to walk; he walked. This attitude—and the hand of fate—had kept him alive for the past eight months.

Once Sapir had arrived at Auschwitz from Hungary and been separated from his family, he had been beaten, herded off to a barracks, stripped, inspected, deloused, shaved, and tattooed on his left forearm with the sequence A3800. The next morning, he had been forced to work in the gas chambers where he suspected his family had been killed during the night. Sapir dragged the dead from the chambers and placed them on their backs in the yard, where a barber cut off their hair and a dental mechanic ripped out any gold teeth. Then he carried the corpses to large pits, where they were stacked like logs and burned to ashes. A channel running through the middle of the pit drained the fat exuding from the bodies. That fat was used to stoke the crematorium fires. The thick smoke, dark red flames, and acrid fumes poisoned his soul.

Sapir lost track of time, unaware of the day of the week or the hour of the day. He knew only night and day. Somehow he escaped execution, the fate of most workers tasked to operate the gas chambers and crematoriums. The Germans regularly killed these workers to keep their activities secret. Sapir, however, was sent to Jaworzno, where he would endure a different set of savageries.

Now, filing out of the satellite camp, Sapir and the other prisoners trudged through deep snow. They walked for two days, not knowing where they were going. Anyone who slowed down or stopped for a rest was shot. As night fell on the second day, they reached Bethune, a town in Upper Silesia, and were told to sit by the side of the road.

The commanding SS officer strode down the line, saying, "Whoever is unable to continue may remain here, and he will be transferred by truck." Sapir had long since learned not to believe any such promises, but he was too tired, too cold, and too indifferent to care. Two hundred of the prisoners stayed put, while the others marched away. Sapir slept where he fell in the snow. In the morning, the group was ordered out to a field with shovels and pickaxes and told to dig. The earth was frozen, but they dug and dug, even though they knew they were digging their own graves.

That evening, they were taken to the dining hall at a nearby mine. All the windows had been blown out by air raids. A number of SS officers followed them inside, led by a deputy officer named Lausmann. "Yes, I know you are so hungry," he said in a sympathetic tone as a large pot was brought into the hall.

Sapir gathered with the other prisoners, starved and almost too weary to stand. The most desperate pushed to the front, hoping for food. They were killed first. Lausmann grabbed one prisoner after the next, leaned him over the pot, and shot him in the neck. He fired and fired. In the middle of the massacre, a young prisoner began making a speech to whoever would listen. "The German people will answer to history for this," he declared before receiving a bullet as well.

Lausmann continued to fire until there were only eleven prisoners left, Sapir among them. Before Sapir could be summoned forward, Lausmann's superior called him out of the hall. The SS guards took the remaining prisoners by train to the Gleiwitz concentration camp, where they were thrown into a cellar filled with potatoes. Ravenous, they ate the frozen potatoes. In the morning, they were marched out to the forest with thousands of others. Suddenly, machine guns opened fire, mowing down the prisoners. Sapir ran through the trees until his legs gave out. He was knocked out by the fall. He awakened alone, with a bloody foot and only one shoe. When the Red Army found him, he weighed sixty-four pounds. His skin was as yellow and dry as parchment. It was January 1945. He would not regain anything close to physical health until April.

Sapir would never forget the promise Eichmann had made in the Munkács ghetto or the call to justice by his fellow prisoner the moment before his execution. But many, many years would pass before he was brought forward to remember these things.

2

AS THE WAR DREW to a close, the world was about to come face-to-face with the vestiges of the horror that Sapir had survived. On April 12, 1945, the Allies opened a road to Berlin. The Rhine River had been crossed weeks earlier, and the British and Canadian armies stormed east across northern Germany in their Sherman tanks. The American armies had encircled the Ruhr Valley, cutting off Hitler's industrial complex and opening up a huge hole in the western front. Only a handful of ragtag German divisions stood between eighty-five Allied divisions and Berlin. A spearhead of the U.S. Ninth Army was already establishing bridgeheads on the Elbe River, just sixty miles from the capital of the Third Reich. To the east of Berlin, 1.25 million Russian soldiers with 22,000 pieces of artillery were on the banks of the Oder River, a mere thirty-five miles away from the capital.

While these forces mustered for the final defeat of Germany, two Wehrmacht colonels flying a white flag from their Mercedes approached the forward headquarters of the British 159th Battalion. They came with an offer of a local cease-fire in order to hand over control of Bergen-Belsen, a concentration camp plagued with typhus located a few miles from the advancing British tanks. That same day, General Dwight Eisenhower, supreme commander of the Allied Expeditionary Force, entered the work camp near the village of Ohrdurf. He shuddered at what he saw.

Reports of the genocidal acts committed by the Germans had reached the Allies over the course of the war. As early as the summer of 1941, code breakers at Britain's Bletchley Park had intercepted transmissions that described in detail the mass executions of Jews in the Soviet Union. In 1942, Witold Pilecki, a member of the Polish resistance movement, had put himself in a position to be thrown into Auschwitz, from which he periodically sent out reports that reached Western governments. Two Slovakian Jews had escaped from Auschwitz-Birkenau at the cusp of the extermination of the Hungarian Jews, and they had provided detailed reports on the number of transports coming to the camp, the nationalities of the arrivals, and their fate in the gas chambers. It was their account that had led to the spate of protests to Admiral Horthy against the Hungarian deportations in 1944, including one from President Roosevelt that stated, "To the Hitlerites, subordinates, functionaries, and satellites, to the German people and all other peoples under the Nazi yoke, we have made clear our determination to punish all participation in these acts of savagery."

Roosevelt had made a similar declaration as early as October 1942. Two months later, British foreign secretary Anthony Eden had announced to the House of Commons that Hitler's aim was to exterminate the Jewish people. The British view at that time, penned by Winston Churchill in a note to his cabinet in 1943, was that after arrest, the German leaders should have a brief trial to ensure their identity and, six hours later, be "shot to death . . . without reference to higher authority." Curiously, it was Joseph Stalin, no stranger to kangaroo courts, who had reined in Churchill with the help of Roosevelt. On a visit by Churchill to Moscow in October 1944, Stalin had insisted that no executions should occur without a fair trial, "otherwise the world would say we were afraid to try them." Still, as the war neared its close, Allied leaders continued to jostle over how best to bring the Nazis to justice.

Plans to capture these criminals were barely in preparation. First, the Allies were having difficulty settling on who should be targeted as a war criminal. The British held the narrow view that the Allies should go after only those major German figures whose "notorious offenses . . . have no special geographical location." The Americans and Russians wanted a much broader definition. This resulted in a confusing number of war criminal lists. Not only did the Allies lack one definitive list, but more important, by April 1945 they had organized only seven investigative teams, numbering roughly five officers and seven enlisted men each, to find these war criminals. In contrast, an Anglo-American operation code-named Paperclip recruited 3,000 investigators to spread throughout the Third Reich to arrest top German scientists and to collect technological information before the Russians got their hands on both. Those charged with tracking down the war criminals did not have so much as an operational code name. Such were the priorities of Washington and London as the war in Europe drew to a close.

Despite the intelligence reports General Eisenhower had read on the German atrocities, he found himself completely unprepared for Ohrdurf. Guided by former inmates, he and his staff saw men in the hospital who had been brutally tortured and were starving, lying shoulder to shoulder, expecting nothing more than death to arrive. In a basement, he saw a gallows where prisoners had been hung by piano wire long enough that their toes touched the floor, delaying death but prolonging the agony that preceded it. In one of the yards, he saw some 40 corpses, riddled with lice, stacked in rows. In an adjoining field, he saw 3,200 more corpses, many with gunshot wounds to the back of the head, next to a pyre of wood clearly intended to destroy all traces of their existence. General Omar Bradley, who accompanied Eisenhower, could not even speak; the hard-nosed General George Patton vomited against a wall. As he left Ohrdurf, Eisenhower told his officers, "I want every American unit not actually in the front lines to see this place. We are told that the American soldier does not know what he is fighting for. Now, at least, he will know what he is fighting *against.*" Once back at headquarters, the shaken supreme commander sent messages to Washington and London demanding that legislators and newspaper reporters come to Ohrdurf. He wanted these crimes documented.

Over the next several days, the Americans liberated larger camps such as Nordhausen and Buchenwald. On April 15, the British finally entered Bergen-Belsen, bringing reporters and cameramen with them to document the 60,000 "living skeletons" who staggered toward their jeeps. An *Evening Standard* journalist wrote, "The indignity of death above ground—the bared teeth, the revealed frame that should be sacred, and once was sacred to some loved one, the piled bodies in their ghastly grayness, the pitiable little thing with claws instead of a hand that was a baby, still within the protecting grasp of an emaciated bone that was once a mother's arm—all on the Nazi death heap." The photographs and newsreels from Bergen-Belsen and the camps that Eisenhower opened to reporters all made a huge impression on the public. The *Jewish Chronicle,* which had published details on Auschwitz after its liberation by the Russians months before, now asked, "Why have we had to wait till now for this widespread revulsion?"

Finally, the flesh-and-blood horror of the Final Solution was revealed, and vividly so, to the public and its leaders. With every day, more monstrous evidence was discovered and documented, and the pursuit of those responsible increased in importance.

By April 13, the once great capital of Germany was in ruins. Frequent air raids had devastated the city. Black smoke drifted through the streets, often obscuring the sun. The wailing of sirens was constant. Berliners threaded their way through the fog to their offices and factories and stood in long lines for food. Life went on. They greeted one another with the words "*Bleib übrig*": "Survive."

At 116 Kurfürstenstrasse, survival dominated the minds of the Gestapo. They had moved into the cavernous building of oversized rooms and marble stairwells where Eichmann had his office after incendiary bombs had ripped apart their main Prinz Albrecht Strasse headquarters. One afternoon Eichmann, who had returned to Berlin the previous December when the Russians had overrun Budapest, came across a number of his fellow Gestapo officers, crowded into a hall where, in the days when the Nazis were advancing across Europe, he used to play his violin accompanied by several of his staff. A table had been set up, and a department official, whose job was to issue forged papers, was taking notes on the new identity each officer wanted so that he could create employment certificates, company correspondence, and other papers. At the back of the hall, standing apart from the crush to get these papers, Eichmann looked on, disgusted by the scene of SS officers now looking to become insurance salesmen and the like to avoid arrest by the Allies.

His chief, Heinrich Müller, came to his side. "Well, Eichmann? What's the matter with you?"

"I don't need those papers." Eichmann patted his holstered Steyr pistol. "Look here: This is my passport. When I see no other way out, this is my last resort. I have no need for anything else."

"If we had had fifty Eichmanns, then we would have won the war automatically," Müller said. Eichmann inflated with pride at the comment.

Eichmann had romantic notions of holing up in his Berlin "foxlair." Since his return from Budapest, where he had narrowly escaped the Russian artillery on Christmas Eve, he had constructed a shelter underneath 116 Kurfürstenstrasse containing a generator, a ventilation system, and enough kerosene, first-aid supplies, water, and food to last several weeks. Outside, he had had his men turn the rubble into defensive positions with tank traps and sharpshooter nests. If worst came to worst, Eichmann had cyanide capsules on hand.

But his plan of holing up in his lair and waiting for the Allied advance was thwarted by Himmler, who had summoned Eichmann to his new headquarters in a castle outside the capital. The Reichsführer-SS, who was more eager than ever to negotiate with the Allies, had ordered Eichmann to assemble 1,200 of the most prominent Jews held in the Theresienstadt camp, northwest of Prague, and to deliver them to the Tyrolean Alps to be held hostage so that Himmler could bargain with their lives.

"I have never been so optimistic. Never. We'll get a better treaty than at Hubertusburg [at the end of the Seven Years' War in 1763]," Himmler said, slapping his leg. "We'll lose a few feathers, but it will still be a better treaty."

In the few remaining hours before the attack on Berlin commenced, Eichmann returned to his office and gathered his dejected unit together. He bid them farewell, saying that he knew the war was lost and that they should do what they could to remain alive. "For me," he said, "there is nothing of interest left in the world other than to fight to the last, and think only of finding my death in this struggle." Then he said harshly, "I will gladly and happily jump into the pit with the knowledge that with me are 5 million enemies of the Reich." Five million was the number of Jews Eichmann estimated had been exterminated during the Final Solution. Despite this pride in his accomplishments, he had already burned all of his department's files.

With that farewell, Eichmann drove south in an armored staff car between the Russian and American forces to Prague to deliver orders to the local SS commander about the removal of Jews from Theresienstadt. From Prague, Eichmann departed for Innsbruck, Austria, to prepare for the arrival of the hostages. On a deserted highway, an Allied fighter plane strafed Eichmann's car. He escaped this attack, only to be caught in a bombing run in an industrial town in northern Tyrol. He was thrown from his car, which was destroyed. It was April 17. The day before, the Russians had begun their final attack on Berlin.

Eichmann was quick to commandeer a tiny Fiat Topolino to continue his journey. When he reached Innsbruck, he informed Franz Hofer, Tyrol's Nazi Party leader, of the impending arrival of 1,200 Jews. Hofer had other things on his mind and was uncooperative. Eichmann then arranged for two hotels in the Brenner Pass to house the hostages. He tried to contact Prague to begin the deportations, but the phone lines were dead. He would have to return to Prague to ensure that Himmler's orders were carried out.

On his way, he stopped in Linz, in Upper Austria, to visit his father, who told him that Himmler's directives were of little import at this late stage of the war. But Eichmann felt the need to follow his orders, and he left his hometown just a few hours after its state police headquarters were bombed into oblivion by an Allied air raid. The American Third Army would soon follow.

In Prague, Eichmann found a wasteland. Most of the SS command had scattered, except for its chief, who told him, "Nothing is left in Berlin . . . The Russians have broken through."

Scrambling to find out what he should do, Eichmann reached Ernst Kaltenbrunner by telephone in Altaussee. Since Reinhard Heydrich's assassination in 1942, Kaltenbrunner had been the head of the

Reichssicherheitshauptamt (RSHA), or Reich Security Main Office, a powerful branch within the SS that ran the domestic and foreign intelligence services, the Gestapo, and the criminal police. He ordered Eichmann to Altaussee to receive further instructions. The Theresienstadt Jews were to be forgotten. Eichmann climbed into his Fiat and motored down the highway, holding firm to an order from a command structure that was crumbling from the top down.

On April 30, the Russians reached the heart of Berlin. The Red Army had swiftly overrun the city with the sheer scale of its firepower. Two weeks before, at exactly 3:00 A.M., a massive artillery barrage from 40,000 guns had heralded the Russians' arrival. Wave after wave of heavy bombers had soon followed. Now their tanks rolled through the streets of central Berlin, blasting apart any building suspected of hiding German soldiers. The Red Army infantry followed, outflanking any street barricades by shooting its bazookas through courtyard walls and basements. Flamethrowers rooted out those hiding in cellars. The bodies of the many who had tried to escape the fighting, civilians and soldiers alike, littered the streets, dust from pulverized brick and stone coating their still forms.

Fifty feet under the Reich Chancellery, in a fortified thirty-room bunker, Adolf Hitler refused to flee Berlin. Over the past two weeks, he had gone from promising a miracle victory at one moment to turning purple with rage, limbs shaking, certain that the war was lost the next. Only his ravings against the Jews remained constant. His command had fallen apart: Himmler, Hermann Göring, and his generals had betrayed his trust by starting treaty negotiations, and his contact with the outside world had diminished to a trickle. With the Russians closing in on the smoldering shell of the nearby Reichstag, Hitler retreated to his room, took a dose of cyanide, and shot himself in the right temple with his Walther pistol. The Thousand-Year Reich was over.

Hitler's faithful—from his inner circle, who had only recently lorded it over the whole of Europe, to the SS officers in the camps, who every day had held life and death in their hands—possessed no power at all. Most of the minor players had already shed their uniforms and fled. Over the past month, the price of a car with petrol, a good forgery, and an authentic Yellow Star had reached outrageous sums. Of the top leadership, only Joseph Goebbels, Martin Bormann, and two other generals were still with Hitler in his bunker when the Führer took his life. The rest of the inner circle had abandoned Berlin in the days and weeks before. Goebbels chose suicide, as did his wife. Their six helpless children had no choice. The two generals also committed suicide. Bormann, Hitler's private secretary, made a desperate dash through the Soviet encirclement. He disappeared, believed to have died, though his death was never confirmed.

When Eichmann arrived in Altaussee on May 2, the lakeside village was teeming with Nazi Party leaders and members of the Gestapo, Sicherheitsdienst (SD), and other units from Berlin. Located in a narrow wooded valley at the foot of the two-mile-high snowcapped peaks of the Dachstein and Totengebirge mountains, the village was perfectly situated to serve as part of the Alpine redoubt that the Allies so greatly feared. The two roads leading into the village could easily be made impassable, and any bombers would have difficulty hitting its center. Eichmann knew, however, that the redoubt was a myth. There was no mountain fortress, nor any coordinated plans for guerrilla operations behind enemy lines. Still, it did provide a retreat from Berlin. Along with other SS officers, Eichmann, who had known the area since he was a boy, had moved his family there as the war had turned against them.

Without delay, he went straight to the villa outside town where Kaltenbrunner was quartered. An aide led Eichmann into the dining room, where their boss was playing solitaire. Kaltenbrunner was dressed in his SS coat, ski pants, and boots. At six foot seven, with tree trunks for arms and a deep scar that ran across his cheek to his sledgehammer jaw, the RSHA's leader was an imposing presence. A family friend from Linz, he had been instrumental in Eichmann's joining the SS, telling him at the time, "You: You belong to us."

"Did everything turn out well?" Eichmann asked, hoping for news from Berlin.

"It's bad," Kaltenbrunner replied.

He asked his aide to bring Eichmann a cognac, and while they drank, he told Eichmann that Hitler was dead. Eichmann was stunned. He had worshiped the Führer, believing that an individual who had risen from lance corporal to leader of all of Germany was worth subordinating himself to blindly. Now Hitler was gone, and the Third Reich was lost.

Kaltenbrunner ordered Eichmann to take some troops into the mountains and establish a resistance. He explained that this would give Himmler some influence in any peace negotiations with the Allies.

The two parted without much ceremony or sentiment. As Eichmann left the room, he heard Kaltenbrunner quietly say to himself, "It's all a lot of crap. The game is up."

Desperate for direction, Eichmann applied himself to his assignment as if the fate of Germany was not already sealed. He recruited several officers in his department, including his personal secretary, Rudolf Jänisch, and Anton Burger, who had been with him since his days in Vienna. They took over the Park Hotel and assembled roughly two hundred men, a disparate collection of Waffen-SS and Hitler Youth, many handicapped by injuries or little military training. Before Eichmann left for the mountains, Kaltenbrunner instructed him to take the Romanian fascist Horia Sima and several of his Iron Guard militia with him on the mission. The RSHA chief was emptying Altaussee of its war criminals to separate himself from them. Kaltenbrunner had delusions that he was of a different breed.

Fearing an Allied attack, a doctor from the local field hospital begged Eichmann to leave the village with his combat troops. After outfitting his men with winter fatigues, weapons, a cache of gold and reichsmarks, and a fleet of trucks, Eichmann led them up into the mountains. He had enough assault rifles and bazookas to wreak havoc on the enemy for at least a month

A heavy snow began to fall, and the men were soon forced to shovel a path for the jeeps and the radio van. By sunrise the next day, the company had reached the mountain village of Blaa-Alm, high in the Alps. During the hike, Eichmann had seen enough of his men to know that they were an ill-trained, disorganized, and, worst of all, disobedient bunch, who would not make for much of a partisan resistance. At Blaa-Alm, he released the worst of the lot, giving each man 5,000 marks, accounting for every financial outlay in a notebook. The soldiers left without protest. Eichmann then ordered weapons training for the remaining troops and sent Burger, a proficient skier, to scout the hamlet Rettenbach-Alm, higher still in the mountains.

When Burger returned, Eichmann led his forces to the hamlet and settled them into some mountain huts. After a few days, an orderly sent by Kaltenbrunner arrived with a directive from Himmler: "It is prohibited to fire on Englishmen and Americans." The order, the last Eichmann received from the Reich, eliminated the need for his motley troops. There would be no glorious last stand. Eichmann's war was over.

3

THE FOLLOWING MORNING, May 8, after a long, sleepless night in the mountain hut, Eichmann informed the men of the directive. They were free to do what they pleased; he planned to visit his family one final time and then hide in the mountains. Given his wartime activities, he had no illusions that the Allies would brand him as anything other than a war criminal. He had to avoid capture.

Alone and on foot, Eichmann descended through the snow to Blaa-Alm, then down to Altaussee. When he reached the village in the late afternoon, he learned that Grand Admiral Karl Dönitz, acting German head of state, had agreed to an unconditional surrender. In the neighboring valley, just across the mountains, American troops were dancing in the streets of Bad Ischl. Allied troops would soon arrive in Altaussee.

Wearing a camouflage uniform and carrying a machine gun, Eichmann slipped through the village to the lake where his family lived. They had rented a small chalet overlooking the water at the end of Fischerdorf Strasse, a road that snaked steeply around the hillside. There was no time for a long goodbye. He had spent much of the war away from his wife and three sons, and he was no longer the man who had met Veronika (Vera) Liebl, the petite, blue-eyed daughter of a Czechoslovakian farmer, at a concert in Linz in 1931.

At the time, Eichmann had been a twenty-five-year-old traveling salesman for the Vacuum Oil Company who had not even graduated from high school. He was from a nice middle-class family of five children and rode his ruby red motorcycle to impress his new girlfriend. The only hint of his politics, such as they were, was his membership in a youth group of a larger German war veterans organization that was militantly nationalist and campaigned against "Jewish Bolsheviks." In 1935, Eichmann and Vera were married in a church, despite the derision of his SS comrades, who looked down on religious rituals. An innocent, uncomplicated Catholic girl, Vera shared her husband's taste in classical music but did not much care for politics and declined to join the Nazi Party. If not for the rise of Hitler and the Third Reich, the two might have lived a quiet existence in Linz. But Eichmann was soon swept away by the SS, and Vera concentrated on raising their three sons. They never discussed his activities, and his infrequent visits and numerous infidelities had created a distance between them. Despite their strained marriage, Vera remained devoted to her husband.

Eichmann had bought a basket of peas and some flour in Altaussee. It was all he could find. Unlike some of his SS comrades, he had not hidden away a fortune in gold and foreign currency. He sorely regretted that he had not personally extorted ransoms from Jewish leaders—they would have gladly given him whatever he asked in exchange for their lives.

"The war is over," he told Vera. "You don't need to worry. It'll be the Americans or British who are coming." But in case it was the Russians who arrived first, he gave his wife a cyanide capsule and one for each of his sons. Then he left instructions for her if anyone came to the house to investigate. He would contact her once he had settled somewhere safe.

Then Eichmann went out by the lake, where his sons—Klaus, age nine; Horst, five; and Dieter, three—were playing and embraced them in turn. While he watched them play, little Dieter slipped and fell into the lake. Eichmann fished the boy out of the water, took him over his knee, and slapped him hard several times. While his son screamed, Eichmann told him never to go near the water again. He might never see his boys again, he reasoned; it was best to leave them with a bit of discipline. To his mind, this was the most a father could do for his children.

"Be brave and look after the children," he told Vera, and then he hiked away.

Without any orders to fulfill or leaders to follow, Eichmann was rudderless. As he climbed into the mountains, the U.S. Army, including a detachment of Counter Intelligence Corps (CIC) investigators looking for Kaltenbrunner, was heading toward Altaussee. By dark, Eichmann had reached Blaa-Alm. Most of the Hitler Youth and other soldiers he had brought into the mountains had disbanded. His own men, the Waffen-SS, and Horia Sima and his guard remained, knowing that they were targets of the Allies. Eichmann spent the night in the village, deciding to head higher into the mountains the next day with as many men as would come with him. He was certain that he could evade capture by staying in the mountains that he knew so well.

At dawn, his long-serving driver, Polanski, asked if he could take one of their vehicles and leave. Now that the war was over, he planned to start a transport business. Eichmann suggested that he take one of the trucks; the fleet was useless to him now. Later that morning, one of his SS officers, Otto Hünsche, who had also gone down to Altaussee to see his family, returned with news that American tanks had just entered the area. Hünsche had evaded them, hiding in the fields outside Altaussee before making his way back to Blaa-Alm.

Eichmann's party hiked to Rettenbach-Alm and put themselves up in some mountain huts. Over the next several days, they scouted the surrounding hills for Allied patrols or Austrian resistance fighters who might tip off the Americans as to their location. They posted signs warning that anybody who entered the area would be shot. But they knew that their discovery was inevitable. While Eichmann was away, his comrades had decided that they did not want to be found with the overseer of the Final Solution. They elected Anton Burger to deliver the news.

"Colonel, we've been talking about the situation. We mustn't fire on the English or Americans, and the Russians aren't coming here," Burger ventured. "You are being hunted as a war criminal. We are not. We feel you'd be doing us a great service if you would leave us and appoint another commander."

The disloyalty of his men stung, but Eichmann knew they were right. Only Rudolf Jänisch volunteered to stay with him. They dressed in Luftwaffe uniforms they had brought with them and discarded their personal papers and anything else that might identify them. After a farewell toast of schnapps, Eichmann and Jänisch walked out of Rettenbach-Alm, heading north.

A year before, in Hungary, Eichmann had met Joel Brand, a Jewish representative who was attempting to trade 10,000 trucks for 1 million Jewish lives. When Brand had glanced down at Eichmann's pistol on the desk, the officer had smiled coldly and said, "Do you know, I often think how glad some of your people would be to bump me off. But don't be too optimistic, Mr. Brand. It may be that times will change, it may be that we shall lose the war, but you won't catch me . . . No, I have made all arrangements against that eventuality."

It had all been bluster. Eichmann was far from prepared to be a man on the run. He had little money, no safe house, no forged papers, and only one young adjunct still loyal to him. As they made their way toward Germany, they found Allied troops everywhere. The net was tightening.

Once the peace was secured, the Allies rapidly occupied Germany. Martial law was imposed, checkpoints were established at bridges and road intersections, curfews and blackouts were set, roving patrols were sent out, and Wehrmacht soldiers were interned in POW camps. The aim was to secure the country, to prevent the development of an organized underground resistance, and to provide routine policing to restore public order without delay. Allied headquarters issued directives to every army group in every sector to arrest and question any Nazi Party members, starting with Hitler's inner circle and continuing all the way down to local group leaders; members of the SD, Gestapo, and other branches of the SS; and high officials from the police, Wehrmacht, Hitler Youth, and propaganda ministry, among many others. The Allied leaders meant to pin Germany down and to remove every last trace of the Nazi state.

Since the liberation of the first concentration camps, the Allies had dramatically increased the number of individuals devoted to capturing the Nazi leadership and other war criminals. The CIC, whose chief job in Germany was to collect intelligence and help secure the U.S. Army against subversive agents, found that there was little to do in this respect at the end of hostilities, so they turned their attention to the most-wanted lists. British intelligence also contributed to the effort, though with less immediate vigor. The Allies had recruited war crimes investigators, whose specific mandate was to gather evidence and to seize those suspected of involvement in the atrocities. In Versailles, Allied intelligence agents pored over captured records and personnel files, developing a registry of war criminals and security suspects. This registry, the Central Registry of War Criminals and Security Suspects (CROWCASS), was added to a long list that had already been compiled by the United Nations War Crimes Commission. By the first week of May, the list contained more than 70,000 names. As British foreign minister Anthony Eden boasted to the House of Commons at the time, "From Norway to the Bavarian Alps, the Allies are carrying out the greatest manhunt in history."

The senior Nazi leadership, identified and targeted by the Allies long before the war's end, was at the top of the list. The day after Eichmann retreated back into the mountains, Colonel Robert Matteson, a thirty-one-year-old Harvard-educated CIC officer attached to the U.S. Third Army, drove his troops into Altaussee. He had been tipped off that Kaltenbrunner was in the area with his mistress. Soon after their arrival, Matteson and his team rounded up at least twenty Nazis and seized the villa that Kaltenbrunner had just left—as well as the wireless station through which he kept in contact with Berlin. A few days later, another tip came from a local Austrian resistance fighter that Kaltenbrunner, his adjunct, and two SS guards were hiding in a hunting cabin high in the Totengebirge.

Guided by four former Wehrmacht soldiers who knew the territory and backed by an American infantry squad, Matteson climbed into the mountains, disguised in lederhosen, an Alpine jacket, and spiked shoes. The party hiked through the deep snow during the night to avoid detection. Five hours later, at first light, they sighted the cabin. Matteson walked the last five hundred yards to the door alone. In his pocket, Matteson had a note from Kaltenbrunner's mistress that he had made her write, pleading for her lover to surrender peacefully to the Americans. Matteson knocked.

An unshaven man in civilian clothes opened the door a crack. "What do you want?"

"I want to come in. I'm cold," Matteson responded, his gun hidden.

The German shook his head no. The CIC agent passed the mistress's note, and the moment the man read its contents, he slammed the door shut. Through the window, Matteson saw the man run across the room and grab a revolver. Another man on the bed reached for a gun as well. Matteson darted toward a wall of the cabin without windows and whistled for his squad. They surrounded the house and called for Kaltenbrunner and his men to surrender. The door opened, and out they came, arms high in the air. At first Kaltenbrunner pretended to be a Wehrmacht doctor, but he was given away by his height, the scar across his cheek, and his Gestapo identification badge, engraved "#2." Kaltenbrunner had ranked behind only Himmler in the SS.

Himmler himself did not go so easily. At the war's end, he brought his staff together, saying, "Well, gentlemen, you know what you have to do now? You must hide yourselves in the ranks of the Wehrmacht." Himmler followed his own advice. Shorn of his mustache and dressed as a sergeant with a black patch over his eye, he tried to pass through British lines with six of his men, but they were caught by a random patrol. During a routine medical examination before his interrogation, Himmler bit into a cyanide capsule hidden in his mouth and died fifteen minutes later.

Other top Nazi leaders soon found themselves incarcerated at the Allied prison in Mondorf-les-Bains, in southeastern Luxembourg. Hermann Göring surrendered in the Alps, insisting that he would speak only to General Eisenhower. Two soldiers unceremoniously hauled the 264-pound Göring, who had been Hitler's second in command, out of his car. Grand Admiral Dönitz, General Alfred Jodl, Field Marshal Wilhelm Keitel, and Minister of Armaments Albert Speer surrendered without protest. Fritz Sauckel, head of the slave la-

bor program, was trapped while hiding in a cavern. On a routine patrol, an American Jewish major identified a bearded Julius Streicher,
the virulently anti-Semitic publisher, who was disguised as an artist,
paintbrush in hand. Hans Frank, the governor-general of Poland,
attempted to hide among German POWs, but he grew so nervous
over the risk of discovery that he slashed his left wrist and neck, barely
surviving. Troops from the 101st Airborne uncovered Robert Ley, head
of the German Labor Front, in a mountain hut very much like the
one in which Kaltenbrunner was found. Foreign Minister Joachim
von Ribbentrop was one of the last to be caught. The son of a wine
merchant, who Ribbentrop had hoped would give him sanctuary, informed the police of his whereabouts. British soldiers arrested Ribbentrop while he was still in bed at his Hamburg hideaway. Wearing
pink-and-white-striped silk pajamas, he sat up and said in flawless
English, "The game is up. I congratulate you."

The most notorious Nazis fell into Allied hands within the first
weeks of the occupation. Every day, more than seven hundred individuals on the automatic arrest list were imprisoned and held for further interrogation in order to discover the nature of their actions during the war for a potential trial. Many of their brethren were dealt
with more swiftly.

Although the Russians took several top Nazis into custody for Allied trials, their revenge was often exacted on the spot—contrary to
Stalin's earlier admonishment to Churchill about the need for fair trials. With the help of local Communists and camp survivors, the Russian secret service, the NKVD, rounded up many suspected Nazi
criminals and shipped them to prisons in the Soviet Union, where
they were never heard from again. Others were executed, their backs
crisscrossed with machine gun bullets.

The Russians were not the only ones to administer rough justice.
After the war was over, groups of Jewish avengers—made up of camp
survivors, resistance fighters, and soldiers from the Jewish Brigade
(settlers in Palestine who had joined a special British army group in
1944)—hunted down and summarily killed Gestapo and other SS
men who had committed crimes against Jews. The Haganah, the underground Jewish defense force based in Palestine, directed some of

these squads. Others operated completely on their own. Often masquerading as British military police, the squads seized their victims at night, drove them to a secluded spot in the woods or by a lake, and then shot or drowned them. One group even carried out a plan to kill 15,000 German POWs held in an American camp near Nuremberg by sprinkling their bread with white arsenic powder. More than 2,000 prisoners became sick, but none died.

With so many hell-bent on rooting out the Nazis, Adolf Eichmann had one advantage: he had not yet been identified as a major war criminal. His name was on the Allied lists, specifically for his "activities" in Czechoslovakia, but at this point he was a mere lieutenant colonel among tens of thousands of entries. The Allies had yet to learn the degree of his involvement in the Final Solution. If Colonel Matteson had been aware of the activities of the chief of Department IVB_4 when he had captured Kaltenbrunner, perhaps Eichmann also would have been captured within days. But given the late start of the Allied investigation into Nazi war crimes, he had escaped.

Eichmann and Jänisch walked and hitchhiked west from Altaussee toward Salzburg. They evaded Allied troops, hiding in fields when they heard soldiers approach, and slept in abandoned barns at night. The fifty-mile journey took several days, but just when they had the city in their sights, an American patrol spotted them, and they were forced to surrender. Eichmann introduced himself as Luftwaffe corporal Adolf Barth, using the surname of his Berlin grocer, but there was little further interrogation. The patrol brought Eichmann and Jänisch to a hastily erected camp, which had a single strand of barbed wire as a fence and no searchlights. It was crowded with German soldiers who had been found wandering around the area, all of them worn-out and hungry and still wearing their uniforms for lack of other clothes. Most wanted some food and a place to sleep, much like the 9 million POWs already held by the Allies throughout northwestern Europe, and there was not much need for security.

As soon as night fell, Eichmann and Jänisch sneaked out of the camp and walked to Salzburg. The dome of the city's main cathedral had collapsed, and many of the buildings and houses by the train station had been razed, but for the most part, Salzburg was one of the few cities in Germany and Austria whose historic center had survived the war. Eichmann knew its prewar beauty well; he had spent his honeymoon there ten years before. For the next few days, the two SS officers hid in the winding cobblestone alleys of the old city, away from the Allied patrols.

One afternoon, Eichmann hiked up to Salzburg's famed eleventh-century castle and looked out at the surrounding countryside. He was convinced that he did not deserve to be on the run: he had only abided by his SS oath of "My honor is my loyalty" and executed the orders given to him. He considered whether he had changed from the man who had brought his bride to this very place a decade earlier. No, he decided, he had not changed. He knew he was not some murderer or villain.

The truth was it had been a long, convoluted road for Eichmann to reach the level of hate-fueled fanaticism that had characterized him in Hungary. Born in an industrial town in Germany, he had been raised in Linz, Austria, by a father who was a middle-class manager, a strict Protestant, and fervently nationalistic. In Linz, also Hitler's hometown, as in Austria and Germany as a whole, the majority of the population saw Jews as racially inferior intruders who represented the twin threats of international capitalism and Bolshevism. But anti-Semitism was not Eichmann's motivation to become a Nazi. The disaster at Versailles following World War I, Germany's need for stability, and, more personally, a desire to wear the same smart brown uniform as others his age were reasons enough.

Eichmann joined the Nazi Party in 1932. He went to Germany, received some military training, read more about National Socialism, and enlisted in the SD, which was headed by Reinhard Heydrich. As a member of the party's intelligence operation, Eichmann was charged with compiling a list of German Freemasons, whom the Nazis considered enemies. Diligent, attentive to detail, and respectful of authority, he caught the eye of Edler von Mildenstein, who was in charge of creating a Jewish affairs office. Given the degree of revulsion Hitler felt toward the Jewish people—as evidenced in 1935 by the enactment of the Nuremberg Laws, which stripped German Jews of their citizenship—it was a good career move for Eichmann.

At the time, Mildenstein had a far less virulent attitude toward Jews than did many others in the SS, believing that sending them to Palestine was the answer to the Jewish problem. Mildenstein charged Eichmann with studying Zionism. Over the next three years, working in the changing landscape of the SS, Eichmann spent his days writing reports on the Jews, monitoring their organizations, trying to learn Hebrew (a failure), investigating emigration plans, and even traveling to Palestine in 1937, while posing as a journalist for *Berliner Tageblatt*. He soon became the SD "expert" on Jewish affairs. Although his opinion of the Jews had hardened—he wrote in one paper that they were "the most dangerous enemy" of the Third Reich—he still thought that emigration was the best way to deal with them.

In 1938, Eichmann won his first chance to put this idea into practice when Germany occupied Austria. Second Lieutenant Eichmann arrived in Vienna to represent the SD in dealing with the 200,000 Austrian Jews. After arresting the Jewish community's key leaders, he used many of them to organize and finance the emigration of the Jewish population. In his office in the Palais Rothschild, Eichmann felt his first rush of power, writing to a friend, "They are in my hands; they dare not take one step without me." For his success and "requisite hardness," he won a promotion to first lieutenant. He also gained the ability to view Jews not as human beings but as stock to be moved from one place to another. After a year in Vienna, he was sent to Czechoslovakia to set up a similar operation there.

The more territory the Nazis occupied, the more Jews came under their control, which meant career opportunities for Eichmann. When Germany seized Poland in September 1939, Heinrich Müller, the new Gestapo chief, assigned Eichmann to run the Central Office for Jewish Emigration, the department responsible for forced deportations of Jews to the edges of German-occupied territory. Emigration was out; deportation was in. After the invasion of Poland, the act that precipitated the Allies' declaration of war, Eichmann's first major task was to resettle 500,000 Poles to make room for ethnic Germans. He was by then adept at uprooting communities and arranging their transportation, but his chief problem was finding places to send them. He formulated a proposal to resettle millions of Jews in Madagascar, a plan brutal in its scope and execution, but one that fell apart due to the vacillation of his superior officers. Nevertheless, Eichmann had proved himself to be an essential part of any planning to do with the Jewish problem.

In the meantime, Jewish families who had been ripped from their homes across Poland and other territories seized by the Germans languished in ghettos and labor camps. But their suffering and deaths were increasingly irrelevant to Eichmann. They were a logistical problem that required solving.

In the late summer of 1941, Heydrich summoned Eichmann to Berlin and told him, "The Führer has ordered physical extermination." Hitler had already mandated the slaughter of Jews in the invasion of the Soviet Union, but now he wanted the same fate extended to every European Jew. Eichmann was sent to report on localized killing operations already under way in Poland under the direction of SS police chief Odilo Globocnik, as well as those conducted by the *Einsatzgruppen,* death squads organized by Heydrich to follow the Wehrmacht into eastern Europe and Russia to eliminate Jews, Gypsies, Communists, and any other "enemies" of the Reich. Near Lodz, men, women, and children were rounded up and loaded into vans into which the vehicles' exhaust fumes were pumped. In Minsk, they were forced into pits, ordered to strip, and then shot by the hundreds. Despite his feelings toward Jews, Eichmann was unnerved by what he saw and told Müller as much. This was no longer a "political solution," Eichmann said. At the same time, he feared that the new policy would obviate the need for his department. This fear of losing his position and power outweighed his misgivings, and after further consideration, he accepted the necessity of ridding Europe of the Jews through extermination.

On January 20, 1942, Heydrich gathered fifteen leading Reich officials with an interest in the Jewish problem at a lakeside villa in Wannsee, a suburb southwest of Berlin. The agenda was to create systematic plans for the Final Solution and to centralize them under the SS. Eichmann prepared briefings on anti-Jewish measures, deportations, and a country-by-country breakdown of the 11 million Jews targeted for extermination. He also took the meeting minutes. Later, he drank brandy with Heydrich and Müller, toasting their leadership, as they sat beside a fire and gazed out at the falling snow.

Though only recently promoted to lieutenant colonel, Eichmann was entrusted with being the "competent official" in charge of coordinating all matters related to the Final Solution at the RSHA. He dispensed with any remaining guilt and discomfort he might have felt about being involved in the mass murder by telling himself that his bosses, "the Popes," had "given their orders."

Eichmann took on his new job with characteristic vigor. He had not set the policy of annihilation, he reasoned, but it was his responsibility to manage its successful execution. The more Jews he brought to the extermination camps, the better he looked to his superiors and the better, he thought, he served the Reich. He excelled in his task, delivering millions of Jews throughout Europe to their deaths. But with each challenge, with each victory, he grew more obsessive about his work, more convinced of its importance, and more drawn to the power he held over life and death. A Jew was no longer a person, nor even a unit to be moved from one place to another. Judaism was a disease that threatened every German. "They were stealing the breath of life from us," he wrote. They needed to be eradicated, and he was the one who would see it through to the end. In Hungary, Eichmann reached the height of his barbarity. He was a living testament to the adage "Power tends to corrupt; absolute power corrupts absolutely."

While looking out over Salzburg in May 1945, Eichmann strove to deny who he had become, but he was not so deluded as to think that the Allies would not hunt him down, particularly given the unusually public role he had played in Hungary. He was keen to return to Germany, knowing there was a better chance of avoiding detection there than in Austria, where he had spent most of his life. But it would not be easy. From his vantage point by the castle, he could see Americans guarding all the roads leading into and out of Salzburg.

He recruited a local nurse to help him and Jänisch escape. She walked them to the checkpoint and told the Americans that these two Luftwaffe corporals were poor and wanted only to return to their country. The guards let them pass.

Eichmann and Jänisch then needed to cross the German border to gain entry into Bavaria. Crouching out of sight by the highway, they watched a funeral cortège and some mourners accompanied by soldiers cross the border without so much as a question from the Americans. But when Eichmann and Jänisch attempted to follow them, the two were stopped. This time, one of the soldiers inspected them more thoroughly and discovered the quarter-inch-long black tattoo on the underside of Eichmann's left arm indicating his blood type. Under his breath, Eichmann cursed Himmler for requiring the tattoos for SS members. While in the mountains, he had tried to burn his off with a lit cigarette, but it was still distinguishable.

The men were taken by truck to a well-guarded detention camp. Eichmann presented himself as Waffen-SS sergeant Barth, but over the next few days, he could not fail to notice that the Americans treated the German officers better than the enlisted men. By the time he was interrogated by an American lieutenant who spoke German, he had concocted a new identity for himself.

When asked his name, he responded, "Otto Eckmann." It was a name close enough to his own that he would answer to it even if distracted. Also, if someone he knew did call out his real name, it might not arouse the suspicion of the guards.

"Rank?"

"Second lieutenant, 22nd Waffen-SS Cavalry Division."

"Born?"

"Yes, of course," Eichmann said, with a glimmer of arrogance, but he added, "March 19, 1905. In Breslau."

It was a year earlier than his actual birth date—simple to remember—and he had chosen Breslau because the city was in Russian hands and had been decimated by repeated bombing campaigns, which, he suspected, would have also destroyed any parish registers or official records.

The American officer noted these details, and after asking a few basic questions about Eichmann's wartime service, he dismissed Eichmann and instructed him to go back to his work detail. The lieutenant had a whole German transport unit to question before the end of the day.

During June, Eichmann and Jänisch were moved from temporary camp to temporary camp, living off combat rations and mourning the loss of the Third Reich. On the journeys between camps, Eichmann witnessed the ruins around him. Wrecked tanks and cars littered the roads, and twisted heaps of metal that had once been airplanes dotted the fields. Bridges had been destroyed and railway tracks severed, and most towns had suffered indiscriminate bombing campaigns, their buildings reduced to piles of rubble. None of this matched the human devastation. Hundreds of thousands of refugees, many of them recently freed from concentration and slave labor camps, packed the roads and filled the villages the POWs passed through. Dressed in little more than rags, their tattered shoes stuffed with newspapers, they hunkered down in hollowed-out and blackened houses or walked in small groups toward some unknown destination, carrying what few possessions they had in cloth bags slung over their shoulders. They hastily dug graves on the sides of the road for forgotten corpses.

At a camp in the Bavarian forest, Eichmann encountered a German officer named Rudolf Scheide, who was acting as an adjunct to the camp commander. Obediently, Eichmann revealed his real name and explained that he wished to be registered under his assumed name, Eckmann. "It is your own business what you do with your name," Scheide told him dismissively. He was dealing with hundreds of POWs arriving by truck every day.

In late June, Eichmann and Jänisch were loaded onto yet another transport and shipped off to yet another camp, at Weiden, fifty miles east of Nuremberg. This camp was a vast barbed-wire enclosure. A sea of soldiers, including more than 2,000 officers, occupied the camp, many of them sheltering in holes they had dug in the ground, as there were few tents. The soldiers used slit trenches for latrines, and there was little food and water for the thousands of men.

Eichmann had fallen a long way since the days in his elegant villa overlooking Budapest, pampered by servants and drinking the finest of wines. Yet Weiden was nothing compared to where he had sent the "enemies of the Reich." While Otto Eckmann labored on his work detail, those enemies, the ones who had survived, were beginning to understand the nature of his position in the SS. Soon Adolf Eichmann would no longer be just one among tens of thousands sought for arrest. He would be a chief target.

4

"HAVE YOU HEARD of Adolf Eichmann?" Captain Choter-Ischai of the Jewish Brigade asked the man across from him, who was only beginning to fill out his tall, wide-shouldered frame after years in concentration camps.

"I heard the name from some Hungarian Jews at Mauthausen," Simon Wiesenthal said. "It means nothing to me."

"Better look it up," Choter-Ischai said, explaining that he had information that Eichmann was deeply involved in Jewish affairs in Berlin and should be arrested. "Unfortunately, he comes from our country. He was born in Palestine."

After the captain left, Wiesenthal combed through the files at the Office of Strategic Services (OSS, forerunner of the CIA) headquarters in Linz where he worked. The information on this Eichmann was scant. There was no first name, only a rank: lieutenant colonel. The entry detailed that Eichmann had been involved in actions in Austria, Czechoslovakia, France, Greece, and Hungary, but there was nothing specific. Wiesenthal noted the name so that he could make future inquiries and returned to his whirlwind of activities in mid-June 1945. Only four weeks before, weighing ninety-seven pounds, he had staggered out of the dark barracks at Mauthausen into the sunlight and seen a gray American tank coming through the entrance. He had collapsed at the sight.

Before the Nazis stormed into Poland, Wiesenthal had been an architect with a rising reputation and a husband with hopes for a family of his own. The Nazis had killed his mother, had taken his wife, and he had suffered such terror on his body and mind that he twice had attempted to kill himself. At the war's end, he feared that if he did not go after those responsible, he would have nothing to live for. While recuperating in Mauthausen, the thirty-six-year-old implored an American army War Crimes Unit operating at the camp to hire him. In a letter to the chief, he chronicled the twelve concentration camps he had survived and offered the names and, remarkably, the ranks of ninety-one individuals, along with descriptions of their crimes: "SS Major-General Katzmann—Responsible for the death of at least 1 million people; Gestapo Commissar Shöls—Timekeeper and schedule-maker for mass killing throughout Galicia; Janowska Commandant Friedrich Warzok—A beast who liquidated at least 60,000 Jews and used to burn prisoners alive in their barracks; Plaszow SS guard Hujar—Winner of numerous wagers by sending one bullet through two heads at a time."

The chief investigator hired Wiesenthal, giving him the power to arrest, and he captured more than a dozen SS members with the help of the American unit before he was transferred to the OSS. The American spy agency was also interested in arresting SS officials, albeit more for counterespionage efforts than for war crimes.

In the month after Choter-Ischai informed him of Eichmann's name, Wiesenthal learned little more about the lieutenant colonel other than rumors from former Mauthausen inmates that he spoke Yiddish and Hebrew fluently. In late July, he traveled to Vienna to gather information for his investigations into former SS officers. He met with Gideon Raphael, a senior agent with the Brichah, the underground organization leading the exodus of Jews from Europe to Palestine in defiance of the British blockade. Raphael handed Wiesenthal a list of war criminals that the Jewish Agency for Palestine (forerunner of the Israeli government) had been compiling in earnest since 1944.

The name Eichmann topped the list. Raphael had more information on Eichmann than the Allies did, though still no first name. His nickname was apparently Eichie. He was reported to be married with one child and had allegedly been born in Sarona, a German Templar colony in Palestine. Again, the report stated that he spoke Hebrew and Yiddish. Most important, it said that he was a "high official of Gestapo headquarters, Department of Jewish Affairs." Wiesenthal knew that this meant that Eichmann had been instrumental in running the extermination camps.

After returning to Linz, Wiesenthal went straight to his boss, Captain O'Meara of the OSS, to discuss Eichmann.

"He's the head of the Jewish branch of the Gestapo," O'Meara said. He encouraged Wiesenthal to track Eichmann down.

Unbeknownst to Wiesenthal, the Allies had been collecting more and more information on Eichmann from their interrogations of captured SS officers, including some who had worked closely with him. They knew of his position as chief of the Jewish section of the Gestapo and the broad strokes of his activities.

A few evenings later, at his apartment on Landstrasse 40, only two doors down from the OSS office, Wiesenthal sat at his desk, looking at his list of names. "Eichmann" was now underscored for emphasis. His landlady entered to clean his room and peered over his shoulder at the list.

"Eichmann!" she exclaimed. "That must be the SS general Eichmann who was in command of the Jews. Did you know his parents live here in this street? Just a few houses along, at number 32!"

An astonished Wiesenthal immediately informed the OSS, but he refused, when asked, to go to the house himself. He could not bear the thought of touching the same door handle as an individual who had had a hand in managing so much death.

On July 28, two OSS agents descended on Landstrasse 32. They interrogated Eichmann's father, who reluctantly admitted that his son Adolf had been a member of the SS, but that was all he knew of his wartime activities. Adolf had visited near the end of the war, but his father had heard nothing from him since. The agents learned that he had been born in Solingen, Germany, not Palestine; that he had three children, not one; and that he was married to a woman named Vera Liebl. On a search of the house, they found not a single photograph of Adolf.

"Is there a picture?" an OSS agent asked, suspicious that the man was hiding something.

The older Eichmann shook his head. "He never liked to be photographed," he said.

Standing in a line of SS men, Second Lieutenant Otto Eckmann waited nervously as Jewish camp survivors stared at his face to see if they recognized him. Armed American guards and Allied war crimes investigators looked on expectantly.

Eichmann had passed the summer safely in his new identity, coming through several standard CIC interrogations on his wartime activities without a hitch. None of his answers had provoked further inquiry, and he spent his days stacking heavy ammunition in an air force warehouse. In late August, the Americans moved him to another camp located at Ober-Dachstetten, to the west of Nuremberg. His adjunct Jänisch was sent to a different camp. Eichmann was isolated among three hundred former SS officers and assigned to a work detail. Nobody there knew who he was.

By late September, lineups of former Nazis were occurring more and more often. None of the survivors recognized Eichmann as they moved down the lines. Contrary to the very public strutting of most SS men, whether in the camps or overseeing deportations, Eichmann had preferred to remain in the shadows. Apart from his time in Vienna and Hungary, he had had his staff meet with Jewish representatives and execute his plans. He also had made a point of avoiding having his photograph taken. For his identity cards, he had always used an official Gestapo photograph and destroyed the negatives. This earlier caution was paying off now. Nonetheless, he was sure that one day he would be discovered in one of the lineups.

In October, Eichmann was called in for questioning at the CIC interrogation center in nearby Ansbach. He was certain he was in trouble when confronted by an experienced investigator who spoke perfect German and who knew the Byzantine intricacies of the SS well enough to catch Eichmann in a lie.

Eichmann talked the investigator through his service, how he had been part of a Waffen-SS division that had battled the Russians outside Budapest, then had served under the famed General Sepp Dietrich in the defense of Vienna at the war's end. As to why he had come into the camp without any papers, Eichmann explained that he had destroyed them after his retreat from Vienna, following standard army procedure. The investigator stopped him several times, probing for military details that any Waffen-SS lieutenant should know but that Eichmann did not. Further, when the investigator put him under pressure, Eichmann could not help but reveal an arrogance that betrayed him as a more superior officer. When the interrogation ended, the investigator told Eichmann that his answers would be verified and that more interrogations were sure to follow.

Even though Eichmann had provided information that would require time and travel to investigate, he feared that he had exposed himself. He returned to Ober-Dachstetten by military bus, shuddering to think how the camp's Polish guards would treat him if they learned his identity. Thoughts of suicide crept into his mind, and he even asked one of the other SS officers, who had been a pharmacist before the war, how much morphine he would need to kill himself. His desperation spiked on hearing that the Allies were about to parade the Third Reich's great leaders into a courtroom in Nuremberg.

Two hours before dawn on November 21, guards awakened the prisoners at Nuremberg to prepare them for their first day of the International Military Tribunal. After many months of political and legal wrangling among the Allies, they had settled on an indictment and a list of twenty-four defendants for the major war crimes trial. The defendants had been interrogated at length. The prosecutors had gathered piles of incriminating Nazi documents, many found hidden in salt mines, stored in country chateaus, or secreted behind false walls in government buildings. Now the trial was to begin in earnest.

The guards gave the prisoners a breakfast of coffee and oatmeal, shaved their faces, and dressed the military men in plain uniforms and the civilians in suits and ties. As had been the case since their arrest, their every movement was watched to prevent any attempt at suicide. Swinging a billy club, the prison commandant warned them that if they misbehaved during the proceedings, they would suffer a loss of privileges. Then they were led in groups of four through the prison, down the covered walkway, and into the Palace of Justice. An iron door was slid open, revealing a steel-cage elevator large enough for the prisoners and their guards.

On the second floor, the guards escorted them into the courtroom and sat them on two long wooden benches, according to the order of their names in the indictment. First row: Hermann Göring, Rudolf Hess, Joaquim von Ribbentrop, Wilhelm Keitel, Alfred Rosenberg, Hans Frank, Wilhelm Frick, Julius Streicher, Walter Funk, and Hjalmar Schacht. Second row: Karl Dönitz, Erich Raeder, Baldur von Schirach, Fritz Sauckel, Alfred Jodl, Franz von Papen, Arthur Seyss-Inquart, Albert Speer, Konstantin von Neurath, and Hans Fritzsche. Of the other four defendants, Ernst Kaltenbrunner had suffered a brain hemorrhage three days before, Robert Ley had hanged himself with a towel in his cell, Gustav Krupp had been found too frail to stand trial, and Martin Bormann was still at large.

Ten guards, with white clubs, white belts, and white helmets, stood to the side and behind the defendants. The rest of the amphitheater-like courtroom was empty. At 9:30 A.M., the doors swung wide. The defense attorneys streamed in and arranged themselves in front of the dock. The prosecutors settled on the opposite side. Interpreters and court stenographers took their positions, and more than 250 journalists took theirs. At 10:00 A.M. sharp, the marshal called for order, and four judges, one each from the United States, the Soviet Union, Great Britain, and France, entered to hushed silence.

After a brief introduction by the tribunal president, the prosecution listed the four-part indictments against the defendants for crimes against peace, war crimes, crimes against humanity, and a conspiracy to commit these crimes. Hour after hour, the indictment was read, a damning portrait of international treaty violations, totalitarian control, aggressive war, slave labor, the slaughter of captured soldiers, looting, the wanton destruction of thousands of villages and cities, and the torture, shooting, gassing, hanging, starvation, and systematic extermination of innocents to clear way for the "master race." Some of the defendants grimaced, wiped their brows, and shifted uneasily in their seats. Others were stone still. Göring mugged for the cameras. Hess groaned miserably, from stomach pain he claimed, and had to be given a shot to relax him. Tears rolled down Ribbentrop's face, and eventually he was removed to sob alone in an adjoining hallway. During the break for lunch, Schirach, the dapper thirty-eight-year-old former leader of the Hitler Youth, turned to a clinical psychologist who was supervising the prisoners and said dryly, "I suppose we'll get steak the day you hang us."

The following day, the defendants entered their pleas of guilty or not guilty. First, Göring answered, with a defiant stare, "I declare myself, in the sense of the indictment, not guilty." The rest followed with not guilty pleas as well. Then Robert Jackson, the lead American prosecutor, stood to give an opening statement. Dressed in a three-piece pinstriped suit with a watch chain dangling from his vest, he spoke with measured intensity.

> The privilege of opening the first trial in history for crimes against the peace of the world imposes a grave responsibility. The wrongs, which we seek to condemn and punish, have been so calculated, so malignant, and so devastating, that civilization cannot tolerate their being ignored, because it cannot survive their being repeated. That four great nations, flushed with victory and stung with injury, stay the hand of vengeance and voluntarily submit their captive enemies to the judgment of the law is one of the most significant tributes that power has ever paid to reason.

Over the following weeks, the prosecution laid out its case on each of the indictments, considering seized Nazi papers and testimonials on how plans for these crimes had been developed by the defendants, the methods they had taken to achieve them, and the orders they had given to execute them. Their guilt was clear, but the trial also made obvious that many other Nazis had had a direct hand in these crimes. One of the names that became most prominent was that of Adolf Eichmann.

Eichmann was first mentioned on the trial's twentieth day. The prosecution quoted a Hungarian Jewish leader writing about the arrival of the Germans in March 1944: "Together with the German military occupation, there arrived in Budapest a 'Special Section Commando' of the German secret police with the sole object of liquidating the Hungarian Jews. It was headed by Adolf Eichmann . . . Commanders of the death camps gassed only on the direct or indirect instructions of Eichmann." The next day, Eichmann was noted as the "Chief of the Jewish Section of the Gestapo," who had once authoritatively declared that 4 million Jews had been deported and then killed in the extermination camps.

Shortly after the restart of the proceedings, on January 3, 1946, SS captain Dieter Wisliceny took the witness stand. Wisliceny had worked with Eichmann for eleven years, and he was also a close family friend. His testimony would lay bare the part that Eichmann had played in the genocide.

In answer to a question from Lieutenant Colonel Smith Brookhart of the prosecution as to whether Eichmann had shown Wisliceny the order from Himmler to begin the Final Solution, the witness said, "Yes, Eichmann handed me the document and I saw the order myself."

"Was any question asked by you as to the meaning of the words 'Final Solution' as used in the order?" Lieutenant Colonel Brookhart asked.

"Eichmann went on to explain to me what was meant by this. He said that the planned biological annihilation of the Jewish race in the Eastern Territories was disguised by the concept and wording 'Final Solution.'"

"Was anything said by you to Eichmann in regard to the power given him under this order?"

"Eichmann told me that within the RSHA he personally was entrusted with the execution of this order," Wisliceny responded. "For this purpose, he had received every authority from the Chief of the Security Police; he himself was personally responsible for the execution of this order."

"Did you make any comment to Eichmann about his authority?"

"Yes. It was perfectly clear to me that this order spelled death to millions of people. I said to Eichmann, 'God grant that our enemies never have the opportunity of doing the same to the German people,' in reply to which Eichmann told me not to be sentimental."

With this stark testimony, the significance and character of Adolf Eichmann was revealed to the general public for the first time. However, since the summer, the Allied investigators had grown increasingly keen on his capture. The CIC had interviewed his wife in Altaussee in August. She had informed investigators that she had had no contact with her husband since they had separated in March 1945. Nor did she have a picture of him to give them.

By early September, interrogations of several other intimates of Eichmann, including Wisliceny, had provided an exhaustive chronicle of Department IVB$_4$'s leader and his close associates. It was clear that he had been alive at the war's end, and his associates doubted that he would have committed suicide. The investigators had several tips as to his whereabouts, among them Altaussee and Salzburg. Later that month, the Allies targeted Eichmann in a special report as "urgently wanted at the Supreme Headquarters of the Allied Expeditionary Force center for interrogation and possibly for trial by the War Crimes Commission." By November, notices distributed to various CIC regions labeled him "of the highest importance among war criminals" and provided a vivid, precise portrait of him:

Age: Approximately 40
Height: 1.78 meters
Weight: 70 kilograms
Build: Gaunt, sinewy
Hair: Thinning on top, dark blond
Eyes: Blue-gray
Face: Prominent features, beak nose
Posture: Erect, military, mountaineer's gait
Dialect: Speaks Austrian accent, strident, hoarse, unmodulated
   voice, always loud

Other identifying marks: Usually carries a walking stick. Motions are strikingly nervous; while talking, he has a nervous cough, a twitch in one corner of the mouth, closes one eye.

Yet at the start of 1946, Eichmann remained undetected after more than six months in Allied hands, revealing the fractured and over-stretched state of the war crimes investigators. Beyond their early targets of the Nazi elite, who were now on trial, the British dragged their feet, and the Americans still did not have enough investigators to handle the number of individuals they had targeted. Further crippling their efforts, the much-vaunted CROWCASS list of suspects was not widely distributed until the fall of 1945, and even then it was too voluminous to be effective.

The Allies had proved more than capable of rounding up tens of thousands of suspects in their automatic arrest categories. They had been photographed and interrogated, and their physical characteristics had been noted. But without a coordinated, fully staffed center for this information, neither Eichmann nor the others who lied about their identities could be exposed in a POW system with more than two hundred American camps in Germany alone.

Nonetheless, individual Allied investigators struggled mightily against these challenges. A few days after Wisliceny's testimony, the CIC issued another bulletin to its regional offices, requesting every lead on Eichmann, who was "at least partly responsible for the extermination of about 6,000,000 Jews," to be followed to secure his arrest. The bulletin warned that Eichmann was "a desperate type who, if cornered, will try to shoot it out. He is a resourceful alpinist and presumably frequently changing his location."

At the Ober-Dachstetten camp, Eichmann was planning his escape. In early January 1946, through the prisoner grapevine, he learned of the testimony of Dieter Wisliceny. He had named his youngest son after Wisliceny. If one of his closest friends was singing to the Allies, Eichmann could be sure that others were as well, perhaps his adjutant Jänisch, who knew of his fake identity. Now that Eichmann had been publicly identified as being the center point of the Final Solution, the price on his head was certain to be high.

For months now, the fear of capture had gnawed at him. He could never be certain who was searching for him, how diligently, whether they had his photograph, whether they had informants. He had survived another Ansbach interrogation, yet it had left him even more convinced that his interrogators did not believe him. Either they would eventually identify him as Eichmann or some Jewish survivor would recognize him. One way or the other, his discovery was certain if he remained in the camp.

Eichmann went straight to Colonel Opperbeck, the camp's top-ranking SS officer. Eight months after the collapse of the Third Reich, Eichmann still felt the need to seek approval before making a move. He revealed to Opperbeck his name and rank, his position in the RSHA, and his desire to escape.

"I have known who you are for quite a while," Opperbeck said. "Since you never said anything to me, I kept it to myself."

They agreed to hold a meeting of the SS officers. That night, they assembled by the latrine, and Eichmann told the officers that he wanted to get out of the camp. He did not reveal his name, only that he feared that the Allies were after him for his political activities. He told the group that he planned to travel to Egypt, where he might find safe harbor.

The officers consented to the escape. One, Hans Feiersleben, suggested that Eichmann stay in Germany for a while. He had a brother who was a forest ranger in northern Germany and could get him a job in an isolated area where the Allies would never find him. Another, Kurt Bauer, advised him to travel first to Prien, southeast of Munich, where Bauer's sister would hide him and assist in his travels.

By the time the meeting concluded, Eichmann had a plan. The other officers helped him forge papers in the name of Otto Heninger. An orderly made an attempt to burn off his SS tattoo. And a woman he used to flirt with at the camp's fence slipped him a Tyrolean jacket and some dye to color his Luftwaffe pants green. With a pair of wool socks pulled over his pants, he would look like any hunter out in the woods.

A few nights later, Eichmann shaved his beard and put on his new outfit. He made his way to a section of the barbed-wire fence out of the guards' view. In the darkness, he gingerly climbed through the barrier, avoiding the razor points. On the other side of the fence, he hesitated, feeling helpless, exposed to any random patrol. He hastened into the woods.

5

IT WAS LATE MAY 1946, and Tuviah Friedman was waiting on a Vienna street for a man he knew only as Arthur. Arthur was the chief of the Haganah in Vienna as well as the leader of the Brichah organization that was helping the twenty-four-year-old Friedman and thousands of other Jews secretly to immigrate to Palestine. Friedman's request to meet with Arthur had nothing to do with this journey, but it was of equal, if not greater, importance to him.

Near the end of the war, Friedman had returned to his little house in Radom, a small industrial city in the heart of Poland that the Russians had freed on their advance toward Berlin. Standing on the street outside the house, he was flooded with childhood memories: his young sister, Itka, pedaling her bicycle and keeping her blond curls from her face with one hand; his daring younger brother, Hershele, playing on the roof; his older sister, Bella, reading one of her precious books; his father showing him the workings of the printing presses; his mother in one of the pretty dresses she made at her shop. His parents, Itka, and Hershele were all dead, thanks to the Nazis, and he still did not know whether Bella was alive. He had survived the ghettos, the slave labor, the murderous whimsy of the SS guards, and a half-planned breakout from a work camp through the sewers. He had ultimately managed to escape only by burying a bayonet into the neck of a German soldier. Standing outside his house, now inhabited by a family that had moved in as soon as the Jews had been cleared from Radom, Friedman knew that this world was dead to him. He would not return again.

He joined the Polish militia and was sent to Danzig to arrest any Germans still in the ruined city. His superior advised him to take the name Jasinki—with his blond hair, he could pass as a Gentile. He reluctantly agreed, wanting the position. Soon he found he had a knack for police and interrogation work, not to mention a real zeal, fueled by his grief and anger, for making his SS prisoners cower in front of him. While in Danzig, Friedman was reunited with Bella, who had miraculously survived Auschwitz.

Over the passing months, he became more and more uncomfortable living a lie, pretending to be Jasinki. Early in 1946, he retired from the military, joined a kibbutz outside Danzig, and a couple of months later contacted the Brichah and began the trek toward Palestine. En route, he met an old friend in the streets of Vienna, who told him about an SS man from there whom they knew from Radom. Friedman marched straight to the man's house, learned that he was hiding in an American POW camp, went undercover to find him, and won his confession. Then he heard of another SS officer from Radom, also hiding in Vienna. Friedman asked to see the Haganah chief, hoping to get his help in gathering evidence against the officer.

A black sedan pulled to the curb, and its driver rolled down the passenger's side window. Cigar smoke plumed out. "Friedman?" the driver asked. He nodded and got into the car.

Arthur Pier introduced himself as he drove. He was tall and slender, and he spoke and dressed like an aristocrat. Though only a few years older than Friedman, Pier had an air of calm competence that impressed Friedman straightaway. He told Pier about his desire to get to Palestine.

"And we're anxious to get you there," Pier said. "I'm a kibbutz member myself, and we need healthy young men like you, Tadek."

Friedman was surprised that Pier knew his nickname, but he said nothing. They arrived at 2 Frankgasse in the center of Vienna. The sign on the door read AUSTRIAN REFUGEE ORGANIZATION, but it was actually the Brichah headquarters, a six-room office that hummed with activity. Pier invited Friedman into his office and closed the door. Friedman explained that before leaving for Palestine, he wanted assistance in getting to Stuttgart to collect testimony against two SS officers.

"What are their names?" Pier asked, paging through a small black notebook on his desk. "This little notebook is the result of two years of hard work in Palestine . . . Konrad Buchmayer? Yes, he's listed . . . There's a Gestapo officer named Schokl in Radom. That must be your man, Richard Schoegl." He made a quick mark with a red pencil by each name. Then Pier looked up at Friedman. "Tadek, a few weeks ago, the leader of your kibbutz told me about you, and about your work in Danzig."

Pier explained that he had emigrated from Vienna when the Nazis had taken over. After a few years helping others get to Palestine, the Jewish Agency had tasked him with collecting evidence on Nazi war criminals from refugees arriving in Haifa. Over the next eighteen months, he had collected dossiers on thousands of Germans, which he had then passed to the American OSS and the International Criminal Tribunal in Nuremberg. Pier told Friedman that at the end of the war, David Ben-Gurion, the leader of the Jewish Agency, had brought Pier and other top people in the organization together and had called on them to go to Europe to lead the movement of Jews to Palestine. This would further their efforts to create an independent state. Ben-Gurion also had instructed them to join the Allies in hunting down war criminals, using the information that Pier had collected. They must be brought to justice, Ben-Gurion had insisted, hammering his fist on the table for emphasis.

Posing as a journalist, Pier had arrived in November 1945, carrying with him a briefcase with a false bottom containing the notebook and gold sovereigns to fund his operation. He had soon found himself overwhelmed by his responsibilities smuggling refugees to Palestine. He was just now putting together a team to go after the war criminals in earnest and to bring them to trial. "This is not an easy job. None of us here works for money," Pier said. "I know you've experience in this, and I am asking you to work with us, to find these murderers."

Friedman listened. He now understood why he had survived the horrors of the war: to do this work.

"Did you ever hear of Adolf Eichmann?" Pier asked, pointing to his name in the notebook.

Friedman told him no, feeling foolish for not knowing who he was.

"You must find Eichmann. I will say it to you again: you *must* find Eichmann." Pier gestured again to his notebook. "I want to be able to put a line through it."

Friedman had his mission. He was one of several men Pier was setting on the trail of the lieutenant colonel he had first known in Vienna. Pier had heard many stories about Eichmann over the past two years, particularly about his deeds in Hungary. He wanted him captured and brought to justice.

The Haganah was not the only group after Eichmann. Other pursuers, operating independently, had some of the same information as Pier and believed that they already had their target in sight. Unlike Pier, however, they wanted immediate justice, not a trial.

Five Jewish avengers, outfitted with British army uniforms and Sten guns, hid their jeep in a grove of trees outside a small village between Linz and Salzburg. They waited for the last of the light to drain from the sky. Their eyes were trained on a small two-story chalet. When night completely enveloped them, they slowly made their way up the hillside to kill Adolf Eichmann.

When they neared the house, one of the men crept forward alone, growling like a dog. He had fought with Tito in his guerrilla campaign against the Fascists in Yugoslavia and was experienced in handling watchdogs. The three massive dogs that guarded the chalet came toward him, and he threw a slab of poisoned meat at their feet. Several minutes later, the dogs were dead. The rest of the group went to the side of the house. A brief glance through the window revealed four men eating dinner. The avengers prepared themselves.

They had traveled to Austria looking for Eichmann in the spring of 1946. They had tracked down his wife in Altaussee and his elder brother Otto in neighboring Bad Aussee. After a month of surveillance, they had followed the two twice to this same chalet. The fact that Eichmann's wife and brother had taken different trains to the village, then went their separate ways to meet these men, had made the Jews suspicious. They had staked out the chalet for several weeks. It was clear that four men lived in the house. They never went out during the day, and a villager would deliver food and other supplies every evening. The avengers were convinced that one of the men was Eichmann. His features and height matched the reports they had collected, and the visits by Vera and Otto Eichmann provided even more confirmation.

On a signal, two of the Jews rammed their shoulders into the chalet door, bursting it open. They leveled their guns at the four defenseless men and told them to stand. The men rose from the table, careful not to make any threatening moves.

"You," one of the avengers barked in German. "Come here!"

"Me?" one of the men replied, trembling.

Two men dragged him out of the house, while the others kept their guns on the ones around the table. Once clear of the chalet, one of the two men knocked their prisoner out with a blow to the back of his head. They carried him back to their jeep and drove several miles into the pine forest. Tossed out of the jeep into the mud, the prisoner came to.

The leader of the group climbed out of the jeep and stood over him. "We are Jews, Adolf Eichmann. We've got a big score to settle with you."

"I swear to you by my wife and children, by the memory of my mother, that I am not Adolf Eichmann. He was a killer. I was only a soldier. You are good people," he pleaded. "Show me mercy."

"You know how much mercy you showed to the Jewish people."

The prisoner confessed that he had been part of the *Einsatzgruppen* and that he had killed some Jews, but only because he had been ordered to do so. He begged them to believe him, telling him that the wife and brother of Eichmann were friends of the chalet's owner. After a few moments, his torrent of words slowed, and he said, "All you can do is kill me."

With that, the avengers fired several rounds of bullets into his chest. They cursed his very existence, then buried him in an un-marked grave.

Adolf Eichmann was still very much alive the morning after the five Jewish avengers shot the man in Austria. He woke up in a bunk hut deep in the woods in British-occupied northern Germany with nine-teen woodsmen, all of them discharged Wehrmacht soldiers. After breakfast, Eichmann and his workmates trudged into the forest with their axes and saws. They called the heavily wooded area in the Lüneburg Heath "the island." For Eichmann, the island, which had neither electricity nor telephone, was an ideal hiding place from his pursuers, who, he saw in one of the rare newspapers that found their way into the camp, were calling him a "mass murderer."

After escaping from Ober-Dachstetten, Eichmann had hunkered down in an abandoned railway station several miles from the camp until the next morning. He had then caught a train to Munich, then one to Prien. He had presented a letter of introduction to Nellie Krawietz, the sister of SS officer Bauer and a striking war widow of twenty-four. She had asked no questions, providing Eichmann with a room at a farm on the town's edge. For the next six weeks, they had met almost daily, though he had revealed little more than that his name was Otto Heninger and he was the divorced father of three chil-dren whom he had not seen since the war's end.

The American military was everywhere in the district, and in February 1946, Eichmann had become increasingly nervous. He had asked Nellie to buy him two tickets to Hamburg; she was to accom-pany him so that they looked like a couple traveling for the weekend. This would be more inconspicuous, he had explained. Having fallen for the quiet, somewhat melancholic man, Nellie had agreed. During the journey, she had pleaded with him to turn himself in to a de-Nazification tribunal so that he would not have to stay underground for the rest of his life. In a moment of carelessness, he had explained that he had been involved in the concentration camps and that his name was really Adolf Eichmann. If caught, he had assured her, he would be imprisoned by the Allies for much longer than a few years—if they did not execute him, the fate they planned for those convicted in the ongoing Nuremberg trial. Nellie had promised to keep his secret and to visit him whenever possible.

In March, Eichmann had walked into the town hall of Eversen, on the southwestern edge of the Lüneburg Heath, sixty miles from Hamburg. He had presented forged documents to the British zone officials stating that he was a Breslau-born, discharged Wehrmacht POW—the same information as his previous identity. The clerk had not questioned any of the details and had approved his resident documents in the name of Otto Heninger. Eichmann had located the brother of SS officer Feiersleben and secured a lumberjack job. He had been working there for several months.

At the end of a long day in a fire-ravaged section of the forest, Eichmann returned to the camp, his clothes and face black from the charred wood. With the other men, he washed himself in rainwater collected in old munitions barrels and then settled down by the campfire, where he ate a watery stew. Into the night, the lumberjacks played cards, drank the local schnapps, and smoked Lucky Strikes. They were a rough bunch, coarse of talk and behavior. On occasion, Eichmann borrowed a violin from one of the rangers, but otherwise he made every effort to blend in. He liked the peace of the woods; he felt safe. For now, this was all he wanted.

On a frosty Vienna morning early in 1947, Arthur Pier and Tuviah Friedman entered the Vienna jail where Joseph Weisl, Eichmann's former chauffeur, awaited trial for war crimes. Friedman had arranged the interview and, as always, was amazed at the doors that had opened when he had mentioned that he worked with the Haganah chief.

The prison commandant loaned them his office for the interrogation. A guard led the twenty-eight-year-old prisoner into the room. Pier leaned back in the commandant's chair, smoking a cigar, while Friedman sat next to him with a notebook and pen. First, Pier led Weisl through some basic questions about his war experiences and how he had escaped to Austria. Then he asked bluntly, "Are you trying to tell me that Eichmann was killed in the war?"

"No, no. I don't know what happened to him. All I know is that about a month before the war ended, the SS officers all changed their ranks—nobody wanted to be higher than a lieutenant."

"What kind of man was he, Weisl?"

"Well, in the last few years, everybody was afraid of him, really terrified . . . He stopped smiling and laughing. I guess he knew too many things."

"You were in charge of the barracks in Doppl for a long time, weren't you? And Eichmann frequently visited Doppl, right?" Pier asked. They had already gathered a dossier on the chauffeur. A few months previously, Dieter Wisliceny, Eichmann's deputy, had been transferred to a prison in Czechoslovakia after the Nuremberg trials. Upon his arrival there, he had provided a wealth of details on Eichmann's associates and had even offered to help track Eichmann down to evade punishment for his own crimes.

Weisl hesitated to answer the question, looking from one of them to the other. Pier offered him a cigarette, and Friedman put down his pen in an attempt to ease him.

"You know, of course, that Eichmann had a mistress in Doppl. Frau Maria Mösenbacher. She was quite a woman, and he spent a lot of time with her," Weisl said.

"Where does she live now?" Pier asked.

Weisl explained that she still lived there. He took the pen and pad from the desk and drew a map of Doppl, indicating exactly where. "She must still have a photo of Eichmann. I saw one there myself. She was very proud of him."

"Tell me," Friedman said. "Does he really know Hebrew?"

Weisl chuckled. "Eichmann spoke to the Vienna Jews, the rich ones, who did not understand any Hebrew. Afterwards, he used to laugh about it because he convinced the Jews that he was born in Palestine."

Pier stood. He and his family were among those that Eichmann had forced out of Vienna in 1938. "That's all for today," he said, waving to the guard at the door and then turning back to Weisl. "You SS men were a fine group, a very fine group," he said sarcastically. "But it's all over. Finished. Kaput."

Friedman and Pier returned to their headquarters at 2 Frankgasse. Over the past eight months, while securing the arrest of many SS officers and gathering a vast collection of documents on war crimes, Friedman and a handful of others working out of the Haganah office had followed many leads on Eichmann. Some of the Nazi's closest staff, including Anton Burger, had been caught and questioned. They had also chased down Eichmann's family and several of his mistresses. Nobody knew where he was.

Friedman and Pier had heard a rumor that he was being held in a German POW camp, and they urged the Allies to inquire at all the camps, but they were unable to supply a photograph of him. Of the dozens of people they had interviewed, not one possessed a single picture. They had a good physical description of Eichmann, but this was nothing compared to a photograph. Now, at least, Weisl might have given them a good lead for obtaining one.

Pier wanted Manus Diamant on the job, and Friedman knew he had made the right choice. The next day, Diamant was on a train from Vienna to Linz.

Handsome and suave, Diamant often played the Romeo agent for the Haganah team in Austria. He had blue eyes and a full mustache, and he could play any role assigned to him with ease and confidence. In a different life, he might have been a great stage actor, but he had been born a Jew in Katowice, in southern Poland, in 1923. When he was eleven, he was stealing swastikas off the Mercedes parked in front of the German consulate. As a teenager, he had seen Nazis pummeling Jewish refugees, a fate he swore would not be his. At eighteen, he had gone to Warsaw with his family and joined the underground resistance. When the Nazis had cleared the ghettos, Diamant had escaped the city with forged Aryan papers, but he had not been able to save his family. At the age of twenty-one, he was in Austria helping Jews escape while posing as Dr. Janowski, a pathologist at a Graz hospital. From there he had gone to Hungary, where he had purchased arms for the resistance and sabotaged German ammunitions trains. Arrested in a roundup at the border, he had been sent to Auschwitz but had managed to convince his guards that he was a Pole.

After the war, Diamant had come to Vienna to work with the

Haganah. He had already earned the confidence of Eichmann's wife in Altaussee, and he had wooed several of Eichmann's mistresses. Every effort, however, had ended in frustration. Vera Eichmann had been closely guarded and offered no hint of her husband's whereabouts or even whether he was alive. The mistresses proved equally unhelpful, none of them owning so much as a snapshot of their former lover.

This time, Diamant prayed, they would have more success. Posing as a former Dutch SS officer, he stopped in Linz to meet with Simon Wiesenthal. Wiesenthal still lived in the town with his wife, who had survived the war. He knew the surrounding area well. Although they worked separately, Wiesenthal and the Haganah investigators often traded tips and contacts. Wiesenthal gave Diamant some insight into Doppl and mentioned some people to connect with in his search for Maria Mösenbacher, Eichmann's mistress there.

After a few inquiries in Doppl, Diamant learned that Fraulein Mösenbacher was an attractive, frivolous woman of forty who was not very well liked and who had often bragged of her relationship with "Adolf," a high-ranking SS officer. Diamant also found out that she had moved and rented a tiny furnished apartment in Urfahr, a town on the opposite side of Linz. For the next week, he followed her, noting when she went to the hairdresser, grocer, pharmacy, and post office and when she returned home to her apartment opposite the pastry shop. So when some groceries fell from her basket, Diamant was there to pick them up. He introduced himself with a smile as Henry van Diamant.

"Thank you. Thank you very much. My name is Maria . . . Thank you."

He tipped his hat and offered to walk her home. Over the next few weeks, he slowly grew closer to her. They met for coffee, then dinner, then a walk in the country. One evening at dinner, he purposefully let his wallet fall open to show his forged Dutch SS identification so as to explain why he could not return to Holland. He bought her blouses and chocolates. To convince her of his avid interest in amateur photography, he gave her some landscape photographs that he pretended to have taken himself but had actually bought. Then one evening at her home a few weeks after they had met, he showed her an album filled with his "family photos" (all bought).

"I also have one," Mösenbacher said proudly, taking a gold-edged album from a shelf. She thumbed through the pages, pointing out pictures of her brother and parents.

Day after day, Diamant had tolerated this vapid woman, who spoke so viciously about the Jews, all to arrive at this point. He prayed that she had the photograph of Eichmann.

"You know, I had many admirers." She stopped at a photo of a man in his early thirties with a long, sharp nose and pursed lips. "This is Adolf . . . He was my regular boyfriend. Who knows what happened to him. He probably didn't survive the war, otherwise he would surely have given me a sign of life."

For the next two hours, lingering over dinner and drinking wine with Mösenbacher, Diamant wanted only to leave so that he could set into motion his plan to get the photograph. The next morning, he went to the Austrian police with a letter from Arthur Pier. A few hours later, the police seized the albums on the pretense of a tip that Mösenbacher was hiding stolen ration cards within them. Diamant could not keep his hands from trembling when he held the photograph.

He returned to Vienna and showed it to Pier and Friedman. "You've done a good job, Manus. This is the murderer of our people." Hundreds of copies were made and distributed to police and Allied investigators throughout Europe. Diamant personally delivered a copy to Wiesenthal, who told him, "Now we know what he looks like. This is the first step in getting him."

6

EICHMANN WANTED TO get out of the woods. Eighteen months as a lumberjack, pretending to be a simple laborer without any family, ambition, or status, had worn on him. The only time he ventured out of the forest was for a Sunday drink at the tavern in Celle and an occasional meeting with Nellie Krawietz. Although Eichmann was safe in Lüneburg Heath, he felt more like a mole than a man. He wanted a new life.

He was reminded of his old one in the newspapers. The capture and confession of the Auschwitz commandant Rudolf Höss had brought Eichmann the "mass murderer" into the headlines again. Höss provided even more proof of Eichmann's involvement in the extermination camps, detailing his frequent visits, his discussions about the suitability of Zyklon B for the gas chambers, and his complete obsession with "destroying every single Jew that he could lay his hands on."

One day Eichmann read that a squad of Jews had seized him at a cabin in Austria, taken him by jeep into the woods, and shot him. According to the killers, he had remained defiant to the end. Eichmann enjoyed that last detail, certain that he himself would prove equally brave in the face of death. More disturbing, however, was a report that chronicled his flight from Ober-Dachstetten, including the exact date of his escape. Either his adjutant Jänisch or one of the SS officers at the camp had told investigators that the escaped Otto Eckmann was actually Adolf Eichmann. At least there was no mention of his new identity, and he was reportedly on his way to connect with the grand mufti of Jerusalem.

As the first winter storms of 1947 whipped the Lüneburg Heath, Eichmann turned his mind to how and where he could build a new existence with his family and without the fear of being revealed at any moment. He began to ask around, discreetly, if anyone knew a route out of Europe. He also plotted to find a way to get his name removed from the wanted lists. His rumored killing by Jewish avengers was not enough to convince war crimes investigators to stop searching for him.

In December 1947, Simon Wiesenthal traveled to CIC headquarters in Bad Ischl, Austria, after a CIC agent called him for an urgent meeting. The agent told Wiesenthal the disturbing news that Vera Eichmann had just applied to the local court for her husband to be declared legally dead "in the interest of her children." According to an affidavit from Karl Lukas of Czechoslovakia, which was included with the application, Eichmann had been shot and killed by partisans in Prague on April 30, 1945. This was a story the CIC agent had been hearing from the Eichmann family for the past year, but now they had a corroborating witness.

From his own investigations, Wiesenthal knew that this was impossible. He had interrogated associates of Eichmann who had met with him in Altaussee in May 1945, just before he disappeared. He had also read the news items about his Ober-Dachstetten escape, and he had heard Nuremberg war crimes testimony from the German officer Rudolf Scheide, who had sworn to American investigators that on June 15, 1945, a prisoner who had first revealed himself as Eichmann wanted to be known as Eckmann before he even reached Ober-Dachstetten. This twice-confirmed alias was distributed to all Allied investigative offices, but with no result. Eichmann would have changed his name again by now. Still, the reports proved that he had definitely not been killed in Prague at the end of the war.

If Vera Eichmann succeeded in her court request, Adolf Eichmann would disappear from the wanted lists of the Allies and the Austrian police. One did not search for a dead man. Wiesenthal was certain that Vera had made her application not so that she could remarry or collect a widow's pension but because she wanted the hunt for her husband to end, and she was probably acting on his command. Although the police intercepted all her mail, Wiesenthal was convinced that Eichmann could pass word to her through other channels if he wished.

The CIC agent impressed on Wiesenthal that he could convince the judge to delay the hearing only for a month. Wiesenthal moved quickly, sending one of his assistants to Prague to investigate this Karl Lukas. Ten days later, he received word that Lukas was married to Maria Liebl, Vera's sister. The judge quashed the application.

It was a minor victory but an important one in light of Wiesenthal's fruitless pursuit of Eichmann over the past two and a half years. His file on the Nazi had grown. He had interrogated almost every one of Eichmann's staff members. He had spent weeks at Nuremberg scouring court records for any mention of Eichmann, a labor that revealed to him the true extent of Eichmann's involvement in the Final Solution. Since then, Wiesenthal had discovered many Nazi documents on the extermination program and the role that Eichmann and his underlings had played in executing it. In Linz, people on the street called the Nazi-hunter "Eichmann-Wiesenthal" because he was known for constantly searching out clues and watching the family.

But his failure to find Eichmann was wearing on him, and in this he was not alone. Manus Diamant had told him about an incident a few months after his success in acquiring the photograph at Maria Mösenbacher's house. Despite the photograph's wide distribution and Diamant's close contact with the Eichmann family (also by posing as a former Dutch SS officer), there were no more clues as to his whereabouts, and Diamant was angry at their lack of progress. One afternoon he went out on the lake with Eichmann's three sons, who had come to call him "Uncle Henry." Sitting in the boat, he became overwhelmed by memories of scenes he had witnessed during the war: children taken from their mothers' arm; Jews fleeing in advance of the black-uniformed SS marching through the streets; shootings and shootings and shootings.

When his mind cleared, he found himself gripping one of the oars and staring at Dieter Eichmann, who was laughing and playing in the summer sunshine. Diamant had the urge to strike down Dieter and the other two boys in revenge. Adolf Eichmann deserved to pay at least *this* price for his deeds, Diamant silently raged. But then he relaxed his grasp on the oar and returned to shore. Vera Eichmann greeted him on his return, commenting that he looked strained. "Nothing happened," Diamant reassured her. "The children all behaved very well." He swore never to go back to the house.

That December, Diamant left Austria. After the United Nations resolution of November 27, 1947, partitioning Palestine for the establishment of a Jewish state, Arthur Pier disbanded his group of Haganah agents and returned to Palestine along with Diamant. A war was expected against the Arab states that opposed the creation of Israel, and they were needed to smuggle arms and prepare a defense.

It was also clear to Wiesenthal that the rest of the world was moving on. The start of the cold war drained the will and resources of the Allies away from pursuing war criminals. The convictions at Nuremberg had satisfied many political leaders that adequate punishment had been meted out for the Nazi atrocities. Follow-up trials there against *Einsatzgruppen* leaders, concentration camp doctors, and Third Reich judges, among others, were in progress. In the end, these proceedings indicted only 185 defendants. There was a scattering of other trials and the de-Nazification court proceedings for those interned in camps after the war. Some 9,600 former Nazis spent time in jail for their crimes, typically serving short sentences. These numbers represented only a small fraction of the 160,000 Germans who Wiesenthal and others estimated were involved in war crimes, from leaders such as Heinrich Müller and Adolf Eichmann; to notorious individuals such as Josef Mengele, who oversaw the selections at Auschwitz and conducted bestial experiments on prisoners; to the rank-and-file soldiers, policemen, and SS troops who participated in the atrocities. They were either released from the POW camps or never caught in the first place. Few people showed any further interest in bringing these criminals to justice.

Only Tuviah Friedman remained in Vienna to continue the hunt with Wiesenthal. The CIC and the Austrian police helped them, but these organizations were more reactive in their efforts than proactive. The two men labored night and day to gather survivor testimonials and any evidence they could find against war criminals. Although they ran separate documentation centers, they often worked together, exchanging information and tracking down individuals on their wanted lists, most recently some of those involved in the Belzec extermination camp. Eichmann was constantly on their minds, but they had run into dead end after dead end in pursuit of him. He seemed to have vanished like a ghost, and their wish for a clue on where he was hiding remained unfulfilled at the end of every day.

One gloomy wintry afternoon, as 1947 drew to a close, Wiesenthal sat in his office, surrounded by the reports of murders, tortures, and other horrors that filled his filing cabinets and teetered in piles on his desk. On the wall opposite him was a large map of the world, with a few lines drawn in pencil representing the routes he had heard war criminals had taken to reach the Middle East and South America. The previous month, Wiesenthal had met a former Nazi intelligence officer who had told him about a secret organization created by SS officers to smuggle Nazis out of Europe. Staring at the map, Wiesenthal could not help but think that if Eichmann had already taken one of those routes, he would never be found.

In Altensalzkoth, a village in the Lüneburg Heath, Eichmann sat at his desk and penned a farewell letter to Nellie Krawietz dated April 1950. He thanked her for her help and companionship and explained that he was leaving for Soviet territory with the hope that the Russians would recruit him. "If you don't hear from me within the next four weeks," he wrote, "you can put a cross through my name."

The morning of his departure, Eichmann put on a suit and tie for the first time in a long while. For the past two years, he had rented a room in the house of Anna Lindhorst, a war widow who lived with her teenage son. After the lumber company had gone under and he had lost his job, he had leased a parcel of land from her and had started a chicken farm. Because of price controls, he sold his eggs on the black market, mostly to the Jewish community in nearby Belsen, the site of the former concentration camp. Eichmann found it ironic.

He often passed by British soldiers in the area and occasionally even sold them eggs, but he wasn't worried. Nobody suspected that he was anything other than a chicken farmer. Eichmann saved his money and waited.

The time had come to make his escape. The previous year, the British had announced a halt in their efforts to try war criminals, and the Americans were preoccupied with the Russians, especially with the divided Berlin. Eichmann's identification card, issued in June 1948, would expire in six weeks. He had obtained it after connecting with some former SS officers in Celle who were involved with an underground network to smuggle fugitives out of Europe.

Before leaving, Eichmann sat down with his landlady, giving her a different story from the one he had written to Nellie in order to confuse anyone who might attempt to follow him. He explained that he was leaving for Scandinavia, where his mechanical engineering experience would help him secure a job. He told her that the forest ranger Feiersleben would come by the next day to look after his chickens. Since their first meeting, Anna Lindhorst had never suspected anything amiss with her tenant, who was always pleasant with her son and paid his rent exactly on time. She believed his story.

Then Eichmann picked up his suitcase and walked away from the heath. After his usual uniform of faded blue overalls, his new clothes made him feel as though he stood out. Under the name Otto Heninger, he traveled by train to Munich, nervous that he might be exposed at any moment now that he had stepped out of the relative safety of the forest. From Munich he journeyed to a town near the Bavarian border. The challenge would be getting across to Austria, then to Italy. Eichmann had memorized every stopping point and contact on the route that the underground network's agent—a man he had contacted through coded advertisements in the newspaper and knew only as "Günther"—had given him. Eichmann had paid Günther 300 marks, one-fifth of his savings, for his help.

The town was swarming with border police, obviously on the lookout for fugitives. Eichmann trembled as he filled out the hotel registration form, and he panicked when his contact missed their rendezvous. (He later learned from the man's associates that he was in the hospital.) After he waited a week, his contact arranged for a local hunter to guide Eichmann across the border. He was glad to leave. Eichmann slung his suitcase onto his back, and the two men hiked along well-worn paths through the woods and into the mountains, not stopping until they reached a cabin high on the slopes. As night fell, Eichmann looked down into the German countryside: after tomorrow, he was unlikely to see the country of his birth again.

As they ate breakfast the next day, the hunter looked out the window and spotted a border guard coming up the path. "Don't worry," the man told Eichmann. "He'll have seen the smoke from the chimney. He probably only wants coffee." Eichmann hid, petrified, in a dusty closet, trying not to sneeze as the hunter and border guard chatted and drank coffee. After the guard left, Eichmann tumbled out of the closet, and the hunter led him along a winding route, away from any patrols, down into Kufstein, Austria. After spending the night in a monastery that was on his list of safe houses, he hired a taxi to Innsbruck. There he had two contacts. The first, a former SS lieutenant, sent him packing, saying huffily, "They really send every damn tramp this way." The second brought Eichmann to an inn near the Brenner Pass, which leads through the Alps between Austria and Italy. French soldiers were active in the area, so Eichmann had to be hidden in the attic, which was full of spider webs and the innkeeper's junk.

Several days later, the innkeeper judged that it was safe to leave and brought him along the edge of the pass. This time, Eichmann was not allowed to bring his suitcase; the innkeeper was afraid it would arouse suspicions if they came across a patrol. A mile past the border into Italy, a black-robed priest on a bicycle met the two men on the road. The priest had Eichmann's suitcase; he had crossed the border without difficulty.

After the innkeeper returned to Austria, Eichmann and his new companion shared a glass of wine to celebrate the successful crossing. The priest arranged for a car to take them to Merano, a Tyrolean village in northern Italy. Eichmann spent the night at a castle, another safe house for fleeing Nazis. The next day, he received a new identity card, issued by the town hall of a neighboring village, Termeno.

Everything had been arranged. To travel across Europe and the Atlantic Ocean to South America, Eichmann had tapped into a network whose tendrils reached throughout the continent, including the Vatican and the highest levels of the Argentine government. His new name would be Ricardo Klement. The underground agent who brought the ID also had a landing permit for his final destination: Buenos Aires.

In February 1945, Juan Perón had brought together the leading lights of the influential German community in Buenos Aires, most of whom were enthusiastic supporters of the Third Reich. The forty-nine-year-old vice president and minister of war of Argentina—a Machiavellian opportunist to his enemies and a graceful, charismatic savior of the masses to his supporters—announced that Argentina was going to end its commitment to neutrality and declare war on Germany. "It was a mere formality," Perón explained apologetically, to save the country from punishment when the fighting ended. There was little secret that Argentina had been a staging area for the Nazis' intelligence-gathering and covert warfare activities in the Western Hemisphere. At the meeting, Perón made it clear that he would not abandon the German community.

Perón came from a long line of nationalistic military officers who were fervently Catholic and who had little taste for democratic principles. From 1939 to 1941, he had lived in Rome as a military attaché and greatly admired Benito Mussolini and the Italian Fascists. Two years after his return to Argentina, he had staged a coup with a handful of other military men. With his courtship of industrial workers, he had earned enough popularity to win the presidential election less than a year after the war. It was more a stamp of approval than an election, since he already ruled the country of 15 million people in everything but name.

After Germany's defeat, Perón wanted to secure the immigration of Nazi scientists and engineers to benefit his country's military research and to promote industrialization. But he also felt that it was his duty to be a friend to the Germans and to others from the Axis states, and he helped any who wanted to come to his country to build a new life, no matter what they had done during the war. He viewed the Nuremberg trials as an "outrage that history will never forgive" and pledged to do whatever he could to help others avoid the fate of their defendants. He was far less welcoming to those who wanted to join the country's large Jewish community, installing a feverish anti-Semite as immigration chief, who published a book saying that Jews "lodge like a cyst in the people where they establish themselves."

Led by the head of the Argentine secret service, Rodolfo Freude, the escape network's agents established bases of operation throughout Europe. Freude was the scion of a wealthy Argentine businessman with significant Nazi connections who had helped finance Perón's presidential campaign.

The network included Carlos Fuldner, an Argentine German and former SS captain close to Himmler; former members of the Waffen-SS and Abwehr (a German intelligence organization); a Croatian ambassador to Berlin during the war; a Spanish journalist; and war criminals from Belgium, France, Czechoslovakia, the Netherlands, and Germany, who repaid the debt of their freedom by rescuing fellow fugitives. Receiving orders directly from Freude at the presidential palace Casa Rosada, in the heart of Buenos Aires, these agents facilitated the financing of operations, dispensed bribes to local officials, arranged safe houses and transportation for their charges, maneuvered between the immigration office and Argentine consulates to produce the necessary landing permits and other paperwork, and coordinated with Vatican representatives.

The network would never have been as effective without the aid of the Catholic Church, most notably that of Bishop Alois Hudal, rector of Santa Maria dell'Anima in Rome. Once a hospice for the poor, the church had become the center of German-speaking Catholics in Italy in the fifteenth century and still flew the German imperial eagle on its spire. Under Hudal, an Austrian and a devotee of Hitler who proudly brandished his golden Nazi Party membership badge, the church harbored and smuggled war criminals out of Europe, working hand in hand with Perón's agents. In 1948, Hudal personally wrote to Perón to request visas for 5,000 Germans and Austrians who had "bravely fought" against communism. He did not accept the term "war criminal," believing that those he helped were innocent of any crimes because they had only executed orders from their superiors. Hudal was aided in his efforts by cardinals above him and priests below him. A string of monasteries and convents in Germany, Switzerland, Austria, and Italy served as refuges along the Nazi ratlines. Pope Pius XII did not officially approve of the Vatican's involvement in the network, but he certainly turned a blind eye to it, primarily because of the church's commitment to act as a bulwark against the spread of communism.

According to a confidential CIC report in 1947, postwar Europe was rife with people on the run. Fake passports, forged identification papers, and willing smugglers were all easy to find. Argentina and the Vatican were not alone in providing sanctuary for former Nazis, many of whom were involved in atrocities during the war. The Allies also smuggled out a number of war criminals, among them former SS officers, who were recruited for intelligence activities against the Soviet Union and its satellites. In fact, the United States and others were using some of the same routes and safe houses to smuggle individuals out of Europe as were Argentina and the Vatican.

However, none of the smuggling operations was run with the same professionalism and on the same scale as the one created by Juan Perón. When Eichmann reached out from the Lüneburg Heath to find a way out of Germany, one of the network's chief operators, Reinhard Kops, who served as a link between Bishop Hudal and the Argentines, instantly picked up his name. Kops was a former anti-Mason expert and Abwehr captain, and he knew Eichmann well from Berlin and Hungary. Eichmann's escape to Argentina would be most welcome. In June 1948, an immigration file was opened for him in Buenos Aires. A landing permit was issued and the Termeno ID arranged. Eichmann needed to be present for the other steps in the process, following a clear path that Kops had helped establish. Eichmann was only one among many whose escapes were fashioned within the same few months, including "the Angel of Death," Josef Mengele; "the Butcher of Riga," Eduard Roschmann; the mass murderer Erich Priebke; the "mercy killer" of the mentally ill and handicapped Gerhard Bohne; and the dreaded SS commandant Josef Schwammberger. Now Eichmann, the last among this group to leave Germany, looked to follow them to the freedom that a country located on the other side of the world and led by a friend of the Nazis would provide.

Traveling as Ricardo Klement, Eichmann left Merano. That evening, he arrived in Genoa. The four-hundred-year-old stone lighthouse there cast its beams across the ancient port, illuminating his escape.

Eichmann went to the Church of San Antonio, situated near the harbor amid a clutch of old pastel-colored houses. He rapped on the door and waited for his next contact, Father Edoardo Dömöter, to answer. The old Franciscan welcomed Eichmann into the presbytery and showed him to his room. Dömöter had been personally recommended by Kops to be in charge of operations in Genoa. He knew that the Hungarian priest was particularly sympathetic to the fleeing Nazis.

The following day, Eichmann presented himself at the city headquarters of the International Committee of the Red Cross (ICRC). He handed the official his landing permit and Termeno ID, along with a letter of reference from Dömöter. This stated that Ricardo Klement was a refugee from the war and could not obtain a travel document from any other source. Without hesitation, the official approved his application for a Red Cross passport. He took Eichmann's fingerprints and photograph, attached one copy to the cardboard passport, and marked it with an ICRC stamp dated June 1, 1950. An elated Eichmann walked out of the office feeling like a real person again. Next he went to the Argentine consulate, where he received his visa, again without hassle. Last, he went to the Argentine immigration office. They checked his papers and subjected him to a standard medical examination. The doctor removed his glasses — perhaps, Eichmann thought, to see if they were part of a disguise. Clearly they were not, and he passed the test.

During his time in Genoa, Eichmann spent his nights playing chess and drinking Chianti with Dömöter. The day before his ship left, Eichmann accepted the priest's invitation to attend Mass and received his blessing. The next day, July 17, 1950, Eichmann walked down to the port with his suitcase. Wearing his new suit, a bow tie, and a black hat, he looked like a traveling salesman. He boarded the passenger ship *Giovanna C* and deposited his bag in his third-class berth. Afterward, he went to the upper deck to watch the departure. Accompanying him on the passage to Argentina were two other former Nazis whom Perón's network had assisted: Wilhelm Mohnke, an SS brigadier general who had been with Hitler in his bunker, and SS captain Herbert Kuhlmann, a commander of a Hitler Youth Panzer division.

As the ship steamed out of the harbor, Eichmann felt a rush not only of relief but also of triumph at eluding his pursuers. Once he arrived in Argentina, the chances of his discovery by the Allies would be next to nothing, especially if he was careful. However, the knowledge that he had irrevocably broken with his fatherland tempered his joy. He put his hand in his pocket and ran his fingers through some German soil he had collected before crossing over to Austria. He promised himself that he would bring his family over to join him once he had settled in and found a job.

The month-long journey to Argentina passed slowly. More passengers boarded the ship in Naples, Barcelona, and Lisbon before it headed south along the African coast to Dakar. There was no relief from the excruciating heat. Then it crossed the Atlantic, the boredom of the endless seas broken only by two terrific storms that saw all the passengers in life jackets and confined to their quarters.

Eichmann had plenty of time to read about his destination. Eight times the size of Germany, Argentina stretched from the dry, wind-swept lands of the south, close enough to Antarctica to suffer its icy blasts, all the way to the tropical jungles of the north. To its west, the Andes rose like a leviathan, many of the peaks reaching over 20,000 feet. And to the east was the Atlantic Ocean and 2,500 miles of coastline. The heart of the country, its Pampas, or fertile grasslands, provided sustenance for its 22 million people. In these plains, one travel writer wrote, "the distances from house to house are too great for the barking of dogs even on the stillest night, a country in which the cocks crow only twice because there is no answer . . . It is the country in which the green goes on and on like water, and the gulls follow the plows as seagulls follow ships." These empty spaces contrasted sharply with the sprawling, seventy-square-mile metropolis of Buenos Aires, where more than a third of all Argentines lived. In a country such as this, Eichmann could hide among the city's millions on the western bank of the Río de la Plata (the river of silver) or in an isolated outpost, far from human contact.

Finally, after a brief stop in Rio de Janeiro, the *Giovanna C* arrived in Montevideo, Uruguay, as the sun set on July 13. It would spend the night there, across the river from Buenos Aires, because ships were allowed to dock in Buenos Aires only during the day. Standing on the bow, Eichmann stared across the water toward the blinking lights of his new home. The next day, he would take on his fifth identity in five years. He imagined all five in an internal conversation.

"Listen," Barth said to Eckmann, "was all this slaughter, all this killing, necessary?"

"And what was won anyway?" Heninger asked before turning to Klement. "What do *you* expect from coming to Argentina?"

Gazing into the distance, Eichmann once again reasoned with himself that he had only ever followed orders, much as any Russian, French, British, or American soldier had done. They had all committed their share of atrocities, he decided. But that was in the past. From tomorrow on, he would once again be able to live without the constant fear of capture, without having to search every face he passed for a sign that he had been recognized.

In the morning, the *Giovanna C* approached the banks of the toffee-colored Río de la Plata where Buenos Aires spread out along a low, level plain. It passed massive dredging machines that carved out the shallow river and docked in the harbor. Eichmann disembarked, carrying in his suitcase everything he owned, and joined the line to the immigration desk. Running over the details of his new identity in his mind, he prepared himself to answer any of the officer's questions.

Name? Ricardo Klement. *Date of birth?* May 23, 1913. *Mother's name?* Anna. *Marital status?* Single. *Profession?* Mechanic. *Born?* Bolzano, Italy. *First language?* German. *Do you read and write?* Yes. *Reli-*

gion? Catholic. *Reason for emigrating?* To find work. *Where are you staying?* Hotel Buenos Aires.

There was no need to rehearse. His passport was stamped without any interrogation, and the officer waved Eichmann into his new country. He had no intentions of ever crossing its borders again.

7

CARLOS FULDNER, the smooth, forty-year-old, multilingual operator of the Argentine ratline, shepherded Eichmann into his new life. He began by finding Eichmann an apartment in Florida, a neighborhood to the north of the city center, and by introducing the newcomer to others whom he had helped escape.

Buenos Aires was awash with refugee German Nazis, Italian Fascists, Spanish Falangists, Belgian Rexists, and expatriate members of the French Vichy government, the Romanian Iron Guard, the Croatian Ustashi, and the Hungarian Arrow Cross. The number of high-level war criminals totaled in the low hundreds, but many thousands more had been members of these groups and, at the very least, complicit in the atrocities of the war. They associated with one another, and some were very close to Perón, working either for his government directly or for state-sponsored businesses.

Eichmann found that Buenos Aires had a firmly rooted German community, with its own neighborhoods, private clubs, schools, and restaurants and even three major newspapers in the mother tongue. This community had predominantly supported Hitler during the war, and many within it shared his antipathy toward the Jews, 300,000 of whom lived in Argentina. The defeat of the Third Reich was seen as a tragedy. As a foreign correspondent wrote in May 1945, "Among all the capitals of the countries at war with Germany, Buenos Aires has distinguished itself by being probably the only one where there were no public manifestations of joy at the fall of Berlin." The blow was softened only by the flood of gold that came from Germany in the days before and after the fall of the Reich.

With Fuldner's introduction, Eichmann felt at ease in his new world. The city itself reminded him much of Europe, thanks in large part to the many immigrants who had come from Spain, Italy, England, and Germany in the early part of the century. Like Paris or Rome, Buenos Aires boasted broad boulevards shaded by plane trees, lavish gardens, elegant plazas centered on triumphal marble fountains, and grand villas and apartment buildings festooned with cherubs and flowers. There were forty-seven theaters, most notably the Colón, designed after the Paris Opéra. Innumerable fine restaurants, esteemed universities, fashionable shops, exclusive clubs, highbrow publishers, and art nouveau cinemas—Buenos Aires had them all. Such was the residents' pride in the continental air of their city that when they were heading for neighboring Chile or Brazil, they would say that they were "traveling to South America."

Buenos Aires was also a modern commercial city that served as the hub of Argentina's vast agricultural and natural resources, as well as its industrial center. Highways and great railway lines radiated out in every direction, bringing in goods from the countryside, and the port, one of South America's largest, sent those goods abroad. Subways ran underneath the towering white skylines, and cars and buses had largely replaced the horse-drawn cabs that had once dominated the streets (although these could still be found in some narrow lanes delivering milk or beef). Many banks thrived downtown, and the stock market bustled with trade.

But Buenos Aires also had poor outlying slums, called *villa miserias,* where hundreds of thousands of people lived in tin or cardboard shacks, a single tap providing water for fifty families. Their plight was made worse by an economy that funneled most of the country's riches to a few hundred families and suffered from rampant unemployment, an exploding budget deficit, and a vigorous black market.

Eichmann had 485 pesos in his pocket when he entered Buenos Aires. With limited money and no work papers, Eichmann might have fallen into the squalor of the *villa miserias* if not for the help of those who had brought him there. Fuldner secured him a job in a metal shop and facilitated the approval of his Argentine ID card from the Buenos Aires police. In October 1950, with these papers in hand, Eichmann was now wholly and completely Ricardo Klement, a permanent resident and legally able to work. Fuldner then hired him as an engineer at his new company CAPRI, which was funded by the government to build dams and hydroelectric power plants in Tucumán. The company was staffed by more than three hundred Germans, including Herbert Kuhlmann, who had traveled with Eichmann on the *Giovanna C,* and dozens of other former Nazis, among them several high-ranking party officials.

On June 30, 1952, Eichmann sipped maté outside his cottage in the remote village of La Cocha in the isolated province of Tucumán, seven hundred miles northwest of Buenos Aires. Surrounded by rugged mountains on several sides and a wide, flat plain to the south, he lived alone, without electricity, running water, or even a nearby grocer or post office. The wintry winds sweeping down from the Andes brought little relief from the hot, dry air.

Eichmann saddled his horse, pulled on a poncho and a leather cowboy hat, and rode down to one of the several rivers that coursed through the area. At the water's edge, he tested the depth of the river and the strength of the current, then noted both in a small notebook. At the end of the week, he would report his measurements to his bosses and collect his salary. Eichmann earned 2,500 pesos a month as a topographical engineer with CAPRI, the company some joked stood for "German Company for Recent Immigrants."

Even when among his countrymen, Eichmann kept to himself and refused to answer any questions about his past. When his supervisor Heinz Lühr, displeased with his sloppy work and haughty attitude, attempted to find out more about Ricardo Klement from his superiors, he was told to drop the matter and learned only that Klement had "gone through difficult things in his past."

After two years of isolation, bitterly brooding over Germany's defeat and having to remain in hiding, Eichmann longed for his wife and three sons to join him. Fuldner had assisted Eichmann in secretly contacting Vera. He first wrote to her from Argentina at Christmas

1950, saying that "the uncle of your children, whom everybody presumed dead, is alive and well — Ricardo Klement," and since then he had sent her money and instructions for travel.

So on the day in 1952 Eichmann was at the river, his family was boarding the ship *Salta* in Genoa. He hated that his wife had to use her maiden name and that his three sons had to claim that their father was dead and they were going to Argentina to join their uncle, but he could not be sure that the hunt for him had ended. Precautions were still necessary.

Three weeks later, Eichmann took the train to Buenos Aires. Soon after he arrived, the country was plunged into mourning with the death on July 26 of Eva Perón, Juan Perón's wife and the people's beloved first lady. Flags were flown at half-mast. Factories and government offices were closed. Under a gray, stormy sky in the capital, people hung portraits of the "spiritual chief" of Argentina at intersections and on billboards, and candlelit processions coursed through the streets.

Two days after her passing, the passengers of the *Salta* disembarked in the midst of a torrential downpour. Eichmann sent two friends to the port to collect his family, a precaution in case they had been detected leaving Genoa. They were taken to a nondescript hotel. When Eichmann appeared in the doorway, his wife cried with joy. Despite her delight, she couldn't help but notice that her husband had aged dramatically. His stoop was more pronounced, his face looked drawn and gray, and his hair had thinned.

"I am your Uncle Ricardo," Eichmann said to his sons, Klaus now sixteen, Horst twelve, and Dieter ten.

Thinking that their father had been dead for years, his two younger sons did not question the statement that the man in front of them was their uncle. But Klaus knew that this was his father. Still, he said nothing. Eichmann gave them 100 pesos each, and the boys ran off to explore. The two youngest bought ice cream and candy, and Klaus, taking after his father, bought his first pack of cigarettes. Later, the family went out to dinner. Eichmann was pleased to be with his boys once again.

Once Eichmann and Vera were alone, she brought out the pile of newspaper clippings she had collected over the past seven years about the terrible crimes he had committed. She wanted an explanation. Eichmann grew frighteningly angry, his face turning into a hard mask. "Veronika," he said bitingly, "I have not done a single Jew to death, nor given a single order to kill a Jew." She never asked him about the past again.

As soon as the railways began running again after Eva Perón's state funeral, they took the Pullman Express to Tucumán, then a truck to Eichmann's remote house. There he revealed the truth about his identity to his sons and told them that they must never tell anyone who their "Uncle Ricardo" truly was. He refused, however, to ask his sons to live under any name other than Eichmann.

Over the next months, the boys rode their horses in the countryside and studied their required one hundred new words (no more, no less, they were instructed) of Spanish every day. They took to calling their father *Der Alte,* "the old man." Vera cooked the meals, cleaned the small house, kept a tight budget to help with their savings, and read her Bible every morning. For the first time since the war began, Eichmann shared a home with his family for more than a few days or weeks at a time. He felt now that he could start his life over.

"Mrs. Eichmann and her sons have disappeared."

Wiesenthal hung up the receiver and immediately made his way from Linz to Altaussee, from which his informant had called, to investigate. This was July 1952. With the aid of the Austrian police, he visited the house at 8 Fischerdorf and interviewed Vera Eichmann's neighbors and relatives still in the area.

The circumstances of their departure convinced Wiesenthal that they had left to join Eichmann. The house was emptied of furnishings, and a hole had been dug in the yard, as if someone had retrieved buried material, perhaps money or documents. The landlord claimed that Vera Eichmann had moved out without alerting him or canceling the lease. He had no idea where she and her three sons had gone. The boys had left school in the middle of the year, neither giving the headmaster an explanation nor asking for copies of their records, which would be needed to apply to another school. A nearby resident claimed that Vera had left for Brazil to marry a wealthy rancher. Her sister offered a conflicting report that Vera had remarried and moved to Germany, but she claimed that she had never met her sister's husband. Soon after, Wiesenthal discovered a file in the German consulate in Graz revealing that Vera had recently received a German passport under her maiden name. Her sons Horst and Dieter could travel under her passport, as they were minors. Klaus had obtained his own passport.

Wiesenthal knew that the family was his last chance to trace Eichmann. Now they were gone, with no way for him to find out where. He had heard rumors that Eichmann was in South America, Germany, or the Middle East, but that was all they were, rumors.

Wiesenthal collapsed into a depression. He barely ate or drank. He suffered insomnia, spending his waking nights with the dead—his friends and family and strangers he would never know. When his wife asked him what was troubling him, he answered, "The Nazis lost the war, but *we* are losing the postwar." Wiesenthal saw his doctor, who told him that his work was "prolonging the concentration camp" for him. The doctor advised Wiesenthal to find a hobby; at the very least, this would reduce his stress. Wiesenthal agreed to think about it but denied any suggestion that he stop pursuing war criminals. In the end, he did turn to collecting stamps and found that he enjoyed it.

His compatriot Tuviah Friedman was finished with war criminals. Over the past few years, he had shuddered at the sight of new policemen in Vienna's streets, many in their late twenties and early thirties. He was convinced that several had been guards in the concentration camps, but police administrators refused to check their pasts. Friedman was told to let bygones be bygones, an opinion that he knew was also prevalent in the newly constituted Federal Republic of Germany (West Germany). His duties at the documentation center were dwindling, since most camp survivors and displaced Jews had resettled in Israel, Europe, or the United States. Friedman's friends urged him to consider his future, saying, "You've sunk yourself in Jewish sorrows and in Jewish tears" for too long. His bride-to-be, Anna, had resolved to immigrate to Israel to study medicine, and Friedman relented. Anna was a Holocaust survivor from Hungary and felt that Israel was the only place where she would feel at ease. He could not deny her this.

Friedman was preparing to leave for Israel when he heard of the disappearance of Vera Eichmann and her sons. Though convinced that he and Simon Wiesenthal were the only two people left who still cared about searching for Adolf Eichmann and his ilk, he knew that he had to go to Israel. He shipped his files of survivor testimonials and other records in two huge trunks to Yad Vashem, a center in Israel recently created to document the Holocaust. Then he left for Haifa to find a job and to wed Anna.

On a return visit to Vienna in December 1952, Friedman met with Wiesenthal. "Tadek," Wiesenthal said, "keep reminding the Israelis about Eichmann: Don't let them tell you to forget it. Let the Israeli government do everything it wants to do—build houses, teach everybody Hebrew, develop a strong army. Fine, very good. But they must also start looking for Eichmann. Make them do something."

Friedman had kept his file on Eichmann. He had not sent it to Yad Vashem. But, he told his friend, he needed to move on.

Gripping Friedman's hand, Wiesenthal insisted, "Think of it. When Eichmann is caught, he will be tried by a Jewish court in a Jewish state. History and our people's honor, Tadek: Both are at stake."

Late in 1953, after a year without news of Eichmann, a miraculous twist of fate gave Wiesenthal his best tip on the fugitive's whereabouts since his search had begun. He had arranged a meeting with an old Austrian baron in Innsbruck to discuss stamps. A devoted monarchist who had suffered under Hitler, Baron Mast told his guest how distraught he was that former Nazis were regaining high positions in the government as if "nothing had changed."

From his desk drawer, the baron passed Wiesenthal a letter from a Luftwaffe colonel who had never liked Hitler and who now lived in Argentina. "Beautiful stamps, aren't they?" the baron remarked. "But read what's inside."

Wiesenthal unfolded the letter and quietly read its contents: "There are some people here we both used to know . . . A few more are here whom you've never met. Imagine who else I saw—and even had to talk to twice: that awful swine Eichmann who commanded the Jews. He lives near Buenos Aires and works for a water company."

"How do you like that?" the baron asked. "Some of the worst of the lot got away."

Astounded, Wiesenthal hurried back to his hotel to transcribe what he had read as well as the sender's name and address. Upon his return to Linz, he phoned the Israeli consul in Vienna and followed up by sending him a package that contained the contents of the baron's letter, a biography of Eichmann, examples of his handwriting, his photograph, and a chronicle of the eight-year search for him. Wiesenthal insisted that if the Israelis followed the trail, they would find Eichmann.

As the months passed without word from Israel, Wiesenthal became distraught over the prospect that no action would be taken, but there was little he could do. He did not have the funds to go to Buenos Aires himself, nor did he speak Spanish. In addition, the Argentine government welcomed former Nazis and was largely hostile to Jews. Even if he found Eichmann, he knew that he would not be able to arrest him and get him out of the country. Still, he held out hope that the Israelis would take some action.

On March 30, 1954, that hope was extinguished as well. The Israeli consul, Arie Eshel, met with Wiesenthal and told him that the Israelis would need more details on Eichmann's location before engaging in an investigation. They did not have the resources to check out every rumor concerning Eichmann. They had enough to worry about, building the state and dealing with the escalating tensions with Egypt. Israel needed to focus on the future, not the past. Eshel suggested that Wiesenthal contact Nahum Goldmann, the founder of the World Jewish Congress and, next to Israeli prime minister David Ben-Gurion, the most influential Jewish leader on the world stage. According to Eshel, Goldmann was interested in what Wiesenthal had learned about Eichmann.

That same day, Wiesenthal wrote a letter to Goldmann. He opened the letter this way: "I have been dealing with Eichmann for years, and even if I was more fortunate with countless other persons, I have al-

ways had bad luck with this case." He repeated the details he had sent
to the Israelis and then pleaded for Goldmann to move aggressively
on the information. He concluded, "I only hope that the man you are
putting in charge of the case will be luckier than I was. In any case, I
would be willing with all my heart to get involved in the case again if
it was of interest to you."

Then Wiesenthal waited once more. He expected a quick response,
but two months passed without word. Eventually, he received a note
from Abraham Kalmanowitz, a prominent New York rabbi and Jewish scholar. Goldmann had passed his material on to the rabbi. Kalmanowitz wanted to know whether Wiesenthal had Eichmann's exact
address, his alias, and certain proof that he was still alive. "This is of
great importance, as we have no reliable witness that Eichmann has
been seen since the end of the war," Kalmanowitz wrote. Wiesenthal,
frustrated, responded that there were many indications that Eichmann was alive, including his escape from Ober-Dachstetten and the
suspicious activities of his wife. As for his address and alias, he did not
have either, but he suggested that they could hire a Spanish-speaking
investigator for $500 to go to Buenos Aires. Kalmanowitz retorted
that Eichmann was more likely to be in Damascus, Syria, according
to the most recent intelligence from his sources. Further, the rabbi
stated, he was "most interested in definite proof of Adolf Eichmann's
whereabouts, as that is the only information upon which our Government will act."

Unbeknownst to Wiesenthal, Rabbi Kalmanowitz had made repeated attempts to spur the CIA to engage in an investigation of Eichmann, starting in the fall of 1953. The rabbi had sent letters to the
U.S. president, the secretary of state, and the director of central intelligence. He also had recruited a New Jersey senator to exert pressure
on Washington. That October, the CIA responded: "We are not in
the business of apprehending war criminals." Further, the agency said,
even if the CIA found Eichmann, its only recourse would be to inform the West German government, which, according to recent law,
had jurisdiction over all war criminals. However, West German chancellor Konrad Adenauer was not much interested in pursuing them
either, having made this statement two years before: "The time has

come to abandon the smelling out of Nazis . . . If we once start on that, nobody knows where it will end." Kalmanowitz had passed Wiesenthal's letter on to the CIA, but this had not spurred the agency to take any action.

Dispirited by his exchange with Kalmanowitz, Wiesenthal wrote a final letter to Goldmann, informing him that a recent report by Reuters that Eichmann had been killed by Jewish avengers in a forest outside Linz was patently false and that Kalmanowitz had proved useless in advancing the investigation into the Argentina tip. Goldmann did not respond. Soon after, Wiesenthal closed his office, packed his papers in boxes weighing almost twelve hundred pounds, and shipped the boxes to Yad Vashem. Like Friedman, he kept his file on Eichmann, but in his mind, he was finished with chasing down this phantom about whom nobody else seemed to care. His disappointment at failing to find the war criminal kept him awake at night and haunted him through the day. In many ways, Eichmann had come to embody the Nazi machine that had first come into Wiesenthal's life in July 1941, when he had been arrested and lined up against a wall with forty other Jews in Lvov. Half the group had been killed with shots to the neck before an evening Mass, signaled by the ringing of church bells, interrupted the massacre.

With battles raging in Korea and the standoff between the West and the Soviet Union escalating in intensity, the world could not be bothered with crimes of the past. "We've got other problems," Wiesenthal was told by his American friends. This seemed to be everyone's attitude, and so the hunt for Eichmann was abandoned.

8

ONE AFTERNOON in late December 1956, Sylvia Hermann welcomed her new boyfriend, Nick Eichmann, into her home. She lived with her parents in Olivos, a mostly German suburb within the Vicente López district of Buenos Aires on the Río de la Plata, ten miles north of the city center. The two made for a striking couple. Nick was tall and fair-haired, with clear blue eyes and a roguish smile. Sylvia was also attractive, with rich brown hair, blue eyes, and an expressive face. She also had a sharp mind and a willful personality. The two had recently met at one of the neighborhood's dance halls and had been out several times since then. Sylvia had invited Nick over to meet her parents, who were German émigrés.

The introductions were made in their mother tongue. Nick sought out the hand of Sylvia's father, Lothar Hermann, a slight man who was blind. Over dinner, they spoke of Germany. Nick proudly said that his father had been a high-ranking Wehrmacht officer who had served his country well. Lothar, a lawyer, said nothing of his own experiences. Later on, the talk turned to the fate of the Jews.

"It would have been better if the Germans had finished their job of extermination," Nick declared.

Lothar was struck by the statement but again stayed silent. What his dinner guest did not know was that Lothar was half-Jewish and that he had been imprisoned at Dachau for socialist activities in 1936. Mindful of the increase in the persecution of the Jews, he had immigrated with his Christian wife to Argentina soon after Kristallnacht. To avoid any prejudice from the German community there, he had made no mention of his family background. Sylvia had been raised a Christian, and few people, even close friends, knew of her father's Jewish lineage or that he had lost his sight due to beatings delivered by the Gestapo.

Lothar did not reveal any of this to Nick and instead carefully steered the conversation in another direction. He saw no need for an awkward scene, and it was not as though the boy was alone in holding this opinion. During the war, the streets of Buenos Aires had been filled with people from the German community carrying Nazi banners and espousing Hitler's hate-filled philosophy. The defeat of the Third Reich had not magically eliminated such sentiments.

Although Lothar remembered every word that was spoken that evening, Nick did not think twice about what he had said. He may have switched his name from Klaus (the Germanic short form of Nikolas), but for his father's sake, it would be wise to remember that he still carried the Eichmann name before spouting such vitriol. Even after six years in Argentina, Adolf Eichmann was still very secretive about his identity and about his true relationship to the boys. When visitors were expected at the house, he often slapped his sons across the face to impress on them the importance of being careful about what they said and to whom. One never knew whom to trust and who might want to betray them.

As he had done every Sunday morning for the past four months, Adolf Eichmann rode the bus from Olivos to the wealthy Florida quarter of Buenos Aires. It was a typically warm and humid summer day in February 1957. He rang the bell for the bus to stop at Liberty Street and then walked at a leisurely pace to a white house with an elegant porch shaded by silver birch trees.

Willem Sassen, a lanky thirty-eight-year-old Dutchman, ushered Eichmann straight into his study. His wife made herself scarce, not liking the frequent visitor, while his two young daughters spied on the guest from the hallway, thinking how sinister and creepy this man, whom their father interviewed for hours on end behind closed doors, was.

Sassen and Eichmann went to work. The Dutchman placed the microphone on the table, inserted a new tape into his reel-to-reel recorder, and pursued his line of questioning on how Eichmann saw his role in the Holocaust.

In a gravely stern voice, broken by frequent draws on a cigarette, Eichmann replied.

I would like to describe the careful bureaucrat in more detail, which could be to my own disadvantage. This careful bureaucrat was joined by a fanatic fighter for my people's liberty. I say it one more time, the louse that bites you doesn't disturb me, but the louse that sits under my collar does. What is useful for my people is holy order and holy law to me. And finally, I have to tell you, I don't regret anything. I am not eating humble pie at all. In the months during which you have recorded the whole matter, during which you have endeavored to refresh my memory, a great deal has been refreshed . . . It would be too easy, and I could perfectly reasonably, for the sake of current opinion, play a role as if a Saul had turned into a Paul. But I must tell you that I cannot do that, because I am not prepared to, because my innermost being refuses to say that we did something wrong.

No, I must tell you quite honestly that if, of the 10.3 million Jews shown by Korherr [an SS statistician], we had killed 10.3 million, then I would be satisfied and I would say all right, we have destroyed an enemy. Since the majority of these Jews stayed alive through a trickery of fate, I tell myself that's what fate had intended, and I have to subordinate myself to fate and providence. We would have fulfilled our duty for our blood, for our people, and for the liberty of all people, if we had destroyed the most cunning spirit of today's mankind. Since that is not the case, I will tell you that our children will have to deal with the agony and misfortune of our failure, and maybe they will curse us.

Eichmann paused, taking off his glasses and running his tongue across his false upper teeth. Sassen knew that whenever Eichmann was nervous and evasive, his lips pursed and there was a slight twitch below his left eye. In this session, however, he was unusually candid, though in his typically elliptical manner.

It was this kind of frank talk that Sassen wanted, and he was anxious to move on to editing these interviews for a biography. He had already approached *Life* magazine about a "real hot story," but since he could not reveal Eichmann's identity, the editor had told him the magazine did not want anything to do with it. Sassen persevered nonetheless, sure that he had the scoop of a lifetime.

After the war, the Dutch journalist, who had served in a special SS corps of war correspondents and propagandists, had escaped to Argentina with his family on board a chartered schooner. On arrival, he had wooed the former Luftwaffe ace and Perón intimate Hans-Ulrich Rudel. Sassen ghostwrote Rudel's memoirs and also became a presidential public relations adviser and a writer for *Der Weg*, the monthly Nazi rag in Buenos Aires. The magazine was produced in the back of a bookstore that served as a meeting place for fugitive Nazis and their sympathizers.

Sassen and Eichmann had known each other for several years (the journalist had escorted Eichmann to his new home in Tucumán), but ever since Eichmann had moved back to Buenos Aires after the collapse of CAPRI, they had seen each other more frequently. During drinking sessions with his fellow fugitives—whether at the ABC *biergarten,* where the waiters clicked their heels on arrival at the table, or on weekend hunting retreats dominated by conversations of war and women—Eichmann spoke bitterly of the war's end and of his own patriotism. "I have been a good German in the past, I am a good German today, and I will die a good German," he said. The only time he showed much passion was when he spoke about setting the record straight on the Final Solution. One night in 1956, over a bottle of wine, Sassen had convinced Eichmann to recount his story, urging, "Let us write a book together to counter the enemy propaganda."

So began their sessions. Eichmann came to the house every week. They spoke for four hours, often drinking a couple of bottles of red wine in an effort by Sassen to relax his interviewee. Other Nazis occasionally sat in on the interviews, curious to hear what Eichmann had to say. After each session, Sassen had a secretary transcribe the recording on a huge roll of paper that his daughter Saskia cut into separate pages with a kitchen knife.

The transcript revealed a man bent on proving that he had done nothing wrong in his role as head of Department IVB_4. He strove to inflate his importance and to place himself among the Nazi elite, while simultaneously arguing that he was not ultimately responsible for any of the killings, because he had just been following orders. He declared that he held no hatred toward the Jews, mentioning a Jewish friend of his youth, and that he would have preferred their emigration from the Third Reich. Yet he also made a fervent case for why the Jews had brought their annihilation upon themselves. In his effort to resolve these opposing points of view, Eichmann ate up hours of tape, and binder after binder was filled with the neatly typed transcripts.

Many of the passages were chilling. He described how he went about his duties: "I sat at my desk and did my work. It was my job to catch our Jewish enemies like fish in a net and transport them to their final destination." He explained how he convinced those within the Nazi hierarchy to follow his methods of deception: "We used the Warsaw example [in reference to the bloody ghetto uprising] like a traveling salesman who sells an article all the more easily by showing a special advertising section." Of his operations in Holland, he said: "I sent my boxcars to Amsterdam and most of the 140,000 Dutch Jews were directed for the gas chambers at Bergen-Belsen, Sobibor and Auschwitz . . . It went beautifully!"

When Eichmann read the transcript, he was displeased with the result and scribbled hundreds of comments and corrections in the margins. He desperately wanted for his memoirs to justify his past activities. He was losing the battle, but to surrender to the truth meant facing the reality and guilt of what he had done. He continued with the interviews, Sunday after Sunday. One afternoon, he lamented that he would have happily run out the rest of his days as a Linz police chief if the war had gone a different way.

His lips twisted into a smile at the thought. Sassen noted every detail.

Returning to the ramshackle section of Olivos after his meeting with Sassen, Eichmann was reminded of how far he was from the position of respect and prominence that he thought he deserved. He rented his modest house from a Jewish landlord, and worse, at least as far as he was concerned, the signatory to his lease was Herbert Kuhlmann. Eichmann had lent money to the Panzer division commander for his journey to Argentina. Since then, Kuhlmann had amassed a fortune in business and lived in the tony neighborhood Palermo Chico, the embassy row of Buenos Aires. Eichmann had needed to go to him in order to get a lease.

Kuhlmann was not the only former Nazi to grow wealthy in Buenos Aires, to inhabit a palatial mansion, and to achieve social prominence in the city. Josef Mengele and many others had also flourished, even in the wake of losing their prime benefactor and protector Juan Perón as a result of a military coup in September 1955. The success of Eichmann's fellow Nazis struck a blow to his pride, and he was convinced that they were running around town declaring, "Beware of Klement. In reality, he is that pig Eichmann."

When Eichmann lost his job in the spring of 1953, he moved his family to Buenos Aires. Every attempt he made to improve his position ended badly. First, he started a laundry with several other Germans. Their Chinese competitors cleaned them out. Next, he invested in a textile store. That, too, went bankrupt, leaving him broke. Afterward, he took an hourly wage job as a transport manager for a sanitation equipment supplier, but he was soon let go. Then he joined some distant relatives to oversee a chicken farm, located forty miles north of the city, that also bred angora rabbits. This business went bankrupt as well, and Eichmann returned to Buenos Aires to take a menial job at an appliance warehouse owned by an ex-Nazi. The birth of his fourth son, Ricardo Francisco, soon after their move from Tucumán was the only happy note in this time of failures. The boy was named after the Franciscan priest who had helped Eichmann in Genoa.

Eichmann was a quiet, introverted presence in Olivos. He walked stooped forward, rarely speaking more than a few words in heavily accented Spanish to his neighbors. He fought with his wife frequently, and her constant reading of the Bible and singing of hymns drove him mad with anger. One night, he snatched the Bible from her hands and ripped it in two before storming off. Nor was he pleased with his older three sons. Despite his lectures on discipline and the need for purpose, he thought they were boorish and intellectually incurious. Klaus was more interested in riding his horse between Buenos Aires and Tucumán to hunt pumas than in studying, and Horst had set his sights on joining the merchant marine. Eichmann's only wish for them was that they did not become soldiers or get involved in politics. They were better off, he advised, working as simple laborers and neither seeing nor speaking of war. Unfortunately for Eichmann, his own beliefs had infected his sons, and they were not nearly as careful as their father would have liked about sharing them with others.

In Coronel Suárez, a village in the Pampas a few hundred miles southwest of Buenos Aires, the Hermann family enjoyed a much more peaceful life than the one they had recently left behind in Olivos. Lothar had started a new law practice, mostly helping workers apply for their retirement pensions. Sylvia had hopes of attending university in the United States, but for now she still lived with her parents, helping out as much as she could.

One day in April 1957, Sylvia was reading the newspaper *Argentinisches Tageblatt* to her father when she came across an article about a war crimes trial in Frankfurt. One of the individuals mentioned as still being at large was the SS officer responsible for overseeing the mass murder, Adolf Eichmann.

She stopped reading and looked up. In an instant, Lothar Hermann recalled the dinner months before when Nick Eichmann had spoken openly about his father having served Germany well and had said that the Jews should have been annihilated.

Sylvia put down the newspaper. She told her father that Nick had never spoken much about his family, saying only that his mother had remarried after the war. She did not even know if his father was alive, although Nick had mentioned that he had been a high-level Wehrmacht officer who had moved the family around Europe, including a stay in Poland. She had never been invited to her boyfriend's home, and even now she wrote to him through a mutual friend because he had not given her his address.

Lothar Hermann knew that many former Nazis had come to Argentina after Germany's defeat. Given the comments that Nick had made about his father's service and the Jews, Lothar was sure that he was the war criminal's son. The fact that Nick had never told Sylvia where he lived cemented his belief.

Lothar knew that he had to tell somebody, to do something. If he contacted the German embassy in Buenos Aires, he was sure they would alert Eichmann. The place was infested with people who still held Hitler in the highest regard. Instead, Hermann decided to write a letter to the Frankfurt prosecutors mentioned in the newspaper article. He told them that he believed that Adolf Eichmann was living in Buenos Aires with his wife and sons.

Several weeks later in Frankfurt, Fritz Bauer received the letter. A state prosecutor had forwarded it to him, knowing well his interest in pursuing war criminals. Lothar Hermann could not have found a better recipient for what he had to convey. Bauer, a man with sagging jowls, a broad round face, and a compact body, was the attorney general of the state of Hesse and the bulldog of the West German court system. Many jurists found him a force to be reckoned with, especially those who had once been loyal Nazi Party members and who resisted efforts to prosecute Nazis who had committed atrocities during the war.

Born in Stuttgart in 1903, the son of a Jewish textile dealer, Bauer began studying law at eighteen, received his doctorate at twenty-two, and became Germany's youngest district judge at twenty-six. From these early days, his fundamental philosophy of law focused on the jurist's responsibility to serve as the constitution's defender against "the state's innate disposition toward the police state." When the Nazis seized power in 1933, the new government dismissed him from his

post because he was Jewish. A few months later, the Gestapo imprisoned him in a concentration camp for his activities in the Social
Democratic Party. Released nine months later, he fled to Denmark,
where he lived until the Germans occupied the country in 1940. After
another stint in prison, Bauer went into hiding and escaped to Sweden with his family in a fishing boat. He spent the rest of the war
publishing a Social Democratic magazine with future West German
chancellor Willy Brandt and considering the legal outlets to punish
the Nazis for their crimes.

Once the war ended, Bauer hesitated to return to his homeland.
He had married a Danish woman and disliked the thought of living
in a country that had supported a man such as Hitler. But after the
establishment of West Germany's constitution, he felt that it was his
duty to help foster the democracy and to resist any future rise of to-
talitarianism. He also believed that coming to terms with the past was
essential to achieving this end.

On his return to Germany, Bauer was appointed a regional attorney general. He rapidly made a name for himself pursuing slander
charges against Otto Remer, a right-wing politician who had labeled
those who had plotted the attempted assassination of Hitler in July
1944 "traitors to their country." (Remer had helped foil the plot.)
Bauer won the case, pushing his point that resistance to government
authority was the obligation of a responsible citizen. A few years later,
he became attorney general of Hesse, where he actively prosecuted
cases against Nazi war criminals. In December 1956, he filed arrest
warrants for Adolf Eichmann and twelve others on the charges of
murder and accessory to murder.

After reading the letter from Lothar Hermann, Bauer realized that
he had in his hands a solid tip as to the location of one of the archi-
tects of the Final Solution. He did not intend to delay. He charged his
senior prosecutor with gathering as much information as possible on
Eichmann, including his war activities, physical description, photographs, last known whereabouts (for both him and his family) — anything that would help this Argentine source positively identify him.
Bauer then sent this information to Hermann in Coronel Suárez,

along with a request for him to find an address for the individual concerned. At the same time, Bauer attempted to convince Interpol to initiate an international search for Eichmann.

Wearing a blue dress, Sylvia Hermann walked down Chacabuco Street, in one of the poorer sections of Olivos. After a ten-hour train ride from Coronel Suárez with her father, she had taken the bus that weaved through the neighborhood, hoping to run into Nick and to find out where he lived. This failed, but she did meet a friend of hers who knew where he lived. She checked the numbers on each house until she reached 4261. The one-story white house surrounded by a low fence was typical of the area. It was no bigger than a few rooms and had a slanted terra cotta roof. She passed through the gate and knocked on the front door. As she waited for an answer, she noticed someone at the curtains. Several moments passed.

Sylvia's father had received a letter from Fritz Bauer with a blurred photograph of Adolf Eichmann, along with a description of him and details of his family. The names and ages of Nick and his brother Dieter, whom Sylvia had also met, matched the description. She and her father were certain that they were Eichmann's sons. Now the question was whether their father was alive and sharing their house.

Sylvia had come defenseless to the door. There was nobody to help her if her purpose was revealed. Adolf Eichmann was obviously a murderer, and if he was in fact hiding in Buenos Aires, he had gone to great lengths not to be exposed. Sylvia tried to appear as calm as possible as she waited for an answer.

A short, stout woman with a toddler in her arms opened the door. Sylvia introduced herself as a friend of Nick's. The woman said that she was his mother and cautiously welcomed Sylvia inside, asking if she wanted some coffee and cake.

Yes, Sylvia said, and thanked her. She smiled at Dieter, whom she spotted across the room. "Is Nick home?" she asked.

"No, he left an hour ago," Dieter replied, surprised to see her.

As she sat down at a table, a man with glasses entered the room. He was in his sixties, the same age Adolf Eichmann would be. He walked with his head bent slightly forward, as if he was inspecting something on the ground.

"Good afternoon," Sylvia said.

He bowed slightly and said in German, "Pleased to meet you, young lady."

"Are you Mr. Eichmann?" she asked bravely.

He did not answer.

"Are you Nick's father?"

He hesitated before saying harshly, "No . . . I'm his uncle." His strident tone matched what she had read in Bauer's letter, but the photograph Bauer had provided was of a much younger man and too blurry for her to be certain whether this was Adolf Eichmann.

Nervously, Sylvia began talking about how she had recently graduated from high school and planned on studying foreign languages at university. She asked the man whether he spoke English or French, and he admitted that he knew a few words of French from his time in Belgium and France during the war. The conversation soon trailed off, but he had become more pleasant toward her.

Before Vera brought in the coffee, Nick walked through the door. Shocked to see Sylvia in his living room, he blurted, "Who gave you my address? Who said you could visit me?"

She replied that some mutual friends had given her his address and that she had merely wanted to see him while she was in Buenos Aires. "Did I do something wrong?" she asked.

The older man said that everything was quite okay and that she was most welcome. Nick fell silent.

Sylvia then said that she had to go and that she hoped to return for a longer visit soon. There was an awkward moment of silence as the older man accompanied her to the door.

"Thank you, father," Nick said. "I'll see Sylvia to the bus."

As they walked down the street toward the bus station, Sylvia said that she was pleased to have met his family but asked why he had addressed his uncle as his father. Nick dismissed the question, saying it was merely a sign of respect. At the station, she said goodbye, telling him that she could make her own way to meet her father. The farther Nick walked away from her, the safer she felt.

When she met up with her father, she recounted everything that had happened. It was clear to them that the man at the house was Nick Eichmann's father and, given many of the other matching details, none other than the hunted Nazi war criminal Adolf Eichmann himself.

9

ON SEPTEMBER 19, 1957, at a motel on a highway between Frankfurt and Cologne, Fritz Bauer sat down with Felix Shinar, head of the Israel Mission and responsible for overseeing the reparations treaty with West Germany. This provided compensation for the crimes committed against the Jews by the Third Reich. Since the two countries had yet to formalize diplomatic relations, Shinar was the closest individual to an ambassador between them.

Bauer got straight to the point, since he did not want to risk anybody seeing them together at that time. "Eichmann has been traced."

"Adolf Eichmann?" Shinar asked, both shocked and excited at the news. He had been contacted by a rabbi in Frankfurt, who had told him that the attorney general wanted to meet on an important matter, but he had not been told what it was.

"Yes. He's in Argentina."

"What do you intend to do?"

It was a question that Bauer expected and one that he had pondered since receiving word from Lothar Hermann that he was more certain than ever that he had found Eichmann and now had an address for him. Bauer knew well the opposition he faced in going after war criminals in West Germany. Over the years, he had received several threats on his life, and files related to these investigations had mysteriously disappeared from his office. Aside from these personal attacks, there was resistance at the highest government levels against burrowing too deeply into the past. Although Chancellor Konrad

Adenauer was untainted by any association with Nazism and had recognized the atrocities committed by Germans with his reparations
agreement with Israel, his primary interest was to create a viable democracy, and he often ignored the wartime backgrounds of those
within his government if he thought they could assist him.

Many of these individuals were far from being innocent of any
crimes. Most prominently, State Secretary Hans Globke had penned
the interpretation of the Nuremberg Laws that had stripped German
Jews of their citizenship. Bauer detested the fact that Globke held one
of the most powerful and influential positions in Bonn. If flushing
out Eichmann brought down Globke, this would be an additional
benefit. But Globke and others like him had strong motives not to
revisit their dark history, making Bauer's attempt to get Eichmann all
but impossible through official government channels.

Before making any move, Bauer had consulted with Georg-August
Zinn about how best to proceed. Zinn was a high-ranking fellow
member of the Social Democratic Party and prime minister of Hesse.
Few options were available to them. Neither had the resources or the
right to launch his own international investigation. The German Federal Police had responded in the negative to Bauer's request to involve
Interpol in a search for Eichmann, explaining that the "political"
crimes of the Nazis were beyond Interpol's mandate. Bauer and Zinn
feared that if they went to the Adenauer government, either nothing
would happen or, worse, someone would tip off Eichmann, and he
would disappear for good. By providing intelligence to a foreign
country, Bauer was aware that he was committing treason, but he felt
that he had no other choice if Eichmann was to be brought to justice.
That is why he had called for the meeting with Shinar.

"I'll be perfectly frank with you," Bauer said. "I can't rely on the
German Foreign Office. I can't rely on the German embassies in
South America. I can't even rely on my own staff. I see no other way
but to turn to you. Nobody could be more interested than you in the
capture of Eichmann. Obviously I wish to maintain contact with you
in connection with the matter, but only if provided the strictest of
secrecy."

"Thank you for the great faith you've shown us," Shinar said, the emotion clear in his voice and face. "Israel will never forget what you have done."

Shinar promised to pass on the message to the right people and that they would soon be in contact with Bauer. The two then left the motel separately.

Not far from the clear blue waters of the Mediterranean, in the former German Templar village of Sarona, stood an old stone house with a red tile roof. It looked like any other house in that historic quarter of Tel Aviv, and the people who passed it every day never gave it a second thought. Nor did they pay any special notice to the diminutive man who came and went throughout the day. At five feet two, with a balding pate, jug ears, and small, piercing gray-blue eyes, he sometimes wore the neat, inexpensive suit of a bank teller and other times wore street clothes, his shirt opened to his barrel chest. He walked with a lively step and a straight back, seeming always to have a place to go, but this was not unusual. Israel was a young country populated by many people with a strong sense of purpose. If anyone overheard him speaking, which would occur only if he wanted to be heard or if his subject was not secret, he or she would hear Hebrew spoken with a slight eastern European accent in short, sharp bursts, much like a Kalashnikov. The man was Isser Harel, chief of the Mossad, the Israeli secret service, and the old stone house was the organization's headquarters.

On a late September day, Harel entered the building and made his way past the few dozen men and women who worked in the warren of rooms. Greeting his two secretaries, who welcomed him warmly, he stepped into his office. The room was furnished with a simple desk and a telephone, a long table for meetings, a plain settee, and a small safe. Harel had just returned from a hastily arranged sit-down at a nearby café in Ramat Gan with Israeli foreign minister Walter Eytan. Eytan had urgent news from Germany that he did not want to share over the telephone: "Adolf Eichmann is alive and his address in Argentina is known."

Harel asked his secretary to get whatever files they had on Eichmann as soon as possible. He knew that Eichmann had played a lead-

ing role in the systematic killing of the Jews during World War II and
that there had been many rumors as to his whereabouts over the years,
but that was about it. The pursuit of war criminals was not one of the
many mandates that occupied Harel during his eighteen-hour work-
days. He had only one individual on his staff tasked with collecting
intelligence on former Nazis, and this was, essentially, an archivist
position, filing and cross-referencing information sent from various
sources around the world.

The Mossad's lack of activity in this regard reflected the lack of interest within Israeli society in confronting the crimes against the Jewish people. Holocaust survivors, roughly a quarter of the population,
rarely spoke of their experiences, both because it was too painful and
because they did not want to focus on the past. They had a country to
forge. Although Israel had passed a law in 1950 allowing for the prosecution of Nazis and their collaborators, no pressure had been applied
by leading government officials to arrest anyone under this law. In
fact, the only major trial in Israel related to war crimes had been that
of Rezsö Kasztner, an Israeli accused of collaborating with Eichmann
in Hungary. The supreme court had eventually ruled that Kasztner
had saved Jewish lives rather than aided in their destruction—but
not until after he had been assassinated in March 1957. Little mention
had been made during the proceedings that Eichmann and his ilk
should be the ones on trial.

But the eagerness of the typically taciturn foreign minister had
stirred Harel. He knew he was dealing with an unsubstantiated tip in
an area that had no relevance to securing Israel, but at least he wanted
to take a look at the file. It was in his nature to need to know, a chief
reason he became the spymaster of Israel.

Harel was the youngest son of Orthodox Jews from Vitebsk, in
central Russia, whose prosperous family business was seized after the
1917 Russian Revolution. Left paupers, the family moved to Latvia,
where a young Isser survived his harsh new surroundings on the
strength of his fists, a sphinxlike calm, and an omnivorous reading
habit—everything from Russian classics to detective stories to Zionist literature. At sixteen, refusing his parents' demands to finish high
school, Isser left home to join a collective farm run by Zionists out-

side Riga. He embraced the lifestyle and the Zionists' ambitions, and a year later, in 1929, when Muslims massacred sixty-seven Jews in Palestine, he decided to emigrate. He obtained a forged identity and traveled with a small gun and a pocketful of bullets. He arrived by ship in Jaffa, the ancient port city at the southern end of Tel Aviv. When British officials searched the passengers for weapons, Harel easily passed inspection, his revolver and ammunition hidden in a hollowed-out loaf of bread.

Harel joined a kibbutz in Herzliya, north of Tel Aviv, where he cultivated orange trees during the day and slept in a tent at night. Though teased as "Little Isser," he was well respected for his seriousness and strong work ethic. He married, left the kibbutz after five years to start his own orange-packing business, and prospered until World War II. In 1942, he enlisted in the Haganah, fearing that Hitler might attack Palestine.

One of his first jobs was to learn whether a German living in an isolated villa was a Nazi spy. Harel crawled across the grounds at night, broke inside, and went through the house room by room until he discovered a counterfeiting operation in the basement. The guy was a mere criminal. After a stint undercover in the British auxiliary army, which ended when he struck a captain for insulting the Jews, Harel was recruited by the Haganah intelligence service, the Shai.

Operating out of a four-room apartment identified by a sign as the Veterans Counseling Service and located above a flower shop only a stone's throw from the police administration center, Shai agents spied on and thwarted the attempts of the British to defeat the Haganah resistance against the occupation. They ran a network of informants and spies, stole records, tapped phones, decoded messages, and built up weapons caches. Though not as educated, cultured, or smooth as many Shai agents, Harel quickly learned the trade and was charged with hunting down extremist Jewish dissident groups such as the Irgun and the Stern Gang. At first he struggled with the overflow of intelligence, much of which was meaningless, and his bosses worried that he might not be able to handle the job. Soon, however, he learned how to read, interpret, and remember the most important details of an operational file, and he earned a reputation for being a bloodhound. In 1947, Harel was promoted to run Shai operations in Tel Aviv, where he developed an extensive network of Arab informants.

On the eve of May 14, 1948, as the British readied to evacuate Palestine and David Ben-Gurion prepared to announce the creation of an independent Jewish state, Harel was alone among Shai intelligence agents in predicting that the Arab Legion would attack the moment the founding of Israel was declared. It was not a mere suspicion. He had personally carried a message to Ben-Gurion from an informant who had just returned from Jordan: "Abdullah is going to war — that's certain. The tanks are ready to go. The Arab Legion will attack tomorrow." Ben-Gurion sent several army units to establish a defense, thwarting the surprise attack. Harel had attracted the Israeli leader's attention.

Two months later, while Israel was still in the midst of war, Harel joined the other four section heads at Shai headquarters on Ben Yehuda Street to reorganize Israeli intelligence and espionage operations. He was selected to run the Shin Bet, the internal security service, one of the three new divisions. In this role, he won the further notice of Ben-Gurion by breaking up the violent Jewish extremist groups for good. However, Harel's most important job was counterespionage, and he soon became an expert in rooting out Arab and Russian spies. In 1952, this skill proved essential when he took over the Mossad. The Institute for Coordination had been formed only twelve months before to resolve the disarray caused by different, often competing, divisions of the secret service with spying missions abroad. The Mossad's first leader proved incapable of managing the organization, a point that the forty-year-old Harel made bluntly to him: "You ought to resign." His first day on the job, Harel met with his beleaguered staff of twelve, who operated out of three small rooms, and said, "The past is over. There will be no more mistakes. We will go forward together. We talk to no one except ourselves." The hunter of spies, who had capitalized on the sloppy and cavalier methods of his targets, was now the master of spies as well, and he brought a disciplined, relentless approach to both roles.

Over the next few years, Harel battled foreign spies and Arab saboteurs in his role as chief of the Shin Bet, while also developing the

Mossad by bringing in some of the best agents from the internal security service. He sent Israeli spies to infiltrate other countries throughout the world and established a significant relationship with the CIA. During the 1956 Suez War with Egypt, he used the intelligence he gathered to support the Israeli forces in their attacks, and he also engineered a disinformation campaign that kept the Egyptians from attacking defenseless Israeli cities. He managed a massive illegal immigration of Moroccan Jews during the same period and scored a coup by securing a copy of a secret speech by Nikita Khrushchev, delivered at the Soviet Communist Party Congress, that criticized the brutal regime of Stalin and signaled a softening of Soviet policy. Although the Mossad was still a small, fledgling agency, it was gaining a reputation as an effective, formidable force in intelligence. With his successes at the Shin Bet and Mossad, Harel soon became known as the *Memuneh,* "the one in charge," of Israeli intelligence, answerable only to the prime minister.

Harel was haunted by what the Nazis had done to the Jewish people. The state of Israel existed in part to make sure the Holocaust was never repeated. But Harel did not delve too far into the history of the genocide, sensing that it was so profoundly evil that it was beyond his ability to understand. Now he sat in silence at his desk and opened the Eichmann dossier. He read transcripts from the Nuremberg trials, captured SS files, testimony from Eichmann's staff members, and numerous reports of Eichmann's whereabouts. Curiously, one report stated that Eichmann had been born in the same village where Harel now had his office. Some of the information was from Yad Vashem, some from Simon Wiesenthal, some from Arthur Pier and his Haganah team — Tuviah Friedman and Manus Diamant. The photograph obtained from Eichmann's mistress was in the dossier. Many of the tips concerning his location came from letters sent to Israeli embassies from people who thought they had seen him.

As dawn broke the next day, Harel turned over the last page in the thick dossier. He was deeply unsettled by the portrait he now had of Adolf Eichmann. Here was a man, Harel surmised, who had assembled the apparatus to kill millions of people, who had separated children from their mothers, driven the elderly on long marches, emptied out whole villages, and sent them all to the gas chambers. All the while, he had been beating his chest in pride for being faithful to the SS oath, a soldier and an idealist. It was clear to Harel that Eichmann had killed without compunction and was an expert in police and intelligence methods. Of this he had no doubt. If Eichmann was still alive, he had managed to elude his pursuers time and again and had removed all traces of his existence over the past dozen years. This new information from Germany, solid as it appeared to be, might be yet another false lead. Nevertheless, given what he now knew about Eichmann, Harel set about finding out if that was the case.

First, Isser Harel wanted to learn what Fritz Bauer knew, how he had come to receive the information, and whether he was a reliable individual with whom to work. Any plan for what they would do if they discovered the war criminal would be premature, but Harel knew one thing for sure: they would require much more than an extradition request to the proper authorities in Argentina to secure Eichmann.

After finding out what he could from Felix Shinar, Harel sent one of his Mossad operatives, Shaul Darom, to sit down with Bauer. On November 6, Darom traveled to Frankfurt and met with the attorney general in his home. Pleased at the rapid Israeli response, Bauer explained that his source was a half Jew living in Argentina who had presented facts about Eichmann that matched known details of his life, particularly regarding his family. The source also provided an address where the family was living with a man of the same age as Eichmann. Given rumors that Vera Eichmann had remarried, Darom questioned whether this individual might be her second husband, a possibility that Bauer accepted but discounted. He had made separate inquiries into Vera's location, sending a police investigator to interview her mother in a town near Heidelberg, Germany. Her mother had stated that she had not heard from Vera since 1953 and that her daughter had married an unknown man and moved to America. Bauer suspected that the mother was lying. He provided Darom with the entire Eichmann file, including a blurry photograph from an SS file. The only thing Bauer held back was his source's identity, wanting to protect Lothar Hermann. All attempts by Darom to persuade Bauer to reveal this information were in vain.

Darom sent a positive report to Harel about Bauer, stating that if he were to paint a portrait of the German lawyer, he would paint him with a book in one hand and a sword in the other. He also explained that Bauer was willing to do whatever it took to get to Eichmann, even at the risk of losing his position, and that his tip seemed solid enough to warrant following up.

Soon after, in January 1958, Harel sent another operative, Yoel Goren, to Buenos Aires to investigate who lived at 4261 Chacabuco Street. Goren had spent several years in South America and spoke fluent Spanish. Harel warned him to be cautious, fearing that the slightest error might announce his presence and send Eichmann fleeing.

Over the next week, Goren made his way several times to Olivos by train from the city center. The part of that neighborhood that was closest to the Río de la Plata featured many grand mansions, the summer escapes of the elite. The farther away from the river he walked, the smaller and more ramshackle the houses became. From the accents he heard on the streets, many of the residents were German, and he even saw swastikas painted on the sides of a few buildings. Chacabuco Street was located on the farthest edge of the district, populated by blue-collar workers who commuted to and from the city. It was an untrafficked, unpaved street, and strangers were eyed with more than a little suspicion. This made surveillance a challenge, but what Goren saw at 4261 Chacabuco convinced him that there was little chance that Adolf Eichmann lived there. A dowdy woman tended a garden the size of a postage stamp, and the house itself was more suited to a single unskilled laborer than the family of a man who had once held a prominent position in the Third Reich. According to what the intelligence community knew, Adolf Eichmann had personally pilfered the fortunes of Europe's most prominent Jewish families, not to mention the limited wealth of thousands of others. There was no way this bon vivant with a taste for the high life could have been reduced to such meager quarters, even in hiding.

Surreptitiously, Goren photographed the home before returning to

Tel Aviv to report to Harel that the "wretched little house" on Chacabuco Street could not possibly shelter Adolf Eichmann, nor had he seen anyone resembling his description enter or leave the house while it was under his surveillance. Goren made this declaration a mere two weeks after being assigned the case.

When Shaul Darom next spoke to Fritz Bauer, Bauer revised his impression of the Israelis. Such a short investigation could not hope to discover a man who had eluded capture for more than twelve years. Darom informed the attorney general that Harel could not move forward unless he knew the identity of Bauer's source. They needed to trust each other on this matter as well as every other. Bauer relented, and they agreed that Bauer would write a letter of introduction for his "representative" to meet with Lothar Hermann. Harel did not want any trace of the investigation to lead back to the Israelis, although after Goren's report, he was already becoming skeptical that Eichmann resided at the Chacabuco address.

Harel borrowed the head of criminal investigations of the Tel Aviv police, Ephraim Hofstetter, to pose as Bauer's representative. Harel wanted him to ascertain how exactly Hermann knew about Eichmann, whether he was reliable, and whether he was holding anything back. Further, Hofstetter should find out the identity of the individual who lived at 4261 Chacabuco. The Mossad chief had tremendous faith in Hofstetter, a sober professional with twenty years of police investigative experience. Polish by birth, Hofstetter had lost his parents and sister in the Holocaust, and he knew of Eichmann from following the Kasztner trial. The investigator spoke German fluently and could easily pass as Bauer's emissary.

At the end of February, Hofstetter arrived in Buenos Aires wearing a thick layer of winter clothes, only to discover that he had come at the height of summer. He was greeted outside the long, one-story airport terminal by the laughter of a man with a pale complexion and a bald pink head: Ephraim Ilani, a Mossad agent who specialized in Arab operations and had taken a leave of absence to study the history of Jewish settlements in Argentina. Ilani had helped Goren briefly in his earlier investigation. Harel had ordered Ilani to work much more closely with Hofstetter, who did not speak more than a few words of Spanish. Fluent in the local dialect of Spanish (as well as nine other languages), Ilani knew the country well and had a wide network of friends and contacts in Buenos Aires thanks to his easy humor and gregarious nature.

The two traveled to Coronel Suárez by overnight train. At 9:30 A.M., they stepped onto the platform of a dilapidated station. Apart from a single road bordered on either side by wooden houses, the remote town was little more than a stepping-off point before the endless grasslands. It was hard to imagine a less obvious place for a clue to Adolf Eichmann's whereabouts.

Ilani inquired around as to how to find the home of Lothar Hermann. The residents and people working in the local businesses were suspicious of the two men, wondering what these foreigners might want with their neighbor. They did not offer to help. At the train station, a taxi driver offered his assistance, but only if they hired him to take them to Hermann's house. As they soon discovered, they could have walked the short distance across the railway tracks. Hofstetter went to the door alone, Ilani staying behind in case there was any trouble. As far as either of them knew, this could be a trap.

When the door opened, Hofstetter introduced himself. "My name is Karl Huppert. I sent you a telegram from Buenos Aires to tell you I was coming."

Hermann gestured for Hofstetter to enter his living room. Hofstetter could not quite place what was wrong with Hermann or the room, but there was something amiss. Aside from a table, a cupboard, and a couple of chairs, the room was bare. Only when he held out his letter of introduction from Bauer and Hermann did not take it did Hofstetter realize that the man was blind. Isser Harel had sent him to investigate a sighting of Adolf Eichmann by a man who could not see.

Hofstetter soon lost his skepticism when Hermann and his wife, who had appeared when called to read the letter, explained in detail how they had first grown suspicious of Nick Eichmann and how their daughter had tracked down his address. Hofstetter found Hermann full of bluster, particularly in regard to his unsubstantiated comments that Eichmann had had plastic surgery and that he had great means at his disposal, but his motives were clear.

"Don't think I started this Eichmann business through any desire to serve Germany," Hermann said. "My only purpose is to even the score with the Nazi criminals who caused me and my family so much agony."

The front door opened, and Sylvia Hermann entered the house, calling hello to her parents. She stopped on seeing Hofstetter, and her father introduced "Mr. Huppert." Without reticence, Sylvia told him about her visit to the Eichmann house.

"Was there anything special about the way he spoke?" Hofstetter asked her.

"His voice was unpleasant and strident, just as Dr. Bauer described it in one of his letters."

Hofstetter questioned whether these letters might have influenced her thinking.

"No," she said bluntly. "I'm a hundred percent sure it was an unbiased impression."

"What you say is pretty convincing," Hofstetter said, struck by the girl's courage and straightforwardness. Everything she said matched the information he had been given before leaving Tel Aviv. "But it isn't conclusive identification. Vera Eichmann may have married again—we've heard many such rumors—and her children may have continued using their father's name." He explained that he needed to know the alias of the person living with Vera and her sons, as well as where he worked. He also would like to obtain any photographs of him or his family, any documents with his name, and, in the best case, a set of his fingerprints.

"I'm certain I'll be able to get you your proof," Lothar Hermann responded. "I've got many friends in Olivos, as well as connections with the local authorities. It won't be difficult for me to get these things. However, it's obvious I'll have to travel to Buenos Aires again, my daughter too . . . This will involve further expense, and we simply can't afford it."

Hofstetter promised that his people would cover any expenses. For the sake of secrecy, he instructed that all their correspondence should be sent to him at an address in the Bronx, New York, care of an A. S. Richter. He tore an Argentine dollar in two and gave one half to Hermann. Anybody with the other half could be trusted.

After two hours of planning and discussion, Hofstetter thanked the family and left. He would report back to Harel that the Hermanns were reliable but that more information was needed and they seemed capable of gathering it. As Hofstetter walked back toward town, the taxi that had taken him to the house pulled to his side. Ilani stuck his head out the back window and jokingly asked, "Can I give you a lift, sir?"

10

ON APRIL 8, Sylvia Hermann and her father visited the land records office in La Plata, the capital of the province of Buenos Aires, thirty-four miles southeast of the metropolis. Their German contact had sent the promised funds, and the amateur detectives were now out to collect the evidence that they had the right man.

A clerk brought them the public records on 4261 Chacabuco Street, and Sylvia read the details to her father. An Austrian, Francisco Schmidt, had bought the small plot in Olivos on August 14, 1947, to build two houses. Eichmann was Austrian, Lothar knew, and he had arrived in Buenos Aires after the war. Schmidt must be the alias he was living under now. Excited by this important discovery, Hermann and his daughter took a train to Buenos Aires to look for confirmation. Through a contact at the local electricity company, they found that two meters were registered at the address under the names Dagoto and Klement. Rather than doubt the Schmidt alias, Hermann surmised that these would be two fake names that Schmidt had come up with to obscure his trail. When Hermann chased down the people who had sold Schmidt the land at Chacabuco, he was given a description that resembled the one that Bauer had sent on Eichmann and that his daughter had confirmed on her brief visit to the house. The seller also told him not only that Schmidt had some scars on his face but also that the rumor was he had arrived in Buenos Aires on board a German submarine in 1945.

The following month, the Hermanns returned to Buenos Aires for five days to continue their investigation. On this trip, they discovered a photograph of Nick and heard another rumor that Adolf Eichmann had lived in the interior of the country for several years after arriving from Europe. Their attempts to find his photograph, fingerprints, or identity documents failed. On May 19, Hermann wrote to Huppert in New York, describing their detective work of the past six weeks. "Francisco Schmidt is the man we want," Hermann wrote, explaining that it was likely he had undergone plastic surgery (hence the scars). He wrote that further investigation would require more funds and that he should "hold all the strings" in pursuing the matter. Hermann was sure his discoveries would be met with a call to action.

The letter from Lothar Hermann wound its way from Argentina to New York and on to the Mossad headquarters in Tel Aviv, arriving in June 1958. Isser Harel was skeptical about its contents from beginning to end. Hermann was too certain and wanted too much control, both qualities that Harel distrusted by instinct and experience.

Note in hand, he broke down each of its assertions. Merely because Schmidt was listed as the owner of the land where a Nick Eichmann lived did not prove that Adolf Eichmann inhabited the house, nor under that alias. The plastic surgery claim was pure speculation. And what purpose did Hermann have in tracking down where Eichmann lived in the late 1940s if he already knew that Schmidt was Eichmann? One investigated the freshest clues, not the most dated. His demand for more funds and to "hold all the strings" reeked of a potential scam.

Harel had made his way to the top of Israeli intelligence by assembling as much information as he could and then putting himself in his enemies' shoes to understand their motivations and to play out their possible next moves. His agents remarked among themselves that "if you showed Isser Harel one side of a match folder, he could tell you without looking what's printed on the other side." He trusted his intuition, and regarding the Eichmann case, instinct told him not only that Yoel Goren was right that the Nazi fugitive could not be living in such squalor but also that the information Lothar Hermann had sent in his report was suspect at best and perhaps wholly fashioned imagination at worst.

Harel cabled Ilani in Buenos Aires to check on Francisco Schmidt. If this proved to be a dead end, the Mossad chief was going to add the Buenos Aires tip to the pile of unsubstantiated rumors about Eichmann's location in his dossier. One such rumor had him operating an import business in Damascus under the name Brunkmann. In another, he was traveling freely between South America and Switzerland under the alias Dr. Spitzer. Still other rumors had him in Cairo stirring up pogroms against Jews or in Kiel, Germany, calling himself Arthur Sonnenburg. Harel had initially thought that the information from Fritz Bauer sounded credible, but now he doubted it just as much as the other tips.

As the summer passed, Harel was occupied by more pressing concerns. He uncovered a Soviet mole infiltrating his agency, and the Middle East was in a state of upheaval as a result of the continued fallout from the Suez War. Earlier in the year, Egypt and Syria had unified to create the United Arab Republic, increasing the status of President Gamal Abdel Nasser, who was openly belligerent toward Israel. The Iraqi king, Faisal II, had been assassinated in July, and rebels now threatened his cousin King Hussein of Jordan. Ben-Gurion had placed the Israeli army on high alert, and any intelligence on what might be the next move of the young state's Arab neighbors took priority. Given the Mossad's limited size and strength, Harel was unwilling to take a single agent away from his or her duties to pursue what was probably a false lead. Only a directive from the prime minister would change his mind.

At the end of August, Ilani reported to Harel that Francisco Schmidt was definitely not Eichmann, nor did he even reside at the Chacabuco Street address. He was merely the landlord. As one of Harel's agents said, "Sometimes you put together the jigsaw puzzle of information and it comes out a horse instead of a camel, and there's nothing you can do with it." Harel shelved the Eichmann dossier; Hermann had the wrong man. The Mossad chief apprised Bauer of his conclusion and severed his correspondence with Hermann. Once again, the hunt for Eichmann was called to a halt.

Some months before, in early March 1958, Kurt Weiss, an operative for the West German federal intelligence service Bundesnachrichten-dienst (BND), had met with a CIA agent in Munich to exchange information on former Nazis who might be involved in spying opera-tions in the Middle East. Both organizations had made it their prac-tice to recruit former SS, Gestapo, and Abwehr agents into their folds, even though they both vehemently denied those agents' pres-ence to the public—and often to each other. Their respective chiefs, Reinhard Gehlen and his American benefactor Allen Dulles, were focused on fighting the Communist threat across the globe. That some of their operatives, including several lieutenants of Adolf Eich-mann, had blood on their hands did not rank as a reason for dis-qualification. These individuals had often proved to be more trouble than they were worth, however, as a number of them had turned out to be double agents or had enlisted their erstwhile comrades to act as informants. This had created a nest of former Nazis, all morally corrupt and of dubious loyalty, clouding the already murky world of intelligence.

At the Munich meeting, Weiss wanted to know if the CIA had any guidance to offer on several names that had come to his atten-tion: Abwehr agent Eberhard Momm, supposedly living in Germany; Franz Rademacher (alias Rosello), a Third Reich diplomat responsible for Jewish affairs who had fled to Syria after the war; Johannes von Leers, a Goebbels propagandist who had escaped to Argentina and then moved to Cairo in 1956 to work for Nasser; and Adolf Eich-mann. According to the BND agent's information, Eichmann had been "born in Israel and became an SS-Obersturmbannführer. He is reported to have lived in Argentina under the alias Clemens since 1952. One rumor has it that despite the fact that he was responsible for mass extermination of Jews, he now lives in Jerusalem."

Simultaneous with these inquiries, the Bundesamt für Verfas-sungsschutz (BfV), the West German domestic intelligence agency charged with combating any Nazi resurgence, was trying to verify through the Foreign Ministry and the German embassy in Argentina whether Karl Eichmann, an individual known by the agency to write for the neo-Nazi journal *Der Weg,* was actually Adolf Eichmann and whether he was living in Buenos Aires under the alias Klement. The embassy responded later that summer that it had no information to that effect and that Eichmann was most likely living in the Middle East.

Someone in the nest of former Nazis who knew of Eichmann's alias was no doubt speaking to the two key German intelligence agencies. Neither of them showed much vigor or enthusiasm in tracking down the war criminal, perhaps not wanting to expose Hans Globke, who oversaw both the BND and the BfV, to any undue attention. Eichmann would have known the state secretary's activities during Hitler's reign very well indeed.

Nor did the CIA take any action. Four years previously, it had been under pressure from Jewish leaders in the United States to investigate reports from Simon Wiesenthal that Eichmann was in Argentina. But the agency had failed to act then, and they failed to act now — not even the simple courtesy of passing along the latest intelligence to their Israeli counterparts. Given the CIA's ties to Globke, who these days was the chief liaison between German intelligence and the agency, and the slew of Eichmann's lieutenants spying for America, it was not in the CIA's interest to stir up the past. And so the fact that Klement was not only Eichmann's known alias but also the name associated with the house where he lived (according to Lothar Hermann) remained unknown.

In San Fernando, an isolated northern neighborhood of Buenos Aires, Eichmann and his three sons were digging a huge rectangular trench in the earth in February 1959. Water seeped in from the sides and bottom, since the land Eichmann had bought was located in a low, flat plain that frequently flooded in the winter from the overflow of the nearby Reconquista River. Once they finished digging, they pumped out the water and sealed the trench. Eichmann wanted his new house to have a foundation that was five feet deep and had walls two feet thick—both measurements triple the standard. He was building a fortress.

Eichmann had purchased the one-fifth acre in late 1958, exhausting his limited savings. He did not want to rent any longer and thought the investment was a good hedge against the plague of Argentine inflation. He was planning for a long future in the country. The land came cheap because of its remoteness and its tendency to flood. There was no access to electricity, water, or sewerage. On the upside, this meant there were also no municipal taxes and few prying neighbors.

Now that the first stage of construction was complete, Eichmann and his sons could start building their home. He had purchased the necessary supplies and arranged for delivery. He had plotted out a schedule of work in exact detail, and he planned to be finished by early 1960. The single-story brick structure would not be spacious, but it would belong to him.

After a series of missteps in his career, he had gained promising new employment at a Mercedes-Benz factory making buses and trucks, located twenty miles southwest of Buenos Aires in the industrial district of González Catan. Hired as a welder in March, Eichmann suspected that there would be room for advancement. Jorge Antonio, a Perón loyalist who allegedly had been connected with the siphoning of Nazi funds into the country after the war, had started the Argentine branch of the German company. Antonio employed more than five hundred people, mostly German émigrés, a number of whom were fugitive Nazis. Once again Eichmann had called on his former comrades for help, and once again they had answered—though more out of pity this time around.

Despite his improving job prospects, Eichmann remained trapped in the past. He bought history after history on the war, scribbling his reactions in the margins of these books. In *Hitler: The Last Ten Days,* Gerhard Boldt criticized the foolishness and cowardly acts of Hitler's inner circle. Whenever Boldt, a former Nazi officer who had been in the bunker with Hitler, appeared in the text, Eichmann drew a line through his name and wrote "Traitor," "skunk," or "scoundrel." In one section, Eichmann scrawled, "The author should be skinned alive

for his treachery. With crooks like this, the war was bound to be lost."
On the last page of the book, Eichmann wrote his opinion of the nature of duty, a virtue that Boldt obviously did not understand: "1.
Every man is entitled to live as he pleases; 2. But then he has no right
to call himself an officer, because; 3. Officer = fulfillment of duty as
specified in the soldier's oath."

Eichmann was increasingly becoming a pariah within the German
community in Buenos Aires because of his obsession with the war.
Over drinks at the ABC *biergarten,* he often raged about the many
people who had betrayed the Third Reich and how things could have
gone differently. At other times, he was merely a dour presence, spare
with words, highly nervous, and known for having a handshake as
weak as a damp cloth.

Eichmann's sessions with Sassen had ended, removing this outlet
for his spleen. In early 1959, Eichmann attempted to articulate his
thoughts on what he had done and how he felt almost a decade and a
half after the war. It would be the introduction to his memoirs.

> I am growing tired of living the life of an anonymous wanderer
> between two worlds. The voice of my heart, which no man can
> escape, has always whispered to me to look for peace. I would also
> like to be at peace with my former enemies. Maybe that is a part of
> the German character.
>
> I would be only too glad to surrender to the German authori-
> ties, if I were not obliged to consider that people may still be too
> much interested in the political aspect of the matter to permit a
> clear, objective outcome. Far be it from me to doubt that a Ger-
> man court would arrive at a just verdict, but I am not at all clear
> about the juridical status that would be accorded today to a former
> receiver of orders, whose duty it was to be loyal to his oath and to
> carry out the orders and instructions given him.
>
> I was but a faithful, decent, correct, conscientious, and enthusi-
> astic member of the SS and of Reich Security Headquarters, in-
> spired solely by idealistic feelings toward the fatherland to which I
> had the honor of belonging. Despite conscientious self-examina-
> tion, I must find in my favor that I was neither a murderer nor a
> mass murderer. But, to be absolutely truthful, I must accuse myself

of complicity in killing, because I passed on the deportation orders
I received and because at least a fraction of the deportees were
killed, though by an entirely different unit. I have said that I would
have to accuse myself of complicity in killing, if I were to judge
myself with merciless severity.

But I do not see clearly whether I have the right to do this vis-à-
vis my immediate subordinates. Therefore, I am still engaged in an
inner struggle. My subjective attitude toward things that happened
was my belief in the necessity of a total war, because I could not
help believing in the constant proclamations issued by the leaders
of the then German Reich, such as: Victory in this total war or the
German nation will perish. On the strength of that attitude, I did
my commanded duty with a clear conscience and faithful heart.

Such was the belief that Eichmann reaffirmed to himself every
day, confident that his pursuers had given up looking for him and
that he would never have to face the justice that he contemplated in
the abstract.

The identifying photo of Eichmann, found by his pursuers in the late 1940s
Bildarchiv Preussischer Kulturbesitz / Art Resource

Simon Wiesenthal, Nazi hunter
© *UPPA / Topham / The Image Works*

Eichmann during the war
© *Roger-Viollet / The Image Works*

Tuviah Friedman, Nazi hunter
Mirrorpix

The Red Cross passport Eichmann used to escape Europe
Buenos Aires Shoah Museum

Eichmann fleeing Europe on the *Giovanni C,* headed for Argentina, 1950

Eichmann in hiding,
Tucumán, Argentina, 1955
AKG Images / NordicPhotos

Dr. Fritz Bauer, attorney general for
the state of Hesse, West Germany
© *Topham / The Image Works*

Isser Harel, Mossad chief
Moshe Milner / Government Press Office, Israel

Zvi Aharoni, Mossad agent in Argentina
Zvi Aharoni

Surveillance photo of Eichmann's house on Garibaldi Street
Zvi Aharoni

Surveillance photo of the area where the Mossad team planned
to capture Eichmann *Zvi Aharoni*

The truck used by Aharoni during surveillance
Zvi Aharoni

Eichmann outside his house, as photographed with a hidden briefcase camera *Zvi Aharoni*

Eichmann's son, Dieter, briefcase camera photo *Zvi Aharoni*

Left Eichmann's daughter-in-law, Margarita, briefcase camera photo

Zvi Aharoni

The Mossad team
Zvi Aharoni

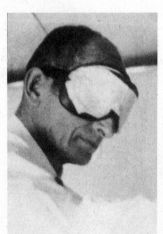

Eichmann in captivity,
wearing blacked-out goggles
Zvi Aharoni

Yosef Klein, El Al station chief
El Al / Marvin G. Goldman Collection

Zvi Tohar, El Al pilot
El Al / Marvin G. Goldman Collection

The El Al plane, Britannia 4X-AGD, used to take Eichmann out of Argentina
Peter R. Keating / Marvin G. Goldman Collection

Eichmann in Ramle
Prison, Israel, April 1961
*John Milli / Government Press
Office, Israel*

Eichmann in the glass booth at his trial, May 1961
Government Press Office, Israel

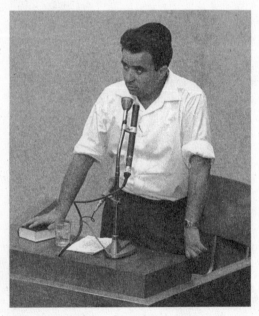

Zeev Sapir testifies at the trial, June 1961
Government Press Office, Israel

11

AT DUSK ON SATURDAY, October 10, 1959, Tuviah Friedman stood on his balcony and looked out over Haifa. The Sabbath rest drew to a close as the sun set, and the city on the northern coast of Israel came alive. People chatted as they poured onto the streets to savor the cool evening at outdoor cafés. Motorcycle engines roared up the steep Mount Carmel streets, and bus brakes squealed on their descent. Friedman could hear neighbors laughing in the courtyard as they headed out. Everyone seemed to be going somewhere. He stared out at the flickering lights of boats in the harbor, knowing that he could not enjoy himself. The envelope in his breast pocket was burning a hole through his chest.

When Friedman had first come to Israel six years before, he had been determined to put aside his hunt for Nazi war criminals, Eichmann most of all. He had floated from job to job before beginning to work at Yad Vashem, helping to organize the collection on Holocaust history and to register the names of Jewish victims. He had started the museum's office in Haifa but then gradually had found himself pressing officials for information on war criminals. He could not help himself, despite his bosses' urging that "we are not a police agency." In 1957, they had let him go. With a small government stipend, Friedman had reopened his documentation center and focused again on the capture of Eichmann. Since then, he had not earned a salary, and his wife, Anna, now a practicing eye surgeon, had supported him and their newborn son.

In the summer of 1959, Friedman had started a correspondence with Erwin Schüle. Schüle was the director of the West German Central Office for the Prosecution of National Socialist Criminals. Based in Ludwigsburg, near Stuttgart, the bureau had opened the previous December after Schüle had successfully prosecuted several Nazis in a highly publicized trial in Ulm. The trial had stirred victims to press for more investigations. Friedman had sent Schüle several files about war criminals he was targeting. He had later asked the prosecutor why he was not interested in finding the "monster who was the devil incarnate," Adolf Eichmann. Schüle had responded that he would indeed be interested in any material that Friedman had, so Friedman had sent a copy of his Eichmann file to Ludwigsburg with a request that the West German government consider posting a reward for the Nazi's capture.

On August 20, Schüle had written that he had a confidential source placing Eichmann in Kuwait. Friedman had presented the letter to his former Haganah chief, Arthur Pier (now Asher Ben-Natan and, at the time, the director general of the Israeli Ministry of Defense), as well as to several heads of Jewish organizations and even to the Israeli police in Tel Aviv. All of them had told him that there was nothing they could do. Nothing.

Now Friedman carried Schüle's letter in his breast pocket, keeping it always with him. He was sure that he finally had a clue as to Eichmann's whereabouts, and yet he was powerless to act on it. His wife tried to comfort him, but he was numb, debating with himself whether to forget the whole affair or go to the press with what he knew.

As he watched and listened to the people of Haifa enjoying a carefree evening, Friedman felt that he had no choice other than to go public. He strode over to the phone, dialed a contact at the newspaper *Ma'ariv,* and gave him a story: Adolf Eichmann, the Nazi war criminal whose sole focus was to clear Europe of Jews, was living freely in Kuwait.

The report, which he credited to the West German prosecutor, prompted a loud public outcry. Newspapers around the globe carried front-page headlines about the war criminal in Kuwait. Friedman gave scores of interviews to Israeli and foreign correspondents, describing the crimes of "history's most infamous killer" and proposing a reward of $10,000 to be set on his head. There were calls for a search to be launched as a matter of urgency. Ten days after the story was published, Friedman was invited to give a speech at a Tel Aviv rally for David Ben-Gurion and other members of his party who were up for election. Friedman implored the prime minister to "issue the orders that the same Eichmann who sent millions of Jews to the gas ovens should be found."

Meanwhile, letters poured into Friedman's documentation center. Some promised that Eichmann would never be found; others offered tips on his true location. One tip had the Nazi living as a hermit in a hilltop house in New Zealand. Among these letters, Friedman received a note posted on October 24 from a Lothar Hermann of Coronel Suárez, Argentina. Hermann explained that he had read the article about Eichmann in a local newspaper and that it was "completely incorrect. The person mentioned does not live in Kuwait on the Persian Gulf. He lives under an assumed name with his wife and four children near Buenos Aires." Hermann offered to provide "precise dates and exact material" and "was prepared to clear up this case completely, provided, however, the strictest secrecy is observed." A rapid exchange of two more letters, including discussions of a reward, convinced Friedman that this Argentine had hard facts on Eichmann's location.

Now dismissing the Kuwait lead out of hand, Friedman copied the letters from Argentina and delivered them to a prominent member of the World Jewish Congress, who promised to pass them on to people who could investigate them swiftly and properly. Friedman felt that he was on the right path.

In early December 1959, suitcase in hand, Fritz Bauer flicked off the lights in his Frankfurt office. He was headed to Israel, this time with certain proof that Adolf Eichmann was hiding in Buenos Aires. The attorney general planned on making his case firmly, and he would not return without the guarantee of a prompt operation. The Israelis needed to act.

Bauer did not dare risk leaving the country with his latest intelligence in written form, but he remembered the details well. According to his source, the fugitive Nazi had escaped from Germany in 1950 with the Catholic Church's aid, hiding in monasteries en route to Italy. There he had been given a new identity and applied for an International Committee of the Red Cross passport. He had traveled to Buenos Aires, obtained an Argentine identity card under his new pseudonym, and begun to work at a series of jobs. The first was at a company called CAPRI, run by an investment firm called the Fuldner Company out of a Buenos Aires address: 374 Avenida Córdoba. The company had dealt with converting waterpower into electricity. Eichmann had lived near the city of Tucumán while working for CAPRI. Later, he had run a laundry in the Olivos neighborhood of Buenos Aires. As of 1958, he still lived in the capital and was still involved with the Fuldner Company.

The intelligence was precise and covered a number of years, almost certainly obtained from someone who knew Eichmann well. None of this information was as important to Bauer, however, as the alias under which the source stated that Eichmann had lived throughout these years: Ricardo Klement. This matched the name to which the electricity meter at 4261 Chacabuco Street was registered. Two independent sources. One name. Klement was Eichmann. No doubt.

Bauer had resolved not to go to Isser Harel with these new details. The Mossad chief had disappointed him by shelving the first tip Bauer had sent, not to mention by relying on a blind man and his daughter to lead the investigation. Instead, Bauer had arranged a meeting with Haim Cohen, the Israeli attorney general. Bauer could not reveal the identity of his source, who was too critically placed. (To this day, it is still a state secret.) He would ask Cohen to exert as much pressure as possible on Harel to act on this information.

After the Hermann experience, Bauer suspected that Harel would demand to know the source's identity or refuse to get involved. However, the past six months had proved to Bauer that he had no option other than to go to the Israelis once again. His initial suspicion that his own government would not act effectively against fugitive Nazis such as Eichmann had been proved again and again. In June, one of his fellow prosecutors in Freiburg had issued a warrant for the arrest of Josef Mengele for his many crimes at Auschwitz. The prosecutor had a known address for Mengele in Argentina and had convinced the West German Foreign Ministry to issue an extradition request. The Argentines first denied that Mengele had ever come to the country (although they knew he had), and when his presence had been proved to them, they had informed the Foreign Ministry that his crimes had been "political" in nature and therefore that further review was needed. The extradition was still pending, giving Mengele plenty of time to escape should he ever feel threatened. Since Werner Junkers, a former high-level aide to Joaquim von Ribbentrop, was the West German ambassador in Argentina, Mengele had likely learned of the proceedings against him and that they would result in failure.

One thing Bauer knew for certain was that there was no more time for delay in catching Eichmann. Even though the Kuwait announcement may have prompted his source to come forward, Bauer feared that it might also have resulted in Eichmann's learning that he was still a target and going to ground. Bauer had since urged his close colleague Schüle, who was now aware of the Argentine investigation, to contact Friedman and reassure him that the Hesse attorney general was making every effort to track down Eichmann. Any more publicity would jeopardize the hunt.

As he headed out of the building and into a waiting car, Bauer hoped that Eichmann had not already made a run for it.

On the road between Tel Aviv and Jerusalem, in the back of a chauffeur-driven sedan, Zvi Aharoni, the thirty-eight-year-old chief interrogator for the Shin Bet, and Isser Harel sat in silence. Aharoni was scanning the reports sent from Lothar Hermann. The Shin Bet interrogator was not surprised that he had heard nothing of the investigation in the past two years. Harel made it his practice to compartmentalize information. His agents knew only what they needed to know—no more, no less. Aharoni was shocked that Harel had relied solely on the Hermanns to conduct the investigation. Aharoni had been in Buenos Aires for six weeks on another mission earlier in the year and could have pursued some of the leads himself. However, one did not question the Mossad chief.

Earlier in the day, Harel had summoned Aharoni and informed him that they were expected at the Ministry of Justice in Jerusalem for a meeting with Haim Cohen and Fritz Bauer. It was only once they were in the car that Harel had told Aharoni about Eichmann and had shown him the files. Cohen had specifically asked for Aharoni to attend the meeting. They knew each other well from several espionage and high-treason cases they had worked together and were both gifted with the same cold, logical intelligence. Both German Jews by birth, neither had kept their faith in a God that had abandoned the Jews to the Nazi barbarity.

As the sedan threaded through the pine-covered Judean Hills outside Jerusalem, Aharoni sensed that his boss was irked at being beckoned by Cohen. The Mossad chief answered only to Ben-Gurion, but he could not dismiss a call from the attorney general. Anyway, Bauer had surely come all this way for a good reason.

The car reached Jerusalem and made its way through the maze of steep streets to the Ministry of Justice on Jaffa Street. The walls of the Old City stood in the distance. They climbed to the second floor where Cohen and Bauer were waiting for them. After a brief introduction, Bauer launched straight into the new intelligence he had received confirming the Klement alias. His bushy gray eyebrows flared while he spoke. He was obviously incensed that the first Israeli investigation had dismissed the Hermanns' reports. A precious eighteen months had passed without action, and Bauer feared that Eichmann had long since moved or switched his name again.

"This is simply unbelievable!" Bauer said angrily. "Here we have the name Klement: Two completely independent sources, who are strangers to each other, mention this name. Any second-class policeman would be able to follow such a lead! Just go and ask the nearest butcher or greengrocer and you will learn all there is to know about him!"

Harel attempted to calm Bauer, assuring him that this significant new intelligence completely changed the dynamic of the investigation. Bauer remained furious. He declared that he would have no choice other than to begin extradition proceedings through official German channels if the Israelis did not act immediately. Though Harel thought that Bauer was probably bluffing, the Mossad chief replied that this would not be necessary. They wanted Eichmann found and were ready to act.

Cohen declared, "I want Zvi to go to Buenos Aires and check out this story once and for all. We can't play around with this any longer."

Harel agreed, sure now that his perception of the Hermann reports had been misguided. Aharoni reacted evenly to the decision, never one to show much emotion, though he glowed inwardly with pride to know that they had such faith in his abilities. Aharoni wanted to know where Bauer had got his information. Bauer was firm that he must keep his source's identity secret, but he insisted that the source and Hermann were unconnected. Aharoni suspected that his intelligence had come from a former SS officer who had recently left Argentina and was looking to curry favor with the West German authorities, either to join their intelligence outfits or to elude a trial for war crimes. At this point, however, it did not matter: the source did look solid. Aharoni would go to Germany to collect the intelligence documents that Bauer had gathered over the past two years. Then he would travel to Argentina. The meeting that had started so tensely ended with warm handshakes.

Aharoni felt the burden begin to weigh on him: his mission would likely be more difficult than inquiring at the local butcher in Buenos Aires, despite what Bauer had said. The fate of Eichmann rested on Aharoni's success in locating and identifying him.

On December 6, Prime Minister David Ben-Gurion welcomed his Mossad chief into his office. Though equal in height to Harel, the man known as the founding father of Israel had a much more commanding presence. He had the lantern jaw and instinctive aggressiveness of a fighter and the wild white hair and curious intellect of an artist. Already in his early seventies, Ben-Gurion was nearing the end of his time as leader of the new nation, but his eyes were as bright and intelligent as when he had announced the establishment of the state of Israel in 1948. Harel and Ben-Gurion were very close, having relied on each other over the past decade not only for Israel's benefit but also for their own hold on its many levers of power.

Haim Cohen joined them shortly, and Harel recounted their meeting with Fritz Bauer to Ben-Gurion, explaining that the Hesse attorney general now had intelligence that identified where Eichmann lived and under what alias almost beyond any doubt. The Mossad chief had told the prime minister before about the search for the fugitive Nazi but never with the conviction that he might be found. Ben-Gurion was impressed by the courage Bauer had shown in coming to them again — this time personally — with the information. Harel advised Ben-Gurion that Bauer had warned that he would push for extradition proceedings in West Germany if Israel did not pursue his leads.

"Prevent Bauer from taking this step," Ben-Gurion said, his voice firm. "If Eichmann is there, we will capture him in order to bring him here."

Harel had already considered such an operation, knowing that it would present enormous challenges that would tax the Mossad's limited resources. A more expedient solution would be to assassinate Eichmann. His people were experienced in this method: one day the Argentine police would discover Ricardo Klement in a car crash or some other mishap, and the world would not need to know that Adolf Eichmann was dead — or that the Israelis had killed him.

Ben-Gurion was unequivocal that he wanted Eichmann taken alive, to stand trial in Israel for his crimes against the Jewish people. Cohen was apprehensive about the legality of such a move, as he had already discussed with Harel. From a purely legal perspective, West Germany had much more of a right to try Eichmann than Israel, which had not existed when the crimes were committed. Nonetheless, Ben-Gurion told the Israeli attorney general to investigate the matter further and arrive at a justification.

As for the operation itself, Ben-Gurion had complete faith in Harel, writing confidently in his diary that night, "Isser will deal with it."

Three weeks later, on Christmas Eve, those in West Germany who looked fondly on the Nazi past acted. In Cologne, two young men painted huge swastikas and JUDEN RAUS (Jews Out) across the walls of a recently constructed synagogue and on a memorial dedicated to those who had fought in the resistance against Hitler. Over the next several days, there was an outbreak of anti-Semitic attacks and demonstrations across West Germany, and police had to be stationed outside synagogues and Jewish cemeteries to prevent further desecrations. In total, 685 Jewish locations throughout the country were painted with swastikas. These were more than the isolated actions of a few hooligans, and Jewish leaders in West Germany asserted that the scene "evoked pictures that bring to mind the November days of 1938."

Chancellor Adenauer promptly broadcast on the radio that these acts were not to be tolerated, but it was plain that much more was needed to tamp down the rise of neo-Nazism. The German Reich Party, a right-wing group with Nazi sympathies, had made gains in the recent election. Membership in militant and nationalistic organizations was increasing, as was the number of newsletters and daily papers, book clubs, and discussion groups whose readers and members hated the "Bonn democracy" and aimed to "correct the accepted facts" about Hitler and German war guilt.

The attacks also highlighted the fact that numerous former Nazi Party officials held many important government posts in the new Germany. They accounted for a third of Adenauer's cabinet, a quarter of the Bundestag, and a sizable percentage of the civil service, judiciary, and Foreign Ministry. In addition, eight foreign ambassadors were former Nazis. Adenauer had stonewalled in the face of a recent campaign, largely organized by his political opponents, against the proliferation of such individuals in the government. Most notably, he had refused to fire Hans Globke, the minister for refugees Theodore Oberländer (a Waffen-SS officer who had once demanded the extermination of the Slavic people), or the interior minister Gerhard Schröder (a former Nazi storm trooper leader).

Also troubling was the fact that the recent war criminal trials conducted by Erwin Schüle and Fritz Bauer had done little to change the "almost nationwide need to pull the blinds on the past," as a *New York Times* reporter described the mindset in West Germany. Even the country's schoolteachers were found to be incorrectly instructing their students on the nature of Hitler's regime. A ninth-grade textbook devoted only a single paragraph to the "Jewish question" during World War II. Extermination camps were not mentioned once. All of these trends drew critical notice in Israel.

Soon after the Cologne incident, the Knesset's Foreign Affairs and Defense Committee asked Harel about the potential of a Nazi revival. Even to these high officials, Harel could not reveal the first major blow he intended to deliver to combat this revival: the capture of Adolf Eichmann. He was more convinced than ever that Ben-Gurion was right: the fugitive's capture, and the public airing of his crimes in a trial, would remind the world of the Nazi atrocities and the need to remain vigilant against any groups who aimed to repeat them. Already the Mossad chief had tasked Aharoni with his mission to Argentina, another agent was investigating the Eichmann and Liebl families in Europe, and Harel was looking into transporting their captive covertly from Argentina when the time came.

Harel had also taken steps to keep Eichmann unaware of the hunt for him in Buenos Aires, particularly after the potentially disastrous announcements by Tuviah Friedman in the press. First, on his advice, Bauer held a press conference in Frankfurt and declared that his office was seriously investigating the presence of Eichmann in Kuwait, saying he had a tip that the fugitive Nazi was in the employment of a sheik and serving as "an influential middleman between German and Kuwaiti companies." Coincidentally, this declaration was made the day before the wave of anti-Semitic attacks. Second, Harel arranged through Bauer for Schüle to contact Friedman once again, urging him to cease his public campaign for a reward for Eichmann. "Please make sure no publications, no speeches, and no proceedings of any kind are conducted in connection with the Eichmann case," Schüle wrote. Third, the Mossad chief used his influence to put an end to a separate investigation by a local Jewish organization in Buenos Aires that had interviewed Lothar Hermann about the contents of his letter to Tuviah Friedman. Fourth, Harel quashed a request by a Knesset member to David Ben-Gurion on December 25 to "take suitable measures in order to bring about Eichmann's apprehension and punishment" by asking the legislator to withdraw his request, because any reply would impair their efforts.

At the Foreign Affairs and Defense Committee meeting, Harel was equally obtuse, but he assured those in attendance, "I am planning an action that, if successful, could mean a death blow to this outburst of neo-Nazism." Now that he was completely behind the mission and had the sanction of the prime minister, he would see this action through to the end.

12

ON MARCH 1, 1960, Zvi Aharoni presented himself to immigration control at Ezeiza Airport, an hour outside Buenos Aires. His Israeli diplomatic papers identified him as Mr. Rodan, a staff member of the Foreign Ministry. He explained in his rough Spanish that he had traveled to Argentina to investigate reports of an outbreak of anti-Semitism in South America. The guard eyed the passport and then its holder.

Aharoni had the kind of long, sober face that made it difficult to divine his thoughts, an advantage in his interrogation work. Those who knew him said that he saw the world as being streaked with tragedy. Over the course of his thirty-eight years, he had tricked death numerous times, and every time he had wondered why he had survived while others had not.

Two weeks before Kristallnacht, the night in November 1938 when Hitler's thugs ransacked Jewish shops and homes throughout Germany, Aharoni left Berlin with his mother and younger brother to immigrate to Palestine. Every other member of his family was killed in the Holocaust.

Living on a kibbutz in the hills of lower Galilee, the youth learned to speak Hebrew, ride a horse, and fire a rifle, and he came to know intimately what it was like to sit in the pitch-darkness and wait for an attack. For most of the next ten years, he carried a gun, serving first as a guard at the kibbutz and then as a member of the Jewish Settlement Police. In 1943, he joined the British army. His unit was stationed in

Cairo, then in Italy, where he interrogated high-ranking German prisoners. At war's end, his attempt at civilian life was thwarted by the
1948 War of Independence, in which he saw heavy fighting. Numerous times he faced certain death: ambushed in broad daylight outside
the kibbutz; caught in an attack by a U-boat at sea; surrounded by
Arabs, alone on a hilltop in Palestine, protected by a single rock,
which was gradually being chipped away by bullets; retrieving a two-
inch mortar in an open field under constant gunfire; finding an unex-
ploded shell inches from his feet. Each time he had lived, while those
fighting alongside him had not.

By the summer of 1949, now a captain and company commander
in charge of two hundred men, Aharoni found himself facing a new
enemy: typhoid. In the hospital, life slowly drained from him. He
was so sick that his wife, whom he had met at the kibbutz, could
not even ask him what they should name their newborn son. Once
again he survived, but he was too weak to rejoin the army. By hap-
penstance, he ran into someone with whom he had served in Italy,
who suggested that he join the Israeli security services. One of their
former commanders was deputy chief of the Shin Bet. Before long,
Aharoni found himself sitting across from Isser Harel at a Jaffa café.
Harel asked him a few questions about his past, then asked what Aharoni thought about the violent, right-wing dissident groups, such as
the Irgun. From Harel's tone, Aharoni knew enough to answer, "I am
absolutely against them." Two days later, he was invited to join the
Shin Bet as one of two men responsible for interrogations. In the following years, he built up the Shin Bet investigations branch, trained
numerous new recruits, and attained the rank of division head, just
below the deputy chief of the entire organization.

Now, newly arrived in Argentina, Aharoni was operating as a Mossad agent for the first time—a far cry from his usual line of work.
Harel, who had waited for him to finish another assignment before
sending him to Buenos Aires, hoped that the interrogator's relentless,
unemotional determination would lead him to Eichmann. At passport control, Aharoni passed his first test when the guard stamped his
documents, allowing him to enter without inspecting the sealed diplomatic pouch under his arm. That pouch contained everything the

Israelis knew about Eichmann, including the most recent intelligence from Bauer, which had taken several weeks for them to obtain covertly.

Waiting outside the airport in the sweltering heat was "Yossef," the security officer at the Israeli embassy, with whom Aharoni had worked for several years in Tel Aviv. On the ride into the city, Aharoni stared vacantly at the thick rows of trees lining both sides of the highway, knowing well that he would soon have to take some risks to prove for certain that Klement was Eichmann. Another "maybe" in the file would be useless. Harel needed a definitive answer before he could launch a mission. Given how long their target had lived freely in Argentina, Aharoni hoped that Eichmann had grown less suspicious and would not flee at the slightest feeling that someone was observing him.

Yossef brought Aharoni to the Israeli embassy—he was the only person there who knew the true purpose of Aharoni's visit. Aharoni locked his Eichmann files in a safe; after long study, he knew most of the facts by heart. Later, Yossef drove him to his hotel. On the way, Aharoni detailed to him the kind of help he would need, particularly since he was alone, unfamiliar with the city, and had a poor grasp of Spanish. In every country, Aharoni knew, there were Jewish volunteers, known as *sayanim,* who were available to assist Mossad agents, whether it was with surveillance, transport, safe houses, or medical aid, or simply by standing on a corner and waiting for a messenger. They did not require compensation, and they knew not to ask questions or to utter a word about what they had done. Without them, the small Israeli secret service would not have had anything like the reach it actually had. Aharoni would need their help.

Two days later, Aharoni drove slowly down Chacabuco Street in a rented Fiat. "Roberto," a twenty-year-old Argentine student with a black pencil mustache, sat next to him holding a street map. Having volunteered for other operations in the past, Roberto kept his inquiries to a minimum.

As they drove past 4261 Chacabuco, Aharoni glanced at the small house with its unkempt garden. He stopped a few blocks away on a side street, pondering how he could get a good look at whoever lived in the house. He fished a postcard of a tropical island, which he had picked up at the airport, out of his pocket and told Roberto to write on the back, "Have just returned. Best regards, George," along with a fictitious name and address. Aharoni told him to jot the name Dagosto (a variation of Dagoto, the name Lothar Hermann had found one of the electric meters at 4261 Chacabuco registered to) and 4263 Chacabuco in the sender box. The address did not exist, but the card would provide Roberto with an excuse to ask neighbors if they knew the sender. Because the postcard lacked a stamp and postmark, Aharoni warned the youth not to allow anyone a close inspection.

Roberto ventured off while Aharoni waited in the car. Two years had passed since Sylvia Hermann had walked down this street. The Nazi fugitive might well have switched neighborhoods, and if he had, he would be very difficult to find in a city of more than 5 million people spread across seventy-one square miles. For all Aharoni knew, Eichmann might have moved to another city, country, or continent.

Twenty minutes later, Roberto reappeared, hurrying back to the car. He waved the postcard and smiled, then climbed into the passenger's seat. He had spoken to a young girl outside the house about the Dagosto family and had peered, undetected, through the windows of 4261 Chacabuco. Nobody in the neighborhood was named Dagosto, but the house was empty, and Roberto had glimpsed some painters working inside. Klement no longer lived at the address. Worse, he had probably vacated the premises very recently. If Aharoni had not been delayed in Israel on that other job, he would have arrived before Klement had moved. Now he needed a new plan.

Across the globe, Mossad operative Yaakov Gat was in a village in West Germany waiting for the return of his partner, Michael Bloch. Harel had recruited the two men to investigate the Eichmann and Liebl families. Bloch, who spoke fluent German, was spending the morning at the local café, chatting casually with villagers to see if they knew anything about Eichmann's family. Every attempt to speak to Vera Eichmann's sister Eva, to see if she knew where Vera lived, had been met by the same wall of silence that Gat had encountered over the previous six weeks with the other members of the family. This was revealing in itself, indicating that the family had something to hide.

Forty years old, tall and slender as a reed, Gat was a Shin Bet agent based at the embassy in Paris. He was in charge of finding East German, Hungarian, and KGB spies who were passing intelligence to Egypt. He was also a leading representative of the Mossad in Europe. Given that Harel ran both organizations, the lines between the two were often blurred. Born in Transylvania, Gat had a personal stake in the operation to find Eichmann. He and his immediate family had survived the Nazis by moving away from the region, annexed to Hungary in 1940, but many in his extended family, including half of his father's family, had remained behind and been sent to extermination camps by Eichmann. At the war's end, Gat had left for Palestine but had been captured and detained in a British camp for illegal émigrés in Cyprus until the state of Israel was declared. Gat's paratrooper cousin advised him that his agile mind and preternatural calm would serve the security services well. He was willing to take a job with them as long as he never had to wear a uniform, as recollections of the fascist Romanian soldiers were still distasteful to him. He underwent a five-week training program, learning self-defense and how to pick locks, open envelopes, handle a camera, break a tail, and surveil a target, among other skills. Then he was sent out into the field to actually learn how to be an operative.

When Bloch returned, he told Gat about a chat he had had at the café. According to the postman, Vera and her three sons had stayed in the town in the early 1950s and then one day had disappeared. No letters had ever come from her, and nothing had been seen or heard of her since. It was the kind of thing a postman in a small town noticed, yet another sliver of information casting doubt on the story that Vera had remarried and moved away, which was the only story her family had offered over the years.

Gat and Bloch took a train to Vienna and, as soon as they arrived, sent their report to Harel. As always, Gat included the facts they had learned. His boss did not want interpretation.

The two also had arranged to meet Simon Wiesenthal, who had something to show them. The independent Nazi-hunter was working

for a Jewish organization that offered vocational training to immigrants to ease their assimilation. Gat had contacted Wiesenthal at the
beginning of the investigation, knowing of his interest in Eichmann. Gat had sworn Wiesenthal to secrecy, but he had kept quiet
about the Argentine operation all the same, explaining only that they
were following up leads on the Nazi's family. Wiesenthal had offered
his help, mentioning that the previous April, he had seen an obituary
for Eichmann's stepmother and that the names listed in the obituary
had included a Vera Eichmann. This seemed strange, because a
woman who remarried usually took her new husband's name. Wiesenthal had helped Gat and Bloch track down several Eichmann
family members and had attempted to find out more about the passports given to Vera and her sons in 1952. The passport file had disappeared from the German consulate in Graz, however, raising more
suspicions. Like Tuviah Friedman, Wiesenthal had urged the Israeli
government to offer a sizable reward for any information on Eichmann's whereabouts.

At his apartment, Wiesenthal spread out five photographs on the
table in front of him and invited the two Israelis to examine them.
One was the picture of Eichmann taken in the late 1930s that Diamant had found in Maria Mösenbacher's possession. The other four
were of his brothers. A few weeks before, Wiesenthal had arranged
to have their photos taken at the funeral of their father in Linz.
"This must be how he looks now," Wiesenthal said, knowing that Gat
wanted to get his hands on a recent photograph of Eichmann. "Probably closest to his brother Otto. All the brothers have the same facial
expression. Look at the mouth, the corners of the mouth, the chin,
the form of the skull."

"Fantastic," Bloch said, nodding his head.

Gat asked if they might take the photos with them. Wiesenthal
gladly gave them copies.

It was clear to Gat and Bloch that Vera and her sons had left Austria without a hint of their destination and that eight years later, they
still wanted nobody to know where they were. Unless she had remarried some other war criminal, Vera must be with Eichmann.

Gat wanted to cut off contact with Wiesenthal, despite his ongoing desire to be of help. Through a source, Gat had learned that Wiesenthal had indiscreetly mentioned in conversation that the Israelis were eager to find Eichmann. Furthermore, Gat was weary of Wiesenthal's questions about payment for his assistance in the investigation. No doubt this would not have been an issue had Wiesenthal known that the Israelis were not just fishing for information but had already dispatched an Israeli agent to Buenos Aires to find him.

On March 4, "Juan," a cherubic eighteen-year-old Argentine who had a permanent smile, entered the gate at 4261 Chacabuco Street. In his hand, he carried an exquisitely wrapped box containing an expensive cigarette lighter. It was addressed to Nikolas Klement, Vicente López, 4261 Chacabuco. Slipped under the ribbon was a note written in flowery script by an embassy secretary: "For my friend Nicki, in friendship, on his birthday."

Juan had instructions from a Mr. Rodan, whom he had just met, to go to the Vicente López address to find out where "Nick Klement" had moved. His cover was that he had a gift to deliver. If asked where the gift came from, Juan was to say that his friend worked as a bellboy at an upscale Buenos Aires hotel, and a young lady had given him a sizable tip to deliver this package. Since his friend was busy, Juan was doing him a favor. Under no circumstances, Mr. Rodan stressed, was Juan to go to the new address. If he got into any trouble, a "friend" would be waiting four blocks away. Then Mr. Rodan wished him good luck.

Unable to find a bell at the gate, Juan shouted out for Nick Klement. The doors and windows to the house were wide open. When nobody answered, he ventured into the yard and around to the back of the house, where a man and a woman were emptying out a brick shack.

"Excuse me please," Juan said. "But do you know whether Mr. Klement lives here?"

"You mean the Germans?" the man asked.

"I don't know."

"Do you mean the one with the three grown sons and the little boy?"

"I don't know," Juan said innocently. Truly, he had no idea.

"Those people used to live here, but now they have moved. Maybe fifteen to twenty days ago." The man suggested that Juan speak to one of the men working in the house and led him inside.

Juan spotted a carpenter in his early fifties and showed him the card and gift. "Can you tell me where I can find him?" Juan asked. "I have to deliver it personally."

The carpenter, who spoke Spanish with a thick European accent, mentioned that the family had moved to a neighborhood called San Fernando, but he did not know exactly where. Helpfully, he offered to take Juan to where one of Klement's sons worked, just a block away. As they approached an automobile mechanic's garage on the next corner, the carpenter pointed out a Motoneta moped that he said belonged to Klement's son. Juan got a good look at the vehicle. Then the carpenter called out, "Dito!" A young man of about nineteen, wearing oil-stained overalls, came over.

"This guy would like to speak to your father," the carpenter told the young man.

Juan did not know whether he was looking for the father or the son, only Nick Klement. He explained the purpose of his visit and that he had just learned that Klement had moved. Dito confirmed this curtly.

"Where have you moved?" Juan asked.

"To Don Torcuato."

Juan hesitatingly offered to give Dito the package to pass on to his father, Mr. Klement, saying that he was doing a favor for his bellboy friend.

"I'd like to know from whom you got that," Dito said.

Juan explained that he did not know the name or anything else about the young lady who had given his friend the package to deliver. Then he asked if he could just have Mr. Klement's address in order to deliver the package himself. Dito refused, saying the area had no street addresses. At last Dito agreed to take the package. Sensing that he had pressed enough, Juan left the garage.

Listening to Juan's report, Aharoni grew excited and thanked him for a job well done. Not only was the trail not dead; they might even

have found one of the fugitive Nazi's sons. He was also personally encouraged that his gambit to deliver the lighter had worked. He had
reckoned that people would be more forthcoming with information
if they thought they were doing Nick a favor. Aharoni had learned
from the file that Nick's birthday was March 3. Now he knew for certain that a German family named Klement had lived at the Chacabuco address until only a few weeks ago. They had four sons, one of
whom was roughly the same age and had a similar-sounding name to
Dieter Eichmann, born March 29, 1942.

Aharoni unfolded his map to locate the two neighborhoods to
which Juan had been told the family had moved. Don Torcuato and
San Fernando were more than three miles apart. Given this discrep-
ancy, as well as the facts that the family did not leave a forwarding
address and Dito had refused to give his, Aharoni concluded that
the Klements had something to hide — another indication that they
might be the Eichmanns.

Hoping that he was on the right track, Aharoni decided to try the
workers at the house again to see if they knew where the family had
moved. Later that day, he brought "Lorenzo," a different *sayan,* to the
house to pose as a salesman. The thirty-five-year-old had the looks,
suit, and smoothness to play the role. Two visits on the same day was
incautious, and the second achieved nothing more than to confirm
that Ricardo Klement had lived there. Still, Aharoni was confident
enough in what he had learned to cable Harel.

That night, he sent a coded message from the embassy to Mossad
headquarters: THE DRIVER IS RED (Klement is likely Eichmann).
He also detailed that their target had recently moved and that he was
attempting to locate him. Once he sent the code THE DRIVER IS
BLACK, Harel would know definitively that Eichmann had been
found, and the operation to capture him could begin.

Aharoni and Juan sat in the Fiat on Monteagudo Street, keeping
watch on the early-evening traffic. It was March 8. Anybody leaving
Dito's shop would have to drive by them to reach the neighborhoods
of San Fernando or Don Torcuato to the north. Aharoni felt that they

would not draw any undue attention to themselves. Even though in most countries, loitering in a car would be suspicious, in Argentina, he had noticed, it was perfectly normal to sit in a car for long stretches of time, smoking a cigarette, reading a newspaper, eating lunch, or engaged in conversation with a friend. So they waited, hoping to follow Dito home.

Since arriving in Buenos Aires, Aharoni had also checked into other intelligence provided by Bauer. None of these inquiries had uncovered anything proving that Klement was Eichmann, nor was there any indication as to where the family had moved. Early that morning, Aharoni had sheltered from a torrential rain under the awning of a house on Avenida Córdoba, watching, for the second day, the doorway to the Fuldner Company across the street, looking for Eichmann on his way into work. Nearly three hours had passed without any sign of him.

Through a Jewish lawyer provided by Yossef, Aharoni had hired a private investigator to find evidence of the arrival of Vera Liebl and her sons in Argentina, as well as any information on the identities of the former tenants at 4261 Chacabuco Street. Again, nothing. There was some possibility of discovering a lead in Tucumán, but he felt that to be a long shot.

Now Aharoni was depending on Dito to lead him to Eichmann, and this was the third afternoon they had spent parked on Monteagudo Street. At 5:15 P.M., a dirt-spattered black moped whirred past the Fiat from the direction of the shop. Its driver, who was in his fifties, wore wide dark glasses, and clinging to him on the pillion was a young blond man wearing overalls. Juan pointed them out, almost certain this was Dito. The moped looked to be the same make as the one Juan had seen in the shop.

That was more than enough for Aharoni, who turned the key and shifted into gear. He followed the moped through traffic, trying not to be seen but also not to lose the moped. Ten minutes later, after a series of turns, the moped turned down a small alley by a railroad station in San Isidro, the neighborhood directly southeast of San Fernando. The young man dashed into a building, then came out two minutes later. Again, Aharoni and Juan followed the moped. When they reached the center of San Fernando, the bike temporarily disappeared among the cars and trucks jammed around the main square. Catching sight of it again, Aharoni turned off the square to follow and found himself abruptly halted by a funeral procession. He could do nothing but grip the steering wheel in frustration as the moped disappeared from view. On the drive back to Aharoni's hotel, the Fiat's electrical system shorted out, and it had to be towed back into the city.

Over the next few days, Aharoni attempted to trail Dito with two other teams of *sayanim*. On the first night, during a heavy downpour, the moped didn't show, but the couple who were watching the automobile shop from a café followed someone resembling Dito to a nearby bus station. On the second night, in a rented station wagon, Aharoni trailed the moped, again with two riders, back to San Fernando. There he switched cars with two of the young Argentines helping him. He almost lost the moped again around the square but managed to keep it in sight. When the bike reached Route 202, Aharoni drew back considerably, since there were only a few cars on the road to Don Torcuato. Just before a railway embankment, the moped stopped at a kiosk on the side of the road. There was only a scattering of houses and wooden huts in the barren, flat land. Aharoni slowed the car. The two riders looked to be staying there a while, prompting Aharoni to drive past and circle back toward San Fernando. Juan was certain that they were following the moped from the shop, but this time he was less sure that the passenger was Dito.

On the third night, Aharoni and Juan trailed a lone young man who left the shop on a moped. When he stopped and went into a house along the way to San Fernando, Aharoni sent Juan out to get a closer look. A few minutes later, he came back and said it was probably not Dito.

Aharoni felt anger well up inside him. A week had passed since he had first sent Juan into the Chacabuco house, and they had learned nothing more. Now they had followed the same individual several nights in a row, risking exposure, and they were still unsure whether they were shadowing the right person. This could not continue. They had to get either the address to which the Klement family had moved or confirmation that it was indeed Dito they were tailing.

"Go back to the garage tomorrow," Aharoni told Juan, trying to temper his frustration. "Tell them your friend is angry. He claims that you never delivered the present and he wants the money from you. Either you get the address where they live so you can speak to Mr. Klement, or at least make sure you have a good look at the boy. Don't tell me you're not sure . . . I need a yes or no."

On March 11, as instructed, Juan returned to 4261 Chacabuco Street to see if any of the workers might tell him more than they had on his first visit before trying the garage again. The carpenter who had helped him before recognized him. After Juan told him the story about how the gift had never been delivered, he asked for Mr. Klement's new address. This time, the carpenter, feeling bad for him, explained that he did not know the street name, but he gave Juan exact directions to the house: go to the San Fernando station; take bus 203 to Avellaneda Street; ask at the corner kiosk for the German's house. If Juan wanted to find the house on his own, that was just as easy. It was an unfinished brick house with a flat roof only a few hundred yards from the kiosk.

"Are you absolutely certain?" Juan asked, not wanting to return to Aharoni with any doubts.

The carpenter nodded. He had done work at the house, and the German still owed him some money. Then Juan asked him about Dito, explaining that he had said he was the son of Klement but that he had never delivered the package. The carpenter thought that Klement had only a young son, no more than eight years old, but that he lived with Dito's mother, who had three sons from her first marriage.

Juan thanked the carpenter and walked over to the mechanic's shop. Dito came out into the yard, recognizing him. "And what do you want this time?" he said.

Juan told his story again, how his friend was potentially facing a fine of 500 pesos.

Dito grew hostile. "How come? If she wanted to send it to my brother, why did she not write down my brother's correct name? There is no Nick Klement. It's Nick Eichmann."

At a café near the Israeli embassy later that night, Aharoni waited nervously for Juan. He knew that sending the young Argentine back to the house was a desperate move, potentially disastrous, but he did not feel that he had any other choice. When Juan appeared, he was stripped of his usual smile and looking worn down.

"What happened?" Aharoni asked worriedly.

Juan explained that he now had specific directions to the family's new house. Aharoni could not understand how *this* would depress him, since that was what they had been searching for over the past week, without success. Juan then admitted, "We followed the wrong person. The name's not Klement. It's Eichmann."

Aharoni could have leapt from his seat onto the table, but he restrained himself. "Ah. Never mind. Don't worry about it," he said.

Juan also explained that on asking where Mr. Klement was, Dito had said that he was in Tucumán on business. Aharoni thanked Juan for his fine work and urged him never to speak to another soul about their investigation. In parting, Aharoni reassured him, "We'll find the right man."

13

AHARONI CRAWLED ALONG Route 202 in his rented station wagon, past a kiosk on the corner to his left. It was late afternoon on March 12, but the sun was still high enough in the sky for him to get a good look at the house. The directions the carpenter had given Juan had played out perfectly so far, and Aharoni had passed several stops on the route of bus 203 from the center of San Fernando. Boosting his confidence that he was on the right track, he remembered coming to this same kiosk a few days before while following the moped.

A railway embankment crossed the road 150 yards ahead, but otherwise the area was level and almost completely featureless. It was a poor, sparsely populated section of San Fernando, without telephone or electrical lines. Fifty yards before the short tunnel that passed underneath the railway, a street turned to the left. On this, Aharoni spotted a one-story brick house with a large wooden door and tiny windows. The masonry was unrendered and the roof flat—just as the carpenter had described. This was the house; Aharoni was sure of it. Apart from a cottage twenty yards up the street, there was not another place within a couple of hundred yards. The house looked more like a provincial jail than a home, an impression reinforced by the barred windows and the low brick wall and chicken wire fence surrounding the property. A wooden shed in the corner of the barren yard could have been an isolation cell.

Driving past, Aharoni saw a woman in a faded sundress sitting on the edge of the porch. A young boy in his underwear, no older than six, played at her feet. The woman was short and thick-bodied, with slightly graying black hair — probably in her fifties. Aharoni suspected that he might be looking at Vera Eichmann and her fourth son, who must have been born after she arrived in Argentina. He continued underneath the railway bridge, stunned at the poverty in which the family was living — worse even than the Olivos house.

Later that night, Aharoni parked fifteen minutes' walk away from the house. It was almost pitch-black, the moon and stars hidden behind clouds. He followed a street that ran parallel to Route 202. Dogs barked in the distance, and as he neared the house, he grew worried that he might run across one of them. But the barking was from somewhere else and had carried across the plain. He was close enough to see the dim light from a kerosene lamp through one of the windows. There was no sign of the supposed stepfather, Mr. Klement, but Aharoni did not expect to see him, since Dieter Eichmann had told Juan that he was in Tucumán.

If Adolf Eichmann lived in the house, he would very likely be back for his silver wedding anniversary a week later, on March 21. Before then, however, Aharoni hoped to confirm that Klement was indeed Eichmann. He needed proof.

In Tel Aviv, Harel excitedly read Aharoni's latest coded message. Although his agent was moving aggressively, chancing his exposure, he was also proving to be more than effective. The Eichmann family had been identified, and Aharoni knew where they lived. In a short while, Harel suspected, Aharoni would confirm whether the man living with the family was Adolf Eichmann himself. Until certain, Harel hesitated to assemble a team for the capture operation.

He drafted a cable to Gat that he cease his actions in Austria. Since they had located Vera Eichmann and her sons, further inquiries might scare the extended family into alerting them. Harel also telephoned Haim Cohen. On the orders of Ben-Gurion, they were to sit down together to finalize the legal justification for the Israelis to capture a German citizen on foreign soil and bring him to trial in an Israeli court. Harel knew that Cohen remained convinced that there was more legal standing for the West Germans to try Eichmann, but they both understood that this was largely a nonissue because their prime minister wanted justice to be served on behalf of the victims of Eichmann's actions.

Two days later, on March 14, at the Waldorf-Astoria in New York, the leaders of West Germany and Israel were meeting for the first time, an occasion of historic and symbolic importance. Ben-Gurion needed to secure a good relationship with Adenauer: this would help tamp down any tensions that might arise were Eichmann caught, although there were decidedly more important issues at stake. In his suite, Adenauer warmly greeted the Israeli prime minister, and the two sat down for a long private conversation. Ben-Gurion hoped to obtain half a billion dollars in economic aid and to further the ongoing illegal arms transfers from West Germany to Israel. Adenauer was looking to bolster his alliance with Israel, a relationship with its own secret military and intelligence advantages for his country. Also critical at that moment was the chancellor's desire to show his people and the international community that the recent outbreak of anti-Semitic attacks was a false representation of the new Germany. He had to exorcise the ghosts of the past.

After the two statesmen concluded their warm meeting, they went to speak to the press. Adenauer expressed how deeply moved he had been by Ben-Gurion and how certain he was that continued reparations served both countries. Ben-Gurion added how pleased he was to have met the West German chancellor, then concluded by saying, "I belong to a nation which cannot forget its past. We do not remember the past in order to brood over it, but in order that we may go on in the certainty that it will not repeat itself. Last summer I said in the Israeli Parliament that the Germany of today is not the Germany of yesterday. Having now met Adenauer, I am convinced that the observation was right." Throughout the meeting, no mention had been made of Eichmann. If Eichmann were captured and were to mention Globke and other ranking members of the Adenauer government, it would be potentially disastrous for the German chancellor. Even so, Ben-Gurion was willing to risk straining relations between the two countries by capturing Eichmann and putting him on trial before an Israeli court.

Back in his Frankfurt office, Fritz Bauer reflected on the meeting between the two statesmen, wondering what impact these discussions would have on the Eichmann manhunt. Despite his ultimatum to the Israelis, they were still moving far too slowly, and he had not had any report of progress since passing his intelligence to Zvi Aharoni several weeks before. No longer willing to depend solely on the Israelis, Bauer had asked the American consul whether the United States would assist in extraditing Nazi war criminals from foreign countries. He was waiting for a response that the Americans would never send. The consul forwarded the request to Washington, but the assistant legal adviser for Europe decided that it was not worth responding to. Although Bauer did not know it, the Israelis were his only hope.

On March 16, Aharoni walked into the San Fernando civil administration headquarters with "Michael," an architect who had emigrated from Israel several years before. After spending a few fruitless days looking into the activities of the Fuldner Company in Tucumán, Aharoni was looking for the proof he needed in the local land records. One did not buy land and build a house without leaving a paper trail.

Using false names and a cover story—that they were interested in purchasing a significant parcel of land for a factory in San Fernando—they requested the names of the people inhabiting the area around where the rail line intersected Route 202. The clerk guaranteed an answer the next day.

Later, as they drove toward the Klement home, Aharoni instructed Michael on their next task. Using a similar cover story—they worked for an American company that was interested in purchasing property in the neighborhood to build a sewing factory—Aharoni hoped to photograph the woman he had seen on the porch to compare with pictures he had of Vera Eichmann.

They parked in front of a cottage adjacent to the Klement house. Michael carried a clipboard, and Aharoni had a briefcase with a camera hidden inside. The lens pointed out of a hole in one side, and a small button by the handle released the shutter. A middle-aged woman appeared from around the side of the cottage. Michael called out a greeting in Spanish and asked her the name of her street. The woman replied that probably none of these dirt side roads had names. Michael explained the reason for his visit, and the woman eagerly offered to sell her house. Inquiries as to who lived next door were less successful. She knew only that they were German and had recently built the house.

While they were speaking, a black-haired woman in her early twenties came toward them from the Klement house. By her looks and accent, she was a native Argentine, and her tone and body language made it clear that she did not like their intrusion on the street. Repeating his cover story, Michael eased her anger, but she was clear that her mother-in-law had no intention of selling the house, nor did she know the name of the street. While Michael was talking to the young woman, Aharoni snapped a couple of pictures. He saw her face turn stern again as she responded that her mother-in-law did not speak Spanish well and could not come out.

When Michael relayed this to Aharoni in English, the woman interrupted him with a nearly flawless command of the language. Aharoni instantly grew nervous, sure that she would notice that he did not have an American accent. She was sharp.

"What's the name of your employer?" she demanded. "What sort of factory were you planning?"

Aharoni wanted to get out of there straightaway. She did not believe them, and if she alerted her husband, he might tell his father about the conversation. This could prove catastrophic.

As Michael began to explain about their sewing factory, she cut him off, wondering why they would want to build in an area without electricity or water. Surely, they were a disreputable company, she declared.

"It's possible there's been a mistake and we've confused the area," Aharoni interjected before turning to Michael and pointing toward the railway. "Let's continue our inquiries on the other side."

They thanked her for her help, retreated to the car, and drove away. Aharoni hoped that he had not just tipped off Eichmann. His aim of getting a photograph of the older woman did not justify the risk. He needed to be more careful.

The next day he learned that their efforts to get a list of landowners also had failed. Apparently, the building office did not keep records on the area because it was sparsely populated, flooded frequently, and lacked any municipal services. Michael had another idea, though. Much of this part of San Fernando had been purchased by a single company, then resold in smaller lots. This company might have the information they needed.

As Michael explored this avenue, Aharoni continued to stake out the house, but he saw no sign of Ricardo Klement. He thought that it might be an advantage to purchase the cottage next door through a third party, as it would serve any operation that the Mossad might launch in the future. He cabled Harel but received a quick reply. "Do Not Buy, Repeat: Not Approved."

The following day, at the embassy, Aharoni met with Michael, who walked toward him waving a piece of paper in the air. "I found the registered owner of plot 14. It's Veronika Liebl de Fichmann."

"I don't know how to thank you. That's exactly what I've been looking for," Aharoni said warmly. He knew exactly what this meant: First, the misspelled name was either a clerical error or an attempt to confuse searchers. Second, they had positively identified the owner of the house as Vera Eichmann. Third, the house was in her name, not her husband's, possibly an effort to keep his name out of the public record. Fourth, and most significantly, she had not remarried, contrary to the story her family was propagating. Otherwise, she would be living under her new husband's name.

Unless Aharoni saw Ricardo Klement and concluded that he did not in any way resemble the photograph he had of Adolf Eichmann, he was certain that he had found the Nazi killer.

"They *looked* like Americans," Margarita said the night after she had confronted the two men outside the house. "They said they wanted to buy a plot of land to build a sewing-machine factory."

Adolf Eichmann, who was very much *not* in Tucumán, listened intently to Nick's wife, trying not to be alarmed by her story. She was right to think that what these men had told her was unusual, if not an outright lie. Although he had been willing to live in an area without water, telephone, or electricity because the land was cheap, an international company such as the one the men had described needed those services, and having them installed would be cost prohibitive. There were scores of better-suited areas.

So who were they? Eichmann knew that the hunt for him had restarted late the previous year. The newspaper *Argentinisches Tageblatt* had carried the announcement that he had been sighted in Kuwait, and a radio program his son Klaus (he did not call him Nick) had heard had detailed how Interpol was actively searching for him. When Klaus had rushed to his house in the middle of the night with this news, Eichmann had gone cold with fear. At the beginning of the year, a fortuneteller had predicted that he would not live past his fifty-sixth birthday.

Eichmann had begun to feel at least partially at peace just before this had all begun to happen. Although his house was a far cry from the Hungarian villa he had once enjoyed, it was his own. His job at the Mercedes-Benz plant was coming along well, and he had recently been promoted to foreman. His two eldest sons, Klaus and Horst, had moved out and started their own lives. Klaus worked as an electrician and rented an apartment with his new wife in central Buenos Aires. Horst was in the merchant marine. Dieter worked as an auto mechanic and would soon be out on his own as well. His youngest boy, Ricardo, was being raised as an Argentine and would never know about his father's role in the war.

Given that he had spent the past fifteen years in hiding, Eichmann was living about as normal a life as was possible. He was still plagued by the past and despised how he was portrayed in the press, as if he was solely responsible for the Final Solution, but there was nothing he could do about that. He had exorcised these demons as best he could with his interviews with Sassen. When he was dead, the truth about his actions would be revealed for all to read.

Those two men lurking around the neighborhood might be searching for him, he thought. They could be Jews, like that Tuviah Friedman, who had made the big Kuwait announcement. Then again, the latest reports were that he was in the Middle East—way off track.

Eichmann swallowed his fear. The strangers could merely have been in the wrong neighborhood. He was not going to disrupt his life because of a single unusual event. Nonetheless, his suspicions were piqued; he would have to keep a closer guard.

His sons, however, had neglected to mention to him the strange circumstances around the cigarette lighter, including how the gift had been addressed to Nick Klement and how the delivery boy had been so eager to know where the family lived. Given that information, Eichmann might well have put the two events together and run.

14

ONCE AHARONI LEARNED about the name on the land purchase record, he wasted no time. The next day, he drove out to San Fernando.
It was Saturday, and he guessed that Eichmann might return from
Tucumán that weekend for his wedding anniversary. Aharoni had
switched cars yet again and was now driving a black DeSoto. Accompanying him was an embassy secretary. They looked like any couple
out for a weekend drive.

Coming from Don Torcuato to the southwest, Aharoni headed
through the embankment tunnel on Route 202. He looked to the
right, to where the Klement house was located, on Garibaldi Street.
(He had eventually learned the name of the street from the land records.) A man was in the yard, taking down the wash. Aharoni slowed
down. The man was at least fifty years old. He had a thin build and
was probably between five feet seven and five feet nine inches tall. He
was balding and had a high, sloped forehead. Before Aharoni could
reach for his briefcase camera, the man collected the last garment
from the line and returned to the house. But Aharoni knew the face.
No question. He had spent hours staring at photographs of it in the
Eichmann file.

"Why are you looking so happy?" the secretary asked Aharoni.

He had not realized that a grin had spread across his face, and his
whole body was electrified. "No, nothing's happened," he said with a
shrug. "I just remembered that today is my mother's birthday. Let's go
and celebrate."

It was the best he could come up with, but she seemed to believe him. Later, he sent Harel a long cable that included the single line of code: THE DRIVER IS BLACK (Klement is Eichmann).

In Tel Aviv, Harel was ready. Over the past few weeks, he had sat at home every night, classical music playing on the transistor radio in his study, running through the many challenges they would face if Aharoni confirmed they had their man.

First, the mission would occur almost nine thousand miles away in a country few of his agents knew and whose language even fewer of them spoke.

Second, the environment would be hostile. Only in the two years since the election of the pragmatic, liberal-minded President Arturo Frondizi had the government turned friendlier to Israel, but there were still many within the halls of power—whether civil or military—who were at best antagonistic to Israel and Jews. Harel knew this firsthand. In 1955, he had been to Buenos Aires when Perón was being ousted from power—there to counter the threat Jews faced from certain quarters. In January 1960, there had been an outbreak of attacks on Jewish synagogues, clubs, and homes, just as there had been in Europe. The city also had a large German community, including some former Nazis, who would add to the danger.

Third, at such a distance, Harel's agents would not have easy, quick communication with Tel Aviv. They would be traveling under false identities, completely alone and without official cover, unable to call on local support because of the mission's secrecy.

Fourth, if they were discovered, they faced imprisonment—or worse—for violating Argentine sovereignty. Israel would incur no end of international political problems, and the black mark against the Mossad would inhibit its activities elsewhere.

Fifth, their target was a former seasoned officer in one of the most deadly security forces in history. Eichmann had intimate knowledge of surveillance and operational tactics, and he knew how to defend himself. During the war, he had been very careful about his security and had never moved around unarmed. Fifteen years may have passed since peace had been brokered with Germany, but Eichmann had spent that time in hiding, and for him the need to stay vigilant remained.

These challenges were multiplied by the fact that the mission was essentially three operations rolled into one. They needed to capture Eichmann alive, without being seen or followed. Then they would have to keep him in a secure location, avoiding detection, for an indeterminate period of time, until the plans for the third part of the mission fell into place—smuggling Eichmann out of Argentina in complete secrecy. Nobody could know who had taken him until he was in an Israeli prison and Harel's people all were safe.

If they succeeded in the mission, the Mossad chief knew that the payoff would match the challenges and risks involved. On a purely professional level, the Mossad would earn its place among the top intelligence agencies in the world. More important, the Jewish people would see justice done to one of the Holocaust's leading organizers. The world would be forced to remember the assembly line of death that the Jews had faced—and it would be reminded that such horrors must never be allowed to be repeated.

Given what was at stake, Harel wanted to be on the ground in Buenos Aires to oversee the mission. High-level decisions might need to be made at an instant's notice, and his agents could hardly wait for cables to and from Israel. But Harel could not participate in the operation itself. He needed someone to select a team, manage the agents, plan the tactical operations, and execute them to the letter—someone he trusted implicitly.

Rafi Eitan, the Shin Bet chief of operations, had been nicknamed "Rafi the Stinker" during the Israeli War of Independence when he had crawled through a sewer system to blow up a British radar installation on Mount Carmel. Born on a kibbutz in Palestine's fertile Valley of Jezreel in 1926, Eitan had an instinct for adventurous missions. As a child, he saw a movie about Mata Hari, a Dutch spy during World War I, and told his mother that he wanted to be a spy. It was much more than an idle fantasy. At twelve, he joined the Haganah, using his youth to elude British suspicion. At eighteen, he was recruited by the Palmach, the Haganah strike force, and participated in the attack on the Atlit detention camp that freed more than two hundred Jewish immigrants held by the British. At twenty-one, he was given command of a reconnaissance platoon that operated behind enemy lines.

On the day the Israeli state was declared in 1948, Eitan was wounded in the leg. He dragged himself back to camp, and once his leg was in a cast, he returned to his battalion to fight. For the rest of the war, he stayed with his reconnaissance platoon, specializing in leading nighttime assaults. His commanders in army intelligence knew that he had nerves of steel, improvised quickly, and killed without hesitation.

Harel called Eitan into his office. One could not picture a more unlikely individual for the long résumé of military actions and secret operations. The thirty-four-year-old was only nominally taller than Harel, with the barrel chest and muscular arms of a farmer. He was extremely nearsighted and wore Coke-bottle glasses that made his eyes seem to bulge out from his face. Often he cocked his head slightly, because he was also deaf in his right ear, another war injury.

Harel recounted the recent developments in the search for Eichmann and Aharoni's work of the previous three weeks. "What are the odds that this man is really Eichmann?" Eitan asked.

Harel explained that they might not know for certain until they had the target in their grasp. Aharoni was still gathering evidence. Then he went on to describe in detail what they faced in attempting a capture on Argentine soil.

"It's a big operation," Eitan agreed with a thin smile. "We've never yet had one like it."

"I'm putting you as the commander," Harel informed him. "A. Take the most suitable men for the job, since you know what it will take to do it. B. Volunteers only. Ask each man if he is ready to volunteer. I don't know how this will end, and if they are caught, theoretically they could even end up with a life sentence."

"None of them will hesitate," Eitan said quietly and confidently.

On Sunday, March 20, Aharoni lay on a mattress in the back of an old Ford pickup, peering with his binoculars through a hole cut in the heavy tarpaulin that covered the back of the truck. The driver, yet another *sayan* arranged by Yossef, was inside the nearby kiosk eating a late breakfast. The truck was parked facing the kiosk, providing Aharoni with a perfect view of the Eichmann house, which was 160 yards away. Although he had already cabled Harel that his investigation should come to an end, since he was certain he had identified their target, Aharoni had one more task. He wanted a good photograph of Eichmann to allay any doubts that Harel might have.

While Aharoni waited for Eichmann to come out of his house, he took a series of shots of the surrounding area for the operations team that would plan the capture. He also sketched a map of the neighborhood.

At quarter to noon, Eichmann unexpectedly walked past the truck from the direction of the kiosk. He had obviously been out early that morning. He headed down Route 202, then turned left before Garibaldi Street, crossing an empty field to get to his house. This time, Aharoni got a long, clear look at Eichmann, who was dressed in brown slacks, an overcoat, and a green tie. He wore glasses, was mostly bald, had a prominent nose and broad forehead, and walked with a slow gait. Aharoni was sure that this was the right man. Unfortunately, Eichmann was too far away for Aharoni to get a good photograph of him.

For the next hour, Aharoni watched Eichmann. When he arrived at the house, he spoke to a boy playing in the garden, straightening the child's shirt and trousers. He swatted at a cloud of flies that surrounded the front door before going inside. Later, he came out wearing casual cotton pants, bought some bread from a baker's horse-drawn cart, and fetched some supplies from the shed. His son Dieter came home, and the whole family went into the house, probably to have lunch.

When the truck driver returned from his breakfast, Aharoni signaled him to leave. On his return to the embassy, he wrote a long report in invisible ink to be delivered to Harel by diplomatic pouch. Aharoni reviewed everything he had learned in detail, then suggested that the operation phase must begin, because any additional steps toward identifying Eichmann might cause him to flee.

Nonetheless, at 9:15 that night, Aharoni returned to San Fernando in a faded red jeep, accompanied by "Avi," an embassy official, and his wife. Aharoni had seen couples parked in the area at night and knew that the two would not attract any attention. Wearing overalls and carrying a pair of binoculars, Aharoni left the jeep and crept toward the house. His aim was to get a peek at the interior, in case the operations team needed to go into the house. It was a very dark night, perfect for the task, but Aharoni soon noticed that there were no lights on in the house. He made his way back to the jeep only a few minutes after he had left it. To his shock, the jeep was gone. Had he gotten lost? he wondered. He walked around the area for a few moments before spying the jeep, fifteen yards away, in the ditch along the side of the road. Aharoni could hardly believe his eyes.

He found Avi and his wife huddled on the ground by the jeep. They had tried to turn the vehicle around without turning on the headlights, in case they needed to make a fast return to Buenos Aires. Avi had not noticed that the street was raised, and he had backed straight into the ditch. Aharoni was livid at their foolishness, but his anger paled in comparison to his fear that the Eichmann family, whose house was less than 150 yards away, would discover them. Either they or their neighbors would notice in an instant that the three were foreigners—and likely Israelis—and Eichmann would know for sure that he was being watched.

"Let's go," Aharoni said, thinking fast. They could not be seen under any circumstances. They ran down Avellaneda Street. Luckily, a bus appeared a few minutes later. At 10:45, when they reached the San Fernando bus station, Aharoni called the only person he could think of who could get the jeep out of the ditch quietly and quickly: Yitzhak Vardi. Vardi was an Israeli financier who had once worked in intelligence for the Israeli Foreign Ministry but who now led the United Jewish Appeal in South America and was based in Buenos Aires.

Vardi understood the critical nature of the situation. Less than an hour later, he drove up to the bus station in his huge Chevrolet, with a tow truck following behind. If they left the jeep in the ditch, it would look very suspicious—Eichmann might even be able to trace Aharoni's alias through the rental agency.

By the time they reached the vehicle, someone had already pilfered one of the tires. While Aharoni put on the spare, some neighbors came out to see what all the lights and commotion were about. The Argentine tow truck driver assured them that nobody had been hurt; it was just a minor accident. The rest of them kept their mouths shut. Aharoni did not see Dieter or his father among the crowd and breathed a little easier. Within a few minutes, the jeep was back on the road. Aharoni thanked Vardi and drove away.

Having not received an order to return to Israel, Aharoni continued his investigation, but he pulled back from the aggressive surveillance of the Eichmann house for the next two weeks, driving by only rarely. Instead, he pursued other avenues. Through a contact in the Argentine police, he uncovered files on Horst and Nick Eichmann. The two had obviously been influenced by their father's politics, as both were suspected of participating in neo-Nazi and right-wing political groups. This made them a danger to any Mossad operation. Through a clerk at the German embassy, Aharoni procured the file the embassy had on Eichmann. From this he learned that the German Foreign Ministry was well aware of Eichmann's presence in Argentina.

Aharoni also traveled to Tucumán to check out the CAPRI company. It took only a couple of days to discover that the company had closed in 1953, contrary to their intelligence that Eichmann still worked there. Aharoni was fairly certain now that the reason he had seen Eichmann in Buenos Aires on almost every reconnoiter of his house over the past two weeks had nothing to do with the occasion of his silver anniversary. He likely worked in the area, a key piece of information.

On Sunday, April 3, Aharoni returned to San Fernando to make one further attempt to get a close-up photograph of Eichmann. He brought two volunteers with him: Roberto, the student who had first brought the postcard to 4261 Chacabuco Street, and "Rendi," a *sayan* who looked old enough to be out searching for a house for his family, which was his cover story. Aharoni had taught Rendi how to hold the briefcase camera and release the shutter. He parked the pickup truck he was driving underneath the railway bridge, seventy-five yards from the house. Then he sent Rendi out.

Rendi cut across the field to the house. Through his binoculars, Aharoni nervously followed him as he walked up to Eichmann and his son Dieter, who were working in the yard. If there was any sign that Rendi was in danger, he planned to rush the house himself. Two minutes passed. Then three. Then four. Rendi continued to speak to the two men as if they were old friends.

At last he walked away, heading toward Eichmann's neighbors, as instructed by Aharoni, to inquire of them how much it would cost to build a house in the area. Then Rendi headed back up to the kiosk, where he waited for a bus back to the San Fernando station. Rendi was confident that he had not been suspected of taking any photographs. Three days later, when Aharoni received the developed film, he was delighted to see that Rendi had taken perfectly focused shots of Eichmann and his son at three or four different angles, all of them up close. With these photographs, Israeli identification experts could confirm what Aharoni already knew beyond a doubt: Eichmann had been found.

In the meantime, Aharoni had received his orders from Harel to return as soon as possible to Tel Aviv to provide a full report. He tied up some loose ends—returning his rental cars and bidding Yossef farewell—and boarded a flight to Paris on April 8. He was satisfied that he had accomplished his mission.

Yaakov Gat welcomed Aharoni at Le Bourget Airport in Paris, where he had a one-day layover before his connection to Tel Aviv. Aharoni returned with Gat to his apartment on the Right Bank, where he showed him the negatives of the photographs of Eichmann. Each man told the other about his investigation. They felt as if they were the only two people in the world in on a great secret. They were both sure that an operation was now inevitable, and both wanted to be on the team.

Aharoni promised that he would ask Harel to include Gat in the operation when he reported his findings in Tel Aviv. Even so, he was not sure that he himself would be included in the mission. It was certainly beyond his expertise, and he had already accepted that he would probably have to return to his interrogation work. Such was life, he thought, feeling a little disappointed.

The next day, Aharoni boarded the flight to Tel Aviv. He was shocked to see Isser Harel coming down the aisle. Harel sat down next to Aharoni, acting as if he were a total stranger. Only after the plane took off did he turn to Aharoni and ask, "Are you definitively sure this is our man?"

Aharoni retrieved a negative from his coat pocket, proud that the Mossad chief was depending on his judgment. "I have not the slightest doubt. Here's the picture."

Harel studied the photograph for a moment and said, "Okay. In that case, we're going to get him."

"Will I be on the team?" Aharoni asked, assuming the worst.

"Did you ever think otherwise? We need you for it."

Aharoni rested his head on the back of the seat, feeling exuberant.

15

AVRAHAM SHALOM WALKED through the terminal building at Lod Airport in Tel Aviv on the morning of April 10, exhausted after an intense undercover operation. He had journeyed several hundred miles across the Arabian Desert in a truck to reach his departing flight. Going through passport control, he took care to remember the details of his alias so as to avoid any problems that might delay a shower and crawling into bed.

As he walked out of the airport, his heart sank when he was met by one of Harel's men. "Isser wants to see you," the man said.

"When?" Shalom asked.

"Now."

Shalom nodded and folded himself into the man's car. After nine years of working for Harel, he knew that his chief would not waste time on a frivolous meeting.

The thirty-three-year-old deputy of Shin Bet operations had the stout body of a wrestler and the kind of common, indistinctive face one usually forgets once the person has left the room. Originally from Vienna, Shalom had lived through one year of the Nazis' occupation of Austria before his well-to-do family immigrated to Palestine. He did not leave unscathed. On the day of Kristallnacht, everyone in his neighborhood knew that the Germans were about to launch attacks on the Jews, but his mother made him go to school anyway. While his teachers looked on, he was beaten so badly by thirty of his classmates, some of whom he thought were his closest friends, that he had to stay in bed for two weeks to recover. He was only nine and was still coming to understand what it meant to be Jewish. Up to then, he had hardly even known his religious faith, since his parents never attended synagogue. He did not return to school. Soon afterward, his father's linen manufacturing company was taken over by the Nazis, and the family was forced from their apartment—and ultimately their country.

In Palestine, unable to speak Hebrew and feeling out of place, he spent much of his first year in silence, a trait he retained, speaking only when absolutely necessary. Like other boys at the kibbutz, he joined the Haganah when the War of Independence broke out. He handled the mortar for his platoon, and on May 15, 1948, he was on the Lebanese border when the Arabs attacked Israel in large numbers. His platoon of thirty men, all of whom he had grown up with at the kibbutz, was cut in half within the first few hours. Shalom went on to participate in battles as a regular soldier before he was recruited to become a scout for Rafi Eitan. Beyond his keen eyes and ears, he had a talent for reading maps and navigating in unknown territory, and he spent the rest of the war operating mostly behind enemy lines.

After the hostilities ended, Shalom rejoined his kibbutz. Unhappy with the communal existence, he moved to Tel Aviv, where he worked briefly as a truck driver. When he met Eitan in the street, his former officer recruited him to join the Shin Bet. Shalom became a commander of counterintelligence activities in divided Jerusalem, then Harel posted him to Paris to run Mossad operations in Europe. There he married an embassy secretary, and for three years he tangled with the Russians—enjoying the war of wits. He returned to Israel to study economics, but occasionally Harel would call him away from his studies to do a job. It soon became apparent that this work suited him best, and he rejoined the Shin Bet under Eitan. Logistics and operational planning were his expertise.

Shalom was the kind of agent that Harel favored: a former member of a kibbutz who had proved himself during the War of Independence; someone who went about his work discreetly and effectively and had a stable home life, which now included a three-year-old son. His integrity was unquestionable, and he was all business. "Isser wants honest men to do scoundrels' work," one of Harel's deputies once explained to a new Mossad recruit. Shalom honored that expectation.

When Shalom arrived at Mossad headquarters in Sarona, Harel sat him down and asked, "How would you feel walking around in a foreign country with a false passport?"

It was a strange question, Shalom thought, considering that Harel knew he never left Israel with anything *but* a fake passport. "I'd feel fine," Shalom said.

"Fine? You can do that?"

Shalom wondered what Harel had planned for him now. For some reason, Harel was obviously hesitant to give Shalom his new orders. Although the chief was dictatorial in his approach to operations, believing he was always right, he nonetheless related to his agents as equals, and often it was clear that he did not enjoy issuing orders.

"Yes, of course," Shalom answered.

"We're going after Eichmann and maybe this time we'll get him."

"Give me some details."

"Aharoni has them. Go see him and ask what he found. Then find Rafi. We have to assemble a team."

The meeting was over. After a visit home to see his family, Shalom traveled to the Shin Bet offices in a dilapidated old building by the clock tower in Jaffa. At this point in the mission, Shalom was focused more on the operational details of capturing Eichmann than on the ramifications should they succeed. Shalom sat down with Eitan, who had been considering the task for a few weeks already, and they finalized a list of people to assemble for the team.

The first choice was obvious to both of them: Shalom Dani, the forger. Dani had escaped from a Nazi concentration camp by fashioning a pass out of toilet paper, and they would need his exceptional skills for all the forged passports, driver's licenses, and other identification documents they would require. The second choice, also obvious to both Eitan and Shalom, was Moshe Tabor. Tabor was not only a strongman—his hands were the size of baseball mitts—but also a technical master who could create suitcases with false bottoms, overhaul a car engine, fix a submachine gun, pick any lock, and build a safe room that would never be discovered.

Harel wanted Zvi Aharoni on the job, even though he did not have much operational experience. From what Shalom had heard, he deserved the spot. His knowledge of the area would be useful, and his skill as an interrogator would prove essential in questioning Eichmann. His name was added to the list.

They also agreed on Yaakov Gat, not only because he was an experienced, cool-headed agent but also because they knew him extremely well, and he would fit seamlessly within the team. Eitan pushed for Peter Malkin, another strongman who had a fine operational mind and who was an expert in disguises. Harel did not know him well, which made him a liability, but he was well suited for the mission. Ephraim Ilani was needed for his encyclopedic knowledge of Buenos Aires and his fluency in Spanish. Finally, they needed a doctor, someone who would keep Eichmann in good health and, if necessary, under sedation, as well as treat any wounds or injuries the team might suffer. Eitan and Shalom knew who would fill this post: "Dr. Maurice Kaplan," a dependable civilian doctor whom they had used a couple of times before on operations. Including themselves, that made a core team of eight. Most of them were Shin Bet—not surprising, given that the Mossad still had a limited number of operational agents.

It was a good team. Each member had almost a decade of experience in Israeli intelligence services. They spoke a wide range of languages—key to keeping their cover. Except for the doctor, they knew one another extremely well and had worked together on numerous assignments. They understood one another's strengths and weaknesses, could communicate without speaking, and, most important, had absolute trust in one another.

Aharoni entered the headquarters of the Israeli police in Tel Aviv a few days after his return to Israel. He carried an envelope with the photographs he had taken of Klement, old photographs of Eichmann

in his SS uniform, and the most recent ones of Eichmann's brothers
collected by Simon Wiesenthal. Harel wanted confirmation from the
police's criminal identification unit that Klement was Eichmann.

For this reason, Aharoni had also shown the photographs to an
Israeli who had met Eichmann in Berlin in 1936. The eyewitness
thought it could be Eichmann, but since it had been almost twenty-
five years since he had seen him, he could not say for sure.

Aharoni handed over the photographs to Israel's best identity experts. A few hours later, he received his answer: there was a reasonable
chance that Eichmann and Klement were the same person. The experts had come to their conclusion by matching characteristics of the
left ear. As they explained to Aharoni, much like a fingerprint, the size
and shape of the ear, as well as the angle at which it joins the face, are
unique to each individual. Although there were eight points indicating that Klement and Eichmann were one and the same — and none
indicating that they were not — there were not enough points of comparison to allow a definitive identification.

Aharoni delivered the news to Harel, who then sent him and Amos
Manor, the forty-three-year-old Shin Bet director, to Jerusalem. There
they met with Haim Cohen and Pinhas Rosen, the Israeli minister
of justice, to present their evidence that Klement and Eichmann were
the same person and to receive legal advice as to whether the operation should go forward. The two top lawyers of the Israeli government gave their approval. Although abducting Eichmann would vio-
late Argentine sovereignty, this was solely an issue of diplomatic
relations between the two countries. In their view, it did not affect
Israeli jurisdiction to prosecute Eichmann, because, they believed,
Germany was never going to pursue extradition seriously, let alone
hold a trial.

With their legal consent secured, nothing stood in the way of the
operation moving to the next stage.

At Mossad headquarters, the staff was busy preparing for the task
force's journey to and stay in Argentina. Given the nature of the assignment and the number of agents involved, this was a complicated

endeavor. All of the agents needed to travel on separate flights, departing from different locations, with forged passports and an array of visas. It was imperative that no agent be tied to another or tracked back to Israel. Further, some of the agents would need to travel out of Buenos Aires with different passports from the ones with which they arrived.

First, each agent had to leave Tel Aviv under one identity. When the agents arrived at their first destination outside Israel, they would be met by Israeli operatives and given new tickets and new identities. These identities needed to match their particular language abilities. One could not give an Italian passport to someone who did not speak Italian. Fluency was not necessary, particularly when one had what Avraham Shalom liked to call "personality." Several of the agents spoke German, others French and English; they also spoke a hodgepodge of other languages.

Travel visas were another challenge, since the Argentine consulate in each country required character references and health documentation. Most of these needed to be forged, and already Mossad and Shin Bet staff were being sent to Paris to undergo inoculations and medical examinations so that their stamped approvals could then be altered and pasted into the passports of the Mossad agents. A couple of agents would bypass this process by being booked into Latin American tours that spent a few days in Buenos Aires (which did not require references or exams), but they would require alternative passports to leave the country. In any event, all of the agents needed at least one completely different set of papers in case the operation was compromised.

Once an agent arrived in Buenos Aires, he would have two rendez-vous times—one in the morning, one in the afternoon—at different locations in order to meet with one or more members of the team who were already in the city. No two agents could stay at the same hotel, and any equipment that could not be bought in Argentina without raising suspicions had to be transported by diplomatic pouch in advance. Some of the items that Eitan had already requested included handcuffs, hidden cameras, sedation drugs, miniature drills and woodworking tools, lock picks, field glasses, pocket flashlights, a forgery kit, and a makeup kit with false teeth and wigs. The sizable amount of money needed for the operation—for renting cars and safe houses, for example—was also transported in diplomatic pouches.

For all these preparations, Harel created a veritable travel agency, and his staff began filling a telephone directory–size book with the matrix of identities, flights, and scheduled meeting points. The simplest error could result in disaster.

Early in the morning of April 16, Peter Malkin strode through the tangled streets of Jaffa's old quarter. The Shin Bet agent had the broad shoulders of a linebacker and a head shaped like a bowling ball. His expressive, youthful face switched easily from a pensive scowl to almost clownish mirth. The day before, he had returned from concluding an investigation into an outbreak of terrorist activity in Nazareth and had met with Eitan. His chief of operations had pointed to Buenos Aires on a map, saying, "We're going to bring Adolf Eichmann to trial in Jerusalem. And you're going to capture him, Peter." What Eitan didn't tell him was that it had taken some effort to convince Isser Harel to include him on the team.

Malkin entered the Shin Bet building and went straight to another meeting with Eitan. They were not alone. Most of the team set for Buenos Aires was gathered for the first time. Malkin felt that they were looking at one another in a new way, as if they were measuring each man to see whether he was up to such a monumental mission.

"Well," Eitan said, easing the tension, "you've all slept on it. Any bright ideas?"

Malkin was reassured that Harel would be on hand in Argentina during the operation and doubly so that Eitan was handling the tactical plans. The two were dramatically different leaders. Harel focused on compartmentalization and rarely took advice from others, his ideas set in his mind before he revealed a mission. In contrast, Eitan brought everyone into the fold and sought their ideas before he decided a course of action.

"We'd just better hope that this man Klement stays put," Avraham Shalom said.

"That's out of our control," Eitan countered. "Why don't we take a look at what we've got."

The shades were drawn on the balcony that overlooked the harbor, and Moshe Tabor turned on the slide projector. Aharoni walked them through a comparison of the photographs of Eichmann in his thirties wearing his SS uniform and the shots he had obtained in Argentina.

Malkin was wary of the Shin Bet interrogator's inclusion in the operation, particularly after hearing about how many risks — careless, in Malkin's view — he had taken to identify the man. Still, the results of his dogged efforts were undeniable. "Run two of them together," Malkin suggested, not sure they were the same man.

Tabor arranged two slides in the projector and put them up on the blank wall. If they were both Eichmann, Malkin was shocked at how haggard and aged the Nazi had become since the end of the war. "It's not easy to tell, is it?"

Aharoni explained the results of the criminal identification unit's work.

"We can't be 100 percent sure until we've got him," Eitan said.

"Once we're sure," Tabor growled, the massive, six-foot-two-inch frame in dark silhouette at the back of the room, "why don't we kill the bastard on the spot?"

"We all share that feeling, I'm sure," Eitan said.

Tabor shook his big, clean-shaven head. "What chance did he give those people at the camps? I saw them, the ones that survived. What kind of consideration did he show them?"

Nobody in the room knew the typically reserved giant as well as Malkin. He and Tabor had recently spent several months together in West Germany on a surveillance operation of scientists who were helping the Egyptians with their missile technology. There the thirty-seven-year-old Tabor had told Malkin about his large Lithuanian family, which had been killed during the Holocaust, and about the extermination camps he had seen at the war's end as part of the Jewish Brigade. Revolted and enraged, Tabor had joined avenger groups operating in Germany and Austria, and he had hunted down, interrogated, and then killed numerous SS men. Tabor had been in his early twenties at the time. There was no question in any of the team members' minds that he would gladly kill Eichmann if given the chance.

Eitan dismissed Tabor's suggestion again, and the matter was dropped. Over the next few hours, and during several follow-up meetings, the team ironed out the operational details. They made adjustments to their cover stories, what equipment they would need, and where they would stay. Ephraim Ilani returned from Argentina to brief them on local customs, including everything from how to rent a car or a safe house to normal behavior at cafés and hotels, traffic conditions, airport procedures, and styles of dress. Since only he and Aharoni had been to Buenos Aires, this was key information. He also detailed the intensive police presence on the streets, particularly with the March crackdown on Peronist terrorist groups in the wake of a series of bombings in the capital.

Most of the time, however, was spent planning how and where they would seize Eichmann. Aharoni showed them his surveillance photographs, along with his sketches of the house and important landmarks (the kiosk, the railway embankment, neighboring houses, and roads). They settled on three different capture methods, knowing that they would decide on one after they had checked out the scene for themselves. The first was snatching him while he was away from the house, perhaps while in the city or before he boarded his bus to return from his job (although they still did not know where this was). The second was a commando raid on his house at night, taking him from his bed. The third focused on seizing him on the street near his house, a possibility given the desolate neighborhood. The timing depended on how they would smuggle Eichmann out of Argentina; Harel was putting together this part of the operation himself.

Each night, Malkin returned to his Tel Aviv apartment alone and read, then reread the Eichmann file. He found himself beginning to fear this individual who had once commanded so much authority and who had executed his plans with such demonic intensity. Malkin knew that the team was relying on him to be the one to physically grab their target, because of his strength and speed, and he began to doubt his ability. Anything could go wrong. He might make a simple mistake that would jeopardize the operation, or a policeman could chance by and catch him in the act. For the first time in his thirty-three years, many spent in dangerous situations, Malkin felt a profound fear of failure.

Malkin was eleven when the war in Europe began, and he immediately joined the Haganah. He had always been a restless youth, spending most of his time in the alleyways of Haifa, roaming the city with a band of other kids, stealing from shops, and then escaping over the ancient walls or down into cellars. The Jewish defense force focused his energies, training him as a courier, teaching him how to hide messages on his person and then conceal them in the crevices of walls. Later, Malkin graduated to breaking into safes and stealing weapons from British police stations at night. In 1947, he enrolled in a Haganah explosives course, learning how to construct makeshift bombs, set booby traps, clear mines, and blow up bridges, all of which were useful when the War of Independence broke out. He joined the Shin Bet after the war, explaining to his recruiters that he had applied because he liked adventure. His patriotism, he imagined, would have been assumed.

Malkin's first commissions were to travel to embassies to train their personnel on the detection of letter bombs. He began to receive occasional counterintelligence assignments and discovered that he had a facility for surveillance and disguise to add to his skills with explosives and lock picking. If he was far away from whomever he was watching, he could easily change his appearance—by walking in a suit for a while, then adding an overcoat and a hat in one hand, then wearing the hat, then ditching the coat and adding an umbrella. If he was closer to his target, he would change his face, wearing a mustache, glasses, false teeth, or a wig. Often he posed as an artist, an easy disguise given his talent for painting.

Beyond focusing on Malkin's various skills and his natural physical strength (which even the giant Tabor humbly acknowledged), Shalom had convinced Harel to use him—despite his habit of bucking authority and his lack of language skills—because he had an extraordinary operational mind. When Malkin looked at a plan, he always found ways to improve it. He saw his work as a game—a serious game, of course, but one that he enjoyed trying to master.

This mission was different, however, and Malkin could not help but think of his older sister Fruma, who had stayed behind in Poland in 1933 when the rest of his family had immigrated to Palestine. She had had a husband and three children of her own. They had all perished in the Holocaust, a tragedy that had destroyed Malkin's father and his younger brother, both of whom had died within a few years of learning of her fate. Malkin himself had forced her memory out of his mind for more than a decade because it was too painful. He could not help thinking of Fruma as he read the Eichmann file.

To distract himself from painful memories and his fear of failure, Malkin focused his every waking moment on the mission ahead, examining the smallest details of the operation and his role in it. He spent hours crafting different disguises for himself and the team and many more practicing the exact moves needed to grab Eichmann. He did much of this at the gym, but he also practiced on his Shin Bet colleagues at work, grabbing them without warning from behind and cutting off their ability to scream. Nobody asked what had come over him—partly because they were used to his antics—but instead just gave him a wider berth in the hallways. Apart from the operations team, only Amos Manor, the Shin Bet director, whose long, energetic stride made him a difficult catch for Malkin, knew why he was practicing his repertoire. Just before Malkin left for Argentina, Manor pulled him aside.

Manor had questioned Harel on the wisdom of diverting many of his top agents—not to mention other resources—to a mission that did little to protect Israel from its many security challenges. Nevertheless, he had provided Harel with everything he needed. Malkin and Manor briefly discussed the operations he was leaving behind. Then Manor, who was the only member of his Hungarian family to have survived Auschwitz, wrapped an arm around his agent's shoulders and said, "Do me one favor. Give his neck an extra little squeeze for me."

The conversation reminded Malkin once again that he absolutely had to succeed.

With the capture plans developing well, Harel needed to devise a way to get Eichmann back to Israel. There were only two options, of course: by air or by ship. His head of administration reported that the latter option had to be ruled out. In the coming month, no Israeli merchant ship or cruise vessel was scheduled to visit South America. Changing course for any of them involved too many complications. Chartering a special ship would require a sixty-day roundtrip journey with multiple stops — too slow and too risky given the need to anchor in foreign ports. If their kidnapping was exposed before they returned to Israel, the ship would be an easy target.

That left air travel. In December 1959, soon after Bauer had come to Israel, Harel had spoken to the manager of El Al, Yehuda Shimoni, about the possibility of sending one of their planes to Argentina. At the time, El Al, the only Israeli civilian airline, did not fly to South America. Shimoni assured Harel, whom he had known well for many years, that technically they were able to fly to Buenos Aires and that they might be able to stage a flight as a test run for future routes to South America. Harel was concerned that a "test run" was a dubious cover and said no more about it.

This would not be the first time El Al had been enlisted in service to the Israeli state, or for covert operations. In September 1948, the civilian airline had been hastily created to transport the first president of Israel, Chaim Weizmann, from Geneva to the newly declared independent state. Because a military flight had been prohibited, the Israelis had transformed a four-engine C-54 military transport, which the Haganah had used to airlift arms from Czechoslovakia, into a civilian plane. They had painted the blue and white Israeli flag on the tail; slapped the name of the new company, El Al ("to the skies"), on the side; outfitted additional fuel tanks to allow a nonstop flight; and furnished the fuselage with seating for the passengers. In fact, Shimoni had been the navigator on that first flight. Since then, the airline had been used in operations to airlift Jewish refugees, sometimes covertly, from Yemen, Iraq, and Iran. There had been other missions, too—particularly when a long-range airplane was needed—and some of the El Al pilots, navigators, and engineers who were routinely recruited for the flights even had a name for themselves: "the monkey business crews."

Now that commandeering an airplane was deemed to be necessary, Harel reopened his talks with El Al. Fortune shone on him when he learned that Argentina was celebrating its 150th anniversary of independence from Spain in late May and that official delegations from around the world had been invited to attend—including one from Israel. It was the ideal cover for an El Al plane. He immediately scheduled meetings with the airline's directors and the Foreign Ministry to arrange for a special flight.

Once this was settled, Harel busied himself with the hundreds of other operational details filling his head. He kept track of all his thoughts by writing notes on little scraps of paper, which mounted up on his desk. Eitan kept him informed of the team's progress, and they decided to split the members' arrival into two stages. Avraham Shalom would lead the first contingent, to confirm that the operation remained a possibility and to obtain safe houses and map out routes to and from Garibaldi Street. Harel personally recruited Yaakov Medad to be the frontman for the operation—the one who arranged for the cars, safe houses, and anything else the agents needed that required presenting papers and being in the public eye. Medad, a Mossad operative, was well suited for the job. Although he was not so gifted with operational or technical abilities, he was able to assume a range of identities—and to switch back and forth between them at a moment's notice—better than anyone Harel had ever known. He took to accents easily, remembered background information to the letter, and, most significantly, had the kind of unassuming, innocent looks that won a stranger's trust in an instant. In Argentina, he would play the scion on vacation, frivolously throwing his family's money around town. Harel also considered bringing on a woman to act as Medad's wife, but he decided to wait until the entire team was in Argentina to see whether this was necessary.

A week before the first team member was set to leave Tel Aviv, Mordechai Ben-Ari, the deputy director of El Al, came to meet with

Harel at his office. The Mossad chief requested the use of one of El Al's Britannia airplanes to bring an Israeli delegation to Argentina for the anniversary celebrations. He also wanted to oversee the crew's selection and asked that Yehuda Shimoni be made available to him for all the arrangements. Ben-Ari explained that this would disrupt their regular flights and cost the company a sizable amount of money, but it was possible. Still, he needed approval from his boss.

Two days later, he received final approval, and the Foreign Ministry, under Golda Meir, who had known of the search for Eichmann since it had begun, gave its assent as well.

On April 18, Harel sat down with Shimoni. Tall with broad shoulders and salt-and-pepper hair, Shimoni was a Dutch Jew who had served as a navigator with the British Royal Air Force (RAF) during the war and had then immigrated to Palestine, where he had joined the ragtag Israeli air force in the fight for independence. When Harel told him the purpose of the mission, Shimoni, whose parents, brothers, and sister had all died in Nazi camps, promised to do everything in his power to help. He suggested Yosef Klein to help organize the flight in Buenos Aires. He proceeded to explain exactly why Klein, the manager of El Al's station at New York's Idlewild Airport, was ideal for the assignment.

"Okay, everyone, let's talk," Harel said, seating himself at the desk in his office. His secretary stubbed out her cigarette, leaving one last trail of smoke to dissipate into the air, and placed a stenographer's pad on her lap.

The small office was crowded with the key members of the Eichmann operation: Rafi Eitan, Avraham Shalom, Zvi Aharoni, Peter Malkin, Ephraim Ilani, Shalom Dani, and Moshe Tabor. Only Yaakov Gat, who was traveling straight to Argentina from Paris, was absent. There was tension in the room, and even Tabor, who was not one for appearances, had worn a starched khaki uniform.

"I want to begin by speaking to you from my heart," Harel said, after taking a deep breath. "This is a national mission of the first degree. It is not an ordinary capture operation, but the capture of a hideous Nazi criminal, the most horrible enemy of the Jewish people. We are not performing this operation as adventurers but as representatives of the Jewish people and the state of Israel. Our objective is to bring Eichmann back safely, fully in good health, so he can be put to trial.

"There might well be difficult repercussions. We know this. We have not only the right but also the moral duty to bring this man to trial. You must remember this throughout the weeks ahead. You are guardian angels of justice, the emissaries of the Jewish people."

The men looked at one another as he spoke. They knew that Harel had dedicated his life to Israel and that everything he did was a matter of principle. He often instilled in his people the same sense of purpose, reminding them before a job that their success would serve a higher purpose. It was this passion that motivated his agents to work for him, despite the risk to their lives, the long periods away from their families, the low pay, the endless hours, and the isolation they felt at not being able to share what they did with those closest to them. But on this day, Harel was particularly fervent and eloquent, and the effect was profound.

"We will bring Adolf Eichmann to Jerusalem," Harel said, striking the table, "and perhaps the world will be reminded of its responsibilities. It will be recognized that, as a people, we *never* forgot. Our memory reaches back through recorded history. The memory book lies open, and the hand still writes."

He turned to Eitan.

"Are your people ready?" he asked, his tone cool, no longer layered with feeling.

"All ready," Eitan replied.

16

ON APRIL 24, Yaakov Gat arrived at Ezeiza Airport. Wearing an immaculately cut suit and a thin tie and carrying a briefcase, he stepped onto the portable staircase that had been rolled to the plane's side and into the harsh glare of the Argentine sun. Gat failed to notice the photographer who had already snapped several pictures of him before he reached the tarmac.

He easily managed passport control, his lack of Spanish not a problem. Instead of taking a taxi, whose driver might later remember where he had dropped off his passenger, he boarded a bus outside the terminal. He was scheduled to meet with Ilani in a couple of hours.

Gat took a seat close to the doorway, as was his habit — just in case of a problem. The bus to the city center was filled to capacity, but there was still no sign of the driver. A policeman was walking around the front of the bus. After ten minutes, Gat began to worry. After twenty, he was convinced that something was terribly wrong.

Suddenly, two men rushed onto the bus, blocking his escape. Gat recognized one of them as the driver because of his uniform. The other placed himself directly in front of Gat and rattled off some Spanish. The Israeli went cold, not understanding what was happening. Then the man showed him a photograph of himself in profile coming off the plane. A rush of panicked questions passed through his mind. Did the Argentine police know who he was? Had they been tipped off? Did they know his passport was fake? Was he about to be detained?

Before he could react, the man had turned to the next passenger and presented him with a freshly developed picture of himself as well. It dawned on Gat that he was a photographer, hoping to cash in on some tourist business. He obviously had a relationship with the driver and the police to hold the bus until he developed his photos. When the man came back around to Gat, he gladly paid for the picture and then eased back in his seat. If he had made a run for it and had been caught, he might have compromised the mission. Such were the dangers, even from the most harmless of incidents.

At five minutes to eleven, he arrived at a café with marble floors and high ceilings in the center of Buenos Aires. As he passed through the revolving doors, he noticed Ephraim Ilani waiting for him, a cup of coffee in his hand and a pipe in his mouth. Since arriving two days before, Ilani had rented an apartment and had stocked it with canned food and some camp beds. Twice a day, he waited at a prearranged street corner, restaurant, or café—a different rendezvous point each time to avoid suspicion—expecting to meet with one of the members of the operations team. As a precaution, he was not informed as to who would arrive or on what day. For the usually gregarious Ilani, passing this much time alone was a dreary chore.

"Pleased to see you! Come, sit here!" Ilani said joyfully in English, rising from his seat.

"How are you?" Gat asked brightly in the same language, projecting his voice. "I've come straight from the airport. I was pretty sure I wouldn't find you still here."

"Let's sit for a while."

Later, they spoke quietly in Hebrew, then left the café to visit the safe house. The next day, Aharoni met them in a similar manner at a restaurant. Since he had left Buenos Aires in early April, he had let his hair grow out and now sported a mustache in an effort not to be recognized by anyone he had had contact with before. Avraham Shalom was expected next.

Shalom, who had traveled with a forged German passport, stepped under the awning outside the Lancaster Hotel on Avenida Córdoba, within walking distance of the Plaza San Martín in central Buenos

Aires. Entering the lobby, he thought he might have been in London, given the oak bar and the aristocratic portraits on the wall. Shalom was used to staying in fleabags—a staple of Harel's thrifty travel policies—but he was playing the part of a businessman, and the hotel suited this role. He wasn't going to complain.

Like his colleagues, Shalom had taken a roundabout route to Buenos Aires. He had flown to Rome under one passport, switching it for another at the Israeli embassy. Then he had traveled by train to Paris, where Shalom Dani had passed him an authentic German passport whose name Dani had carefully changed by a few letters to create a new identity. Shalom had then flown to Lisbon, surrendering his passport to the Portuguese authorities until he was ready to board his plane to Buenos Aires. Inexplicably, he had forgotten his assumed name when the policeman had asked for it so that he could return the passport. Usually, Shalom used some kind of mnemonic device, relating syllables or letters of the first name with the last, but this time his mind had gone blank. Luckily, he had spotted his green passport in the pile and pointed to it, saying confidently, "That one's mine." The policeman had handed it to him without a second thought.

This blunder had soon been followed by another, when he saw the team's frontman, Yaakov Medad, boarding the same flight, something that most definitely was not supposed to happen. If either of their passports was recognized as a fake, the authorities would reexamine all of the passengers' papers. Again, disaster had been avoided, and Shalom and Medad had made a special effort not to so much as glance at each other during the long flight.

A third bad omen came when Shalom handed over his passport at the Lancaster reception desk. The receptionist, a man in his early fifties, took one look at his papers and said, "Compatriot. You're from Hamburg. I'm from Hamburg."

Shalom felt his heart fall into his shoes. He spoke with an Austrian accent and dialect, and the attendant, whose age and nationality were consistent with the possibility that he was a former Nazi, would know that he did not speak like a German from the north.

Hoping to put him off, Shalom said that he was actually from a small town outside the city. Remarkably, the receptionist replied that he was from the same place. Shalom was astounded. What were the chances? He made haste with the hotel forms, took the keys to his room, and walked away, certain that he had made a dubious impression. He planned on switching hotels the next day, just in case.

He had little time to worry, as he had to leave the hotel straightaway in order to make his 6:00 P.M. rendezvous at the corner of Avenida Santa Fe and Avenida Callao, roughly a twenty-block walk due west through the bustling downtown. He arrived at the same moment as Aharoni and Gat.

"What do you want to do, Avrum?" Aharoni asked after very few pleasantries.

Shalom was the advance team's leader, charged by Harel with answering one important question: should the mission go forward? The Mossad chief did not give him any guidance as to what this meant. They had worked together far too long for that to be necessary. Shalom understood that he needed to shadow Eichmann, check out his movements, and see whether there was a suitable location for his capture. At this point, they had only the surveillance reports from Aharoni, and, although Shalom and Aharoni had known each other for years, they had never worked together on a job.

"Let's go to his house," Shalom decided. There was no reason to delay.

"It'll be dark," Aharoni said.

"We'll go."

Aharoni led them to his rented car and drove the hour and a half out of the city to San Fernando at the height of rush-hour traffic. By the time they reached their destination, the sun had set completely, and a slight mist hung in the cool evening air. The lack of streetlights in the area was proof of its isolation. As they passed underneath the railway embankment on Route 202, heading toward the kiosk and bus stop, Shalom saw small, alternating red and white lights up ahead and to his right. Soon he realized it was someone walking with a double-headed flashlight. When the car's headlights illuminated the man's face, Shalom instantly recognized Eichmann.

"That's him! That's the man," Shalom whispered as the car passed Eichmann.

An excited Aharoni stepped on the brake and pulled off to the right, as if he expected Shalom and Gat to jump out and grab Eichmann.

"Stop that! Drive away!" Shalom said harshly. "He'll think that something's wrong."

Aharoni lifted his foot from the brake and steered the car straight, too horrified at his mistake to utter a word. Gat watched from the back seat, hoping that Eichmann would not turn around to see what had caused the car to slow down and veer right. Thankfully, he did not.

They drove a little farther down Route 202.

"Go after him and see if it's him," Shalom instructed Gat. Aharoni stopped long enough to allow Gat to jump out. Gat crossed the street, keeping one hundred yards between himself and the man. The lights from the car disappeared, and it was almost completely dark. Gat watched the red and white lights move sharply to the left; that must be the side street Garibaldi. He followed and saw the man walk twenty yards farther before turning toward the pillbox of a house. It matched the photographs Aharoni had taken.

A half-hour later, Aharoni picked up Gat on the other side of the embankment.

"Eichmann," he said simply. He was elated that they had found him on the first night.

Shalom was sure that he had already seen enough to report back to Harel. It was a Tuesday, and Eichmann was probably returning from work, having taken the bus. If this was the case, it was possible that he returned home at a predictable time every day. He walked along an empty street to a house in an unlit, isolated neighborhood. It could not be better, Shalom thought, despite his policy never to be too confident.

Early the next morning, April 27, Shalom met with Ilani, the only team member working out of the embassy. He passed him a single code word to send to Tel Aviv: CARROT. The mission should move forward.

Later that day, Harel received the message. He called Eitan, giving him the go-ahead for the rest of the team to travel to Buenos Aires.

He was scheduled to leave himself in seventy-two hours, and he still needed to complete the plans for smuggling Eichmann out of Argentina.

Harel had already finalized the date when the special El Al flight would leave Tel Aviv: May 11. This suited the Foreign Ministry delegation, who would arrive a week before the anniversary celebrations in Argentina, and it met with El Al's scheduling demands. In addition, and importantly, the date provided the most operational flexibility. They needed to limit the window of time between when Eichmann was captured and when the plane left. The longer the team needed to hide the Nazi, the greater the odds of discovery, particularly if a search for Eichmann was launched. At most, they had a seven-day time frame before the plane needed to return to Israel. Any longer, and the plane's presence would attract attention. In the best-case scenario, they would capture Eichmann, secure him in a safe house for a day, and then fly him out of Argentina the next day. To add to the flight's cover story, the press was informed early of the diplomatic visit, and tickets were even put on sale to the public for those seats not taken by the delegation.

The main risk of staging the operation in the days before the anniversary was that security within Buenos Aires and at the airport would be at a heightened state of alert. In particular, his team would need to be sure to avoid random roadblocks at their two greatest moments of exposure: first, when bringing Eichmann to the safe house right after his capture and second, when transporting him from the safe house to the airport and into the plane. However, the advantages of the flight's cover story far outweighed these risks.

Now that the mission had begun in earnest, Harel hurried to coordinate the transport element, knowing that he would have to rely on El Al employees—civilians all—to execute it. There were scores of what would normally be mundane logistical details: arranging the crew, the flight plan, passenger bookings, fuel, airplane service, landing clearances, and telex communications with Argentina. But these were far from mundane on this occasion, because El Al had never flown to Buenos Aires before. Nothing could be allowed to delay the plane. Some of those same El Al personnel would be needed to help survey the airport and to provide cover for getting Eichmann onto the plane. Most dangerously, every precaution would have to be taken so that the return flight was not stopped, redirected, or, in the worst case, forced down should it be learned that Eichmann was on board. If this were to happen, it would require extraordinary measures on the part of those chosen to fly and navigate the plane, and the whole crew would be at risk. Finally, everybody selected to be involved in the flight had to be able to be trusted to remain absolutely silent.

Harel dispatched Yehuda Shimoni to spearhead the team's activities in Buenos Aires. The following day, Harel met with the chief pilot, Zvi Tohar, and the two men charged with selecting and vetting the crew, Adi Peleg and Baruch Tirosh. Harel knew El Al security officer Peleg and head of crew assignments Tirosh well. They had worked in the security services before joining the airline. He did not know the tall captain with the trim mustache and stiff bearing of an English gentleman so well. But Tohar had come highly recommended by El Al.

A German Jew, he had escaped to Britain during World War II and volunteered for pilot school with the RAF. After the war, he had immigrated to Israel, flying hundreds of missions during the struggle for Israeli independence, many of them bringing supplies and ammunition into besieged settlements around Jerusalem under heavy Arab fire. He had joined El Al in the early 1950s, when there had been only a few Israeli pilots, most of the rest being foreigners who had volunteered for the Israeli air force during the War of Independence. In 1953, Tohar had become the first Israeli El Al captain, and since then he had shown his flying skills and levelheadedness as captain of numerous proving flights for new El Al planes.

"Look, friends, this is the situation," Harel began, gravely serious. "We have a flight to carry an Israeli delegation to the Argentine anniversary. On the return journey, we will be bringing Adolf Eichmann back with us."

The three men remained silent as the Mossad chief outlined the broad strokes of what he envisioned. He wanted only Israelis to be selected for the flight, cabin, and ground crews. They were to be trustworthy and extremely capable. Every technical detail was to be attended to with extra care. The flight crew would also need to be prepared to take off quickly from Buenos Aires and, potentially, to make evasive maneuvers.

"What do you have to say about this?" Harel asked.

Tirosh was eager to affirm that they could handle the assignment, although they would need two full crews, given the distances of the flights. He also offered ideas on how they could throw off pursuers by filing a false flight plan for the return journey. Peleg was noticeably moved by the prospect of the mission. Shortly after the Nazis had come to power in Germany, his father, a successful merchant, had been beaten and forced to drink liters of castor oil. Soon after that, he had died of a heart attack. Unlike his two colleagues, Tohar was reserved, stating that he "appreciated the importance of the affair." Nonetheless, Harel sensed an eagerness from the pilot to be part of the operation.

Before the meeting ended, Harel stressed that he wanted to limit the number of stops on the flight back from Buenos Aires. The normal flight required three intermediate stops for refueling—for example, Recife, Brazil; Dakar, Senegal; and Rome, Italy—before reaching Israel. This provided too many opportunities for the plane to be seized.

"Will you be able to manage with only one stop?" Harel asked Tohar.

The captain understood the abilities as well as the limitations of the new Britannia 300 series, the most advanced planes with the longest range in the El Al fleet. In December 1957, he had flown the Britannia's proving flight from New York to Tel Aviv, a 5,760-mile journey, the longest distance ever traveled nonstop by a commercial plane.

"It is a very long flight," Tohar said. "Let me check it out."

Before concluding the meeting, Harel insisted that the three breathe not a word about the flight's secret purpose. Nobody else needed to know until they had Eichmann safely on board and had cleared Argentine airspace. For all intents and purposes, it was a diplomatic flight, nothing else.

"See you again in Buenos Aires," Harel said, as he shook each man's hand.

Two hours later, Tohar rang the Mossad chief to tell him that a flight with only one stop in Dakar was doable at a level of risk that he was willing to take. But there were no guarantees. At some point over the Atlantic Ocean, they would pass the point of no return.

Lying flat on their stomachs at the top of the railway embankment, their faces inches from the tracks, Shalom and Aharoni trained their field glasses on Route 202 and on the house seventy-five yards away. It was their third night of surveillance, and they awaited Eichmann's return home. Their lookout post required them to stretch out on rocks and railroad ties, exposed to the unpredictable April downpours. Overgrown grass and weeds along the embankment offered some cover. As often as every five minutes, a train came down the tracks leading to and from Buenos Aires. First the rails vibrated, then a light approached, then the train passed with an earsplitting screech and boom, emitting a cloud of sooty smoke.

They had no trouble getting out of the way in time, and the discomfort was a negligible concern, but the lights from the trains presented a risk that they might be spotted by someone in the neighborhood. Still, the site, fifteen feet above the surrounding terrain, was the best place for surveillance.

After the 7:30 train passed, they kept an even more careful watch. On the previous two nights, at 7:40, the green and yellow bus 203 carrying Eichmann had stopped at the kiosk. Lights appeared on the road. Aharoni checked his watch: 7:38. He shared a look with Shalom. They had their target's schedule down. Their operation depended on his adherence to it.

Eichmann and a woman descended from the bus, then split apart. After the bus moved away, Eichmann turned on his flashlight, walking slowly, head down, toward his house. Shalom had been struck by Eichmann's pathetic existence, living in such a shabby neighborhood without electricity or water, dressed like a simple factory worker in threadbare clothes. Given the power he had once held, it was hard for

Shalom to believe that this was the same man — even though he had studied Aharoni's reports in Tel Aviv himself. As on the previous two nights, Eichmann circled his house before entering. Initially, the Mossad agents had thought that he was making sure nobody was lurking about. Then they had realized that Eichmann was merely checking on his vegetable patch.

Shalom and Aharoni watched the house for a few more minutes, then scrambled down the embankment. Gat picked them up on the road at the prearranged time, and they returned to the safe house, which they had dubbed Maoz (stronghold), to review the day's activities and to plan for the next day. They had spent the morning reconnoitering Buenos Aires harbor, just in case the plan with the El Al plane fell through. It was clear to all of them that they needed to spend much more time at the harbor in order to figure out the best way to get Eichmann out by boat. More pressing was their search for suitable safe houses.

In addition to Maoz, a grand second-floor apartment in an exclusive neighborhood where they could meet and hunker down if the operation was exposed, they needed to rent another safe house to hold Eichmann until they moved him out of the country. Such a place had many requirements. It had to be a large house in a fairly wealthy area so that several expensive cars could be seen coming and going without attracting attention. It had to be private, therefore freestanding, and preferably with a fenced garden and an attached garage so that they could bring the prisoner directly into the house without anyone catching sight of him. The location had to be remote, but not too far from either San Fernando or the airport, and accessible by a variety of routes. There could be no caretaker on the premises.

Yaakov Medad reported that he had leads on two houses in San Fernando, as well as several others elsewhere. They decided to split into two teams and to spend all of the next day checking out the addresses. If none was suitable, Medad would need to try Ilani's contacts in Buenos Aires before turning to real estate agents or random newspaper listings. In the best-case scenario, they would rent their house from a local Jew, explaining that they wanted to use it for the Israeli delegation coming for the anniversary celebrations. If circumstances demanded, they could call on their landlord to turn a blind eye. Following Harel's operational philosophy, they planned everything based on the worst-case scenario.

The men did not finish their discussion until midnight. Then they left Maoz and returned to their hotels, collapsing exhausted into their beds.

In New York, Yosef Klein could not fathom why El Al headquarters wanted him to be in Argentina—or why it had to be immediately. The young station manager already had all he could handle running the airline's activities in New York. What did they want with him in South America, where he had no experience? But that was what the telex message detailed in its shorthand: "Go to Buenos Aires. Meet up with Yehuda Shimoni. Arrive by May 3." There had to be some mistake. He telexed back: "There is probably some error. What do I have to do with Argentina?"

He received a reply that there was no error, and it had been signed by the El Al director himself. After some more back-and-forth with headquarters, Klein learned the route that Shimoni was taking to Argentina and booked himself onto the same Swissair flight from Rio de Janeiro to Buenos Aires. That way, he might be able to find out more before he arrived in Argentina. He expected that they were going to put together some kind of charter flight. The thirty-year-old bachelor planned to have some fun on the trip and to spend several days vacationing in the newly built Brasilia, about to be inaugurated as Brazil's capital, where the government had commissioned astonishing modern architecture. Before the Nazis had invaded his native Poland, Klein had wanted to be an architect.

As Klein was packing his bags, Luba Volk, a onetime El Al corporate secretary who had retired and moved to Buenos Aires with her husband and three-year-old son in 1958, also received a telex from El Al headquarters: "You are hereby appointed El Al representative in Buenos Aires for the purpose of all activities required vis-à-vis the government agencies, national airline, and travel agents, with regard to the Britannia flight carrying the Israeli official delegation for the 150th anniversary of Argentine independence. We are sending two representatives, Yehuda Shimoni and Yosef Klein, to assist you in everything connected to the operational side of the flight."

The thirty-five-year-old was not surprised by the first part of the message. Over the past two years, her former bosses had tried several times to win her back; they valued her efficiency and graciousness. To keep her at least partly within the El Al fold, they had hired her on a freelance basis to investigate opening a route to Buenos Aires to serve the large Jewish community there. She thought it very strange that two senior El Al officials were being sent to be her assistants in managing a single flight—regardless of its diplomatic status. But the message was clear. She was told to meet them at the airport on May 2. Loyal to the airline, she did not question the request.

17

"THE INITIAL TEAM has located Eichmann and reported good chances for the operation," Harel said, standing across from David Ben-Gurion in the prime minister's Jerusalem office. It was April 28, and the Mossad chief was scheduled to depart for Buenos Aires the next day.

"Are you certain that the man was Adolf Eichmann?"

Harel detailed the reasons they were, but he had really come to see Ben-Gurion to receive his farewell blessing. The prime minister was still hesitant about his joining the task force. Top-level officers within the Israeli intelligence community, particularly those at Aman (military intelligence), had lodged serious complaints that the mission was draining precious resources away from their primary responsibility to defend Israel from its Arab enemies, an argument that had merit. Harel had taken the top Shin Bet men and the limited staff of the Mossad away from their usual duties. In the past month, his own attention had been dedicated almost exclusively to the mission, and now he would be abroad for another three to four weeks. They would not know what intelligence or threat they might miss because of the Eichmann operation until it was too late. Furthermore, there were sizable risks if Harel was arrested. Having any intelligence agent caught on foreign soil was a problem; having the chief of Israel's security services caught would be a disaster.

Harel understood all of this, but he wanted to be on the ground in Buenos Aires to make sure everything went well. He felt that the mission was too important and too complicated to be left in anyone's hands but his own. Its success or failure would be his responsibility. Once again, he explained his reasons for joining the team to Ben-Gurion, and the prime minister assented, asking only when he would be back.

"Three to four weeks," Harel estimated.

Ben-Gurion came around his desk and shook Harel's hand. "Dead or alive, just bring Eichmann back with you," he said. His brow furrowed as he reflected on this. "Preferably alive. It would be very important, morally, for the young generations of Israel."

There was nothing further to say, and Harel hurried from the office to visit with his daughter, Mira, who was a student at the city's Hebrew University. He then returned to Tel Aviv, nervous over his impending departure but needing to mask his emotions during an interminable, ill-timed dinner with the intelligence services chief of an Israeli ally. Once his guest left, Harel spent the night preparing his new identity. He packed his bag with a suit of cheap clothes, suitable for someone with the leisure to spend hour after hour hanging around cafés throughout Buenos Aires. Harel planned on using these cafés as his mobile operational headquarters.

Before hurrying to his plane, he said goodbye to his wife, Rivka. Just as he had instructed all his agents to tell their wives, he explained to Rivka that he would be away for a month on a "special mission" and that there would be no possibility of writing her. She sensed that her husband was unusually stressed, but she did not ask what was troubling him. One of the disadvantages of his job was the wall of silence that surrounded much of their everyday life. His daughter knew only that he was a "government official."

There was one aspect of this mission that Harel had kept even from his operatives. Once they had Eichmann in their hands, he hoped to launch a commando raid to seize Josef Mengele, whose ghastly acts ranked him second only to Eichmann as a target of Nazi-hunters. The Freiburg prosecutor's attempt to extradite the Auschwitz doctor had failed, leaving him at liberty, but Mengele was thought to be living in Buenos Aires, according to intelligence that the Mossad had recently gathered. Everything known about Mengele's whereabouts was written in code in a slim notebook that Harel made sure to slip into his breast pocket before leaving his house. One mission had become two.

On Sunday, May 1, with a Buenos Aires road map spread out on the dashboard of their old Chevrolet, Shalom and Gat spent the day driving around San Fernando. The two had worked closely together in Europe, and very little needed to be said as they surveilled the operations area.

They were canvassing all the highways, as well as every street and dirt path, leading into and out of the area in every direction. Finding the best route was essential for the day they had Eichmann bound and gagged in the back seat of their capture car. The most direct route from Garibaldi Street to the city was obvious, but it was critical that they find a route with the lightest traffic, no construction sites, and the least chance of a spot check by the police — a common occurrence with the Peronist terrorist threat and the anniversary celebrations. The numerous streetcar crossings throughout the city also posed a problem. In many areas, one could not drive for more than a few blocks without having to wait for a streetcar to pass and the barrier to lift.

They needed to map out a new route from Garibaldi Street to each safe house they found, along with several secondary routes in case there was trouble. Shalom knew to trust his instincts in deciding where it was okay to be a little reckless. That did not mean, however, that they did not have to thoroughly assess each risk well in advance. To do any less was "worse than criminal," as Shalom was fond of saying.

Their other main priority was to find a suitable safe house in which to keep Eichmann before their flight out of Argentina. Their house searches had been surprisingly fruitless. The places that Medad had viewed did not meet their requirements, usually because the houses always came with the services of a caretaker. The listings in the newspapers and from real estate agents were for sales rather than rentals. They needed to find a rental soon in order to prepare it for the prisoner.

Another problem was the issue of cars, as Aharoni had first discovered in his March investigations. He had managed to deal with this, since he had used only one vehicle at a time. Because of the economic difficulties that Argentina faced, few new cars were available. Buenos Aires's roads were littered with twenty- and thirty-year-old cars, either abandoned or waiting to be towed. Rentals were expensive, difficult to find, and utterly undependable. Either the battery was on the verge of dying, the tires were threadbare, the radiator was ready to explode, or the car inexplicably broke down after only a few miles. In addition, most rental cars were battered and rusted. Considering that the team required several automobiles for reconnaissance and house hunting, this was troublesome indeed. Further, each time Medad rented a car, which required that he show identification papers and put down a large amount of cash (sometimes $5,000) for a security deposit, he risked exposing their presence in the country. Most challenging of all, they needed a pair of reliable large sedans, an even rarer breed of vehicle in Argentina, for the capture itself.

Fortunately, finding both safe houses and a sufficient number of cars turned out to be a matter of persistence and cash, both of which they had in ample supply. Even so, Shalom wanted to alert Harel to the delay and to run through with him what they had discovered in their surveillance of Eichmann. They had been out of contact for several days now. Once Shalom and Gat had finished with their reconnaissance of the roads around San Fernando — their map marked with the most advantageous routes into the area — they drove to Ezeiza Airport, where the Mossad chief was set to arrive that evening.

While Gat remained in the car outside the single-story terminal, Shalom stood among the throng of people waiting for passengers to clear customs and passport control. He made sure that Harel, who looked worn from the long journey, saw him, but neither of them acknowledged the other. None of the team had been told where Harel was staying, so Shalom followed him onto his bus. Harel exited the bus in the city center, only a few blocks from the Plaza de Mayo. He then entered the Claridge Hotel on Tucumán Street. Shalom caught up with him before he entered his room, arranging a meeting later.

The Mossad chief sat down with his team at Maoz that night. Shalom detailed what they had learned from their surveillance over the past four days. Harel listened closely, occasionally nodding his head. No interpretation was necessary. He agreed that Eichmann's strict routine and isolated neighborhood were ideal for the operation.

Then Medad explained their difficulties in finding safe houses. "We can't be too choosy about the location or interior . . . nor be put off by the high prices," Harel replied, saying much the same thing regarding their search for adequate cars.

Before Harel returned to his hotel, he told them about the preparations for the El Al flight. Since the plane was scheduled to leave Israel on May 11 and depart Buenos Aires on May 14, "we will have to make the capture on May 10 at the very latest," he concluded.

They had nine days.

Through his connections with officials at Swissair, Yosef Klein flew first class to Rio de Janeiro and was well rested when he arrived on May 2 for his connecting flight to Argentina. The trip was going to be an enjoyable, relaxing jaunt, centered on arranging the flight of the diplomatic delegation. In the cabin, he met Yehuda Shimoni; they exchanged hellos and sat down together. As the plane prepared for takeoff, they caught up briefly on each other's lives. Klein noticed that Shimoni, whom he had known since joining El Al in 1952, was unusually tense and asked him if anything was wrong.

"Look, this is not going to be something simple," Shimoni said, leaning toward him and speaking in a hush. Fortunately, there were few other passengers in the first-class cabin. "We have a major assignment. There is likely one of the Nazi strongmen who escaped from Europe in Buenos Aires. The Israeli Secret Services suspect they have located him, and they are following him. There's a good chance that he is the right man. If they do get hold of him, it will be our job to get him out of Argentina and into Israel. And for this purpose, there will be a special flight, under certain covers."

Yosef Klein could hardly believe what he had just been told. He was too shocked to utter anything other than "We'll do it, if it's possible."

Shimoni then explained that they were after Adolf Eichmann, and he described briefly what the Nazi officer had done during the war. Klein remained silent, and Shimoni reassured him that his task had nothing to do with catching Eichmann. They were there only to assist with the flight.

For a while, the two sat in silence, and Klein was overcome by memories of the past: Nazis driving his family into a Hungarian ghetto only a couple of weeks after his parents had decided not to escape across the Slovakian border. Stepping off the freight train in Auschwitz, guards separating his father and him from his mother and younger brother and sister. His father saying that Yosef was seventeen, not fourteen, to try to keep him alive. Looking at the smokestacks that towered over the rail yard. Shuffling between labor camps, surviving only because of his father. Parting from him when put to work constructing an underground aircraft plant near the Austrian border. Turning fifteen as a prisoner; spending his days pouring concrete, cutting down trees, and loading coal; struggling to stay alive while others either died in their bunks or were shot by the guards. Nearly being killed during Allied bombings of the installation. Five days and five nights of suffering the crush of human flesh in a freight car destined for an extermination camp. Stumbling out of the train to see American tanks send his guards fleeing.

Klein thought vaguely that he might have seen Eichmann in the Hungarian ghetto before his family was deported, but he was unsure. After all, fifteen years had passed since the war, time spent putting his life back together, first finding his father, then immigrating to Israel, serving as a meteorologist in the Israeli air force, and later joining El Al. Through all those years, he had attempted to erase from his mind those scenes from his past, but he had never succeeded completely.

As the Swissair flight continued toward Buenos Aires, Klein found these memories supplanted by doubts that he would be able to help the operation. He had no experience in any such activities, and even if he was only arranging the flight, he had never been to South America, let alone Buenos Aires. He did not speak Spanish. He did not know the airport, its procedures, or any of its people. What if he could not get everything done on time?

When the plane began its descent to Ezeiza Airport, Klein was already beginning to get hold of both his anxieties over the operation and his emotions regarding the past. But when flashbulbs popped the moment he stepped onto the tarmac, he jumped. Both he and Shimoni thought the mission had already been compromised, and them with it, but they soon realized that a photographer was just trying to make a buck off the tourists. The situation's absurdity provided a welcome relief.

In the terminal, they were met by Luba Volk, her husband, and an individual from the Israeli embassy, who introduced himself as Ephraim Ilani. Volk sensed straightaway that her two El Al colleagues were distracted and worried. Already that morning, her suspicions about their coming to Argentina had been piqued when Ilani, whom she knew only slightly, had telephoned, saying that he wanted to follow her husband and her to the airport to meet Shimoni and Klein. Now Ilani explained to Shimoni and Klein that he had booked a different hotel from the one Volk had reserved for him. Volk and her husband drove Shimoni and Klein to the second hotel, noticing again how anxious they seemed. On the ride home, she remarked to her husband, "There is something more going on with this flight than just the delegation."

Later that night, Klein and Shimoni sat down with Isser Harel in a café in the city. The Mossad chief spoke in a very matter-of-fact tone. Shimoni would be departing in a few days, leaving Klein on his own. "What your job really entails," Harel said, "is to make all the arrangements for the flight."

He spoke at length about how Klein would be responsible for everything from the plane's arrival to its departure. Klein needed to establish relations with the relevant Argentine ministries, as well as the service companies and other airlines that would accommodate El Al, since it had no infrastructure in the country. Furthermore, Harel wanted Klein to survey the airport, its facilities, and its customs and passport procedures and to recommend the best way to get their prisoner on board the plane.

"We're not here just to do a job," Harel said, sensing that Klein needed some encouragement. "This is the first time the Jewish people will judge their murderer."

On May 3, Yaakov Gat spent yet another morning in a café, expecting Peter Malkin and Rafi Eitan to walk through the door. Yet again he was disappointed. They were late. Moshe Tabor, who had landed the day before, had met with them in Paris, but he did not know the reason for their delay. If they had been caught attempting to get into Argentina with false passports, Ilani, at the embassy, had yet to receive word.

The team forged ahead without them, continuing their surveillance of Eichmann, tracking his movements to and from work to see if there was a better spot to grab him than outside his home. They applied themselves to securing proper safe houses, and after forty-eight hours of intensive searching, their efforts were rewarded with two buildings. Both happened to be owned by Jewish families, although they had no idea why Medad wanted to rent their properties.

The first was located in a quiet neighborhood of Florencio Varela, a town eighteen miles southwest of Buenos Aires. The large two-story house, code-named Tira (palace), had several advantages: easy access to both the capture area and the airport, an eight-foot wall around the property, a gated entrance, no caretaker, and a rear garden and veranda obscured by trees and dense shrubs. It was by no means perfect, however. The property was situated on a long, narrow plot of land with neighbors on both sides. The house lacked an attic or basement to hide the prisoner, and the utilitarian layout of the rooms, all built with thick walls, made it complicated to construct a secret room to protect against the eventuality that the police raided the place. Still, it would serve well as a backup to the other safe house, which they considered perfect in every way but one.

Code-named Doron (gift), their second find was more a villa than a house. The architect had designed a sprawling affair with several wings on multiple levels and a maze of rooms unpredictable in their placement, size, configuration, and entrance. With little effort, they could build a secret chamber that would take the police hours, if not days, to find. The villa was a couple of hours from Garibaldi Street, and there were several routes into the area. The extensive manicured grounds surrounded by a high stone wall also limited spying by nosy neighbors. The only drawback was that a gardener serviced the property, but they felt that they could keep him away.

The team now focused completely on planning the capture itself.

After their first day's work in Buenos Aires, Shimoni and Klein met with Harel at a café, their faces revealing their extreme agitation. Shimoni explained that the Argentine protocol office was not prepared to welcome the Israeli delegation until May 19, a week later than they had expected. There was no way to negotiate with them without drawing too much attention to the flight.

After the El Al officers left, Harel discussed the repercussions with Shalom. Either the team would have to postpone the capture date or risk holding their captive for ten days, until the plane could take off on May 20. Neither was a good option. Delaying increased the odds that Eichmann would change his routine or, much worse, that he would discover that he was being shadowed and run. Extending his imprisonment in the safe house gave those looking for him — whether his family, the police, or both — more time to find him, and the team would have to endure waiting day after day in seclusion.

Shalom felt that they should postpone the operation by at least a few days. Harel feared that even this minor delay would give Eichmann a chance to elude their grasp. Needing time to think — and hoping to discuss the situation further with Rafi Eitan if and when he arrived — Harel put off making a decision. One thing was certain: the news heightened the risks for everyone involved.

On the evening of May 4, Eitan and Peter Malkin finally arrived in Buenos Aires. Only the doctor and the forger had yet to arrive to complete the team. Eitan and Malkin had been held up in Paris with documentation problems, then Eitan had been bedridden with food poisoning, and they had had difficulty rebooking a flight.

Shalom collected them at their meeting place in a 1952 Ford clunker. With the operation only six days away, they wanted to go straightaway to San Fernando.

As they drove north, a light rain fell and a cold, blustery wind picked up. Knowing the roads in Buenos Aires thoroughly by this point, Shalom took them to San Fernando by the shortest route. On the way, he updated the new arrivals on the operation. By the time they neared the neighborhood, the drizzle had turned into a downpour, but Malkin still recognized some of the landmarks and streets he had studied in Aharoni's reports. Suddenly, Shalom came to an abrupt stop. They were on a street running parallel to Garibaldi. Two young soldiers materialized on either side of the car. One held a red flashlight; both were armed and carrying truncheons. Shalom stayed calm; he had run across enough roadblocks and spot checks to know that this was routine. In his pidgin Spanish, he explained to one of the soldiers that they were tourists, searching for their hotel. The soldier did not reply, focusing his light first on Shalom, then on the license plate. Rain streamed off the brim of his hat as he contemplated whether they were a threat. After an age, he waved them on, to the relief of the three Israelis.

Several blocks away, Shalom pulled over to the side of the road. "We'd better leave the car here . . . I'd hate for those soldiers to see it again."

Within an instant of exiting the car, they were drenched from head to foot. Malkin hiked across a field pocked with mud, cursing that he had worn a suit and dress shoes. But when he reached the lookout post on the railway embankment, he forgot about everything except the house on which his binoculars were now trained. The post was perfectly positioned, and Malkin was able to see Eichmann's wife clearly through the front window. Then he checked his watch. According to Shalom, Eichmann would arrive within the next few minutes.

Since the first day Malkin had read the file on the Nazi, his presence had loomed ever larger and more evil. In Vienna alone, on his first assignment to force the Jews out of Europe, Eichmann had shown his true nature. He enjoyed striding through the Palais Rothschild, where the Jews lining the hallways retreated from him in fear. He also enjoyed publicly humiliating the city's Jewish leaders by striking them across the face or calling them "old shitbags" in meetings.

After the pogrom led by SS men in civilian attire, during which forty-two of Vienna's synagogues were set afire and more than two thousand families were driven from their homes, Eichmann was remorseless, arriving at the Jewish community's headquarters to announce that there had been "an unsatisfactory rate of disappearance of Jews from Vienna." Already in 1938, the thirty-two-year-old reveled in being called a "bloodhound."

Reading about Eichmann's activities had only started the process of demonizing him for Malkin. His fear of failure when it came to grabbing Eichmann also played a part. But the greatest factor was confronting his own family's loss in the Holocaust. Before Malkin left Israel, he visited his mother and, for the first time, asked her what had happened to his sister Fruma. He learned that she had attempted to get out of Poland with her family but that her husband had not been convinced that they needed to leave. Malkin spent most of that night staring at his sister's photograph and reading the letters she had sent their mother before being shot in a camp outside Lublin. In each one, Fruma had asked if he was all right, while all along she and her family were running out of time because the killing machine that Eichmann had helped build was coming for them.

Now, his hands numb from the cold and rain, Malkin held the binoculars up to his face, and a thousand thoughts about Eichmann, his sister, and the operation coursed through his brain. He saw a bus approach down Route 202. It stopped at the kiosk, and a man in a trench coat and hat descended onto the street. In the darkness, Malkin was unable to see his face, but there was something about the man's deliberate, leaning stride that matched his vision of Eichmann.

"That's him," Shalom whispered.

Malkin stared down from the embankment. The sight of the lone figure walking through the driving rain burned in his mind: this was the man he had come to capture. Malkin was already calculating the type of takedown he would use and where on this stretch of road he would make his move.

What neither Malkin nor Eitan knew was that Zvi Aharoni had traveled for part of the way with Eichmann that night. In an attempt to track where their target boarded bus 203, Aharoni had gone to the station in Carupa, eight stops from San Fernando, dressed in overalls like many workers in the area. As he boarded the old green and yellow bus, he caught sight of Eichmann seated in a row halfway down the aisle, among the throng of factory workers and secretaries. Aharoni made sure to look away, so as not to be caught staring, and handed the driver the 4 pesos for the ticket. If the driver asked him a question in Spanish, he would surely draw attention to himself. Fortunately, he did not.

As Aharoni walked down the aisle, he noticed that the only empty seat was directly behind Eichmann, who was oblivious to Aharoni as he passed. He slid into the seat, barely noticing the steel springs that jutted through the worn leather seats. Aharoni was close enough to be able to reach out and put his hands around the Nazi's neck. As the bus shuddered to a start, he felt a rush of emotion that left him physically weak. Severely distressed, he could not wait to get off the bus at the San Fernando station. If there was ever any doubt in his mind that they were after more than just a man, this brief encounter dispelled that notion. They were closing in on evil itself.

18

THE DAY AFTER his arrival, Rafi Eitan instructed everyone to meet at Maoz. Since receiving word that the operation was going ahead, he had grown coldly determined. He knew what needed to be done, and there was no way he would allow Eichmann to elude or escape them — even if it meant taking the extreme measure of strangling him, as Moshe Tabor had earlier proposed. Now that Eitan had seen where Eichmann lived for himself, they could move forward with planning how exactly to take him.

In the living room of the Buenos Aires apartment, the agents ran through what they knew. It was clear from all their surveillance that they should capture Eichmann on his walk home. Kidnapping him from his bunker of a house introduced too many variables, including the possible actions of his wife and sons and the chance that he had a weapon. It was also unlikely that they would find a better location than an isolated stretch of road at night.

Still, there were many questions: Where between the bus stop and his house would they seize him? How would they position their cars? Would Malkin hide in the ditch beside the road and ambush him, or should they pull up alongside him in a car and grab him that way? Who would drive? What would they do if Eichmann ran? They discussed the numerous possible variations, all of them having already spent hours both alone and together on the same subject. They agreed that they should take him as soon as he turned onto Garibaldi Street, away from any passing traffic. But the question of where the cars were to be placed was a stumbling block. Eitan wanted to do some daytime surveillance with Malkin before they finalized the plan.

As for the operation's timing, they had all heard that the El Al flight was not due until May 19 and that perhaps they should postpone the capture. Eitan made it clear to everyone present that Harel had decided there would be no delay. The chief reasoned that it was better to risk holding Eichmann for longer than first planned than to let him slip through their fingers. What was more, if they scheduled the capture too close to the flight's departure, there might be unforeseeable delays (Eichmann might travel out of the city or get sick), and they would not be able to postpone the plane without setting off any alarm bells. May 10 was still the date, and it was not open for debate, despite anyone's misgivings.

The team ran through their individual responsibilities for the coming days. The strain was beginning to wear on the advance team, who had spent almost two weeks working round the clock — all the while under the stress of avoiding detection. There was still much to be done, and Eitan added one more task to the list. They were to practice grabbing and getting Eichmann into the car. Every second would count.

At Ezeiza Airport, Yosef Klein was making rapid progress on the arrangements for the El Al escape flight. Over the past few days, he had met with officials at the national airline Aerolineas Argentinas, and TransAer, a private local airline that flew Britannias. They both offered their services and outlined standard airport procedures. In his tours of the terminal, airfield, and hangars, Klein had taken care to befriend everyone from the baggage handlers, customs officers, and policemen to the service crews, maintenance workers, and staffs of both airlines. He intimated that this diplomatic flight might be a test run for regular El Al service to Argentina. When that happened, El Al would need to hire local staff. Given how little most of the airport workers were paid, the potential to earn higher wages with El Al made everyone more than helpful.

Now well acquainted with Ezeiza, Klein was certain that Eichmann could not be brought onto the plane through the terminal building, even if he were concealed in a trunk or some other contraption. There were too many customs and immigration officers, and with the heightened security from both the terrorist attacks and the anniversary celebrations, little escaped their attention. He needed to find another place to park the El Al plane that would allow the Mossad to get Eichmann on board.

When Klein visited the TransAer facilities that afternoon, he found the ideal spot. The airline's hangar was located at the edge of the airfield, where there were fewer guards. Since the airline flew Britannias, Klein could easily explain that El Al wanted to park its plane there should any spare parts or special maintenance be required. When he asked the private airline if this would be possible, it agreed.

Meanwhile, Luba Volk, who had not yet been informed of the flight's true purpose, was at the Israeli embassy with Yehuda Shimoni, completing the various letters to the Ministry of Aviation that formally requested permission for El Al to enter Argentine airspace and land at Ezeiza. She did not have an office, and she needed the help of the embassy's secretarial staff because she was not completely fluent in Spanish. Just as she was about to sign the letters, she got nervous and put down her pen. She had a premonition that if she signed her name, there would be trouble in the future.

"Maybe it would be a good idea if you signed the letter instead of me," she said, turning to Shimoni. "After all, it's a onetime flight."

"No, no. That doesn't make sense. You're the official El Al representative in Argentina," Shimoni explained. "If I sign it, they could refuse."

Volk relented and penned her name.

On the evening of May 5, behind closed doors at Maoz, Shalom Dani was forging a passport. In his left hand, he held a magnifying glass. With his steady right hand, he fashioned a typewriter-perfect letter E with a fine-tipped black pen. On the table in front of him and scattered throughout the small room were the accouterments of his craft: a multitude of colored pens and pencils, inks, dyes, small brushes, X-

Acto knives, clumps of wax, a hot plate, seals, cameras, film, bottles of photographic developer, and a small store's worth of paper in every color, stock, and weight.

The forger had arrived only a few hours before, carrying with him several suitcases and boxes labeled FRAGILE that contained these supplies. He had buried the more suspicious items, such as the seals and some of the paper stock, among the more typical items that would correspond with the profession on his passport: artist. Dani's appearance—thin, pale, hollow-cheeked, bespectacled, and melancholic—matched the description. He had come straight to the safe house, which he suspected he probably would not leave, even to take a walk, until the operation was over. He needed to create dozens of different passports, driver's licenses, insurance cards, IDs, and other papers for the team.

None of the team knew that Dani was slowly being weakened by heart problems, and, at only thirty-two years old, he was not about to tell them. He wanted in on this job. Dani's family had been removed from their Hungarian village into a ghetto when the Nazis had occupied the country. His father had been killed at Bergen-Belsen, and Shalom, his two siblings, and their mother had been shuffled between various camps until he had crafted passes that had freed them. They had hidden out in an Austrian town until the end of the war. Shalom had then turned his natural artistic talents to forging immigration papers for Jews to settle in Palestine. After the Israeli War of Independence, he had studied at the École Nationale Supérieure des Beaux-Arts in Paris and had then joined the Mossad. In the mid-1950s, his work—forging old French and Moroccan passports for eighteen hours a day, seven days a week—had allowed thousands of Moroccan Jews to escape to Israel.

Dani had still been living in Paris, working for the Mossad and studying the art of stained glass, when Harel had tapped him to come to Argentina. The team had relied on his passports and identification papers to get into Argentina, without a single problem. Dani was not one to accept praise easily, and he no doubt would have been surprised to learn that his colleagues valued him above anyone else on the team.

He and Moshe Tabor worked alone at Maoz while the others were out and about in Buenos Aires. Tabor was punching out a set of license plates for the capture cars and rigging a system to change the plates in seconds. He was also tinkering on a contraption that would turn the back seat of a car into a kind of trapdoor, allowing them to conceal Eichmann in the narrow space between the trunk and the seat. Occasionally, Tabor checked in on Dani, mesmerized by his abilities. He had seen him work before, flawlessly mimicking documents and intricate seals, no matter the script, language, or alphabet. He could do so under any conditions, even in a moving car under intense pressure. Once Medad got the keys for the safe houses Doron and Tira, Dani would be left on his own at the apartment, so Tabor tried to keep him company for as long as possible. He also built a cache in the fireplace for the forger in case any unwanted visitors came to the house and he needed to destroy his papers.

Late that night, Malkin returned from his second surveillance of Garibaldi Street and saw Dani huddled over his table in the half-lit room. Malkin thought that he looked like a character from a Dickens novel. "When did you get here?"

"A couple of hours ago. You saw him?" Dani asked, not wanting even to say the name Eichmann.

"He was playing with his little boy in the house," Malkin said, remembering how normal Eichmann had looked earlier that night tossing his son in the air. "It was like any of us with our fathers."

Malkin regretted the words as soon as he said them, knowing the forger's past. Dani changed the subject. "Did you bring your painting supplies with you?"

"Just a few things," Malkin said. "It didn't seem important."

"I know," Dani said, having given up a chance to be an artist in order to work for Israel. "I know."

As the operation day approached, the team intensified their efforts on all fronts.

Shalom scouted routes from Garibaldi Street to the safe houses. The city's police presence was growing as the anniversary celebrations neared and dignitaries arrived from around the world. Shalom mapped out three separate routes to each safe house, each with backup routes along the way in case a road was blocked or they were followed. He planned to drive along each route the day before the operation to make sure there were not any last-minute changes along the way.

He also assisted Medad and Ilani with the search for suitable capture cars that could pass for diplomatic limousines. Eventually, they came across two cars that matched their requirements. The first was a black Buick limousine, which was only four years old—fresh off the factory floor by Argentine standards. The second was a large circa 1953 Chevrolet sedan that needed work, but Tabor could overhaul an engine as easily as winding a watch. Deposits of $5,000 secured both vehicles—although the owner of the Chevrolet looked warily at Medad when he brought the money in twenty-dollar bills. In addition to the cars, Medad leased several more apartments as safe houses. The team now had more than ten residences to use in case they missed the El Al flight and needed to stay in Buenos Aires for a long time.

The surveillance of Eichmann continued unabated, performed mostly by Malkin and Eitan; when they were busy, Aharoni took over. Every one of the trips to San Fernando was a risk. On one occasion, two railway workers inspecting the tracks came toward them, and they had to hurry away before any questions were asked. Another time, Eitan made an illegal turn into an intersection and was stopped by a policeman. The jeep they were driving had a broken reverse gear, and they had to push it back out of the junction. This probably played to their advantage, as the policeman sympathized with them enough to let them drive off without inspecting their papers or issuing a ticket.

Despite the risks, the surveillance was necessary. It was important that Eichmann was maintaining his routine. Day after day, the former Nazi showed up at the exact same time. Malkin wanted to know every single one of his movements from the bus stop to his house, going so far as to calculate the number of strides Eichmann took to get there. He also was learning the neighborhood: when traffic was heaviest on Route 202; how often the trains passed; who lived and worked

in the area and when they walked the streets. All of this might prove
critical in the operation.

Many hours were also required to prepare for the prisoner's arrival
at Doron. They stocked the place with more beds and with food, as
well as with all the equipment they had brought from Israel. They reinforced the security bars on the windows and changed the locks
throughout the house. Tabor surveyed the house and found a spot in
the attic to hide the captive in case of a search. He moved some support beams slightly and was now building a false wall that opened on
a hinge. When complete, it would look like part of the house. The
only, and increasingly worrisome, obstacle to their work was the gardener. He was a simple, gentle man, but suspicious about all the activity at the house. There were only so many errands away from the
grounds on which they could send him.

Whenever all of the team members were together at Doron, they
practiced using Tabor's mechanism for changing the license plates.
They would have to be able to do it in the dark, quickly, since they
expected to change plates right after the capture and potentially a second time before reaching the safe house. Practicing that procedure
was nothing compared to the repeated, sometimes painful, rehearsals
of the snatch. These were held in the garage at Doron. With a stop-
watch running, one of the operatives would play Eichmann walking
down the street. Malkin or Tabor would grab him, and two others
would help get him into the car. Eitan wanted this action down to
less than twelve seconds, without giving Eichmann a chance to so
much as scream. The team practiced ten to twenty times a night,
wanting the movements to become automatic.

Throughout, they wondered what Eichmann would do when they
confronted him. Would he resist? How capable would he be? Although he was physically weaker than Malkin or Tabor, he had once
been a member of Reinhard Heydrich's SD. These were men known
for their toughness and ruthlessness, men trained to kill and to use
any means to see their will realized. The agents played out various
scenarios in case he put up a major struggle, and few finished the session without a bruise or two.

At the end of the night, one of the team always went off to update Harel, and the others returned to the city, sometimes grabbing a late dinner together before returning to their hotels, devouring rather than savoring their meals, since breakfast and lunch were usually brief and taken on the run. They took walks together in the city or caught a quick drink just to relax. Eichmann and the critical day ahead were rarely out of their thoughts.

On a chilly Sunday, May 8, "Dr. Maurice Kaplan," an anesthesiologist at a leading Tel Aviv hospital, took a taxi into Buenos Aires. In his early forties, of medium height, and wearing a sharp, expensive suit, he looked most at ease, although he was traveling with false papers on a mission that could land him in an Argentine jail if things went badly. This was not the first time the Israeli secret service had called on Kaplan, but because he was a Holocaust survivor, this mission was special to him. The doctor knew Rafi Eitan well and had even treated him for wounds on several occasions. For cover, he had told his hospital that the army had called him up for his annual reserve duty.

After meeting Eitan and Shalom at a designated spot in the city, he was whisked off to San Fernando to take a look at the capture site. Kaplan would be waiting in one of the cars in the eventuality that Eichmann had to be sedated. Afterward, the men drove to Doron, where the doctor was introduced to the rest of the team. Only Tabor and Malkin were there at the time, preparing the prison cell. The room was freezing.

"We're glad you're here," Malkin said, shivering. "I hope you've had some experience with treating double pneumonia."

"Oh, I understood this to be a vacation." The doctor grinned. "I thought I only had one patient to worry about."

They liked him immediately.

In the city, Isser Harel actually was ill. The stress of the operation and his constant movement among eight to twelve cafés a day had left him with a fever and a thick cold. Nevertheless, this was no time to rest. He crossed the street from the Israeli embassy and entered a Chinese restaurant, taking a seat in the back. The Israeli ambassador was to join him for lunch. The two had not met since the Mossad chief had arrived, nor did the ambassador know that an operation was in the works. It was time he was informed, and Harel feared that he might resist, given that this was a grave intrusion into his territory.

Arye Levavi came into the restaurant alone and sat down with Harel. It was one of the last places anyone would expect the ambassador to dine, and it was doubtful that he would be recognized.

Harel explained why he was in Buenos Aires, then said, "The government has approved the operation, but I thought you might object."

"I have no objection," Levavi countered, welcoming the news. Although he doubted that the Mossad could pull off the capture without anyone realizing that Israel was responsible, the operation was already at such an advanced stage that there was no point in suggesting a different path to arrest Eichmann. He told Harel that when the Argentines learned about it, there would be "dramatic diplomatic difficulties." This was a consequence Harel had already accepted.

Harel recommended to the ambassador that some volunteers be assembled at the embassy beginning on May 10, in case the operation was exposed early and there were vigilante attacks on the embassy. He explained that Eichmann's sons were connected to radical, strongly anti-Semitic nationalistic groups. Levavi said that he would see to it. He would tell his staff that this was a precautionary measure for the Israeli delegation's arrival.

That Sunday night at Doron, Rafi Eitan gathered the operations team together. It was time to finalize exactly how the capture would unfold.

A drawing of the area where Eichmann lived was pinned on the wall. A broken blue line showed the path Eichmann took each day from the bus stop on Route 202 to his house on Garibaldi Street. Bus 203's route through the area was designated with a solid green line, and the surrounding streets were in solid red. Key landmarks, including the railway embankment and kiosk, also were detailed. The Eichmann house was indicated with a black X.

Aharoni, who had discussed everything with Harel, outlined the plan. The two cars would station themselves on Route 202 between

Garibaldi Street and the embankment, facing toward the bus stop where Eichmann alighted. Malkin and Tabor would hide on Garibaldi Street, near the house, and would jump on the target. "As soon as we see that you've secured him," Aharoni explained, tapping the place on the map, "we'll swing around the corner, pick you up, and take off . . . Fast and simple."

"Let me see if I understand you," Malkin said, hardly veiling his frustration. He and Aharoni had opposing personalities, and the operation was testing their already limited patience with each other. "Tabor and I are supposed to stay exposed, out in the open, until you decide to arrive with the car? A question: What if a policeman happens by—or even an ordinary pedestrian?"

Aharoni replied calmly that they would watch out for that and would respond with deliberate speed. Malkin erupted, shouting that he would not be involved in anything so amateurish. Eitan cut him off before tempers grew even more heated.

In Malkin's view, a plan was only a suggestion for how things might proceed; at the end of the day, it was always the target who dictated their actions. Since Eichmann's actions were beyond their control, anything could happen. The team could stage everything perfectly on the basis of what they knew about Eichmann's routine, but if he came back from work late or accompanied by somebody else, the operation would need to be flexible enough to adjust to that. If Malkin and Tabor were hiding alone on the roadside, their choices would be too limited and they would be too vulnerable. Malkin's fear that the operation could turn bad ran very deep. He thought about the many possibilities every night, and given Aharoni's limited operational experience, Malkin was not about to accept the Shin Bet interrogator's plan just because he had run through it with Harel.

Malkin stood up and went over to the map. He had an alternative plan, one he had developed with Eitan and Shalom. One car would be stationed on Route 202 in the exact position that Aharoni had suggested. This car would turn on its lights, in order to dazzle Eichmann as he walked toward them. The second car would be parked on Garibaldi Street, facing away from Route 202, with its hood up—as if it had broken down. As Eichmann drew near, Malkin would say something to him in Spanish to distract him before he grabbed him. Then Tabor and Eitan would assist in dragging him into the back seat of the car. This would limit their exposure before Eichmann was put into the vehicle, and if for any reason their target grew suspicious, they could walk away.

Everyone, including Aharoni, saw the advantages of this plan, but they could see a major vulnerability as well. What if Eichmann panicked upon seeing a car he did not recognize parked yards from his house at night? He might race across the field toward his house or dash back toward the bus stop and kiosk. Malkin argued that this was unlikely. It would be up to Harel to settle the debate.

The team then turned the discussion to another issue, and this time everyone agreed without question: they must switch safe houses. The gardener was on the premises too often and could not be persuaded to stay away. He needed only to mention the strange activities at the house to the wrong person, and the whole operation would be compromised.

With the capture date rapidly approaching, every detail of the plan was scrutinized and scrutinized again. Any mistake could cost the agents their freedom, but worse in their minds, it might allow Eichmann to keep his.

19

ON MAY 9, RAFI EITAN drove to San Fernando on reconnaissance. He turned onto Route 202, near Garibaldi Street, and suddenly found himself at the scene of an accident. A car had collided with a motorcycle, and the police were on hand. Before Eitan could turn around, a policeman, supporting a bloodied motorcyclist, appeared at the driver's window.

"Hospital," the policeman said.

Eitan watched dumbfounded as his back door was opened and the motorcyclist deposited in his car.

"Hospital," the policeman repeated.

There was nothing for Eitan to do but to nod enthusiastically and drive off with the man to get him medical treatment. Eitan had doubted that the team would be ready for the capture the next day, particularly since they were moving safe houses, but now he had another reason to hesitate: he did not want to risk being seen by the police in the area two days in a row.

Later that morning at the Café Molino, one of the city's grandest coffeehouses, he sat down with Harel. Aharoni and Malkin also were present. With his voice lost in the constant hum of conversation from the surrounding tables, Eitan detailed why they should postpone the capture by a day. Harel was reluctant. Once he set a plan in motion, he did not like to change it. In this case, he was especially worried that Eichmann might take flight. But Eitan was absolutely clear that the team needed more time, and Harel assented. He had to admit that his men looked harried and exhausted. They could have said the same of their chief, who had dark half-moons under his blood-shot eyes. Then the conversation turned to the capture plan. Eitan related their stalemate from the night before, pointing out Malkin's insistence that a car be parked on Garibaldi Street, hood up, for the snatch.

Malkin felt Harel's eyes boring into him as Eitan was speaking, but the chief acknowledged that it was important that Malkin be at ease with the plan, since he was the one charged with grabbing Eichmann. He asked pointedly what would occur if Eichmann became unnerved by the car: "What if he leaves the road and cuts through the field to reach his house?"

"He will continue straight ahead," Malkin stated firmly. The only reason, he explained, for going with the first plan—keeping both cars on Route 202—was to avoid making Eichmann suspicious, but this did not seem worth the risk of not being able to get a car to Tabor and him after they had seized Eichmann.

Harel and Aharoni looked unconvinced.

"Look, imagine you're Eichmann . . . You see a car with its hood up. It's maybe thirty yards to your house. What do you do?" Malkin paused for effect. "You're a proud man, a former SS officer, a creature of habit and routine. A little dialogue goes on in your head. You're a little ashamed of yourself even to be feeling such fears. After all, it has been fifteen years. You can't run away from every single suggestion of the unknown . . . You continue on."

Again Harel said that he might easily cross the field to get home.

"I've seen plenty of Nazis in shiny boots," Malkin said. "They will not walk through the mud unless they absolutely have to."

The Mossad chief contemplated Malkin's explanation. Then he stood up from the table, directing his hard gray-blue eyes at Malkin. "All right. I agree. But, Peter, it's on your head."

The three agents left the café. Even with the one-day reprieve, they barely had time to finish their preparations, including transferring everything from Doron to Tira, constructing a room in which to hide

Eichmann, overhauling one of the capture cars again, surveying the roads, verifying that Eichmann maintained his routine, and practicing the snatch. They also needed to check out of their hotels, move into their assigned safe houses, and assume completely different identities. There was to be a complete break with who they had been since first arriving in Argentina. If they had to run, the authorities would not have a trail to follow.

But at least they agreed on the plan for the capture. Now they needed only to execute it.

In West Germany, Fritz Bauer had no idea how close the Israelis were to seizing Eichmann. As far as he knew, the investigations might have fizzled again, and he was growing increasingly impatient over the long silence. He had risked too much by handing over the intelligence on Eichmann for nothing to come of it. Less than a week earlier, he had written a note to Haim Cohen, demanding to know what was happening and threatening to pursue other avenues as previously outlined.

On May 10, Bauer received his reply from Cohen. "I assure you this matter is being attended to intensely," Cohen wrote. "We expect to be able to report exact details shortly. Until then, we, and that includes you, have to be patient, and in the interest of the matter, I implore you to calmly wait for further information." The message was clear: Bauer was to hold tight.

Tuviah Friedman was also in a state of suspense. He had not made any further announcements about Eichmann after receiving letters from Erwin Schüle stating that any action might jeopardize the ongoing investigations. From what Friedman understood, the follow-up investigations by the World Jewish Congress proved that the information Lothar Hermann had provided was yet another false clue in the hunt for Adolf Eichmann.

As for Simon Wiesenthal, his brief flurry of activity with the Mossad had contributed nothing other than adding several more pages to his file on Eichmann. Contact had been abruptly cut off and no explanation given to Wiesenthal. In spite of his obsessive efforts to find Eichmann over the fifteen years since the Nazi's disappearance in the postwar chaos, Wiesenthal was resigned to the fact that the fugitive would elude justice for many more years to come.

As Eichmann was returning to his house on Garibaldi Street after work on May 10, a black sedan pulled up beside him. The driver rolled down his window and asked in Spanish how to get back to Buenos Aires. Eichmann gave him directions, very ill at ease with how closely the four men in the car seemed to be watching him. Before the sedan disappeared into the night, Eichmann noticed that its license plates were from the city. Why, then, would they need directions? Could this somehow be related to the two men who had approached his daughter-in-law Margarita six weeks before?

As soon as he got home, he told his wife about the black sedan. He brushed it off as nothing—at worst, the secret police doing a routine check in the area—but Vera was worried. Eichmann ate his dinner and smoked one cigarette after another, but he did not play his violin as he usually did. Lately, he had been practicing a piece by Andreas Hofer, "My Love, Do Not Forget Me," a break from his favorites, Mozart and Haydn. That evening, he was too tired. In bed that night, his wife slept uneasily next to him, dreaming about her husband in a white shirt that suddenly turned crimson.

Neither of them had anything to fear from that black sedan—the Mossad team had no reason to approach him so obviously. But now Eichmann was wary.

"We're planning for the operation to take place tomorrow," Harel told Yosef Klein earlier that evening. "So, just be aware of that. Suppose we get discovered—the police might get hold of the story somehow. I just want you to be aware."

Klein got the message. If he felt threatened or heard that the operation had been compromised, he was to go straight to the embassy for protection. Harel also advised him to make himself as visible as possible at the airport throughout the next day. That way, he could not be implicated in the capture.

Once they had discussed these preventive measures, their meeting followed the usual format. Klein had drawn a picture of the airport—its every entrance, building, runway, and guard position, as well as the locations of some windows and doors. He had also outlined the routine movements into and out of the airport, as well as staff shift changes. He had learned how Harel liked to do things. For each and every aspect of the flight—servicing and stationing the plane, moving the crew into the airport, boarding passengers, and many other details—Harel had wanted to know every alternative and possibility. Then he had tested each against the other, dismissing some, recommending others. After this review, he had ranked the scenarios in order of preference and determined the possibility of switching between them in case the unexpected occurred.

Klein told Harel that one such unexpected situation had developed already. Earlier that day, when he had gone to TransAer's maintenance area, he had found soldiers and police everywhere. He was still not sure why this was the case, but he had heard that the Americans were using one of their hangars for military aircraft. Whatever the reason, El Al could no longer use this spot. They needed a new location. Their second alternative had already been selected: the facilities of Aerolineas Argentinas. Although these facilities were closer to the main terminal than TransAer's, the area was poorly lit at night and guarded by only a few soldiers. What was more, it could be accessed without passing through the entrance to the main terminal.

With his usual barrage of questions, Harel zeroed in on the main weaknesses of using the national airline. With standard procedures, they would tow the plane to the terminal an hour before departure, which meant there would be too much activity around the plane when they wanted to get Eichmann on board. Klein suggested that they inform Aerolineas Argentinas that they wanted to use all their facilities except their towing equipment, which they were unaccustomed to using on Britannias and which might damage the plane. After fielding an interrogation from Harel as to whether the airline would grow suspicious at the El Al request to taxi to the terminal and then to the runway by itself, Klein had the go-ahead to set it up. With Shimoni scheduled to leave the next day to coordinate the plane's departure from Israel, Klein would be alone to handle all these matters.

They still needed to determine the best way to get Eichmann through security and onto the plane, but Harel had to go.

At Tira, Moshe Tabor rushed to prepare the safe house for the prisoner's arrival. He had chosen a ten-by-twelve-foot room on the house's second floor for the cell. First, he placed a bed with a cast-iron headboard in the room. Then, with one-inch nails, he secured heavy wool blankets over the two windows and the four walls to muffle any sound from Eichmann. He rigged a bell in the room that could be activated from the front gate or the living room if the house was about to be searched. He was in the middle of constructing two separate spaces to serve as hiding holes, both padded heavily with blankets. One was underneath the veranda, where there was a foot and a half of clearance between the wooden floor and the concrete foundation. The other was in a small storage space above the room.

In another part of the house, Aharoni was attempting to teach Malkin the few phrases in Spanish that he would say to Eichmann before grabbing him, something to put their target temporarily at ease. At first Aharoni tried "Can you tell me what time it is?" and then "Excuse me, please?" Malkin, who had unusual difficulty with Spanish, settled for a simple "*Un momentito, señor.*" Meanwhile, in the garage, other team members, including Shalom and Gat, were cleaning and polishing the two capture cars to make them look worthy of their diplomatic status. They also continued to practice changing the license plates and putting the prisoner in the hollow behind the back seat, using Tabor's hinged seat construction.

They interrupted all this activity for one final meeting with Isser Harel to go over the plan. In several cars, they drove to the center of Buenos Aires, to the safe house Ramim (heights), a collection of adjoining apartments in a tall new building. Those not at Tira also assembled there, including Shalom Dani and Ephraim Ilani. Ramim had been chosen so as to limit the number of people going in and out of Tira the night before the capture.

Harel stood before his men, and they went instantly silent. "You were chosen by destiny to guarantee that one of the worst criminals of all time, who for years has succeeded in evading justice, would be made to stand trial in Jerusalem," he began, saying each word deliberately, his voice firm, much as he had during the speech he had given before they had left Israel. "For the first time in history the Jews will judge their assassins, and for the first time the world will hear the full story of the edict of annihilation against an entire people. Everything depends on the action we are about to take."

It was a stirring beginning. Then the Mossad chief got down to business. He reviewed the capture plan and the responsibilities of each member. From the lead car, the one stationed on Garibaldi Street, Malkin would make the first move on Eichmann, and Tabor would follow. Aharoni was to drive, and Eitan was to remain out of sight, ready to lead the team and to assist where necessary. In the second car, parked on Route 202, Shalom would be the driver, Gat would act as lookout, and Dr. Kaplan would be on hand to administer any medical procedures required.

Then they talked contingencies.

What should they do if they were to learn that Ricardo Klement was not Eichmann? This was still a possibility, albeit a faint one, thanks to the investigations of Aharoni. Still, his identity was the first thing they needed to verify. If they discovered that they had made a mistake, Harel instructed Malkin and Tabor to drive Klement several hundred miles north of the city and drop him off with some money. Then they were to cross over the border into Brazil while the rest of the team got out of Argentina.

What would happen if Eichmann managed to escape and reach his house? Harel commanded them to break into the house, using whatever means necessary, and to grab him there. If the police chased them before reaching the safe house, they were to use every evasive maneuver in their repertoire, to break every traffic law, and even to use the second car, the one driven by Shalom, to ram any pursuers.

What if they were caught with Eichmann? "Under no circumstances whatsoever are we to let him go or allow him to escape," Harel insisted. As many of the team as possible were to slip away, but once they were surrounded, Harel wanted Eitan to handcuff himself to

Eichmann and ask for the authorities' ranking officer. Eitan was then to declare that they were Jewish volunteers, operating without governmental authority. They had heard that this notorious Nazi war criminal was living in Buenos Aires and wanted him brought to trial. Until they were promised that their captive would be held pending an investigation, Eitan was to do everything in his power not to be separated from Eichmann.

Although the team had always known the stakes involved in the operation, hearing what they were to do if they were caught made the risks even more tangible.

"Are there any questions?" Harel asked.

Thinking of his wife and two children (his daughter barely six months old), Yaakov Gat asked, "If there's a problem with the authorities, and they arrest us with Eichmann, how long can we expect to sit in jail in Argentina?"

"I checked," Harel replied, not surprisingly. "Maximum, ten years. But with diplomatic influence, maybe two or three."

"Who looks after our families?" Gat then asked, knowing it was a question the others wanted answered as well.

"I'm responsible," Harel said firmly. "I'm in charge."

Not one of the team doubted for an instant that their chief would follow through on his word. He was a difficult taskmaster, but his loyalty to his people was unquestioned.

Harel then told the men that if Eichmann did escape during the capture and the police were on their trail, they had to get out of Argentina fast. He suggested that they take a train out of Buenos Aires; the airports and hotels were sure to be searched first. Apart from the doctor, they all had enough experience to handle themselves.

Balancing this grim slate of contingencies, Harel reassured his men that he had complete trust in their skills and resourcefulness. In his view, their success was guaranteed. With that, he finished by wishing good luck to every one of them. They were now on their own.

Some stayed at Ramim for the night. Others returned to Tira or went to the safe house they had leased in the same neighborhood. Each man spent time mulling over the next day's operation.

Lying in his bed at Ramim, Shalom knew that despite their preparations, there were many opportunities for the operation to go terribly wrong. The traffic in the area was undependable. A neighbor might be walking along one of the adjoining streets and see them take Eichmann. The Nazi might manage to shout out, and someone might hear him—perhaps one of his sons. A police blockade might be set up in their path, or a reckless driver might hit their car. Or their vehicle might break down. Tira might prove unapproachable because of a random patrol. Despite these possibilities, Shalom understood that the time to take their chances had come.

In his room at Tira, Malkin tried on a new pair of fur-lined leather gloves. He had bought them partly to ward off any numbness from the cold, but also because he did not want to physically touch this man, this killer. Memories of his family dominated his thoughts, followed by a rush of fear that he might fail his team and, in some way, all the people who had died because of Eichmann. To push away this fear, he kept repeating to himself, "I'm going to catch him."

20

WHEN THE MOSSAD TEAM awoke on May 11, they faced a long day of nervous anticipation. Tabor and Malkin double-checked that the safe house was ready and finished the hideout. Shalom, Gat, and Eitan drove to San Fernando and back to check that no obstruction had appeared along the return routes they had chosen. Aharoni made a rushed trip to a garage to buy a new battery for the Buick limousine. By early afternoon, however, they had run out of ways to pass the time.

Everyone involved in the capture operation waited at Tira. Between games of chess and gin rummy, they looked for anything other than the operation to talk about, but it was useless. Some retired to their rooms to relax—maybe even sleep—but they were all back in the living room after a short while, more on edge than ever.

Malkin was one of those who attempted to lie down. He slowed his breathing to calm himself, but he kept thinking of Eichmann approaching him in the darkness and would then grow agitated.

An hour before they were scheduled to leave, Malkin splashed some water on his face and dressed for the operation. He pulled on a wig, along with a blue wool sweater and black pants, and for a long time stared at himself in the mirror, mentally charging himself up. Then he went downstairs, to find that almost everyone else was ready. Tabor had also covered his bald head with a wig and wore a heavy overcoat, looking even more gargantuan and imposing than usual.

The other operatives had outfitted themselves in jackets and slacks. A few wore ties, to look more like diplomats, but they were not in disguise. Only Malkin and Tabor would be outside the car.

Dr. Kaplan sat on one of the couches, his medical bag drawn close to his side. Obviously ill at ease, he was idly shifting chess pieces around the board, his face blank.

Before they left, Eitan reviewed their plan one more time. He offered no eloquent words of inspiration. Each of them knew what he needed to do. It was half past six, time to go.

Adolf Eichmann started his day as usual, rising from bed at the crack of dawn. He shaved, washed himself with a pail of water, and then had breakfast. Before he left, his wife told him about her nightmare. She warned him to be careful, but he told her there was nothing to worry about. He left his house, caught bus 203 at the kiosk, and began his daily two-hour trek to work. He switched buses twice, catching the one for the final leg at the Saavedra Bridge, which separated the city center from the outlying districts of Buenos Aires. This bus was usually filled with the same people every day, mostly his fellow workers at the Mercedes-Benz plant. Typically, he never said much to the other passengers during the twenty-mile ride southwest of the city. Some of them knew his name, Ricardo Klement, but that was about it.

Once at the plant, he clocked in like everyone else and put on a pair of dark blue Mercedes-Benz overalls to keep from dirtying his pants and shirt. As foreman, he spent the morning walking the assembly line, inspecting the work in progress. When the 12:30 P.M. whistle blew, Eichmann took his lunch break, alone, at the same restaurant a block away from the plant at which he ate every working day. An hour later, he returned to work exactly on time and finished out his shift. Typically, he left the plant in time to catch the 6:15 bus back to the Saavedra Bridge, but that evening he had a short trade union meeting to attend. Otherwise, it was just another day. This was not the existence he had imagined for himself when he had been climbing the ranks of the Nazi Party, enjoying ever more the power and the spoils of his position. Eichmann remained embittered over the past, but as aimless as his life was now, at least he was free.

Aharoni turned the Buick limousine off the highway, heading toward Route 202 in the darkness. Eitan sat by Aharoni's side, and Tabor and Malkin were in the back. Only a blustery wind and the distant rumble of thunder broke the silence. They all kept their eyes trained on the road, though occasionally they glanced at one another, recognizing how much each depended on the others for the success of the operation — and, potentially, for their own freedom or even lives. This realization bonded them together in a unique way. There was also a touch of fear in the air, but they had long since become accustomed to tuning out that feeling so that it barely registered.

At 7:35 P.M., they reached Garibaldi Street. Shalom, driving the Chevrolet, had taken a different route to the target area, but they arrived at the same time. Gat was next to him in the passenger's seat, at relative ease because he knew they had a good plan. More than that, he had faith in the team. In the back seat, the doctor was silent, looking at the operatives through different eyes. They were almost a different breed, so calm in the moments before the operation began.

In five minutes, the bus would arrive. They had not wanted to be in the area for too long before the capture to avoid drawing attention to themselves, but now they needed to move to get into place. On Route 202, Shalom stationed the Chevrolet facing Garibaldi Street and turned off the headlights. Behind them, between their car and the railway embankment, a truck was parked. Its driver was preoccupied with eating his dinner, and Shalom had to hope that he would stay that way. There was nothing they could do about him now.

Aharoni stopped his limousine ten yards in from the highway on Garibaldi Street, facing toward Eichmann's house. Tabor and Malkin stepped out into the cold and opened the hood. Tabor leaned over the engine; he would be concealed from Eichmann when he turned onto his street. On the limousine's front left side, Malkin also bent slightly over the engine, as if to watch. Eitan slipped into the back seat, his forehead pressed against the cold glass as he kept his eyes trained on the bus stop. Staying in the driver's seat, Aharoni stared in the same direction through a pair of night vision binoculars. Their backup car was in place, roughly thirty yards away. Again, there was no reason for them to speak, only to wait and watch.

A minute before bus 203 was scheduled to show, a boy wearing a bright red jacket, probably fifteen years old, pedaled down Garibaldi Street on a bicycle. He stopped at the limousine's side. Aharoni stepped halfway out of the car; he was the only one of them who spoke any Spanish. They needed to get the boy out of there. He asked what was wrong and if they needed some help. Tabor dropped the hood down, and Aharoni smiled at the boy, saying, "Thank you! No need! You can carry on your way." Malkin waved him away as well. The boy took off, his unzipped jacket swirling around him in the wind as he disappeared in the darkness. A storm was definitely coming.

Then 7:40 P.M. passed, and the bus had not yet arrived. Three minutes later, they saw the lights of a vehicle approaching from the direction of San Fernando. They had spent enough nights on the railway embankment to know that the lights were from the bus.

Malkin prepared himself, running the words "*Un momentito, señor*" over in his head and gauging where in relation to the road and the car he would make his move. Tabor prepared to drop the hood and help Malkin. Both reminded themselves that they were not to hurt Eichmann. Every care must be taken that he not be injured. They also had to keep him from screaming, which complicated their effort, but they had practiced plenty. Malkin was to seize him by the throat, spin behind him, and drag him toward the open car door. Tabor would grab his legs and help throw him into the back seat with Eitan. They had no guns, nor any need of them. Guns would only amplify the risk if the police caught them on the road.

The lights from the bus cut through the night, but instead of stopping opposite the kiosk, the bus kept going past the second capture car and underneath the railway embankment, and then it was gone. It had not even slowed down near its usual stop. Instantly, a rush of doubt overcame the team. Had Eichmann altered his schedule or gone on vacation? Had he simply returned early from work? Or, worst of all, had he learned of their presence and fled from Buenos Aires?

Malkin looked toward the house, noticing that only a lone lamp was lit. Usually after Eichmann returned at day's end, there was a lot more light and activity. He was definitely not home. But this did not rule out the possibility that he had run or had taken the week off. After all, because of the rush to switch safe houses and to finalize their plans, they had not been there the previous two nights to see Eichmann come home at his usual time.

Each man remained in his position as the surge of expectation that the capture was about to take place slowly ebbed. Nobody wanted to give voice to the concern they all shared: they might have missed their opportunity. The wind continued to strengthen; the thunder from the approaching storm grew closer, and now there was an occasional burst of lightning in the distance. Every few minutes, a train roared by on the tracks.

Five minutes passed. Then ten. Another bus approached from San Fernando. The team readied for action, but this bus did not stop either. The possibility that Eichmann had missed his usual bus was losing credence.

Shalom and Gat stood alongside Route 202, looking toward the limousine to see if there was any movement. According to their plan, if Eichmann did not show up by eight o'clock, they would return the next day. The longer they stayed in the target area, the greater the chances that the police or someone else would come upon them. Behind them, they heard the sudden start of an engine. They whirled to see the truck that had been parked to their rear take off down the highway. At least the driver was no longer a concern.

After taking a few steps closer to Garibaldi Street and seeing no activity at the limousine, Shalom decided to wait. He did not want to go over to talk to Eitan because if somebody was watching them, this would connect the two cars. Until he saw the limousine roll away, he planned to remain where they were on Route 202.

As the deadline to leave arrived, Aharoni turned in the seat and asked Eitan, "Do we take off or wait?"

Eitan had already made his decision when the first bus had passed without stopping. He knew he was jeopardizing their chances to return the next day by remaining in the area for so long, but he also knew that the team was more ready now than it ever would be again. It was worth the risk. "No, we stay," he said adamantly.

One minute passed. Then two. As before, they all stared down Route 202. Standing side by side, Tabor and Malkin were certain that Eichmann was not coming and that they would have to spend more nights thinking and mentally preparing for the moment they grabbed their target. They waited for the word from Eitan to close the hood and pack up.

At 8:05 P.M., headlights broke the darkness once again.

Nursing a hot tea with brandy, Isser Harel sat alone in a café not far from Tira. He had checked out of the Claridge Hotel early that morning and had stashed his suitcase in a railway station locker. If the operation was exposed or he was tailed, he could disappear without a trace. Nonetheless, he was so miserable with fever that making such an escape seemed an insurmountable task.

He checked his watch: almost eight o'clock. His men would already have Eichmann in their grasp—if everything had gone as planned. He did not expect anyone to come to the café to inform him of their success, or otherwise, for at least another forty-five minutes. He kept his mind off what might have gone wrong by focusing on what he expected Vera Eichmann to do when her husband did not come home that night.

She would not go straight to the police, of that Harel was sure. Even if she did, she would be reporting a missing husband—a not altogether novel occurrence in any city and certainly not one worth marshaling the Argentine forces for. Only if she revealed that Ricardo Klement was Adolf Eichmann would a serious search be launched. Surely, she and her sons would check the local hospitals and his workplace before exposing the truth. Harel's Mossad team would have at least a couple of days before any of this unfolded—maybe more. Then again, they could not rule out a hunt by Eichmann's sons or by his Nazi associates and their friends in the German community.

These thoughts were idle reflection until he knew the result of the operation. He stared at the hands on his watch, with every passing minute growing more and more anxious to know what was happening on Garibaldi Street.

Bus 203 came to a screeching halt opposite the kiosk.

Shalom was already back at the wheel of his car, ready to start the engine and turn on the headlights. Gat sat beside him in the passenger's seat. At the limousine, Tabor repositioned himself over the engine, hidden from sight. Aharoni raised his binoculars again, and Malkin and Eitan looked toward the bus stop, unable to see whether Eichmann was getting off the bus.

Two people exited the bus. The first was the stout woman who usually arrived with Eichmann at 7:40. She stepped down and turned left, away from Garibaldi Street. The second passenger was obviously a man, but even with his binoculars, Aharoni could not discern whether it was Eichmann. The bus pulled away, moving toward the embankment and past the Chevrolet.

The man walked toward Garibaldi Street.

"Someone's coming," Aharoni whispered to Eitan, "but I can't see who it is."

Eitan stared into the darkness, but his vision was not what it had been in the past when he was leading night ambushes against Arab troops. He saw nothing.

Shalom flicked on his headlights, and they all knew at once that the figure cast in silhouette was Eichmann. The way he walked—bent forward, a determined gait—was unmistakable. Unusually, he was not carrying his flashlight to warn passing cars of his presence.

"It's him," Aharoni declared.

The two words electrified Eitan. He looked to make sure Malkin and Tabor were in their positions, then he prepared to burst out of the car should he be needed.

As Eichmann approached Garibaldi Street, Aharoni spotted him slipping his hand into the right pocket of his trench coat. Immediately, he suspected that Eichmann was reaching for a pistol. He must know that something was wrong.

"He may have a revolver," Aharoni said hurriedly. "Should I warn Peter?"

"Yes, tell him to watch the hand."

Malkin was focused on counting out in his head exactly how many steps away Eichmann was, wanting to meet him a few feet from the tail end of the limousine. Lightning coursed through the sky, and he feared that if it struck any closer, Eichmann might be able to see him. A roll of thunder followed as Malkin edged forward. He was certain that if Eichmann made a run across the field, he could catch him long before he reached his house.

Twenty yards away now.

Just as Malkin passed the limousine driver's side door, Aharoni held out his hand. "Peter, he has a hand in his pocket. Watch out for a gun."

Malkin was startled. Nobody should be saying anything to him, he thought. He did not want to be hearing anything about a gun. His every move had been practiced without a weapon being in the equation. This changed everything.

Eichmann turned the corner. Fifteen yards away now.

Malkin heard his target's footsteps and saw how he was leaning into the wind, collar upturned, his right hand deep in his pocket. Eichmann glanced at the limousine as Aharoni turned over the engine, but he did not alter his steady stride.

Malkin kept moving forward. He knew he would have to change how he grabbed Eichmann. First, he had to make sure that Eichmann never freed his gun — if he had one — from his pocket.

Five yards.

Malkin stepped directly into his path, and Eichmann slowed down. "*Un momentito, señor,*" Malkin said, the words coming out uneasily. He locked eyes with Eichmann and saw panic as Eichmann's eyes widened in fear. Suddenly, the Nazi stepped back. He was about to run.

Without hesitation, Malkin sprang forward, one hand reaching out to keep Eichmann's right arm down. His momentum, coupled with Eichmann beginning to retreat, sent them both pitching to the ground. Malkin grabbed hold of Eichmann as they rolled into the shallow, mud-slicked ditch that ran alongside the road. Landing on his back, Malkin tried to keep one hand on Eichmann's right arm and the other on his throat to prevent him from calling for help. Eichmann kicked and struggled to free himself, managing to loosen the grip on his throat. At that moment, he screamed.

Aharoni revved the engine to drown out the bloodcurdling wail. Meanwhile, Tabor moved toward the ditch to help Malkin. Eitan also jumped from the car. The shrieking continued. The Eichmann house was roughly thirty yards away, close enough for somebody outside to hear, or somebody inside if the windows were open. They had to silence him and get out of there. When Tabor reached the ditch, Eichmann was pressing his feet against its side to gain some leverage against Malkin, who was holding him from behind. The more Eichmann struggled, the harder Malkin held on to him. There was no way he was going to get loose.

Tabor grabbed Eichmann's legs, eliminating any further chance of resistance. Eichmann went slack and stopped screaming, surrendering himself. Malkin rose to his feet and, with Tabor, carried the captive out of the ditch and over to the limousine.

Shalom waited with Gat and the doctor on Route 202, desperate to know what was happening. The moment Eichmann had turned onto Garibaldi Street, they had lost sight of him. Then they had heard screaming. Now there was silence. Seconds crept by as if they were hours. They could not move until the limousine did.

Eitan helped Malkin and Tabor shove Eichmann into the back seat. Tabor went to close the hood as Malkin kept his gloved hand over their captive's mouth, and Eitan covered Eichmann's eyes with a pair of motorcycle goggles whose lenses were obscured with black tape. Once Tabor had slid into the passenger's seat, Aharoni gunned the limousine. Twenty-five seconds had passed since Malkin had first reached for Eichmann.

Aharoni took a left at the end of the street while the others bound Eichmann's hands and feet, pushed him onto the floor, and covered him with a heavy wool blanket. An inspection of his trench coat pocket revealed that he did not have a gun, only his flashlight.

A hundred yards away from the Eichmann house, Aharoni shouted in German, "Sit still and nothing will happen to you. If you resist, we will shoot you. Do you understand?"

Malkin released his hand from their captive's mouth, but he did not utter a word.

"If you resist, we will shoot you. Do you understand?"

Again no response. They thought he might have passed out.

Aharoni kept driving, heading due east, even though Tira was located to the southwest of Buenos Aires. If anybody saw the cars leave the area, they would point the police in the wrong direction. Eitan turned around and noticed that their backup car was nowhere to be seen.

"Where are they?" Malkin asked.

A moment later, headlights appeared. Shalom brought the Chevrolet alongside the limousine for long enough to receive a thumbs-up: they had Eichmann. The relief on his face was clear as he sped ahead of them to lead the way.

As Aharoni settled about a hundred yards behind the Chevrolet, he once again addressed the captive, this time in Spanish. "What language do you speak?"

He did not reply, remaining still on the floor of the limousine, breathing heavily. Then, three minutes into the drive, he said, in flawless German, "I am already resigned to my fate."

This was all they needed to hear. Their captive was alive and well. He spoke native German, and given his acceptance of his fate, he clearly knew why he was being kidnapped. It was as close to an admission that he was Adolf Eichmann as they could hope for.

Eitan grasped Malkin by the hand and congratulated him on the capture. Malkin sat back, relieved. Though the operation had not gone perfectly, they had succeeded in bringing Eichmann unharmed into the car. Now they had to get back to the safe house without being caught.

A mile away from Garibaldi Street, Shalom veered onto a dirt side road off Route 202 and stopped by a copse. Aharoni followed in the limousine. Tabor and Gat jumped out of their respective vehicles and exchanged the black and white Argentine license plates for blue diplomatic ones. Every one of them had forged Austrian diplomatic papers in case they were stopped by the police or at a checkpoint, but the plates lessened the chances of that happening.

Less than a minute later, they were on the road again, following the route that Shalom had charted after two weeks of reconnaissance. They drove at the speed limit and took special care not to break any traffic laws or to get in an accident. Eichmann remained silent. Halfway to the safe house, they came to one of the two railway crossings on the way to Tira. As they approached, red lights flashed, and the barriers lowered. There would be at least a ten-minute wait, but there was no way around the crossing.

An increasingly long line of cars idled behind them. Once again, Aharoni warned Eichmann that he would be shot if he uttered a word. He lay compliantly still underneath the blanket, his breathing settled. The four Israelis in the limousine attempted to look at ease — difficult, given the circumstances. Drivers paced beside their cars and smoked cigarettes while they waited for the train to pass. Music spilled through the open doors. The storm that had threatened a downpour moved away without breaking.

At last the train passed, and the barriers lifted. The lines of traffic slowly moved forward. Shalom drove away, with the limousine close behind. They traveled through the next crossing without having to stop. Ten minutes out from Tira, Shalom took a wrong turn, but Aharoni continued on the proper route. Shalom spun the car around and soon caught up. Five minutes away, they stopped again on a side road, switching the diplomatic plates to a new set of Argentine ones.

As they neared the safe house, Eitan began reciting the "Partisan's Song" in his head. Written by a Jewish resistance fighter in Vilnius during World War II, the words went like this:

> Never say that you walk upon your final way
> Though leaden clouds may be concealing skies of blue
> Because the hour we have hungered for is near
> And our marching steps will thunder: We are here!

At 8:55 P.M., the two cars pulled in front of Tira. Medad was already there, ready to open the gate. Aharoni steered the limousine straight into the garage, and the door was closed. Adolf Eichmann was now a prisoner of the Jewish people.

21

EICHMANN SHUFFLED into the safe house, held between Shalom and Malkin. The entire team brought him through the kitchen and upstairs to his prepared cell. Nobody said a word to him. Only Aharoni was to speak to him, and for now the interrogator was silent. They crowded into the small bedroom outfitted with a bed, two wooden chairs, and a table. A light bulb dangled from a cord in the ceiling.

For a moment, Eichmann remained standing in the middle of the room, the operatives getting their first good look at him. His trench coat was coated with mud from the struggle in the ditch, and the goggles covered his eyes. He was silent, standing with his back straight as a board, arms down at his sides. Only his hands moved, clenching and unclenching in nervous fits.

Aharoni sat Eichmann down on the bed, and they stripped him. He was completely compliant and looked helpless in his frayed, grubby underwear and socks. Aharoni wondered how this pathetic creature could be Adolf Eichmann, once master of the lives of millions of Jews. Dr. Kaplan stepped forward and inspected Eichmann's body and mouth for any hidden cyanide capsules. He removed his false teeth and examined those as well.

Eichmann broke the silence, his voice strained but clear: "No man can be vigilant for fifteen years."

At first Eichmann had thought that thieves were attacking him on Garibaldi Street, but he had realized that his kidnappers were Jews after being warned in German that he would be shot if he made any sound. He had begun to tremble at that stage, but he had settled down a little during the long drive. Now it was obvious to him that they were checking for poison capsules.

The doctor checked the prisoner's vitals, to make sure he was not on the verge of collapse. Then, at the direction of Aharoni, he inspected Eichmann's body for any distinguishing marks, as listed in the Mossad's file. They did not have fingerprints to prove definitively that they had captured the right man, but if these characteristics matched—and, more important, if they were able to get a confession—all doubt would be eliminated in their minds.

The doctor found several scars that matched the ones described in medical certificates and witness testimonies, including an inch-and-a-half-long pale scar below his left eyebrow and one above his left elbow. When the doctor inspected the top of his left arm, however, there was no SS tattoo—only uneven scar tissue, perhaps a sign of the tattoo's removal.

Aharoni wanted to begin his questioning straightaway, when his subject was at his most unbalanced. He may not have been an experienced undercover operative, but as an interrogator, he was without equal in the Shin Bet. He never used force, knowing it only led to false confessions. Instead, he wore his subjects down with staccato bursts of questions, twisting them in their own lies and hammering them with known facts until the truth was the only way out. He had studied applied psychology and, under CIA purview, had apprenticed in Chicago with John Reid and Fred Inbau, the authors of the standard text on interrogation.

Before the questions began, Malkin and Shalom dressed their prisoner in loose pajamas, laid him flat on the bed, and handcuffed his left ankle to the bed frame. They left his goggles on, rendering him vulnerable and disoriented.

At 9:15 P.M., Aharoni asked his first question. He was prepared for a long night. He had Eichmann's entire file memorized so that he never had to delay asking a follow-up question.

"What's your name?" Aharoni asked in a commanding tone.

"Ricardo Klement," the prisoner answered.

"What was your previous name?"

"Otto Heninger."

Aharoni grew tense. He had never heard the name, and the manner in which his subject was responding, coolly and credibly, surprised him. He changed tactics, deciding that only indirect questions would bring about a confession.

"When was your third son born?"

"On March 29, 1942."

"What is his name?"

"Dieter."

"How tall are you?"

"Five feet, eight inches."

"What is your size in shoes?"

"Nine."

"What size in shirt?"

"Forty-four."

The answers came almost as quickly as the questions, and at this point, they matched what Aharoni had in the file. The prisoner was not lying.

"What was the number of your membership card in the National Socialist Party?" Aharoni asked, keeping up his rapid pace to prevent Eichmann from having a chance to prevaricate or attempt to deceive.

"889895," he said definitively and without pause. This was Eichmann's number. It was a critical admission, yet given as if Aharoni had asked for the color of his eyes.

"What was your number in the SS?"

"45326."

Klement was Eichmann. It was a certainty. Now Aharoni wanted to hear him admit it. He looked across the bed at Shalom, who was equally anxious to hear the prisoner confess to his true identity. Then he continued.

"When did you come to Argentina?"

"1950."

"What is your name?"

"Ricardo Klement."

He was still resisting, but his hands were trembling slightly. He must have known that he had revealed himself already with his party numbers.

"Was your SS number 45326?"

"Yes."

"What's your date of birth?"

"March 19, 1906."

"Where were you born?"

"Solingen."

Aharoni was there. He knew it. He asked firmly, "Under what name were you born?"

"Adolf Eichmann."

Joy swept over the team, and Aharoni and Shalom shook hands vigorously over the prisoner. Gat later described the moment as like the sun coming out at night. They had their man.

A few seconds after his admission, Eichmann spoke again, this time in an ingratiating tone. "You can quite easily understand that I'm agitated. I would like to ask for a little wine, if it's possible—red wine—to help me control my emotions."

Aharoni replied that they would bring him something to drink.

"As soon as you told me to keep quiet, there in the car, I knew I was in the hands of Israelis," Eichmann continued. "I know Hebrew. I learned it from Rabbi Leo Baeck. *Sh'ma Yisrael, Ha'Shem Elokeinu—*"

Aharoni cut him off, refusing to listen to Adolf Eichmann say the holiest prayer in the Jewish religion, one recited in the morning and at night by the faithful. It was the prayer spoken at the hour of death, and millions of Jews had come to utter it because of Eichmann. Everybody left the room to calm their emotions and to avoid attacking the prisoner.

Once they had settled themselves, Aharoni returned to his questioning for another hour, asking more about Eichmann's family: the birth dates and birthplaces of his sons and brothers, of his wife, and of his extended family. They already knew they had their man, but if he later tried to argue that he had been tortured into a false admission, these details, which Adolf Eichmann alone could know, would prove otherwise.

Eventually, Eitan called an end to the interrogation. They had yet to send someone to report to Harel. He would be eager to know the results of the operation and that Klement had admitted his true identity.

Shalom and Aharoni first drove into Buenos Aires and dropped the Buick limousine off in a parking lot. Medad would pick it up the next day and return it along with the Chevrolet. He planned on telling each rental agency that his wife was sick and he would rent the car again in a couple of weeks (saving the $5,000 fee). If the police were to look for the vehicles, they would find them back in the rental lots, traceable to an identity that existed by virtue of Shalom Dani. While the interrogation was in progress, Tabor had wiped every inch of the limousines clean of fingerprints and had removed the hinged back seat and the spring mechanism that allowed the license plates to be switched.

When they reached the café, it was a few minutes shy of midnight. The chief was paying his check, ready to move on to the next location on his list. Over the past few hours, he had run through every conceivable scenario of what might have happened to make his men so late—everything from all of them being under arrest to their having had an unqualified success in their mission.

When he saw Shalom and Aharoni, disheveled and tired though they looked, Harel glimpsed the excitement in their eyes. They sat down at the table, and Shalom told him directly that they had captured Klement, and that he was, beyond a doubt, Adolf Eichmann.

"The moment I saw you," Harel said, "I knew you had done it. How was it?"

Shalom recounted the operation. Aharoni was taken aback by his chief's muted praise and his stiffness as he listened to the account. But Shalom, who had worked more operations with Harel, knew that his mind had already moved on to what was to come next: getting Eichmann to Israel.

They parted ways soon after. Harel hurried to a nearby restaurant, where a *sayan*, recruited by Ilani, was expecting him. Harel recognized "Meir Lavi" by the placement of a certain book on his table. Lavi had been moving from café to café for as many hours as Harel, not knowing the purpose of his actions nor whom he was supposed to meet.

Harel greeted him but dispensed with any small talk. He instructed Lavi to go to Ilani and say, "The typewriter is okay."

"That's all?" Lavi asked, disappointed that he had spent so many hours waiting to do nothing more than pass along a message that seemed like so much gibberish.

The look on Harel's face informed him otherwise.

"I'll go to him at once," Lavi said.

Harel's message to Ilani, which translated to Eichmann being in their hands, would be passed on to Mossad headquarters, then to David Ben-Gurion and his foreign minister, Golda Meir.

Instead of flagging down a taxi, Harel chose to walk to the railway station to collect his bag. With each step through the streets of Buenos Aires, breathing in the cold fresh air, he slowly realized the significance of what they had accomplished. For a short while, he allowed himself to enjoy their success.

At the house on Garibaldi Street, Vera Eichmann waited for her husband to return. It was approaching midnight, and although she had expected him to be late because of his union meeting, she had not expected him to be this late. He rarely deviated from his daily routine. He should have long since been home and in bed. He had to go to work the next day. Something was wrong.

She had heard a car race past the house after eight o'clock, but besides that, she had not heard anything strange. It was possible that he had been involved in an accident of some kind; maybe he was in the hospital. But she expected the worst—what she had always feared: that those from whom he was running had finally caught up with him. She had convinced herself—perhaps out of necessity—that he could not be guilty of the horrible crimes they had described in the newspapers. Her conscience was clear on that, willfully naive though she was. Even so, she had never doubted the necessity of their remaining in hiding in Argentina.

She was going to tell her sons that he had not come home. They would launch a search for him; find him; get him back.

At midnight, Malkin gently rapped on Eitan's open door.

"I'm going back," he said the moment his operations chief looked toward him.

He explained that just before Eichmann's interrogation, he had suddenly realized that the Nazi did not have his glasses. A subsequent search of the limousine had revealed nothing. Malkin had mulled over the consequences if the glasses were found on Garibaldi Street. Vera Eichmann would have immediate proof that her husband had been abducted and grounds for a police search, even if she did not reveal his identity.

Eitan considered the risks. "I'm not sure you should."

"Listen, let me take care of it," Malkin urged. "You know I won't do anything dangerous."

After some more wrangling, Eitan assented, and Malkin left Tira to drive alone into San Fernando, where he caught a late-night bus. A cold, wet wind blew across the plain as he slowly walked toward Garibaldi Street, making sure there were no policemen, nor anyone else, around. A single kerosene lamp still burned in the Eichmann house. They still expected him back, Malkin thought.

He retraced his movements throughout the capture, searching the road and the ditch with a small flashlight. He spotted some broken glass in the mud by the side of the road but no frames. Nothing. Malkin continued to look in the scrub brush beyond the ditch, but it was fruitless. Someone might see him if he lingered too long.

A few hours later, he arrived back at the safe house. While waiting for Tabor to open the gate, something jumped on his back. Malkin spun and reach behind him to flip his assailant over, then he realized he had grabbed a fistful of fur. A white cat had pounced on him. He released the yowling cat, cursing not only it but also himself for being so on edge. By the time Tabor came out, Malkin was able to smile at his reaction, and he let the cat into the house out of the weather.

The house was quiet and cold on his return. The thick masonry walls deadened any sound but kept a chill in the air. That was not to say that everybody was sound asleep under piles of blankets. Far from it. With Shalom and Aharoni staying at a different safe house, there were only five operatives at Tira—Eitan, Malkin, Medad, Gat, and Tabor—to watch the prisoner and to stand guard in the front and back of the house in case it was approached. Only two of them could sleep at a time.

It was unlikely that anybody had discovered where they were holding Eichmann—yet. Every precaution had been taken to ensure that they had not been followed. Even so, this was only the first night, one of ten to come, maybe more, until Eichmann could be flown out by El Al. Plenty of time for the police, the Argentine security services, or the expatriate Nazi community to find them. The Mossad team just had to sit, wait, and hope that their precautions would keep them safe.

Each man had already considered when and how the news might break that Eichmann had been taken. Vera Eichmann would probably hold off before going to the police, but she or her sons could easily alert friends in the network of former Nazis still in Argentina. Some of them had influence within the government and the army. Or they might go looking themselves. If a public search was put together, it might take only one mistake, one indiscretion, for somebody to tip off the police and lead them to the house. The potential scenarios were endless.

If the police came, Eitan was to handcuff himself to the captive and demand to see their superior. The rest of the men were to try to get away. But what if it was not the police who came? They might find themselves having to hold off an assault. If this were to happen, there was no way that they would allow Eichmann to get away. Tabor had already resolved to take Eichmann into the crawlspace he had devised above the cell, where he would strangle him.

Then there was the potential that their prisoner might stage his own breakout. Eitan had already instituted a twenty-four-hour watch in rotating three-hour shifts. He wanted a guard in the room with Eichmann at all times. He wanted the door always open, the light always on, and he planned on sleeping in the adjoining room, just in case. What was more, he wanted the goggles to remain over the prisoner's eyes until he was in Israel. This not only reduced his chances of escape, but also, if he somehow did manage to get away, he would not be able to identify them. Eitan figured that their prisoner was already crafting a plan for how to get out of the house.

Throughout his first night in captivity, Eichmann was restless, perhaps considering the possibility of flight. He had refused to eat anything and did not sleep. As he lay in bed, flat on his back, his face repeatedly twisted and then relaxed, seemingly beyond his control. Depending on which of his facial features was clenched or eased, he expressed a range of emotions: anger, spirited resistance, easy calm, deep introspection. He sometimes tried to adjust his body, clanking the handcuffs attached to his thin ankle against the iron bed frame.

Blindfolded, stripped of any objects that he might use to spring the lock on his manacles, and guarded around the clock, Eichmann could plot and move about all he wanted. There was no realistic way to escape. But the agents knew that their prisoner was a schemer with cunning intelligence who had escaped from several POW camps and eluded his pursuers for years. They needed to be vigilant.

22

ON THE MORNING of May 12, Gat sat Eichmann up in bed. He was still blindfolded, and his ankle was still chained to the bedpost. Gat gave him a glass of orange juice and spoon-fed him some eggs and crackers, which Eichmann ate fastidiously. He remained submissive and silent, uttering not a word of complaint. His hands shook constantly.

Aharoni arrived at the safe house soon after breakfast and sat down in front of the prisoner, a notebook and pen on the table by his side. In his clipped, staccato German, he took up his interrogation where he had left off.

"I just have a few simple questions for you," he said. "Answer them, and we won't have any problems."

"Yes, sir," Eichmann answered obediently.

"Why did you use the name 'Otto Heninger' last night?"

"That was my name for more than four years."

"Where was that?"

"In Germany. I worked there as a lumberjack before coming to Argentina."

Without any reluctance, Eichmann chronicled his escape at the end of the war, from his last meeting with Kaltenbrunner, to his going into the mountains, to being imprisoned by the Americans, to his escape across Europe to Argentina. He preened over outfoxing his enemies, and he showed no hint of remorse for anything he had done in the past.

"Why didn't your family live under the name Klement, like you?" Aharoni asked, knowing well that this had been Eichmann's undoing when his son Nick had met Sylvia Hermann.

"You don't expect me to ask my family to lie for me," Eichmann said in disgust.

Aharoni was incredulous at the comment. Eichmann's wife and sons had been lying for him for years. The answer was typical of many the interrogator would receive, as Eichmann twisted reality to suit his ego. On the prior instructions of Isser Harel, Aharoni switched to questioning Eichmann about other former Nazis living in Argentina. First he asked him if he knew the whereabouts of the Auschwitz doctor Josef Mengele.

"No, I don't know that."

"I suppose you don't even know if he's in Argentina?"

Eichmann shook his head.

"And Martin Bormann?" Aharoni asked. Hitler's private secretary, who was convicted in absentia and sentenced to death at Nuremberg, remained at the top of the list of Nazis who had yet to be found. "Do you know anything about his whereabouts?"

"No, I have no idea."

"But didn't your friends help you with the false papers you needed to reach Argentina?"

"That was a long time ago."

Aharoni offered Eichmann a drink, which he refused. He changed the subject again, this time inquiring what Eichmann's wife would do when he did not come home. They needed to know what to expect.

"Nothing," he said confidently. "She's frightened. She doesn't understand."

"What about your sons Nick and Dieter?"

"They will know something has happened."

"Will they go to the police?"

Eichmann said that he thought they would not, at least not straightaway. As for the former Nazis in the German community, he suggested that they would be too worried about saving their own skins to do much about finding him. It was clear to Aharoni that

Eichmann thought little of his former colleagues and also that he was telling the truth.

The interrogation continued for several more hours, the two men sitting a few feet apart in the small chamber. Eichmann remained calm and forthcoming, at least about his own life. Eventually, Aharoni felt there was a comfortable enough exchange between them that he asked, "Are you prepared to come and stand trial in Israel?"

"No. Definitely not. Number one: I did nothing wrong," Eichmann said forcefully, as if he had been waiting for the question. "All I did was follow orders. You could never prove that I did, that I committed a crime. Number two: What, what do I have to do with Israel? I'm a German. You can put me—if, at all, if I did commit any crime, I should be judged in Germany. Or in Argentina, I am a citizen here. But not in Israel."

"You must be joking," Aharoni scoffed. Haim Cohen had advised him that it would be better if Eichmann came willingly to Israel and wanted, if possible, a signed statement to that effect. "You know that nobody will put you on trial except the Israelis. So, it's Israel or nowhere. Don't worry. It won't be a kangaroo trial. It will be a proper trial. You will have a lawyer."

"I will think about it," Eichmann eventually said.

Aharoni ended the interrogation; Eichmann would recognize soon enough that he had no other option. For now, Aharoni needed to report back to Harel on the most pressing issue: what the Eichmann family would do when he did not come home.

Nick Eichmann was installing a control box for an elevator shaft in the city when his younger brother Dieter appeared suddenly. Short of breath and panicked, Dieter blurted out, "The old man is gone!"

The screwdriver in Nick's hand clattered to the floor.

Dieter hurriedly recounted how their father had not come home the night before. The two sons had been bothered by the repeated reports in the press announcing a fresh search for their father. Their fears had been heightened by that strange encounter in April with the two men who had claimed to be looking to buy property in the area. The incident with the limousine driver asking for directions two nights before had further aroused their suspicions. Now that he had vanished, they immediately thought that he must have fallen victim to an assault, probably by Jews, maybe even by Israelis.

Together they rushed from the construction site. Their middle brother, Horst, was away in the merchant marine, which meant it was up to the two of them to find their father. They traveled across Buenos Aires to see Carlos Fuldner, the man who had helped their father get into Argentina, who had provided him with employment over the years, and who remained one of the leading figures within the expatriate German community. Dieter and Nick did not know where else to turn. At this point, they were also scared that whoever had gone after their father might also want to abduct their mother and younger brother as hostages.

Fuldner was calm and more reasoning. He told Eichmann's sons that there were three plausible reasons why their father had not returned to Garibaldi Street. First, the police could have arrested him and kept him overnight in jail for drunkenness or some other infraction. Second, he could have been involved in an accident and been taken to the hospital—or even the mortuary. Third, his pursuers could have found him, as his sons suspected, and these individuals, whether vigilantes or state sponsored, had kidnapped or already killed him. These were the options, plain and simple, and a search needed to be launched, starting with the hospitals and police stations around San Fernando. The area around the house also should be searched for any signs of a struggle and, potentially, a body. They should also visit the Mercedes-Benz plant to see whether Eichmann had shown up for work the day before.

Nick and Dieter left to start the hunt, hoping that Fuldner and the other members of the German community would rally to help. They also planned to visit Willem Sassen, who was a friend of their father's and had many contacts in the city.

Their inquiries at the San Fernando police station and nearby hospitals came up empty. Vera Eichmann went straight to Mercedes-Benz, where she learned that Ricardo Klement had worked the entire day before and had then stayed late for the union meeting. He had not shown up for work that day, and the supervisor informed Vera that Eichmann would lose his job and benefits if he did not return to work soon.

A search around Garibaldi Street uncovered Eichmann's broken glasses, pressed into the mud in the ditch. There was no question now. He had been taken.

The day after the capture, Isser Harel returned to his string of city cafés. His every attention had shifted to getting Eichmann out of Argentina before the operation was exposed.

Yosef Klein joined the Mossad chief at one of his cafés. News of the capture did not have as much of an impact on the El Al station chief as Harel's warning that the potential risks of their activities had just escalated, particularly since they were unsure as to what the Eichmann family would do. The conversation turned to the flight, specifically to how they would move their prisoner onto the Britannia now that they had finalized the plans for parking the plane in the maintenance area of Aerolineas Argentinas.

They ran through the range of possibilities, some originated by Harel, others suggested by Klein. "Let's do it this way," Klein would suggest. "Okay," Harel typically responded. "I'll consider that, but how about doing it in another way . . . And a third way . . . And how about . . . ?" The flow of ideas—including one that involved a harness and a set of ropes and hooks to lift Eichmann onto the plane—evolved into three possibilities.

The first centered on secreting Eichmann onto the plane in a crate stamped as diplomatic cargo. In the second, they would hide him in one of the caterer's carts that were forklifted on board before departure. The third plan involved dressing Eichmann in an El Al uniform and passing him through inspection with the crew. All three had their strengths and weaknesses, depending on the intensity of the police presence, roadblocks, passport control, and whether or not the operation had been compromised. Since Harel had only forty-five minutes with Klein before needing to move on to his next café, they postponed making a decision to further investigate the pros and cons of each plan.

Later that day, the Mossad chief sat down with Avraham Shalom.

Since Eitan was overseeing the safe house, Harel needed someone to spearhead the escape. "You are in charge of getting Eichmann out," Harel informed his deputy head. "Make a plan."

The El Al flight was to be Shalom's chief focus. He needed to consult with Klein on airport procedures and to acquaint himself with the place and its people. He also needed to map out safe routes and arrange documents and disguises for the day they transported Eichmann to the airport. Most important, he had to finalize the most advantageous method to get Eichmann on the plane, using either one of the three plans discussed with Klein or his own scheme.

Shalom was instructed to survey the port of Buenos Aires: was there a way to smuggle Eichmann out of the country by ship? Over the past few days, Harel had been plagued by the concern that someone might connect Eichmann's disappearance with the arrival of the first-ever El Al flight to Argentina. If the two events were linked—and this was certainly conceivable—government forces or vigilantes could easily stop the plane before it had a chance to take off. A contingency plan was essential.

Meanwhile in Tel Aviv, the pilots, navigators, flight engineers, radio operators, pursers, aircraft maintenance technicians, and flight attendants whom El Al had selected and the Mossad had cleared were receiving phone calls or notices in their mail slots that they had been chosen for a flight carrying a special diplomatic mission to Buenos Aires for the 150th anniversary of Argentina. Except for Zvi Tohar, the chief pilot, none of them knew the flight's true purpose.

For those locked down at Tira guarding Eichmann, the Britannia could not arrive soon enough. Only twenty-four hours had passed since they had captured the man, and they already felt oppressed by their duty in ways they had not anticipated. They had mentally prepared themselves for the risks of holing up at the house, possibly having to face an assault from the police or from Eichmann's sons and associates if they were located. Every time a car braked on the street outside, they were unnerved. But not one of the team had foreseen the soul-hollowing effect of inhabiting the same space as Adolf Eichmann.

Their prisoner had already proved to be no threat. He was obedient to the point of subservience. When they had brought him to the bathroom for the first time, he had asked permission before having a bowel movement. When finished, he had asked if he could have some toilet paper. Tabor was reminded of German prisoners after the war who would polish the heads of nails when ordered to do so without so much as a mutter of protest.

Eichmann was also clearly too scared to attempt any resistance. When told to stand, he would obey but would tremble uncontrollably. Earlier that afternoon, when they had brought him out for some exercise, he had asked if they were taking him outside to kill him. Their assurances to the contrary did little to relax him.

Now that it was clear that Eichmann was no threat either to them personally or as an escape risk, they were overwhelmed with disgust at having to be so close to him. This was the man who had driven many in their own families to their deaths. They had to feed him, to dress him, to shave him, to accompany him to the bathroom, and to tend to his every discomfort. It would have been easier had they felt only hatred toward him, but unexpectedly, he looked and acted too pathetic and sheepish to inspire that emotion. They were contemptuous of his presence, especially when they considered those they had lost because of his actions. But most of all, they were burdened by other unsettling emotions, namely their frustrating inability to reconcile the pitiful nature of their prisoner with the fact that he had been responsible for the deaths of so many Jews. This conflict cast a pall over the house.

That evening after dinner, they were looking forward to the arrival of Judith Nesiahu, an operative whom Harel had summoned to Buenos Aires to play the part of Yaakov Medad's wife at the safe house. Nesiahu was an orthodox Jew who had emigrated from Holland in 1940 before most of her family was wiped out in the Holocaust. She had served in the army during the War of Independence and had worked undercover for the Mossad on several operations, including one in Morocco, coordinating the passage of Jews to Israel. When required, she would pose as a Gentile, violating her strict religious practices whenever in public. With her thick glasses and stocky figure,

Nesiahu would never play the honey pot to lure spies, but she was unflappable, multilingual, bold, and completely devoted to serving Israel. When one of Harel's lieutenants had informed her five days before that Harel wanted her to leave for an overseas mission, she had simply replied, "Very well." The bemused lieutenant had asked her whether she was interested in knowing the purpose of the assignment or its location, and her answer had been that she expected he would tell her when it was necessary.

Nesiahu arrived at the house with Medad, who had already warned her about the "besieged" atmosphere. Her primary role was to prevent the neighbors or any other visitors from growing suspicious of their activities by making sure that she was seen enjoying the garden and taking leisurely walks with Medad, but her presence promised to break the monotony of the male-dominated atmosphere. The team was also hoping that she might be able to help with the cooking, since they had shown themselves to be inept at making anything more complicated than eggs.

Eitan and Malkin both knew Nesiahu, and they greeted her warmly before introducing her to the other operatives as well as to the doctor. She was excited to be involved in the operation, having learned from a short meeting with Harel only hours before that they had captured Adolf Eichmann. For a brief spell, her enthusiasm lightened the mood. But once she saw the prisoner later that night, and how he lay motionless on the mattress apart from the involuntary clenching of his face, she regretted her earlier enthusiasm. "The thought of cooking or washing up for him makes me sick to my stomach," she admitted to the others. "I shudder even to think of touching anything that he's touched." Thus the oppressive mood returned to the house.

In the early hours of May 13, Peter Malkin, who was on watch, decided that he could not bear to be idle, merely staring at the sleeping Eichmann. He dashed down the hall and retrieved some colored sketch pencils from his disguise kit and the only paper he could find, *The South American Handbook,* a guidebook he had bought in Paris.

Gripping a brown pencil, Malkin opened the book to a map of

Argentina. With an intensity born of contempt and unwelcome idleness, he began to sketch the sleeping figure on top of the map. The emerging portrait was of a man with dead eyes looming under spectacles, narrow bloodless lips, and the cheekbones of a cadaver. Malkin moved from that rushed portrait to another, of Eichmann in his SS uniform, a swastika on his armband. This time he painted Eichmann as he imagined the Nazi during the war, his bearing stiff, his eyes inflamed and all-seeing.

On another page, Malkin drew Eichmann carrying a machine gun, depicting it pointed at Poland and Hungary. He also drew almost comical portraits of Hitler and Mussolini facing each other on opposite pages. Eichmann continued to sleep, Malkin keeping an ear out for footsteps in the hall. He did not want the others to know what he was doing. Still he drew, now moving to a pastel portrait of his parents side by side, hands touching. Their eyes looked downward, as if they were watching him. And last, he sketched his sister Fruma from his youthful memory of her: big eyes, deep with concern and love. For a moment, Malkin eluded the depression that hung over the house. Then he was relieved from his watch and went to try to sleep.

May 13 began much as the day before. They woke Eichmann up, fed him breakfast, and shaved him. Downstairs, they had the radio on, and during the breaks in the tango music and soap operas, they listened intently for any mention of Klement or Eichmann that might reveal that his capture had gained the notice of the police. Nothing. They also scoured the morning newspapers, which Medad had gone out to buy. There were details of an insurrection plan by Peronists, which had been disrupted, weapons and propaganda seized. There was another long article on the massive upcoming anniversary parade featuring 10,000 soldiers, 160 tanks, and more than 100 planes flying overhead. Ella Fitzgerald was going to make her debut in the city that night. No mention of Eichmann. This offered little relief. The police or security services might not post notice of Eichmann's disappearance so as not to tip their hand.

None of the Mossad team at Tira expected that the risk of discovery or the strain of living with Eichmann would ease in the days ahead. Their only aim was to be rid of the Nazi war criminal by sending him to Israel.

Back in Israel, Yaakov Caroz, a Mossad department head, had just received the cable from Buenos Aires. He set off through the streets of Tel Aviv to inform the country's top leaders of the capture.

A stop at the prime minister's office revealed that Ben-Gurion was away at his retreat at the Sde Boker kibbutz. Unless a meeting was absolutely necessary, his secretary told Caroz, it would be better to meet with him on Sunday. Caroz agreed and hurried over to the office of the foreign minister, Golda Meir. She delayed an appointment and asked him to join her on the balcony of her office. As soon as they were alone, the slight, spirited foreign minister, with her dark gray hair bound tightly in a bun, asked him why he had come.

"Adolf Eichmann has been found."

"Where is he?"

"All I know at this point is that Eichmann has been captured and identified."

Meir caught her breath and placed the palm of her hand squarely on her chest. Such was her emotion that she had to lean on Caroz to keep from falling. A few moments later, she said, "Please, I beg of you, if you hear anything more, will you come and tell me?"

Caroz left Meir to deliver the message to the chief of staff of the Israel Defense Forces, who offered his congratulations; he also wanted to know more. But Caroz had only the spare coded cable from Buenos Aires. THE TYPEWRITER IS OKAY offered little room for elaboration.

It would be two more days before Caroz made the car journey several hours south of Tel Aviv to Sde Boker, in the Negev desert. Bodyguards led him to a cottage, where Ben-Gurion welcomed him into his small, book-lined study.

"I've come to inform you that Eichmann has been found and his identity established beyond doubt."

Ben-Gurion took a second to digest the news, then asked, "When will Isser be back? I need him."

"In a week, I would say. I couldn't say precisely."

Later, Ben-Gurion wrote in his diary, "This morning I met a messenger from Isser, who told me that Eichmann has been identified and captured and will be flown here next week (if they manage to get him onto the plane). Isser will return later. If it does not turn out to be a case of mistaken identity, this operation is an important and successful one."

Like his Mossad chief, Ben-Gurion allowed himself only a modicum of excitement. The mission was not yet complete.

23

AT THE HOUSE of Willem Sassen, on Liberty Street in the quiet, leafy neighborhood of Florida, mayhem reigned. It was May 13, two days since their father had disappeared, and Nick and Dieter Eichmann were still frantically trying to put together a search party. They had arrived in the middle of the night, pounding on the door. Sassen's wife and daughters had retreated to a bedroom, not sure what was happening but fearing some kind of violence. The youngest daughter, Saskia, thought the two boys, with guns tucked in their belts like outlaws, were crazy. Downstairs in the living room, voices raised, the men argued over who could have taken Eichmann and what they were going to do about it.

Eventually, Sassen took the two brothers in his car to see if they could discover any trace that might lead them to him. Some of his associates thought that he might have fallen down drunk on his way home from a bar and hurt himself. But the boys had their father's smashed glasses to prove this was not the case. Their inquiries around San Fernando had not come up with anything either. Nobody had seen anything on the night of May 11.

The boys knew that they needed more help than Sassen could provide, not only to find their father but also to protect their mother and younger brother in case the same individuals who had taken their father came to take them as hostages. Nick and Dieter had hawked some gold rings and watches for three guns—a .22-caliber pistol, a .38, and a .45—at a pawnshop. Already it was becoming clear to them that they could not depend on the German community for help. Besides Fuldner and Sassen, most of their father's associates wanted nothing to do with them. They were more worried about protecting themselves. As for the police, the two brothers could not get their help without revealing their father's true identity, which might place him in even more danger than he was already in. Instead, they decided to turn to their connections in an organization called Tacuara.

Tacuara was a radical nationalist organization founded a few years before by a group of young, mostly bourgeois high school and university students, who had first mobilized to protest against the secularization of the education system. The name was taken from the makeshift weapon that had been used by gauchos in the fight for Argentine independence—essentially a knife tied to the end of a stalk of sugar cane. Fiercely Catholic, Tacuara had been modeled on the Spanish Falange, led by José Antonio Primo de Rivera. It was militant, fascist, and anti-Semitic. Its members favored violence to achieve their ends, which included freeing Argentina from liberal democracy, capitalism, and the Jewish influence. New members swore an oath of allegiance in a graveyard, cut their hair short, trained in militant camps, wore gray shirts and armbands stitched with the Maltese cross, addressed one another as "comrade," idolized Hitler and Mussolini, used the Nazi salute, and spread anti-Semitic and nationalist propaganda. They were often seen roaming the city on motorcycles.

Though not Tacuara members themselves, Nick and Dieter shared similar political views and had friends in the organization. The idea of a group of Jews, potentially Israelis, operating illegally inside Argentina was anathema to Tacuara, and some of its members rallied to find Eichmann, to protect his family, and to hunt down his abductors.

Without her knowledge, Luba Volk was providing camouflage for the escape. As part of her duties for the special El Al flight, the airline's headquarters had instructed her, on the advice of Isser Harel, to book private passengers for the return trip to Israel. They had sent Volk stacks of printed posters and flyers to help her promote the flight, which she had done over the past week through her contacts in the Buenos Aires travel industry. She had sold almost all the seats, but there was one stumbling block: the minister of aviation. She needed his permission to fly private passengers, but given that there was no reciprocal agreement between El Al and Aerolineas Argentinas, she doubted that he would approve her request. The tickets were sold with this proviso. Her superiors at El Al said that they understood this risk, but most unusually, she thought, they wanted her to forge ahead nonetheless.

On May 14, she received her answer from the Ministry of Aviation. Her request had been denied; the flight would have no private passengers. Disappointed, Volk wanted at least to do a good turn for an elderly Israeli woman who was sick and needed surgery and who hoped to return to Tel Aviv for the operation. Volk submitted a "stretcher case" application to the minister for permission to fly the woman to Israel, unwittingly exposing the flight to even more scrutiny by the Argentines.

Yosef Klein did not know of the request. Although he regretted being unable to reveal the flight's purpose to Volk, he was told to keep her in the dark. In any event, he had his hands full. The plane would arrive in five days. Klein had secured all the clearances and was finalizing the services (fuel, catering, cleaning) for the Britannia. He knew where the plane would be parked and had secured permission to taxi it under its own power from the maintenance area to the gate. He continued to befriend the airport staff, who now allowed him to walk unchallenged through security and around the airport. Klein had also introduced Shalom and the recently arrived El Al security chief, Adi Peleg, to the airport staff. Together, the three men reconnoitered the airport in order to plan the most discreet way to get Eichmann onto the plane.

Occasionally when they met, Harel would pointedly remind Klein of the "historic importance" of what they were doing. "Everything is going to work. Hang on, hang on," Harel would say. Klein always left these meetings with Harel not only with more confidence in his abilities but also slightly choked up at the thought of helping to bring Adolf Eichmann to justice. Harel's encouragement eased his worries over the operation's danger and his role in making sure it went off successfully.

Now that he was in charge of getting Eichmann safely out of Argentina, Avraham Shalom had no intention of leaving the operation solely in the hands of a civilian, even one as competent as Klein. Over the past two days, he had scouted out the harbor with Aharoni and Ilani. They were the only three members of the Mossad team apart from Harel not bound day and night to Tira. The southern quay was bustling with stevedores and customs inspectors overseeing the unloading and loading of cargo: too busy. The northern quay, where the cruise ships normally docked, offered more opportunities, particularly since it was winter in Buenos Aires. Still, Shalom was skeptical of any plan to smuggle Eichmann out by boat, mainly because of how long the journey to Israel would take and how exposed the ship would be at the various ports along the way. There had even been brief mention of getting a submarine to take Eichmann out of the country, but this had been abandoned as a wild fantasy. The El Al plane was still their best option, so that was the avenue on which Shalom concentrated his attention.

Most of his reconnaissance time was spent at the airport, where he posed as a diplomatic official helping to arrange the El Al flight. He promptly determined that the guards watching the side entrance to the maintenance area would be easy to deceive. They were more concerned about theft than other kinds of security breaches. With Eichmann dressed in an El Al uniform, perhaps sedated by the doctor, they should be able to get him through without difficulty. Smuggling their prisoner on board in a caterer's cart or a diplomatic crate would be too complicated. Shalom liked simple and straightforward. He planned on passing through security every few hours over the next five days so that the guards were as used to seeing him as they were to seeing Klein.

Next there was the question of how soon the plane could take off, who would give permission for it to leave, and what to do if there was a delay. Shalom thoroughly interrogated Klein and Peleg about every eventuality. The escape from Argentina had to be as meticulously planned as the capture itself.

Shalom and Eitan were both distressed, therefore, when Harel proposed a new mission.

"The search for the doctor is to be given the highest priority," Harel said as he set his coffee cup down on the café table on May 15. He went on to explain that he had sent orders for two more Mossad agents to come to Buenos Aires. They would participate in a commando raid to capture Josef Mengele—if they found him—and bring him back to Israel on the same plane as Eichmann.

Eitan and Shalom had heard the reports about Mengele being in Argentina, and there had been some talk prior to leaving Tel Aviv about looking for him while they were there. Even so, Harel had never indicated to them that he wanted to take the doctor on the same mission.

"Look, Isser," Eitan said, "I'm not sure that we will be able to bring the two of them safely to Israel. So, I don't want to risk another operation."

Harel had waited to spring the assignment on the team, but with Eichmann secured at the safe house and no news of any search for him being in progress, the time had come. He relayed his plan to go after Mengele in no uncertain terms to Eitan and Shalom.

"Try to catch a lot," Eitan said with a tight smile to defuse the tension, "and you will catch nothing."

Although Eitan and Shalom were clearly not supportive of this second operation, Harel would not be dissuaded. They had specific leads on Mengele, and Harel could not live with himself if he did not pursue them while they were in Buenos Aires. He had shuddered at the stories Amos Manor had told about the Auschwitz doctor—stories that had come from his own experiences. After those conversations, Harel had burned within his bones, as he described it himself, to get the doctor.

Harel instructed Eitan and Shalom to tell Aharoni to push Eichmann harder on Mengele. The Mossad chief was sure that their prisoner was lying and knew precisely where Mengele lived.

Later that day, Aharoni asked Eichmann once again about Mengele. Now in his fourth day of captivity, with no idea whether it was night or day or how long they would keep him blindfolded and bound to the bed in this tiny room, the prisoner was steadily losing any resistance as to what he would reveal. At first Eichmann again told his story about not knowing Mengele at all. But after repeated questioning, he revealed that they had met once, by accident, at a restaurant in the city. The doctor had offered Eichmann free medical care, he remembered.

But Aharoni insisted that Eichmann must have met Mengele on more than one occasion. Surely he knew where he lived. Eichmann denied this vehemently, adding that he feared for his family should he say anything. Aharoni told him that he could wait months for him to answer the question. Nobody was looking for him. Hours later, Eichmann confessed that Mengele had once said something about staying in a boarding house run by a German woman named Jurmann. He did not know the address, but it was somewhere in Vicente López. The Pensión Jurmann already appeared in Harel's coded notebook. This proved that their intelligence was good.

Feeling as though he was making progress with Eichmann, Aharoni pushed him again to sign a statement that he would willingly come to Israel and stand trial. Aharoni had prepared a sample text to that effect for Eichmann to copy and sign. To Aharoni's frustration, Eichmann held out. At one point, he suggested that he would go to Austria instead.

"Stop insulting me!" Aharoni snapped. "It will be either Israel or nowhere at all. Either you agree or you refuse. But do not cloud the issue. If you have committed no wrong, then you have nothing to fear. Think about it. We have lots of time."

That night, Harel visited Tira to see Eichmann and congratulate his agents on the successful capture. Earlier, when he had seen Eitan, Harel had been shocked by his grave demeanor. Now Harel found the rest of the team equally dispirited. He had always suspected that it would be stressful to watch over Eichmann, but he did not understand the debilitating morale until he went upstairs that evening to see Eichmann himself.

The prisoner was lying on the bed in his pajamas, the goggles over his eyes. He made no move to sit up until told, and even then, he was retreating in his presence. Harel was stunned at how ordinary and pathetic Eichmann was.

Despite Eichmann's attempts to convince Aharoni that he had been only a "small cog" in the Nazi machine, Harel knew that Eichmann had implemented operations across Europe. He had stripped whole populations of Jews of their rights, expropriated their wealth, forced them into ghettos, and then deported them to camps to be exterminated either immediately or through months of hard labor. He may not have killed Jews with his own gun, but his efforts had been even more devastating. On his arrival in Budapest, he had called the city's Jewish leaders into his Majestic Hotel office and promised, "Once victory is achieved, the Jews would be free and allowed to do what they wanted. In general, I am no friend of force and hope that things go well without it." The next day, Eichmann had sent his transportation chief to Vienna to finalize the railway details for the delivery of the Hungarian Jews to Auschwitz. Over the following months, while one Jewish community after another in Hungary had been destroyed, Eichmann had cavorted around Budapest, sleeping with his mistresses and drinking himself into a stupor at the city's fine restaurants. When Rezsö Kasztner had urged Eichmann to allow some Hungarian Jews safe harbor in Budapest, Eichmann had flown into a rage, saying, "Once I've said no, it's no . . . Get me straight, I've got to clear the Jewish shit out of the provinces. No arguments or tears will help."

That someone who looked like a postal clerk, someone so average in appearance and temperament, could have been responsible for killing millions of Jews was a horror in and of itself. Harel later described the feeling he had that night. "The sight of that miserable runt, who had lost every vestige of his former superiority and arrogance the moment he was stripped of his uniform and powers of authority, gave them a feeling of insult and profound scorn. Was *this* the personification of evil? Was *this* the tool used by a diabolic government? This nonentity, devoid of human dignity and pride, was *this* the messenger of death for six million Jews?"

Harel's visit had only a temporary effect on the mood in the house, and he instructed Eitan to allow each operative a day's leave away from the house on a rotating schedule. While putting on his overcoat to leave, he told the team, "I know what you've all been through. All you have to do is hang on for a couple of days longer." But as he closed the door behind him, Harel feared that if something went wrong with the El Al plane, they would have to remain weeks longer, not days.

On May 16, the hunt for Mengele began in earnest. Through Ilani's seemingly endless network of *sayanim*, Harel recruited an Israeli couple, who were originally from Argentina and were back in the city to settle some family matters, to check out the boarding house. For the moment, he had decided, it was best not to divert any of the core team from their primary duties. When he met "Hilel" and "Neomi Pooch" for the first time, they looked and spoke like the natives they were: ideal for his purposes. Harel was straightforward about who they were looking for. The Pooches required only a short description of the horrendous experiments Mengele had performed on Jewish twins to volunteer wholeheartedly.

They went to work that day, keeping watch over the Pensión Jurmann, a large house encircled by a white fence set on a narrow lane. They didn't see anybody resembling the photograph they had been shown, and a few discreet inquiries around the neighborhood told them that there were no Germans living at the boarding house. Harel grew anxious on hearing these reports. He had two separate sources both pointing to the Pensión Jurmann. The Pooches needed to be more proactive in finding out who lived there. Harel sent Hilel Pooch back to the neighborhood with a cover story and instructions to walk around until he met up with the postman.

After spending several hours roaming the streets on May 17, Hilel found the postman and explained that he was searching for his uncle, a doctor, with whom he had long since lost contact but who he thought still lived in the area. His name was Dr. Menelle, Hilel said, altering the name slightly.

"Dr. Menelle," the postman repeated, thinking the name over. Then he pointed toward the house surrounded by the white fence. "Oh yes, he lived over there until a few weeks ago, maybe a month."

"Ah, my bad luck. So I've come just a little too late. Did he leave his new address?"

The postman shook his head.

"Do you know who's living there now?" Hilel asked, suggesting the new tenants might know.

"He's an engineer from South Africa. Why don't you ask him?"

Hilel thanked him and ventured off toward the house to keep the mailman from becoming suspicious of his questions. Hilel had no intention of knocking on the door.

Although Harel was upset to hear that they might have missed Mengele by a few weeks, at least they knew they were on the right track; they had picked up the trail.

Back at the safe house on May 17, the mood had darkened further. The days and nights were always the same. Two of the Mossad team kept a vigilant guard in case the police showed up. The constant worry that they might be discovered frayed their nerves.

And then there was the prisoner. One team member watched Eichmann at all times, whether he was eating, sleeping, going to the bathroom, taking a shower, exercising in the garden, or lying stretched out on the bed. Their obedient prisoner continued to inspire loathing and an almost stifling depression in his captors, as if he were draining all the light and oxygen from the house.

The boredom was also oppressive. Apart from listening to the radio for any hint of news about a hunt for Eichmann, there was not much constructive they could do when not on guard duty. The house had a few books in English, but those who could read that language had already exhausted the supply. To pass the time, they played chess; stared out the windows, watching the neighbors going about their lives; took naps in their rooms; and even invented games, such as an apple-eating contest. The inactivity only gave them the opportunity to dwell on their fears and their revulsion toward Eichmann, a vicious cycle.

A few tasks did offer relief from the strain of watching over Eichmann. Tabor was supervising the building of a large wooden crate to smuggle their prisoner into the airport. On the inside of the crate, they attached four leather straps to secure the prisoner's arms and legs. They also drilled fifty breathing holes into the wood. They labeled the crate DIPLOMATIC POST — FROM: ISRAELI EMBASSY, BUENOS AIRES — TO: FOREIGN MINISTRY, JERUSALEM. Tabor also constructed a concealed chamber in a caterer's cart that Yosef Klein had managed to smuggle out of the airport. The plan was to bring Eichmann on board as part of the El Al crew, but they might need these containers as backups—or to bring Mengele onto the plane should he be found.

The team spent that night preparing the extensive documentation—including an Israeli passport, a visa, a driver's license, health certifications, and an El Al badge—needed to pass Eichmann off as crewmate Zichroni. Under Malkin's supervision, Eichmann was given a close shave, had makeup applied to his face, had a dark, closely cut wig placed on his head, and was dressed in a nice suit. He looked startlingly younger and more imposing, more like his wartime photograph. The effect disturbed everyone at Tira, but not as much as Eichmann. He was convinced that they were preparing him for his execution, despite their assurances to the contrary.

Shalom Dani came to the safe house to prepare the documents. He had suffered his own isolation at Maoz, frequently unaware of what was happening and lamenting that he had not been part of the capture. As a result, he felt useless, but without him, his compatriots assured him, the operation would never have stood a chance. Dani wanted to face Eichmann personally, to tell him what he had done to his family. This was his opportunity. But as soon as Dani entered the cell, the color drained from his face, and his hands began to tremble. He said nothing to Eichmann, other than directing him how to pose for the photographs, telling him to angle his chin this way or to turn that way for the camera.

The minute the photographs were taken, Dani got out of the room. He told the others that he had not expected such a rush of emotions. "To even be in the same room with him, I had to force myself not to feel anything," he said, before withdrawing into one of the other rooms to work on his forgeries. When he emerged, he handed Eitan the documents and left Tira, forgetting to say goodbye to the others. He had only one thing on his mind: leaving and never going back.

Peter Malkin was on guard when Eichmann suddenly asked, "Are you the man who captured me?"

"Yes, my name is Maxim," Malkin answered hesitatingly.

Even though Eitan's express orders were not to speak to the prisoner, Malkin wanted to know why Eichmann had orchestrated the slaughter of his people and how the Nazi had been capable of such acts. With Eichmann speaking in German and Malkin in Yiddish, the conversation was rough and stuttering.

Malkin remembered when he had watched Eichmann playing with his young son outside his home. "Your boy, he reminds me so much of my sister's son," Malkin said.

"What happened to him?"

"Nothing happened," Malkin answered bitterly. But then he continued, "There is only one thing I know: Your boy is alive, and the boy of my sister is dead."

"Are you going to kill me?" Eichmann asked.

"No. We're going to bring you to trial, to a fair trial: a chance you never gave your victims."

Then he asked Eichmann, "How did you come to do what you did?"

"It was an order. I had a job to do."

"Just a job?" Malkin said incredulously.

"Are you not a soldier? Don't you have your orders? You captured me. Why did you do it? Because of an order."

"Yes, I got an order to capture you, but there's a big difference between you and me. I had an order to catch a criminal. But you went after innocent people. They had done nothing wrong at all. You followed those orders because you hated these people."

"No . . . I, in a way, I love Jews."

Malkin could hardly believe what he was hearing. This was too much. "You love Jews? Then what were you doing in the SS in the first place?"

"I wanted them to have their own country. I wanted to send them away. We didn't want to do anything to the Jews. At first, we just talked about cleaning the Jews from Germany. But there was no nation that would accept them. We talked about Madagascar and all kinds of other plans. I even went to Israel in 1936."

Clearly, Malkin thought, Eichmann was already preparing his defense.

Night after night, they talked. Eichmann would speak in a cloyingly innocent tone, as if he was aiming to please. He would service his ego by boasting about his prominent position in the SS, yet at the same time he would claim that he had not been the one responsible for the decisions that had been made. Malkin was sickened by his denials and his inability to view his actions against the Jews through anything other than the prism of a Nazi mindset—even after fifteen years. His complete lack of empathy for his victims was jarring, even as he claimed to "love" the Jews.

24

ON A CLEAR, BRIGHT Tel Aviv afternoon, May 18, the Israeli delegation for the Argentine anniversary celebrations boarded the Bristol Britannia 4X-AGD at Lod Airport. Photographers snapped pictures as the delegates climbed the mobile staircase into the long, sleek plane with the Israeli flag painted on its tail. At the top of the steps, Abba Eban, the head of the delegation, smiled for the cameras and waved goodbye to the dignitaries who had come to see them off.

Tall and distinguished, Eban had only recently been elected to the Knesset after serving for a number of years as the Israeli ambassador to the United States, as well as at the United Nations. Forty-five years old, he was a rising star in Israeli politics and had helped David Ben-Gurion win reelection the year before. Though a member of Ben-Gurion's cabinet, Eban was a "minister without portfolio"—that is, not in charge of any department—which made him ideal to serve as the Israeli emissary on this occasion. Ben-Gurion had personally informed Eban several days before that the flight was being sent to Argentina to collect Eichmann.

So when Eban boarded the plane, he was already tense. With him in the delegation were General Meir Zorea, chief of the Israel Defense Forces' Northern Command, and a number of Foreign Ministry officials and their families. None of the others had the slightest idea of the flight's special purpose, although Zorea would no doubt have approved. After World War II, he had been a member of an avenger group that had hunted down and killed Nazis. All of the passengers were scheduled to return to Israel on American civilian airlines—ostensibly because the Britannia was needed back earlier for its regular routes.

However, every effort at secrecy could not keep the crew members from suspecting that there might be more to this flight than El Al had told them. First, there were three men in El Al uniforms whom none of them had seen before. They sat together and made no effort to do any work (though they were listed on the crew manifest as a navigator, flight engineer, and flight attendant). Second, only a limited number of El Al employees participated in "monkey business crews." When enough of them were brought together for a flight, it usually meant there was a hidden agenda. After checking the crew roster, Captain Shmuel Wedeles, one of two copilots selected by Tohar for the mission, was sure there was an ulterior motive. A Viennese Jew who, as a child, had seen a mob force an elderly rabbi to eat pork before setting his beard on fire, Wedeles had escaped alone to Israel; the rest of his family had died in the Holocaust. He had been a Haganah fighter and a pilot in the War of Independence. As soon as he saw Yehuda Shimoni on the plane, he asked him bluntly, "Who are they bringing, Mengele or Eichmann?" Shimoni denied the implication, but his look of astonishment told Wedeles everything he needed to know.

The chief purser was also suspicious. When he asked his friend Tohar what was going on, the pilot cryptically said, "You won't be sorry you've been chosen to participate in the flight."

Once all the passengers had settled into their places and the crew was ready, loudspeakers in the terminal building and outside on the tarmac boomed in Hebrew and then English, "Announcing the departure of Flight 601, Tel Aviv to Buenos Aires." The four turbo-propelled engines hummed to life, and the Britannia, nicknamed "the Whispering Giant," taxied toward the runway. At exactly 1:05 P.M., the wheels lifted off Israeli soil, and the journey to Argentina began.

The passengers first had a short jaunt to Rome, then a nine-and-a-half-hour flight to Dakar, where they would pick up a second El Al crew. After a brief layover, they would travel for six hours across the Atlantic to Recife, where they would refuel a final time before flying seven and a half hours south to Buenos Aires, scheduled to arrive there on the afternoon of May 19.

There was nothing especially difficult about the flight, except that the cockpit crew had never flown to South America before. The chief navigator, Shaul Shaul, had to purchase navigational charts for South America in New York because El Al did not have any in its possession. This was new territory for everyone involved.

May 20 was the target date for smuggling Eichmann onto a plane and out of the country. This gave Harel only two more days to find Josef Mengele. Hilel Pooch had visited the post office in Vicente López but had discovered that Mengele had not left a forwarding address. Further inquiries around the neighborhood elicited no new information. Either people were protecting him or he had covered his tracks well.

The boarding house address was not the only piece of intelligence in Harel's notebook. He also knew that Mengele's alias several years before had been Gregor Helmut and that he had owned a mechanical equipment shop close to where he was supposed to live. Although the Mossad chief was still insistent on finding Mengele, the hesitancy of both Eitan and Shalom to divert their focus from Eichmann had made an impression on him, and he decided not to involve his team in the search.

So Harel provided Pooch with a new cover story: he was looking to purchase a large order of special screws that he had heard were made by Helmut's shop. When the young Israeli arrived at the shop and told the secretary that he wanted to speak to the owner, Gregor Helmut, about an order, she turned skittish and retreated to a side room. Pooch heard some urgent whispering, then the secretary returned. She eyed him for a long while, then crisply said there was nobody at the shop named Gregor and they were unable to help him.

When Pooch reported back to Harel, the chief felt that they were on the right track but they needed to be more aggressive. More agents were required to survey the shop and, potentially, to search the boarding house to see if Mengele had truly left.

Later that day, it became clear that clandestine behavior had become much more difficult in the city, whether to transport Eichmann to the airport, to sneak him onto the plane, or to launch an operation to seize Mengele should he be located. With international delegations arriving, security was tight. All of the major roads and those leading between the airport and the capital were awash with police patrols. Shalom had found it all but impossible to map a route to the airport that circumvented police checkpoints.

Radio reports indicated that security was going to get even tighter. Bombs, likely set by Peronist terrorist groups, had exploded at the state-run telephone company and gas office, damaging both significantly. The government was calling for a lockdown and launching a manhunt for the culprits—a move that put Tira in even more jeopardy than before.

That night, Nick and Dieter broke through the front door of a Jewish synagogue in the city, brandishing their guns. A former SS officer whom they knew through their father had tipped them off that Eichmann might be in the synagogue's basement. Their search revealed nothing. The synagogue was empty, and they left without a confrontation.

Throughout Buenos Aires, Tacuara members were out patrolling on their motorcycles, watching the airport as well as the bus and train stations. They also staked out synagogues and checked the hospitals and morgues in every neighborhood. The heavy police presence did little to slow their search.

Nick and Dieter had no idea whether their father was still alive. For all they knew, he might have been taken outside the city and shot, his body buried. His assailants might well be long gone by now. With each passing day, the two brothers grew more and more desperate.

Some of the young firebrands who were helping them were convinced that they needed to make a bold gambit if they had any chance of finding Eichmann. They were certain the Israelis were behind the abduction, and they suggested kidnapping the Israeli ambassador Levavi, offering him in trade. If the Israelis balked, they would torture the ambassador until Eichmann was returned.

This plan was too rash for Nick and Dieter. A former SS officer helping them warned, "Don't do anything stupid. Stay reasonable. Or you will lose everything, absolutely everything." They decided to rely on searching alone.

"Let me ask you this," Malkin said to Eichmann in the early-morning hours of May 19. "When it was determined that the policy was not to be resettlement but death, how did you feel about that?"

"There was nothing to be done. The order came down from the Führer himself."

"But how did you feel?"

"There was nothing to be done."

"I see. So you turned into a killer."

"No. That's not true. I never killed anyone," Eichmann insisted, explaining that he had tried to avoid spending much time at the extermination camps — and besides, they had not been under his direct control. "I was involved in collection and transport," he explained.

Malkin did not understand how Eichmann could be convinced that his actions had been moral and proper, that he had done nothing wrong. The order had come from his superiors; he had obeyed them. Duty had demanded it.

Eichmann went on to explain how diligent he had been in making his schedules. Malkin interjected, "You do realize we are talking about innocent people here? Small children? Old men and women?"

Eichmann was unfazed by this statement, and Malkin realized that he was completely immune to any regret for his actions. In the end, Malkin was more affected by the discussions than Eichmann. He had never thought it possible for someone to be so emotionally crippled and impervious to feeling. He returned to his drawings, unnerved and saddened. Although sometimes he felt an urge to strike Eichmann because of his lack of pity, he also felt incredibly sorry for him.

Later that evening, during his watch, they picked up the conversation again. Eichmann spoke of his love for red wine, and Malkin considered it harmless to give him a glass. For eight nights straight, he had been bound to the bed. At least he could feel human again for a moment, Malkin thought.

A few minutes later, he returned to the cell with a bottle of wine and a record player that belonged to Medad. Malkin poured the wine and guided the glass into the prisoner's hands.

"I do like wine so very much," Eichmann said after draining the glass.

Malkin drank his more slowly. He placed a record on the player and then lit a cigarette for Eichmann. Flamenco music filled the small, stuffy room.

The prisoner sucked deeply on the cigarette until it was almost at its butt.

"Don't burn your fingers," Malkin advised him.

"Why are you doing this for me?" Eichmann asked, more at ease than he had been since his arrival at the house.

"I don't know. But I don't hate you," Malkin replied, realizing that they had built a strange kind of relationship over the past eight days. "I just felt it was something I wanted to do for you."

Eichmann was silent.

Malkin remembered the statement that Aharoni had been trying to get Eichmann to sign over the past week. This might be their opportunity. "Eichmann, I think you are mistaken about not signing the papers to go to Jerusalem," he said.

"I don't want to go. Why can't I go to Germany?"

"I'm not going to force you to do it. If I were you though, I would sign the papers, and I will tell you why. It's the only time in your life that you will have the opportunity to say what you think. And you will stand there in Jerusalem and tell the whole world what you think was right, in your own words."

Eichmann finished his second glass of wine, obviously mulling over the idea. Then he asked to be allowed to stand and to remove his goggles. Malkin obliged, knowing that Eichmann had already seen his face on the night of the capture. Still, he kept careful watch. This might be a trick, an attempt to escape.

At last Eichmann said, "Where is the paper?"

Aharoni had prepared a draft statement for Eichmann to copy, saying that he was going of his own free will to stand trial in Israel. Malkin passed him the paper, along with a pen. Eichmann read the draft, then leaning on the night table, he wrote his statement in neat German.

I, the undersigned, Adolf Eichmann, declare of my own free will that, since my true identity has been discovered, I realize that it is futile for me to attempt to go on evading justice. I state that I am prepared to travel to Israel to stand trial in that country before a competent court. I understand that I shall receive legal aid, and I shall endeavor to give a straightforward account of the facts of my last years of service in Germany so that a true picture of the facts may be passed on to future generations. I make this declaration of my own free will. I have been promised nothing, nor have any threats been made against me. I wish at last to achieve inner peace. As I am unable to remember all the details and am confused about certain facts, I ask to be granted assistance in my endeavors to establish the truth by being given access to documents and evidence.

Once finished, he turned to Malkin and asked, "What date should I put, yesterday's or today's?"

"Just leave it May 1960."

He nodded and signed the paper "Adolf Eichmann, Buenos Aires, May 1960."

"You have done a very good thing. You won't regret it," Malkin said, allowing him another cigarette before refastening the goggles over his eyes.

Suddenly, they heard footsteps charging down the hall, and Medad burst into the room in his gray pajamas. "What the hell are you doing?" he yelled, looking at the wine and cigarettes. "Throwing a party for this murderer?"

Malkin attempted to justify himself, but the Czech-born Medad was livid, his face flushed. "You amuse *him* with my music? This butcher of my family?"

Hearing the shouting, Eitan, Gat, and Nesiahu all rushed to the room. Malkin tried to explain, showing them the signed statement, but they were preoccupied with calming down Medad, then berating Malkin for disobeying orders and speaking to the prisoner.

Eventually, everyone settled down, and Tabor relieved Malkin of his watch. As Malkin retreated down the hall, Eitan stopped him long enough to say, "Good work."

Captain Shmuel Wedeles was at the controls. At 6:25 A.M. on May 19, en route from Dakar to Recife, he pointed the Britannia down through the clouds over the South Atlantic, and they crossed over the Brazilian coast. They were on track with their flight plan.

Fifteen minutes later, they reached the radio beacon of Campina Grande, eighty nautical miles from Recife, the altimeters indicating they were now at 10,000 feet. Wedeles shifted onto a course heading southeast toward the airport. Then he contacted air traffic control.

"Recife Control, this is El Al 4X-AGD from Dakar to Recife, heading 135, altitude 7,500, descending, estimating Recife on the hour."

"Roger, El Al," the controller radioed in return. "Maintain course. Report when reaching 2,000."

At an altitude of 4,000 feet, the forecast cloud base, the Britannia had yet to descend out of the clouds. In another few minutes, they would be at the airport. Forty nautical miles away, they reached 2,000 feet. Wedeles prepared to contact air traffic control to inform them of their position when the plane finally cleared the clouds. Suddenly, he saw an expanse of green straight ahead. The plane was heading into a hilltop forest. Wedeles immediately pulled back on the stick, bringing the nose of the plane up. Simultaneously, he pushed the engine throttles forward, increasing the speed of the plane to prevent the aircraft from stalling. The plane leveled off, just above the treetops. Everyone in the flight cabin stared out the window as they flew less than a wingspan over the forest.

"My God, the Brazilians think and talk meters, not feet," a member of the cockpit crew exclaimed as Wedeles continued to fly level with the treetops. The Israelis measured altitude in feet, as was the rule in Europe, the United States, the Middle East, and Africa. If the cloud base had been a hundred feet lower, they would not have made it.

Ten minutes later, at 7:05 A.M. on May 19, the Britannia landed safely in Recife. The Israelis' troubles were only beginning.

Tohar wanted to depart as soon as they had refueled and cleaned the plane, an hour at most. To their surprise, when they taxied toward the terminal building, they found a red-carpet reception, including a local band and hundreds of onlookers, waiting for them. Representatives of the local Jewish community cheered their arrival. The airport commander, who was outfitted in a stiffly starched uniform bedecked with medals, welcomed their "overseas strangers to beautiful Brazil."

After the awkwardly staged reception, the crew and delegation disembarked to stretch their legs and grab a coffee in the airport terminal. A few of them bought souvenirs and fruit from the vendors who lined the airfield's perimeter fence. Half an hour later, when Shaul and his fellow navigator, Gady Hassin, attempted to enter the airport control tower to file their flight plan and collect meteorological reports for the journey to Buenos Aires, they were blocked by a soldier who angrily waved them back, barking, "No passage!" The soldier was undaunted by Shaul's imposing presence—six feet five inches tall, and with piercing, humorless eyes—likely because he was the one armed with a carbine. Hassin went to fetch Tohar, but even the captain's presence achieved nothing. The soldier was clear: "The commandant is asleep. Nobody is to disturb him."

Tohar feared that the real reason for their flight had been exposed. To avoid attracting undue attention Tohar backed off.

As the standoff continued, a waiter from the terminal's cafeteria approached. He was in his late twenties and, most likely, a Mossad operative stationed at the airport in case such a situation arose. He spoke briefly with the guard in fluent Portuguese, then told Tohar, "Have patience. I will go into town, and, with any luck, I'll be back within a half hour with a solution." He pedaled away on his bicycle.

Half an hour later, an elderly man, who was the secretary of the local Jewish community center, entered the airport terminal carrying a leather bag. He approached the soldier and said that he had a message for the commandant. The soldier disappeared with the bag, and the commandant himself appeared a few minutes later. In a bravura performance, he slapped the guard twice in the face, delivering a withering curse, then looked straight at Tohar.

"Captain," he said, "why didn't you tell me that you wanted to talk?"

The bribe paid, the Israelis filed their flight plan. Three hours and twenty-five minutes after landing in Recife, the Britannia moved down the runway and lifted gracefully into the sky.

On the way to the airport to await the arrival of the El Al plane, Shalom and Aharoni saw that the whole of Buenos Aires was bustling in anticipation of the anniversary celebrations. Flags flew from every window, people filled the streets and cafés, and tango music played in the public squares. Soldiers and police were stationed everywhere as well, stopping cars and checking documents. The two Shin Bet agents knew that bringing Eichmann to the airport under these conditions was a huge risk. In case they were searched, their prisoner would need to be incapacitated, and his papers would have to be in perfect order.

After being delayed by a traffic accident, they reached Ezeiza Airport. They spotted Isser Harel and Yosef Klein among the crowd of people who had come out to see the first Israeli plane land in Argentina. A host of diplomats from the Argentine Foreign Ministry were on hand, along with a military band and a ground crew ready to roll out the red carpet. This sort of welcome was standard for arriving international delegations. Also in the crowd were many Israeli embassy staff members and scores of people from the local Jewish community, including more than one hundred children holding small Israeli flags. All were eager for the Britannia to land.

But the plane was late. Two hours passed. Klein ran about the airport, anxious to find out what was wrong. He learned that there had been some trouble with the plane receiving clearance to take off in Recife, even though all the clearances had been arranged well in advance. Harel shared Klein's nervousness, but there was nothing either of them could do but wait and hope.

At last, at 4:05 P.M., three hours later than scheduled, the Britannia descended from the sky and touched down onto the runway with a screech. The waiting band struck up the Israeli national anthem, "Ha-

Tikvah" ("The Hope"). Klein followed the plane's approach toward the terminal.

Eban emerged from the plane to the fervent waving of Israeli flags. He greeted the Argentines and, to the surprise of everyone, delivered a short speech in perfect Spanish. Eban betrayed no sign that his presence was anything other than a diplomatic gesture of goodwill. Standing on the tarmac in front of the plane, Luba Volk enjoyed the moment, proud that her arrangements for the reception had gone smoothly. Then she noticed several men in El Al uniforms whom she did not recognize descend from the plane. As Yehuda Shimoni followed them off the plane, she approached him. After a short greeting, she asked pointedly, "Who are those people?"

"Best regards to you from General Ben Arzi," Shimoni said, taken aback by her question and avoiding it altogether by bringing up her former boss, the head of El Al. "He asked me to remind you that he's still very much interested in you accepting his offer to return full time."

Instead of responding to his comment, Volk said, "I had an unpleasant surprise from the Aviation Ministry. I wanted to take a stretcher case, but they refused."

"You did *what?*" Shimoni said, shocked.

"What's the matter with that? It is within my authority as the representative here."

"I don't know . . . This is very bad. Okay, it doesn't matter. You're not involved in what happens from here on in," he said strangely. Seeing her look of bewilderment, he added, "I feel very badly about not being able to tell you what this flight is all about."

A stewardess from the flight appeared, wanting to speak with Volk. Her conversation with Shimoni ended abruptly, before she could ask him what on earth he was talking about. Distracted by her own conjectures, including one that involved someone using the plane to take Josef Mengele out of Argentina, Volk tried to concentrate on greeting the rest of the crew as they filed into the airport terminal.

Captain Tohar then debriefed his crew, telling them to enjoy their sightseeing in Buenos Aires but to be back at their hotel by early evening the next day to prepare for departure. Nobody was to be late. Arye Friedman and Mordechai Avivi, the plane's mechanics, thought that they, too, would be able to enjoy Buenos Aires, but Adi Peleg informed them that they were to stay with the airplane overnight in Aerolineas Argentinas's maintenance area. Peleg explained that they needed to maintain a careful watch because some "hostile agencies" might want to sabotage the Britannia.

Shalom and Aharoni watched all this take place without making their presence known to any of the arriving passengers or crew. They were at the airport to reconnoiter the route to the airport one more time and to ensure that the plane was positioned correctly for the next day. Once this was done, they left for Maoz for a final meeting about the escape operation.

In a café near the airport's Hotel Internacional, shortly after the plane's arrival, Harel sat down with Tohar and Shimoni. Both men looked exhausted. The captain kept their close call before landing in Recife to himself. Instead, he made it very clear that he was ready to do whatever Harel asked of him or his crew — with one stipulation: he categorically refused to land the plane in Brazil again. The Brazilians were untrustworthy. That was fine with Harel, since he wanted to fly straight from Buenos Aires to Dakar anyway, to avoid any opportunity for the Britannia to be stopped in South America.

With that settled, Harel outlined the plan, which was to get Eichmann onto the plane disguised in an El Al uniform. He would need the crew to go through security with their captive. Tohar and Shimoni thought this was a better idea than smuggling him through in a food cart or diplomatic crate. Shimoni told Harel about the stretcher case that Luba Volk had requested and his fear that this might have raised suspicions, but the Mossad chief discounted that and instructed Shimoni just to make sure that there were no unwanted passengers on the flight. Their only point of disagreement was the departure time. Harel wanted to leave as early as possible the next day, but Tohar argued that the crew needed more rest, given the long flight to Dakar and then Tel Aviv. They were testing the Britannia's limits as it was.

The added burden of a tired crew was tempting disaster. Harel acquiesced. They would leave close to midnight on May 20.

Tohar went straight from the café to the Hotel Internacional to meet with his crew before they headed into the city. He gathered the other two pilots, Wedeles and Azriel Ronen; the navigators, Shaul and Hassin; and the flight engineers, Shimon Blanc, a survivor of the Dachau concentration camp, and Oved Kabiri, together in his suite. This was the team responsible for getting the Britannia safely back to Israel. Tohar thought they deserved to know the purpose of their mission. Except for Wedeles, everyone was astonished by Tohar's explanation, although not everyone in the room knew who Eichmann was. Then he told them that they were going to fly nonstop from Buenos Aires to Dakar and asked his navigators to chart a route and his flight engineers to ensure that the Britannia was capable of the effort. He made it clear that if the reason for their flight was discovered, they might have to take evasive action.

Sobered and fully briefed as to what they had to do, the crew disbanded.

On the other side of town, at the safe house Maoz, Harel joined part of the team. Malkin, Tabor, and Medad remained at Tira to guard Eichmann. For once, Harel did not make a grand speech about the historical importance of their mission. He was all business: schedules, documentation, disguises, routes, cars, backup plans, the Mengele search, cleanup, escape plans for those not taking the flight.

Eitan left early to check on Tira, and the meeting broke up around midnight. Sleep was not on the agenda for any of them.

In the dark hours of their last night at Tira, Rafi Eitan thought he heard someone moving outside. He ran through the house, alerting the other team members. Tabor hurried to Eichmann's cell and prepared to bundle the prisoner into the hiding space above the room, while others peered out the windows, looking for any movement. One agent searched the front of the house, another the back. It was a false alarm.

Everyone settled back down, though the mood was still anxious, everyone desperate to be free of their prisoner and back in Israel. No one had a chance to rest; they were all busy either with guard duty, returning the house to its original condition, going over their new identities and documents, or cleaning up — collecting any items (binoculars, tools, passports, clothes, maps, and so on) that needed to be thrown out or destroyed before they left. Throughout the night, Eichmann sat on the edge of his bed, obviously aware that something was about to happen.

As dawn approached, the team faced the final stage of its mission. Then it would be time for the members to make their escapes.

25

ON THE COLD, WINTRY morning of the escape flight, tensions at Tira were sharper than at any other time during the mission. Even as they were preparing for their departure, the team members knew that many things could go wrong once they left the safe house.

Although there had not been any mention of Eichmann in the newspapers or on the radio, the police or security services might have kept deliberately silent about a search, and it was doubtful that the expatriate Nazi community would announce that it was on a manhunt itself. Beyond the danger of discovery by either of these forces, the team also ran the risk of being stopped by a random patrol, giving Eichmann a chance to indicate that he was being held against his will—even though Dr. Kaplan would have him sedated for the drive to the airport. The sedation itself was a challenge, despite Kaplan's experience as an anesthesiologist. The team also faced the possibility of an accident on Buenos Aires's chaotic roads, or the guards at the airport might prove to be more diligent than usual. And, of course, there were the dangers surrounding the flight.

By early afternoon, the team had finished most of its preparations and had nothing to do but wait—more time to contemplate what might lie ahead. The safe house was all in order. Malkin had done a test run with his disguise for Eichmann, who once again was afraid that they were getting ready to kill him. The doctor had put him on a strict diet in order to reduce the risk of complications resulting from the sedatives. Everyone had shed his or her old identity for a new one, and Eitan had reviewed the plan for getting Eichmann to the airport that evening.

Outside Tira, the other operatives were busy with their own responsibilities. Aharoni removed any traces of his presence at the safe house where he had been staying. Then he donned a suit and tie, looking every inch the chauffeur, and flagged a taxi to the Israeli embassy. There Yossef provided him with a new Chevrolet limousine with diplomatic plates in which to bring Eichmann to the airport. He also gave him a new diplomatic passport that identified him as a member at the South American desk of the Israeli Foreign Ministry, and an international driver's license. His days as a German businessman were over. Aharoni left the embassy in the limousine and went to have it thoroughly inspected at a garage. They needed to be extra careful.

At Maoz, Shalom Dani rushed to finish the last of Eichmann's documents. He even had an official medical certificate from a local hospital stating that he had suffered head trauma in an accident but that he was now cleared to fly. Harel had earlier arranged for a *sayan* to fake the injury, check in at the hospital, and obtain an authentic release form. Dani easily changed the volunteer's name to Zichroni, Eichmann's alias. Now he was finalizing Zichroni's passport.

Tabor spent most of the day at the airport. After inspecting the Britannia with the two mechanics, he set about preparing a secret compartment to hide Eichmann in case the plane was searched. He built a hinged false wall in front of one of the lavatories in the first-class cabin. When Tabor was finished, no one would have suspected that there was a bathroom in that part of the plane.

Avraham Shalom also was spending a fair amount of time at the airport, ensuring that the guards whom he had befriended over the past week had not been shifted to different posts and that they knew he would be coming in and out of the gate throughout the day. He reconnoitered the roads from Tira yet again, finding no new checkpoints along the routes he had chosen. Still, there were scores of security men in the city and around the airport; Shalom was nervous about the drive with Eichmann.

He shared his concerns with Harel, who had stationed himself at a restaurant in the airport terminal to coordinate the day's activities. Although some police and soldiers took their meals in the large hall, the restaurant was always crowded, the conversation and clanking dishes were deafening, and people were constantly milling in and out of its doors. Harel could stay there for hours, meeting all his operatives for their briefings, without anybody giving him so much as a second glance. Given the plane's scheduled departure at midnight, he was ready for a long day.

Harel listened to Shalom with understanding. More than any other member of his team, Shalom constantly replayed the scenarios of everything that could go wrong and the backup plans that were in place in the event that something did. These scenarios had kept him awake most nights over the past few weeks.

Even in these anxious hours before smuggling Eichmann out of the country, with so much on the line, Harel still held out hope of capturing Mengele as well. The newly arrived Mossad men were expecting his call ordering a commando operation the moment the Auschwitz doctor was found.

It was not to be, however. Harel had sent Meir Lavi, the *sayan* who had met with him on the night of Eichmann's capture and to whom he had given the message about the typewriter, to attempt to gain entry to the boarding house in Vicente López. Lavi, who pretended to have a package to deliver, failed in his attempt, but he did manage to reach the tenant on the phone. She did not speak Spanish, and when they switched to English, her accent revealed her to be American, not German.

Hilel Pooch went to the house a few hours later, wearing overalls and a tool belt. He told the woman that he had been called to fix the water heater. Pooch identified her as an American as well and noted that she acted perfectly at ease, openly offering her name. Although she refused him entry to the house because she had not been informed about any repair call, it was obvious that she was neither German nor hiding anything. Mengele was gone.

Lavi and Pooch delivered their reports to Harel in the early evening. Harel was very disheartened. He had prayed for a lucky break, but time had run out on them. The hunt for Mengele would have to wait for another day. At 7:30 P.M., Shalom and Aharoni arrived in the smoky, cacophonous restaurant and informed him that the team was ready for the transfer to the airport. Having received confirmation from Klein that the plane and the El Al crew also were ready, Harel gave his operatives the go-ahead.

Back at Tira, the team prepared for their departure. Those traveling to the airport dressed in El Al uniforms and packed the last of their belongings. After the doctor gave Eichmann a thorough physical examination, Malkin went into his cell to apply his disguise.

Earlier in the evening, Eichmann had become highly agitated when Aharoni had informed him that they were taking him to Israel that night, cautioning him not to resist. But now he seemed relaxed, resigned. Malkin dyed Eichmann's hair gray and applied makeup to his face, aging him further by drawing lines on his forehead and around his mouth and shadowing the skin underneath his eyes. He glued a shaggy mustache onto Eichmann's top lip. Then he dressed Eichmann in a crisp white shirt, blue pants, polished shoes, and an El Al cap with a blue Star of David on the front.

Soon after Malkin had finished, Aharoni arrived with Yoel Goren, one of the Mossad operatives who had come on the El Al flight. Goren was the one who, more than two years before, had investigated the house in Olivos and discounted the possibility that Eichmann could possibly live in such a ramshackle place. Despite his false assessment, Goren was an obvious choice to aid in this last chapter of the mission because of his fluent Spanish and knowledge of Buenos Aires.

The men led the prisoner down into the kitchen and sat him in a chair. On the table was a needle and a tube. Dr. Kaplan entered the kitchen, glad to be of use after ten days of idleness. He rolled up Eichmann's right sleeve and then soaked a cloth with alcohol. As he moved to press the cloth against Eichmann's arm, the prisoner recoiled.

"It isn't necessary to give me an injection," he said. "I won't utter a sound . . . I promise."

"Don't worry," the doctor said. "It's nothing, just something to control your excitement."

Aharoni added, "You have a very long journey ahead of you. The medication will help you to overcome all the strain."

The doctor moved to inject the needle into Eichmann's arm.

"No, no . . . I'm not excited at all," Eichmann insisted.

"Please," Malkin said. "We have to do this. We have orders."

Eichmann capitulated and laid his arm in his lap. The doctor inserted the needle into a vein and attached the tube to the needle. Then he administered a dose of sedative. Eichmann soon faded, mumbling, "No, no. I don't need it."

"We're ready to travel," the doctor said, his finger on Eichmann's pulse.

At 9:00 P.M., Yaakov Gat and Rafi Eitan grabbed Eichmann under the arms and brought him into the garage. He was conscious but barely able to speak. He looked drowsily at the others, all in their El Al uniforms, and said, "I don't look right. I have to put on a jacket." They had not dressed him in one because it would restrict access to his arm, but they were encouraged that Eichmann actually seemed to be trying to assist.

Gat jumped into the limousine's back seat and drew Eichmann down beside him. The doctor also sat in the back, ready to inject his patient with more sedative if the situation warranted it.

"Don't worry," Eichmann mumbled again, understanding more than his listless eyes revealed. "You can rely on me. I won't need any more injections."

Aharoni started the engine, and Yoel Goren slid into the passenger's seat. Malkin opened the gate for them—he and Nesiahu were staying behind at Tira in case there was a problem and the rest of the team needed to return to the house. Eitan and Tabor were to follow in another car. The limousine turned out of the driveway and into the night.

Meanwhile, Captain Wedeles gathered the El Al crew members who had yet to be informed of the reason for the flight in a secluded corner of the Hotel Internacional lobby. The seven individuals included the radio operators, pursers, and stewardesses. All of them had spent the past twenty-four hours having a splendid time in Buenos Aires, dining on huge Argentine steaks, touring the city, and shopping. They were unsettled to see how serious Wedeles looked and were curious as to why Yosef Klein and Adi Peleg were standing beside him.

"We're advancing the return departure," Wedeles said. "Please be downstairs in an hour. No shopping. No nothing. After that, you're to stick with me. If I get up, you get up with me. If I sit down, you sit down—because I want you all around me at all times."

"You're participating in a great event," Peleg said, stepping forward to explain. "Don't ask me what it is, but we're taking a very important person back with us to Israel. I will tell you his identity later on."

"We'll be boarding the plane in three cars at the maintenance area," Wedeles continued. "In one of the cars will be that man."

The crew members were not terribly surprised by the meeting, as most of them had sensed all along that there was something unusual about the flight. They all made sure they were packed and ready on time. Before they left, Luba Volk arrived at the Internacional.

Klein approached her in the lobby. "Are you going to the airport?"

"Of course," Volk said. Although she now knew there was much more going on with this flight than met the eye, she still planned to see her friends off.

"Please, please, do me a favor. Don't go to the airport," Klein said softly. "It's dangerous, and unfortunately I can't talk about it . . . but don't go to the airport. Just forget it. Remember that you have a young boy."

Volk saw that Klein almost had tears in his eyes, and she promised not to go. She bid him and the others goodbye and returned home, knowing well that it was her name that appeared on the stream of papers filed with the Aviation Ministry for the flight.

The crew climbed aboard the minibus that was idling outside the hotel entrance and waited. Nobody asked any questions. Klein had already left, on his own, to check that everything was ready for the flight.

At the airport, in the Argentine national airline's maintenance area, Avraham Shalom looked at his watch. It was a few minutes past ten. Captain Zvi Tohar, several of his flight crew, and the two mechanics had spent the past two hours checking the plane. Tohar reported that everything was in perfect order. Shalom then went to survey the entrances to the airfield, to make sure there was no special security on duty nor anybody suspicious lurking around. Finding no cause for concern, he went to the terminal, where he informed Harel of as much. Then he made his way to the airport parking lot to await Eichmann's arrival.

In the aeronautical services office in the control tower, the navigators Shaul Shaul and Gady Hassin pored over the most recent meteorological data between Buenos Aires and Dakar, studying the high-altitude forecast charts for wind distributions, temperatures, and areas of expected turbulence. A direct path between two points was rarely the most efficient way to fly. Any tailwinds they found or headwinds they avoided might prove to be the difference between success and failure, particularly given how far they were pushing the Britannia's maximum range with their long nonstop flight, the likes of which had never been attempted with this plane.

Once they had finalized their route, they checked carefully through the NOTAMS (notices to airmen) for forbidden flying zones, restricted altitudes, and expected military air exercises along their path. Then they filled out their flight plan for air traffic control—a plan that did not resemble in the least the one they had just mapped out. As far as air traffic control was concerned, they were planning on traveling to Recife, then on to Dakar—just as on their incoming flight. Anything else would cause unwelcome questions to be asked. Although they had scheduled their departure time for 2:00 A.M. on May 21, Tohar wanted the landing wheels up by midnight, throwing off anyone who planned to interfere with the flight.

Aharoni drove conservatively on a circuitous route to the airport, avoiding the checkpoints on the major roads. Eichmann was quiet in the back—almost too quiet for Aharoni and Gat. They feared that he might be acting drowsier than he actually was to prevent the doctor from administering any more sedative; then, at an opportune moment, perhaps while boarding the plane, he might scream out for help and ruin everything.

Apart from keeping an eye on the escort car behind them and watching out for random patrols, there was not much else to think about for the hour-and-a-half drive. They were forced to stop at one railway crossing, but otherwise the journey was uneventful. The cars managed to avoid every checkpoint until they reached the airport's main entrance, where they were waved through because of their diplomatic plates.

At a preappointed spot in the parking lot, they met Peleg and the minibus carrying the crew. Shalom also was there. It was almost 11:00 P.M. Someone ran to alert Harel, and he came striding out into the lot. He looked into the limousine. Eichmann appeared to be asleep, but Dr. Kaplan assured Harel that he was able to see and hear, though not alert enough to know what was going on around him. More important, he was unable to offer any resistance. Gat was still not reassured but kept his fears to himself. Harel gave the order to move out to the maintenance area where the plane was parked.

Peleg took over the escort car that Eitan had driven to the airport. Shalom sat by his side in the passenger's seat. Both of them had gone in and out of the airport often enough to know the guards by their first names. They would lead the convoy through the gates into the maintenance area. Behind them was the limousine, driven by Aharoni, and last was the minibus with the plane's crew.

The line of vehicles drove back out through the main entrance and onto the highway for several hundred yards before making a right turn. This took them along the fence surrounding the airport until they reached another gate. Harel had wanted them all to act slightly drunk and raucous, thereby explaining why one of their crew was passed out in the back seat, but Shalom had decided to dismiss that suggestion. He knew the guards well enough, and any untoward behavior might raise suspicions.

When they stopped at the gate, an armed sentry approached the first car, where he recognized Peleg and Shalom. He raised the barrier and waved them forward, pleasantly shouting, "Hi, Israel!" The lim-

ousine and minibus slowed down long enough to give the guard a
glimpse inside to check that everyone was wearing an El Al uniform.
They drove into the airport, keeping away from the lighted hangars,
and made their way to the national airline's area.

"Be absolutely silent," Gat warned Eichmann as they neared the
Britannia. "We're about to go onto the plane."

The prisoner did not even register the warning. The limousine
stopped at the bottom of the steps, where Tohar was waiting for them.
Spotting a policeman walking toward the convoy, Eitan jumped out
of the back of the escort car.

"Do something with the policeman," Eitan whispered urgently to
the captain.

Tohar hurried toward the official and steered him to the back of
the plane, where he wouldn't be able to see the steps.

When the way was clear, Gat lifted Eichmann out of the limousine. His legs had almost no strength, so Yoel Goren supported him
from the other side. The El Al crew filed out of the minibus.

"Form a circle around us and follow us up the steps," Eitan ordered.

Wedeles was right behind Eichmann as Gat and Goren brought
him up the steps. The prisoner's feet dangled limply, hitting each step
as the men climbed up. An airport searchlight panned across the
gangway. Wedeles put his hand on the small of Eichmann's back to
help push him upward. Everyone was crowded closely around, making Eichmann all but indistinguishable in the mass of El Al uniforms.
Then they were all on board the plane. On the tarmac, Aharoni took
a few deep breaths in relief, and Yosef Klein reassured himself that
their part in the mission was almost complete.

Inside, Gat and Goren brought Eichmann to the back of the plane
and sat him in a window seat in the first-class cabin. Gat took the seat
across the aisle, and the doctor sat directly behind just in case. Of the
five remaining first-class seats, Goren took one, and the others were
filled with El Al crew members. A stewardess sat next to Eichmann
and covered him with a blanket. She still did not know who he was
and speculated that he might be some kind of scientist.

"Pretend to sleep," Gat instructed them all.

A purser dimmed the overhead lights and drew a curtain across the entrance to the cabin. If customs or the police boarded the plane before takeoff, they were to be told that the relief crew was getting some rest. Eichmann remained oblivious to what was happening around him.

At 11:15 P.M., the Britannia's doors were closed, and Tohar fired the engines. Then the plane taxied to the terminal.

As the Britannia neared the apron in front of the terminal building, Isser Harel felt the reverberations from its engines against the window. They had Eichmann on board. Once the crew passed through customs and the Mossad operatives who were returning on the flight had boarded, they would be set to take off. That moment could not come soon enough for Harel. He constantly expected the police or a band of former Nazis to rush into the airport demanding that the flight be stopped.

Harel left his table in the restaurant and met with Klein, who assured him that everything was ready. Harel then hurried outside the terminal, where Eitan and Shalom had just arrived by car from the hangar. They reported that the transfer of Eichmann onto the plane had gone flawlessly. Eitan and Shalom were staying behind with Malkin to return the cars and remove the last traces of their presence before decamping from Argentina themselves. They shook hands, wishing each other luck on their respective journeys.

Harel headed back into the passenger lounge, where he was joined by Aharoni, Tabor, and the two Mossad agents who had come on the El Al flight. Medad entered the lounge last, his car having broken down on the way to the airport. The agents had piles of luggage to take back to Israel.

Klein approached Harel. "You surprise me with this crowd!"

"They're all my people. Don't worry," Harel reassured him, although even he thought they had overdone it in terms of numbers.

Still concerned, Klein walked away. At 11:30 P.M., he received word that the plane was ready for takeoff. Porters had loaded the luggage onto the plane, but the customs and passport control officers had yet to appear to allow Harel and his entourage, as well as a few El Al crew members who were also waiting, to board the plane. Since there were no other flights leaving at that late hour, it was not likely that the officials were busy elsewhere.

Minute after minute passed with no sign. As midnight approached, Harel and Aharoni paced nervously back and forth in the passenger lounge. Had someone spotted them carrying Eichmann onto the plane? Had the airport been tipped off that there was something suspicious about the flight? Was there going to be a raid? Harel contemplated sending word to Tohar to depart without them, but he decided to wait a few minutes longer.

Then Klein managed to locate a customs official. The tall, heavily bearded officer walked into the lounge and apologized for the delay. From his sheepish grin, they knew it had merely been a mix-up. The officer gestured them toward the exit and stamped their passports, wishing each of them a hearty "*Bon viaje!*"

As Harel crossed over to the Britannia and climbed the stairs into the plane, he noticed a man in a suit dashing out of the terminal from another exit and speaking urgently with an airport official. Harel had a sinking feeling that something was wrong. Then the plane doors were closed behind him.

In the cockpit, Tohar ran through the preflight checklist with his crew. Electrical system. Check. Fuel quantity. Check. All gauges indicate proper functioning. Check. As Harel was belting himself into the cockpit jump seat, Tohar ordered the flight engineer to start the engines. All four propeller engines fired without any problem.

Following procedure, Tohar called the control tower. "El Al is ready to taxi. Request clearance to Recife." Then he gave them the checkpoints and altitude that Shaul had provided for their false flight plan to Brazil.

The tower responded. "El Al, proceed to runway. Hold for takeoff clearance en route to Recife."

They were almost away, thought Harel. The man he had seen run out of the terminal wasn't a problem after all. Regardless, Harel wished that they were already in the air.

Tohar released the brakes, and the Britannia rolled forward on the taxiway to its takeoff position. As the plane cleared the airport terminal, the tower radioed again. "El Al, hold your position. There is an irregularity in the flight plan."

Everyone in the cockpit froze. Harel was certain that they had been discovered. Tohar did not seek further clarification from the tower. Instead, he halted the plane and turned around in his seat to see what Harel wanted to do. The rest of the cockpit crew was silent, hardly able to breathe.

"What happens if we ignore the tower's command and take off for Dakar?" Harel asked.

The cockpit crew knew that Tohar was an Israeli air force reserve pilot and that he had experienced enough tight situations to do what needed to be done. Tohar doubted that the Argentine air force was on standby, but if the flight left without clearance, a fighter plane might be scrambled. He could fly the Britannia low to the ground and evade the radar, first heading south instead of north to Recife, throwing off their pursuers for a while. However, he told Harel, the risks were substantial.

"There's still one more option," Tohar said with deliberate calm. "Before having the Argentine air force put on our tail, we should check and see if they really know that Adolf Eichmann is on board. Let's not create a problem that doesn't exist."

Harel nodded, even though any further delay would give the authorities time to alert the air force or to prevent the Britannia from leaving altogether.

Tohar turned to Shaul. "They are saying there's an irregularity in the flight plan. So, let's send the guy who prepared it to the tower to find out what is going on."

Shaul was the senior navigator; it was his responsibility.

"If you don't return in ten minutes," Tohar warned, "we'll take off without you."

Klein was standing on the apron beside the airport terminal, completely at a loss as to why the plane had stopped. He had checked and rechecked everything. There was no reason the Britannia should not have departed—unless its secret passenger had been exposed. Klein attempted to gain eye contact with someone in the cockpit, but nobody was moving, nor did they open a window to call out to him.

After what felt like hours, Klein saw one of the pilots gesture for stairs to be brought to the plane's side.

Then the Britannia's doors opened, and Shaul stepped out. Klein met him at the bottom of the steps. "What the hell is happening?"

"The tower wants something to do with the flight plan," Shaul said.

Klein felt momentary relief at the explanation, even though he knew this might merely be a pretext. It was highly unusual for a plane to be stopped and the navigator called out.

"Shall I go with you?" Klein asked.

"No, wait. I'll do it alone."

Shaul entered the tower, unsure of who or what awaited him, only that if he did not return to the plane within a few minutes, the Britannia would depart without him, leaving him in the center of a firestorm. The thirty-year-old father of two slowly climbed the stairs like a man approaching a hangman's noose.

"What is the problem?" he asked the controller in English, looking around for any sign of the police. There was none.

"There's a signature missing," the controller said, holding the flight plan up in his hand. "And what is your en route alternate?"

Shaul composed himself. It was a simple mix-up. "Pôrto Alegre," he responded before adding the detail to the plan and signing the document. Then he rushed back down the steps and outside.

"Everything's okay. Something was missing on the flight plan," Shaul said to Klein, not stopping on his way back to the plane.

The relief in the cockpit was palpable as Shaul recounted what had happened. The doors closed again, and Tohar called the tower. "This is El Al. May we proceed?"

"Affirmative."

At 12:05 A.M. on May 21, the plane accelerated down the runway and lifted off.

At half past midnight, Nick Eichmann learned from someone in his search party that an Israeli passenger plane had departed Buenos Aires for Recife. Nick was certain that his father was on board. With the help of a former SS man, he alerted a contact in the Brazilian secret service to the flight and asked him to intercept the plane when it landed—exactly the threat that the nonstop flight to Dakar aimed to counter.

All that remained between Eichmann and Israel was a transatlantic flight that had never before been attempted in a Britannia—a flight with only the slimmest margin for error.

26

WHEN THE BRITANNIA cleared Argentine airspace a few minutes into their journey, there was an uproar of excitement in the cabin. The "El Al crew" in the first-class cabin rose from their seats to embrace one another and to cheer their success. Wedeles and a few of the other real crew members who knew the special passenger's identity also joined in the celebration. The spontaneous outburst surprised Harel, and although he hesitated to inform everyone else on the flight, secrecy was now pointless. He gave Adi Peleg the honor.

The El Al security chief brought the crew together and declared, "You've been accorded a great privilege. You are taking part in an operation of supreme importance to the Jewish people. The man with us on the plane is Adolf Eichmann."

The announcement sent a shock wave of excitement through the crew. The stewardess sitting next to Eichmann felt her heart drop in her chest. She could not believe that this skinny, helpless man who was nervously drawing on a cigarette, his Adam's apple bobbing up and down in fright, could be Eichmann. In disgust, she stood up and moved away from him, while the others continued with their celebration. Aharoni sat back in his seat and drank a double whiskey. He knew exactly who the prisoner was and the feat it had taken to seize him.

In the cockpit, the mood was much more sober. The plane gained altitude, and Tohar steered due northeast across Uruguay and out over the Atlantic, following the course that Shaul had set out which gave them the best chance of reaching Dakar. The flight engineer and navigator checked each calculation, which was then rechecked by their alternates.

The chief pilot, both navigators, and Shimon Blanc had supervised the Britannia's proving flight between New York and Tel Aviv in late 1957. The nonstop journey had covered a distance of 5,760 miles in fifteen hours, but in a plane stripped of its seats, its galleys, and anything else deemed unnecessary—including passengers. They had also had the benefit of a strong tailwind of roughly 65 miles per hour. For that flight, they figured the maximum still-air range of the plane to be around 4,700 miles.

Buenos Aires to Dakar was a 4,650-mile flight. They were expecting the plane to fly near the performance ceiling for the aircraft, along a route where the forecasts predicted they could expect tailwinds. But they were carrying some four tons of additional weight, which compelled the aircraft to fly 2,000 to 3,000 feet lower than on the proving flight, consequently consuming roughly 5 percent more fuel per hour. And there was no guarantee that the wind conditions would be to their advantage.

Shaul and Tohar were confident that they would reach Dakar, but they were also aware that anything could happen. They might lose an engine, which would force them to fly lower and to use more fuel. The forecasts had predicted 40-mile-per-hour winds, but they might actually be half that. This particular Britannia, the 4X-AGD, also might burn fuel at a faster rate than the performance charts indicated. Over a thirteen- to fourteen-hour flight, slight deviations could add up to create big problems. At best, they might have to divert to another airport, perhaps in Abidjan, Ivory Coast. At worst, they might run out of fuel over the Atlantic. Margins for error were always built into flight plans for safety's sake, but those margins had been considerably reduced for this operation.

Hour after hour passed as they flew over the blank expanse of the Atlantic, heading first toward the small volcanic island of Trinidad, 680 miles east of Brazil, then almost due north toward Dakar. Periodically, the radio operators called in for revised weather forecasts, the navigators adjusted the route, and Harel popped his head into the cockpit to ask if everything was on track.

In the first-class cabin, Eichmann remained as docile as he had been in the safe house. The doctor had stopped administering the sedative once they had boarded the plane, but he allowed Eichmann only small meals in case he needed to inject the prisoner again. Harel also instructed his guards to stay vigilant, even though Eichmann was handcuffed and goggled, fearing that he might attempt to kill himself. The prisoner smoked heavily and fidgeted constantly in his seat.

Now that they were in flight, most of the El Al crew kept their distance from him. There was only one confrontation that exposed their underlying emotions toward the Nazi war criminal. On first hearing that he was on board, the head mechanic, Arye Friedman, was too overwhelmed to do anything but weep. In Poland, his six-year-old brother, Zadok, had been dragged away and killed by a German soldier, and Arye had endured many more nightmares in ghettos and concentration camps throughout the war. During the flight, Friedman confronted one of the guards with Eichmann, yelling, "You give him cigarettes! He gave us the gas!" Eichmann said nothing, looking in Friedman's direction but unable to see him because of the goggles. The mechanic took a seat opposite the prisoner and stared into his face, seeing only Zadok and his mother as he relived the past. Then he stood and walked out of the cabin.

Yosef Klein concluded his business in Buenos Aires the morning after the flight left. He paid any outstanding bills for services rendered to El Al and then caught a flight with Aerolineas Argentinas back to New York. There was no time for that sightseeing trip in Brazil he had planned on his journey out. Klein's reward had been seeing the taillights of the Britannia disappear into the night with Adolf Eichmann on board.

On his flight back to the United States, Klein sat next to a reporter from the *Daily Express* (London) who was hammering away at his Hermes typewriter on a story about the honeymoon of Princess Margaret, Queen Elizabeth's sister. It was a "big exclusive," the reporter told Klein, explaining that he had chartered a plane to fly over her beachside villa. Klein smiled knowingly, wanting to say, "If you only knew what exclusive is sitting right here beside you."

Early on May 21, Eitan, Malkin, Shalom, Dani, and Nesiahu awakened at Tira, heartened that Eichmann was no longer their responsibility and that their mission had gone so well. They had a few loose ends to tie up: They erased all vestiges of their presence in the various safe houses. They burned or disposed of any material they did not plan on taking with them. And they returned the last of their cars. There was no mention of Eichmann in the papers or on the radio, and Ilani assured them that the embassy had not heard anything about any government-driven search for any Nazi war criminals.

The last task remaining for the operatives was to get out of the country. Dani and Nesiahu were booked on flights the next day, but with the anniversary celebrations in full flow, no flights were available for Eitan, Malkin, and Shalom. So, late that morning, they bought three tickets for an overnight train that would take them to Mendoza, on the border between Argentina and Chile. There they would take another train through the Andes to Santiago. Harel had assured them that the announcement about the capture would not be made until they were safely back in Israel.

Red lights flashed in the Britannia cockpit as Tohar descended toward Dakar.

They had flown for close to thirteen hours and far beyond the 4,650 miles projected. Shaul had adjusted their flight path and altitude during their Atlantic crossing to find more favorable winds. The time for jokes, as when the captain had gone through the cabin asking if anybody had a lighter because they needed all the fuel they could use, had passed. They had long since crossed the point of no return, and they would either reach the coastline where the Dakar airport was located or they would not. The gauges indicated that the plane was dangerously low on fuel.

The cockpit was silent, everyone focused. Tohar stared out the window, looking for land. The lights continued to flash. This would be close, very close. The flight engineers and navigators knew this without looking at the gauges. If there was a problem in Dakar, if the runways were shut down for any reason, they would not have enough fuel to fly around the airport to wait to be cleared for landing or to divert to another airport. And that would be *if* they even made it to the coastline. Nevertheless, the cockpit crew remained certain that they would, even though there was only a few minutes' worth of fuel left in the tanks.

The landing wheels had already been lowered by the time they sighted land, and they had alerted the airport control tower long before of their arrival. Tohar steadily decreased their altitude and finally, after thirteen hours and ten minutes of flying, made a smooth landing on the Dakar runway. He killed two of the engines as soon as the plane had slowed down sufficiently, unsure that they had enough fuel to taxi to the terminal.

Harel congratulated the cockpit crew on the successful flight, but he was worried that the Argentine authorities had contacted Dakar in the meantime, advising them that the El Al plane might be carrying a suspicious passenger. If this was the case, a thorough search of the plane was guaranteed. So before the steward opened the plane's door, Dr. Kaplan injected Eichmann with more sedative, and Gat sat down next to him. Once again, the curtain was drawn across the first-class cabin, and the lights were extinguished.

While an airport services crew refueled the Britannia, one of the El Al crew rushed into the cabin to alert Gat that two Senegalese health inspectors were coming. Gat heard someone speaking in French approaching. He placed Eichmann's head on his shoulder and pretended to be sleeping himself. The inspectors gave the cabin only a cursory look. The rest of the stopover went smoothly. The crew loaded more food onto the plane, and Shaul and Hassin filed their flight plan to Rome, even though they were going straight to Tel Aviv.

Before they took off, Harel warned the captain that the Senegalese were not the last threat. He did not want to fly anywhere near the North African coastline, fearing that the Egyptians might either force the Britannia to land in their country or shoot it out of the sky if they found out that the plane was being used to bring Eichmann to Israel. Nobody in the cockpit needed to be reminded of this possibility.

Only five years before, an El Al Constellation that had skirted Bulgarian airspace had been shot down by a MiG 15, killing all fifty-one passengers and seven crew members on board.

Shaul and Hassin had already plotted out a 4,500-mile, eleven-hour route that would keep them far from Egyptian airspace. They both knew that the tailwinds over the Mediterranean were much stronger than those in the South Atlantic, meaning that the journey would not test the plane's limits in terms of fuel in quite the same way as the journey to Dakar had done. Still, the flight would take three hours longer than the direct path.

An hour and twenty minutes after touching down, the Britannia left Dakar. It flew up the west coast of Africa, then northeast to Spain. The plane passed over the Strait of Gibraltar during the night, gathering speed from the tailwinds as it turned almost due east toward Italy. The flight deck informed air traffic control in Rome that they would be heading on to Athens. The Britannia then flew southeast across the Mediterranean before the radio operator alerted Athens that they would go straight to Tel Aviv. The Israelis crossed over southern Greece, skirting Turkey, before turning toward Israel. They avoided Egyptian airspace by more than one hundred miles, and the flight was flawless.

With the plane approaching Israel, Harel washed his face, shaved, and put on clean clothes, preparing for the rush of activity that was awaiting him on arrival. He informed his men of their duties on landing, then stared out the window, eager to see the Israeli coastline appear out of the steadily lightening sky.

At 6:55 A.M. on Sunday, May 22, Zvi Tohar spotted the sliver of land on the horizon. He lowered the landing gear, and fifteen minutes later, the Britannia's wheels touched down in Israel. There was no celebration as there had been when they had left Buenos Aires. The crew had been flying for almost twenty-four hours straight, and the operatives watching Eichmann had not rested either. Relief was the emotion that prevailed throughout the aircraft.

Tohar taxied the plane to the terminal so that most of the crew could disembark. Harel made sure to shake everyone's hand. The captain also praised the efforts of the crew, warmly thanking each of them as they stepped off the plane. Customs officials attempted to board, but they were informed that there would be no inspection of the cabin. The doors were closed, and Tohar taxied the plane to the El Al service hangars, far from the terminal.

Two cars awaited them. In the first was Mordechai Ben-Ari, the deputy head of El Al; in the other was Moshe Drori of the Mossad. Drori boarded the plane first, but his congratulations were soon forgotten when it became clear that he had not made preparations for the transport or detention of Eichmann. "I have been waiting for you and your instructions," Drori said weakly, his explanation doing little to placate Harel, who stormed off the plane.

Harel strode into one of the hangars and found a grease-smudged phone with which to ring Shin Bet headquarters. "The monster is in shackles," he told one of his lieutenants before ordering a van. A short while later, a windowless black van appeared beside the plane. Tabor and Gat escorted a trembling, blindfolded Eichmann down the steps and into the back of the van. Harel explained to Gat that he was to take Eichmann to the secret Shin Bet detention center located in an old Arab house on the edge of Jaffa. Gat nodded, suggesting that since most of the guards there were Holocaust survivors, they identify the prisoner as a high-priority spy. Revealing his true identity might provoke an attack. Harel agreed, and the van drove off.

The Mossad chief then hurried toward Jerusalem. He hoped to see Ben-Gurion before his standard ten o'clock cabinet meeting. He did not want to draw attention to himself by breaking into the meeting.

His longtime driver, Yaki, sped through the Judean Hills into the city. The wind rushing through the open window offered little relief from the scorching heat. They arrived a few minutes before the meeting. A secretary led Harel into the prime minister's office.

"I brought you a present," Harel said.

Ben-Gurion looked up from his paper-strewn desk, surprised to see Harel.

"I have brought Adolf Eichmann with me. For two hours now he has been on Israeli soil, and, if you authorize it, he will be handed over to the Israeli police," Harel continued.

Ben-Gurion was stirred by the news, and for a few moments, he was silent. "Are you positive it is Eichmann?"

It was not the response Harel expected, and he was slightly taken aback. "Of course, I am positive. He even admitted it himself."

"Did anyone who met him in the past identify him?"

"No," Harel said.

"If that's the case, you have to find someone who knew him to go and inspect Eichmann in jail. Only after he has been officially identified will I be satisfied that this is the man."

Harel understood Ben-Gurion's reticence, knowing the implications of any announcement he made. Even so, there was not a shred of doubt in his own mind that they had their man. Only a few hours later, Moshe Agami, who had been a Jewish Agency representative during the war and had met with Eichmann in Vienna, was brought to the cell where the prisoner was being held. Within a few minutes, Agami had confirmed that this was the man who had made him stand at attention in his office in the Palais Rothschild in 1938 while he pleaded for permission for the Jews to immigrate to Palestine. After Agami left the cell, Benno Cohen, the former chairman of a Zionist organization in Germany in the mid-1930s, also identified Eichmann. Harel phoned the prime minister and delivered the news.

At last Ben-Gurion allowed himself to relish the operation's achievement. He wanted to announce the capture the next day. Harel asked him to wait; some of his operatives were still in South America.

"How many people know Eichmann is in Israel?" Ben-Gurion asked.

Already more than fifty, Harel admitted.

"In that case, no waiting. We're going to announce!"

Early the next morning, May 23 — another blisteringly hot, cloudless day — Eichmann was brought in front of Judge Emanuel Halevi in Jaffa. When the judge asked for the prisoner's identity, he answered without hesitation, "I am Adolf Eichmann." With his voice cracking, Halevi charged him with crimes of genocide and issued his official arrest warrant.

Harel then cabled Haim Yitzhaki, his contact with Fritz Bauer in Cologne. Harel and Haim Cohen, now a justice on the Israeli Supreme Court, both thought the Hesse attorney general deserved to be told of the mission's success before it hit the news.

Later that day, in a restaurant in the center of Cologne, Bauer awaited Yitzhaki, who had called for an urgent meeting but was now late. Bauer feared that something had gone horribly wrong with the mission. Finally, Yitzhaki entered the restaurant and crossed quickly to the table, his hands and clothes smeared with grease from changing a flat tire. When Bauer heard the news about Eichmann, he jumped from his seat, tears welling in his eyes, and kissed Yitzhaki on both cheeks.

Now it was time for the rest of the world to know.

At 4:00 P.M., Ben-Gurion entered the Knesset chamber. There were rumors that the prime minister had a special announcement to make, but none of the members, nor any of the press, had any idea what he was about to reveal. Nevertheless, they excitedly packed the hall and the public gallery. Just moments before Ben-Gurion rose to address the assembly, Isser Harel and Zvi Aharoni slipped into the gallery. It was the first time Aharoni had ever been inside the Knesset, and he was awed by its subdued grandeur.

Then Ben-Gurion stood at the podium, and the chamber hushed. In a solemn voice cracking with emotion, he announced, "I have to inform the Knesset that a short time ago one of the most notorious Nazi war criminals, Adolf Eichmann—who was responsible, together with the Nazi leaders, for what they called the 'Final Solution of the Jewish Question,' that is, the extermination of six million of the Jews of Europe—was discovered by the Israeli Security Services. Adolf Eichmann is already under arrest in Israel and will shortly be placed on trial in Israel under the terms of the law for the trial of Nazis and their helpers."

Nobody moved. The members were rooted to their seats, either unsure whether they had heard the prime minister correctly or that what he had said was true. Slowly, people realized the enormity of the statement, and it was as if the air had been knocked from their chests. "When they had recovered from the staggering blow," an Israeli journalist reported that night, "a wave of agitation engulfed the hearers, agitation so deep, that its likes had never before been known in the Knesset." Many went pale. One woman sobbed. Others leapt from their seats, needing to repeat aloud that Eichmann was in Israel in order to come to terms with the news. The parliamentary reporters ran to their booths to transmit the sixty-two-word speech, which had been delivered in Hebrew.

Ben-Gurion then stepped down and left the hall. Nobody was quite sure what to do as the chamber buzzed with the news. Harel and Aharoni slipped out as discreetly as they had entered.

Golda Meir then attempted to deliver her scheduled speech about a recent survey by the Foreign Ministry on Israeli international relations, but few listened to what she had to say.

Eichmann. Captured. That was all anyone in the chamber heard. Eichmann. Captured. Within hours, all of Israel and the rest of the world would be as captivated by the dramatic announcement. The stage was set for one of the century's most important trials.

27

ON MAY 25, AVRAHAM SHALOM took a bus back to his hotel in Santiago, Chile. He, Eitan, and Malkin had arrived in the country three days earlier, after a breathtaking journey by steam train from Mendoza through the Andes. On the day of their arrival in the capital, southern Chile had suffered a devastating earthquake, the most powerful in recorded history, which had killed thousands and sent tsunamis surging across the Pacific. Shalom had only just that day been able to send a cable to Mossad headquarters, notifying Harel that they were safe.

He idly looked over the shoulder of a passenger ahead of him, who was thumbing through a newspaper. There, in bold letters, he saw EICHMANN. Stunned, Shalom stumbled off the bus at the next stop. At a corner stand, he bought a whole bundle of papers, most carrying the headline BEN-GURION ANNOUNCES THE CAPTURE OF ADOLF EICHMANN. Nobody was supposed to know about the operation until they were back in Israel. When Shalom showed Eitan and Malkin the newspapers, they were equally angry, but there was nothing they could do about it.

A few days after that, they secured flights out of the country. By chance, Shalom and Malkin were both routed through Buenos Aires and spent a worried hour on the tarmac at Ezeiza before takeoff. At last they arrived back in Israel.

When Shalom returned home to his wife, he realized that she knew that he had been on the mission. A visit from Yaakov Gat several days before, assuring her that her husband was okay and would be home soon, had made it clear. Shalom knew that she would never utter a word about his involvement.

Others on the team had similar experiences, despite their firm denials to the contrary. On the evening of the announcement, Moshe Tabor was with his wife in a cinema in Tel Aviv when the film was interrupted by the news. Turning to him, she said, "You were in India, I thought?"

Tabor attempted to deflect his wife's attention, but then she told him that the toy pistol he had bought for their son was stamped from Argentina.

At Malkin's first Sabbath dinner with his family, his brother talked of nothing else. Malkin pleaded ignorance, wanting to know what had happened while he was in "Paris" for the past month. His mother pushed him to tell them where he had really been.

"Look, didn't you get my letters?" he asked.

"They were like all your letters. They could have been written last year or tomorrow . . . Were you involved with this?"

Malkin desperately wanted to tell her that he had been and that he had avenged his sister. "Please, Mama . . . Enough. I was in Paris."

Aharoni made the same excuse when his brother called him unexpectedly, wanting to know when he had come back. "I'm not naive," his brother probed. "I know you were away for over two months, and I heard Ben-Gurion on the radio. I can add two and two together. Or can I? Well done!"

A Shin Bet secretary, who had also tied Aharoni's absence to the news, embraced him on his first day back in the office. No words were needed.

All of the operatives were proud of their success, but it was the nature of their work that, as far as they knew, they would take the secret of their accomplishment and the dangers they had faced to their graves.

Eichmann was being held just outside Haifa, in northern Israel, at a fortified police station code-named Camp Iyar. He was confined to a ten-by-thirteen-foot cell that contained only a chair, a table, and a cot. The lights overhead were never extinguished, and a guard sat with him at all times. Another guard kept a steady watch through an opening in the reinforced door to make sure there was no contact between the inside guard and the prisoner. The prison commandant feared not only that Eichmann might commit suicide but also that there might be an attempt on his life. As added precautions, his food was always tasted before serving, and none of his guards had lost family members in the Holocaust.

On the afternoon of May 29, at 4:30, two men crossed the courtyard from the station headquarters to the prison block. Commander Ephraim Hofstetter and his chief inspector, Avner Less, were members of Bureau 06, the police unit organized to collect evidence, interview witnesses, and interrogate Eichmann for his eventual trial. Hofstetter, who had met with Lothar Hermann early in the hunt, was the first one chosen for the unit and its elected chief deputy. He had selected Less, a keen criminal investigator and Berlin native whose father had been gassed at Auschwitz, to question the prisoner.

The two men entered the interrogation room, a large space furnished with a plain desk and several hard chairs. They were prepared for an extended campaign to get Eichmann to talk. Secret microphones had been installed in the room. These were to be used if Eichmann did not agree to have the sessions recorded. Once they had settled themselves, Hofstetter called for Eichmann to be brought in. He had met the prisoner a few days before in Tel Aviv, where he had been a witness at Moshe Agami's and Benno Cohen's formal identification.

Two guards led Eichmann from his cell to the room. The prisoner, in a khaki shirt and pants, looked tense, standing at attention until he was told to sit down.

"You recognize me, I presume? I am Colonel Hofstetter of the Israeli Police."

"Yes, sir," Eichmann replied in a sturdy, clipped voice, though both investigators noticed that his hands, underneath the table, were shaking uncontrollably.

"Mr. Eichmann, I'm told you're willing—eager in fact—to give your version of your role in the so-called Third Reich? Is that right?" Hofstetter asked, expecting the reply to be far from that.

"Yes, that is right."

"You are fully aware that you are not being coerced in any way?"

"Yes, sir."

Ever helpful, Eichmann also agreed to allow recording equipment in the chamber.

The commander continued, "Then Captain Less will stay here with you and take your statement."

"I think we should begin with your curriculum vitae," Less said.

To their surprise, Eichmann began to speak at length about his personal history. As first the hours and then the days passed, however, Less noticed that the prisoner's forthrightness was far from honest—in fact, it was a deception in itself. As he had in captivity in Buenos Aires, Eichmann was rehearsing how he would defend himself in court, following the course taken by his compatriots at Nuremberg. Between chain-smoking cigarettes, he lied about his personal involvement in the atrocities until confronted with contradictory evidence, and whenever that occurred, he stated that he had been merely following orders.

Despite his obfuscations, Eichmann never believed that he would be given a trial. He expected that the Israelis would deliver the kind of justice that he remembered from his days in the Gestapo. In the second week of June, a guard interrupted the interrogation, explaining that he was to bring Eichmann to see the judge. As they blindfolded him, Eichmann staggered, his knees giving way, and he cried out to Less, "But, Captain! I haven't told you everything yet!" He calmed down only after being assured that the judge needed to see him so as to extend the order of his detention.

While Eichmann was being held at Camp Iyar, the impact of Ben-Gurion's announcement continued to spread. In Israel, the shock over the capture developed rapidly from pride in the accomplishment, to demands for swift revenge, to a more settled view that justice could be delivered only in terms of the letter of the law.

There were many disparate opinions, all hashed out in endless reams of newsprint and hours of radio airtime, on who should ultimately try Eichmann: Israel, West Germany, or an international tribunal. Ben-Gurion was clear about his intentions. "The Jewish state is the heir of the six million murdered, the only heir," he wrote to a representative of the American Jewish community who wanted Eichmann extradited to West Germany. Therefore, in his view, the trial should be held in Israel to fulfill that country's "historic duty" to those killed. As for the half million Israelis who were Holocaust survivors, the majority agreed that a trial should be held in Israel. Nevertheless, they were cautious about the possible repercussions. Since the war, most had kept to themselves the sufferings they had experienced at the hands of the Nazis. They were well aware that a trial would mean a painful exposing of past wounds.

The capture also had international implications. The Argentine government was in an uproar as soon as press reports revealed that the capture had taken place on its soil by "Israeli agents." Arturo Frondizi had no choice but to protest, since he was already enjoying tenuous relations with his military, which clearly viewed the action as a violation of Argentine sovereignty and wanted to use it to highlight his weakness. Frondizi was also under pressure from right-wing nationalists and Nazi sympathizers within the country.

On June 1, the Argentine foreign minister, Diógenes Taboada, summoned the Israeli ambassador Levavi to demand an official explanation and the return of Eichmann. "I don't think this is possible," Levavi said. Two days later, the Israeli government delivered a communiqué explaining that a group of "Jewish volunteers, including some Israelis," had been responsible for finding Eichmann. These volunteers had "made contact" with Eichmann and received his written permission to take him to Israel, where they had handed him over to the Israeli security services. The letter concluded that Israel regretted *if* these volunteers had violated Argentine law but that the "special significance of bringing to trial the man responsible for the murder of millions of persons belonging to the Jewish people be taken into account." Ben-Gurion followed this formal communiqué with a personal letter to Frondizi, repeating that there had been a "supreme moral justification" for the volunteers' actions.

The Argentines clearly did not believe that dubious story. Taboada again called for Eichmann to be returned and those responsible for the capture to be punished. The diplomatic war of words escalated, and even though Frondizi wanted to bury the affair by quietly bringing the matter to the UN, others in his government were intent on more strident measures. His UN ambassador, Mario Amadeo, a Catholic nationalist and erstwhile supporter of Benito Mussolini, led the charge in New York. Contrary to Frondizi's wishes, Amadeo pushed strongly for Eichmann's return, as well as for a UN vote of condemnation against Israel. The UN called an emergency Security Council meeting to discuss his complaint. Despite a stirring speech from Golda Meir in defense of Israel, Amadeo won not only his condemnation but also an order for Israel to make "appropriate reparations." Attached to the resolution, however, was a statement declaring that the UN understood that Eichmann should be brought to justice. The stalemate between the two countries persisted until late July, when Levavi was declared persona non grata in Argentina and forced to leave. In the end, this was the only action required for Frondizi to save face.

Even so, some in Argentina were keen to punish the Israelis. Unable to strike against them directly, right-wing groups unleashed a string of attacks on the Jewish community in Argentina. Tacuara carried out the worst of the incidents, beating up several Jewish students at the University of Buenos Aires and chanting "Long live Eichmann. Death to Jews." One student was shot, and later, in a vicious assault, Tacuara radicals branded a swastika onto the chest of a teenage girl whose father was suspected of having helped the Israelis. Nick and Dieter Eichmann hung a swastika flag in front of their Garibaldi Street house and talked tough.

Vera Eichmann called upon the Argentine courts to instigate proceedings against those involved in her husband's kidnapping. On July 12, a judge approved the case and launched an investigation, aided by the Argentine security services. None of Harel's team was in harm's way, but Luba Volk, who had signed her name to numerous documents related to the El Al flight, was still in the country. One afternoon when she was driving to her house in Belgrano, she sensed that a car was following her. After a few turns, she was certain of it, but whether it was the police or some vigilantes, she did not know. She went straight to the Israeli embassy, where security officials instructed her not to leave her house alone at night and to watch over her son carefully.

Volk tried to ignore the fear she felt, carrying on with her day-to-day activities as much as she could. A week later, she and her husband were called to the office of Joel Baromi, the acting Israeli ambassador. Baromi informed them that he had reliable intelligence that the Argentines, prompted by the proceedings brought by Eichmann's wife, were going to arrest Volk for her connection to the flight.

"Get out of this country as soon as you can, and by any means you can — legal or illegal," Baromi advised.

The next day, Volk and her family packed their most important belongings into a few bags and boarded a small plane to Uruguay. After a couple of weeks in Montevideo, she and her son traveled to Israel. Her husband followed shortly after, his business career in shambles because of his hasty exit from Argentina and the rumor that he was actually a Mossad agent.

By the fall, relations between Argentina and Israel had improved, and the case instigated by Vera Eichmann faltered. Investigators failed even to discover the names of those who had returned on the El Al flight. The Mossad had covered its tracks too well. In addition, the impetus to continue with the inquiry met with resistance, no doubt because of the embarrassment of various Argentine agencies, including the police and security services, at having been outwitted.

The other major player in this drama was West Germany. Chancellor Konrad Adenauer publicly chastised Israel for the kidnapping and for its commitment to trying the war criminal. He was supported by a host of his country's top newspaper editors, who demanded that Eichmann be extradited and "tried by judges instead of by avengers." But Adenauer never made any serious attempt to extradite Eichmann, knowing that the Israelis would not relinquish their right to try him. Still, as the trial approached, Adenauer grew increasingly worried about what Eichmann might reveal about the war activities of his national security adviser, Hans Globke. Israeli and West German officials made back-channel efforts to ensure that the trial did not embarrass the chancellor's government.

THE ACCOUNTANT OF DEATH and EICHMANN'S STORY, PART I: I TRANSPORTED THEM TO THE BUTCHER were the headlines in the German magazine *Der Stern* and the American magazine *Life*, respectively. Throughout the fall of 1960, both magazines published serial installments of Eichmann's memoirs, drawing millions of readers across the globe into the mind and history of the Nazi war criminal. One issue recounted a scene in late 1941 when Eichmann had seen the first preparations for exterminating the Jews: "General Heydrich ordered me to visit Majdanek, a Polish village near Lublin. A German police captain showed me how they had managed to build airtight chambers disguised as ordinary Polish farmers' huts, seal them hermetically, then inject the exhaust gas from a Russian U-boat motor. I remember it all very exactly because I never thought that anything like that would be possible, technically speaking." Such statements revealed Eichmann's callous disregard for his victims' suffering.

The memoirs came from the 850-page typescript that Willem Sassen had made from his taped interviews with Eichmann. Within days of Ben-Gurion's announcement, Sassen had approached publishers around the world to sell the rights to the interviews. For a share of the proceeds, he even convinced Vera Eichmann to grant permission for the sale. She later declared that she had had no idea of the nature of their content.

Even before publication, word of the memoirs' existence prompted a firestorm. The chief of the German intelligence agency BND, Reinhard Gehlen, petitioned the CIA to determine whether the memoirs were genuine and "if so, how much material is damaging to members of the West German government, so as to suppress these memoirs if desirable and possible." Ultimately, CIA director Allen Dulles convinced *Life*'s editors to eliminate the single mention of Globke. The Mossad had learned of the memoirs several days after kidnapping Eichmann, and they had secured a partial copy themselves, knowing it would make their case against Eichmann all the more solid.

While Eichmann's shocking admissions and reminiscences riveted the rest of the world, Avner Less and the others in Bureau 06 used the memoirs to challenge Eichmann's web of lies, half-truths, and denials in their ongoing interrogations. The inquiry resulted in more than 275 hours of tape, totaling 3,564 pages of transcripts. Bureau 06 also confronted Eichmann with hundreds of documents that pointed to his involvement in the genocide. These documents, among more than 400,000 pages that were collected, came from a range of sources, including war archives in West Germany and the United States and the collections of Tuviah Friedman and Simon Wiesenthal.

On the day of Ben-Gurion's announcement to the Knesset, Wiesenthal received a cable from Yad Vashem informing him of the capture and stating, "Congratulations on your excellent work." After taking a moment to gather himself over the unexpected news, he turned to his teenage daughter, Pauline. "You never saw your father when you were a baby. You were asleep when I went to work looking for this man and asleep by the time I came home. I don't know how long I will live. I don't know if I will leave you any fortune at all. But this cable is my gift to you. Because through this cable I am now part of history." In the months that followed, Wiesenthal presented Hofstetter with everything he had on Eichmann. He volunteered to look for further incriminating records. He also provided important information on the defense strategy of Robert Servatius, Eichmann's lawyer, through an informant close to the Eichmann family.

Friedman was equally forthcoming. On the evening of May 23, he heard the news by telephone. His friend in Tel Aviv had to repeat himself before Friedman could take it in. Feeling weak, he walked out of his office to a newsstand, where there was already a late edition plastered with Eichmann's face. Several days later, Friedman met with Bureau 06, presenting his four-hundred-page file on Eichmann. At long last, his years of obsessive searching, uncovering every detail he could find on the man, had a use: proving Eichmann's guilt.

In their collection of evidence, Bureau 06 investigators sought more than incriminating documents and the confessions of Eichmann himself. They wanted witnesses, people who had had contact with Eichmann during the war, people who could testify to the atrocities committed against the Jews in every country occupied by the Nazis. One of these witnesses, who had seen Eichmann in the days before the clearing of the Munkács ghetto in Hungary, was Zeev Sapir.

On November 1, 1960, Sapir went to the offices of Bureau 06 for an interview. Many men and women had come forward on their own, but Sapir was not one of them. An Israeli association of Hungarian survivors had suggested his name, and only after the Bureau 06 investigators had contacted him about the possibility of testifying did he agree to discuss his searingly painful memories of the war.

After being rescued by the Red Army in January 1945, Sapir had spent months recovering in a hospital. A Russian officer had invited him to return to Moscow with him for Passover, and from there Sapir had traveled to Bucharest, where he had been helped by the American Jewish Joint Distribution Committee, which had given him some money and allowed him to spend some weeks in their displaced persons camp. He had bought a suit with the money; the new clothes had made him feel human again. Sapir had then returned to his hometown of Dobradovo, but there had been nothing left for him there. Back in Budapest, while registering his name with the authorities, as was required at the time, he had spotted his elder brother's name in an entry that was a week old. Sapir had searched everywhere for him; he had always thought that his brother had died in a Hungarian work camp. Then, a few weeks later, on a train to Vienna, he had seen his brother's face reflected in a mirror, and they had been reunited. Together, the brothers had traveled to Austria and, through the Brichah network, by boat to Palestine. Sapir had joined a kibbutz and, like many other refugees, had participated in the fight for an independent Jewish state. Later, he had married, started a family, and worked as a teacher. It was still difficult for him to speak of the past, but he had never forgotten it.

Now, as he sat in front of the Bureau 06 investigators, the memories came out of him haltingly: the Munkács brickyards, Auschwitz, the Dachsgrube coal mines. He also told them about when Adolf Eichmann had gone into the ghetto in Munkács and announced that the Jews had no cause to worry. Days later, he explained to the investigators, he and the rest of his village had been shipped off to the extermination camp.

28

IN THE VALLEY below the Old City stood Beit Ha'am, the House of the People, a white stone and marble four-story edifice in the middle of modern, chaotic Jerusalem. On April 11, 1961, at 8:55 A.M., one hundred police and military guards with automatic weapons surrounded the building. Inside, Adolf Eichmann, dressed in a dark blue suit and tie and wearing thick horn-rimmed glasses, was brought into the courtroom and directly into a bulletproof glass booth on the left side of the converted auditorium. He sat facing the empty witness stand. Two guards stood directly behind him.

Already seated in the hall, the 750 spectators gazed at him with unblinking eyes. Straight ahead of them, on the first level of a three-stepped raised dais, were the five prosecutors and two defense attorneys in their black gowns, seated at tables, side by side. Above them were the court stenographers and clerks.

For five minutes, there was little movement in the hall. Eichmann sat stoic and still, rarely glancing beyond his glass booth. There was muffled conversation as those gathered attempted to understand how this single man, with his remarkably ordinary face and measured demeanor, could be responsible for so much death. They would have been less taken aback if a monster had been clawing at his chains. Cameras and microphones, hidden in the acoustically tiled walls, recorded every moment for the world to see and hear.

At last the three judges walked into the court and took their places in high-backed chairs at the top of the dais. In quiet but stern Hebrew, the presiding judge, Moshe Landau, opened the proceedings. "Adolf Eichmann, rise!"

Eichmann snapped to his feet the instant the judge's words were translated through the headset hanging around his neck.

"Are you Adolf Eichmann, son of Adolf Karl Eichmann?"

"Yes," he answered.

When instructed by the judges, Eichmann turned toward them, his jaw slightly cocked, his face still impassive. Landau began reading the indictment, head down, hands together as if in prayer.

"First count. Nature of Offence: Crime against the Jewish People. Particulars of the Offence: (a) The Accused, during the period from 1939 to 1945, together with others, caused the deaths of millions of Jews as the persons who were responsible for the implementation of the plan of the Nazis for the physical extermination of the Jews, a plan known by its title 'The Final Solution of the Jewish Question.'"

Landau's words were like drips of water against a stone. The indictment went on for an hour: fifteen counts, numerous charges within each. He had uprooted whole populations. He had assembled Jews in ghettos and deported them en masse. He had committed mass murder at the extermination camps of Auschwitz, Chelmno, Belzec, Sobibor, Treblinka, and Majdanek. He had enslaved Jews in forced labor camps and had denied their rights as human beings. He had inflicted inhuman torture and suffering. He had plundered the property of Jews through robbery, terror, and torture. He had been directly involved in the deaths of one hundred children in Lidice, Poland. He had operated across Europe as well as in the Soviet Union and the Baltic countries Lithuania, Latvia, and Estonia — always, always, with the intention of "destroying the Jewish People."

When the judge asked Eichmann for his plea, he answered with the same phrase for each count. "In the sense of the indictment, no." This was the exact statement Hermann Göring had used at Nuremberg.

Directly after Eichmann's plea had been heard, Gideon Hausner, the forty-five-year-old attorney general, a man of stout figure and hooded blue eyes, began his opening speech. He had the flourish of a man who knew he was speaking for history.

> When I stand before you here, Judges of Israel, to lead the Prosecution of Adolf Eichmann, I am not standing alone. With me are six million accusers. But they cannot rise to their feet and point an accusing finger towards him who sits in the dock and cry: "I accuse." For their ashes are piled up on the hills of Auschwitz and the fields of Treblinka and are strewn in the forests of Poland. Their graves are scattered throughout the length and breadth of Europe. Their blood cries out, but their voice is not heard. Therefore I will be their spokesman.

The trial was launched. Following the direction and aim of David Ben-Gurion, it was as much about laying bare the Nazi program to exterminate the Jews as it was about prosecuting a single man. For the next fifty-six days, Hausner unfolded his case against Eichmann, placing him at the nexus of the Holocaust. He presented Eichmann with the Avner Less interrogations, captured German documents, statements from his former collaborators such as Auschwitz commandant Rudolf Höss, pages from the Sassen interviews, and witness testimony. Throughout the prosecution, Eichmann remained composed and alert. Every time he entered his booth before a session, he wiped his desk and chair with a handkerchief, then arranged his papers about him as if he were preparing for a day at the office. Usually, he kept his eyes focused on the prosecutor. Occasionally, though, his head would jerk to the left, seemingly involuntarily, or he would draw in his cheeks to the point where the skin was tight against the bones of his face. "In moments like these," one witness recounted, "he is somewhat like the Eichmann we would like to see: an inexplicably merciless face, sending a shiver up my spine."

On May 28, Zeev Sapir was called to the witness stand. While making his way into the chamber, Sapir looked at Eichmann and felt an overwhelming rush of pride and elation at seeing the enemy of his people sitting between two Israeli guards. After one of the judges swore him in, the young assistant prosecutor Gabriel Bach began his questions. The first were easy: name, town of birth, date the Germans arrived. Then he was asked about the clearing of Dobradovo.

"How many Jews were you in your village?" Bach asked.

"One hundred and three souls, including children of all ages," Sapir responded. He continued to speak, as the memories of what had been lost there came back to him.

Bach then inquired about when Sapir had heard that an important SS officer was expected in Munkács. Sapir described the roll call and the man named Eichmann coming into the ghetto at the head of a party of German and Hungarian officers.

"You see the accused here. Can you identify him as the man whom you saw then?"

Sapir stared again at Eichmann, who was sitting in his booth, eyes averted, scribbling something in his notebook. The name was the same, but the man across from Sapir was missing the uniform, the weapon, and the aura of power. What was more, seventeen years had passed. "It is hard to compare," Sapir said. "He's different from what he was, but there is some resemblance that I can see in him." The witness then recounted the horrors that had awaited him after Eichmann had departed the camp. The memories were still fresh and raw.

Sapir told the courtroom that he never saw his parents or his younger brothers and sister again after the selection process at Auschwitz. He almost broke down when he remembered the ages of the little ones: eleven, eight, six, and three. The courtroom was silent as he recounted his march from the coal mines and then the SS officer Lausmann preparing to massacre those who could not continue: "A pot was brought into the room, and we all thought that there was food in it. But he took us, one by one, bent each down into the pot and shot him in the back of the neck."

Sapir was having trouble standing upright on the witness stand. A clerk brought him a chair. He sat down uneasily and held his bowed head in his hands. He did not touch the glass of water offered to him. The prosecutor offered to waive the question about how he had ultimately escaped, but Sapir wanted to tell his story. He had earned the right. He wanted to tell them that he had been forced to eat frozen potatoes to survive and about the indiscriminate shootings in the forest. Judge Landau allowed it. When he had finished speaking, Sapir raised his sleeve and showed the courtroom his Auschwitz tattoo: A3800.

At that time, it was impossible to know what role his testimony would play in the trial's outcome, but the important thing for him was that the facts of what he had experienced because of Eichmann were now known. Indeed, given the exhaustive coverage of the trial in the newspapers and on radio and television, Sapir's story, like every other aspect of the trial, became known across the globe.

Several of the agents whose successful operation had made the trial possible came to see Eichmann in his glass booth. Most didn't bother with more than one session; they were busy with other operations. It was enough to know that they had succeeded in bringing him to justice.

Once Hausner finished presenting his case, the defense took over, claiming that the Nazi state had been responsible for the crimes. Eichmann had merely followed orders, and his role in the atrocities had been limited and carried out without any particular willingness on his part. In fact, Servatius argued, Eichmann had actually wanted to save the Jews by promoting their emigration. At last Eichmann spoke in his own defense.

Given his clipped, military tone, one might have expected straightforward answers, but Eichmann spoke in long-winded, elliptical passages whose beginnings were often bewilderingly contradicted by their endings. His arguments seemed to make perfect sense to him, however, as did his long excursions into the intricacies of the Nazi hierarchy, full of indecipherable SS jargon. The translators had a burdensome task in relaying his statements. As for his guilt as an accomplice in the murder of millions, he explained:

From the point of view of human guilt, a question which I have to judge in a much graver manner, because in this respect I must sit in judgment with myself—in this respect I must admit that I have played my part, though under orders. From the legal point of view, as a recipient of orders, I had no choice but to carry [them] out. How far the fact that I had to carry out part of the deportations and that the Jews who were thus deported found their death, how far I am legally guilty is a question which, in my opinion, should be left until the question of responsibility has been examined.

Eichmann rarely backed down over the next fifty hours of cross-examination, even when caught in a skein of his own lies. The Sassen tapes proved damning, particularly in terms of demonstrating Eichmann's willingness and vigor in executing his duties against the Jews. He won many of the exchanges, most of them when Hausner attempted to overreach by implicating Eichmann in every facet of the Jewish genocide. To the chagrin of the Adenauer government, Eichmann reminded the attorney general that Hans Globke had also played a role, but because Globke was never called to testify, this mention had little impact.

Throughout the cross-examination, Eichmann was a formidable presence, unmoved by the attorney general's many attempts, some ill-advised, to force him into an admission of legal guilt. Still, Eichmann could not elude the weight of evidence against him, particularly that related to his actions in Hungary.

After closing statements on August 14, the judges adjourned the trial. Four months later, they returned with their verdict. Eichmann was found guilty on all counts of the indictment, but he was acquitted on several individual charges within these counts. As Eichmann listened to the judges read their 211-page judgment, he slowly lost control of himself. His face twitched, and he looked frantically from side to side.

At the end of the second day, Eichmann gave a statement, repeating many of the arguments he had used in his defense. On Friday, December 15, 1961, Judge Landau asked Eichmann to rise and delivered the sentence:

> For the dispatch of each train by the Accused to Auschwitz, or to any other extermination site, carrying one thousand human beings, meant that the Accused was a direct accomplice in one thousand premeditated acts of murder . . . Even if we had found that the Accused acted out of blind obedience, as he argued, we would still have said that a man who took part in crimes of such magni-

tude as these over years must pay the maximum penalty known to the law . . . But we have found that the Accused acted out of an inner identification with the orders that he was given and out of a fierce will to achieve the criminal objective . . . This Court sentences Adolf Eichmann to death.

It was the first — and to this day only — sentence of death by an Israeli court.

Eichmann was motionless, his lips drawn together as if he was forcing himself to suppress even the slightest reaction. His throat and the collar of his shirt were soaked with sweat. Eight minutes after the session began, the bailiff called, "All rise!" and the judges filed out. The trial was over.

Eichmann appealed the judgment, and hearings were held in March 1962. While he waited for the decision in Ramleh prison, the heavily guarded garrison outside Jerusalem where he had been kept throughout both sets of proceedings, he penned his second autobiography. This was his third attempt to tell his story. The Sassen interviews had been his first; a memoir he wrote while at Camp Iyar between interrogation sessions with Avner Less had been his second. Each time, his aim had been to justify his role in the Holocaust and to place his actions in what he saw as the best possible light: three documents created more for himself than for anyone else.

Eichmann began to meet with the Reverend William Hull, a Canadian Protestant missionary in Jerusalem. On his own initiative, Hull petitioned the Israelis to allow him to act as Eichmann's spiritual counsel. At first Eichmann refused, but Hull persisted, and eventually the two met in Eichmann's prison cell for the first of thirteen sessions. Hull wanted to save the soul of the Nazi war criminal by having him repent his sins, confess to his past deeds, and confirm that "the Lord Jesus Christ was his Savior," a tall task given that Eichmann had spent the past seventeen years convincing himself exactly why he did not need to seek forgiveness for what he had done.

Eichmann joined in these discussions with his usual seriousness of purpose. He explained to Hull that he believed in God but that his study of other religions, as well as of Nietzsche and Kant in his "search for peace through truth," had turned him away from organized religion. He believed in a pantheistic God, one found in nature and in all things. Hull convinced Eichmann to renew his study of the Bible (he refused to read the Old Testament because it was "Jewish fables"), but beyond this, the minister had no success apart from engaging Eichmann in conversation. Eichmann did not fear God's judgment: "There is no Hell," he declared. What was more, he refused to confess: "I have not sinned. I am clear with God. I did not do it. I did nothing wrong. I have no regrets." Hull pressed him on this, but Eichmann was rigid in his self-made faith.

On May 29, 1962, Eichmann's appeal was denied. He flushed with anger when the five-judge panel restated the reason for the guilty verdict. Later that same day, he pleaded for clemency to the Israeli president. Two days after that, at 7:00 P.M., the commissioner of prisons, Arye Nir, who had overseen Eichmann's incarceration for two years, advised his prisoner that this plea had also been denied. Eichmann had run out of options, and Nir crisply informed him that he would be hanged at midnight.

Eichmann requested a bottle of white wine, cigarettes, and a paper and pen. Seated at the desk in his cell, the always present guard nearby, he wrote a final letter to his wife and sons. Then he shaved, dressed in brown slacks and a shirt, and brushed his teeth.

By 11:20 P.M., when Rev. Hull arrived, Eichmann had drunk half the bottle of wine, had smoked his cigarettes, and was unnervingly calm.

"Why are you sad?" Eichmann asked the minister. "I am not sad."

They spent twenty minutes together, but any final-hour repentance from Eichmann was not forthcoming. "I have peace in my heart. In fact, I am astonished that I have such peace . . . Death is but the release of the soul."

Two guards and the commandant entered the cell. Before they bound his hands behind his back, Eichmann asked for a moment to pray. He retreated to a corner for a minute and then announced, "I am ready."

Accompanied by Hull, Eichmann was escorted down the prison corridor. He walked the fifty yards briskly, and Nir had to order the guards to slow down. The group entered the makeshift execution chamber through a hole that had been knocked through one of the walls. Formerly, the third-floor room had been the guards' quarters. A wooden platform had been built over a hole cut in the floor. A rope hung from an iron frame. Bureau 06 chief inspector Michael Gold-mann and Rafi Eitan, who had come to see Eichmann to his end, were waiting for them as witnesses to the execution. Over the past few months, Eitan had interrogated Eichmann several times at Camp Iyar about how the SS had been organized and operated.

The guards placed Eichmann on the platform and tied his legs to-gether. He stared at Eitan and said sharply, "I hope, very much, that it will be your turn soon after mine."

A white hood was brought out, but he refused it. He looked at the four journalists selected to witness the execution as they scribbled on their pads. A coiled rope, lined with leather to prevent abrasions, was placed over his head.

"Long live Germany," Eichmann declared. "Long live Argentina. Long live Austria . . . I had to obey the laws of war and my flag. I am ready."

Two guards moved behind the curtain of blankets that shielded the trapdoor's release mechanism from the prisoner. The contraption had been rigged in a way that only one of the two buttons actually opened the platform's flaps.

Eichmann smiled thinly and called out, "Gentlemen, we shall meet again soon, so is the fate of all men. I have believed in God all my life, and I die believing in God."

It was exactly midnight. The commandant yelled, "Ready!"

Eichmann half-closed his eyes, looking down at the trapdoor un-derneath his feet. His face was ashen.

"Action!"

The two guards hit their buttons, and the platform opened with a clang. Eichmann fell ten feet into the room below without a sound. The rope went straight, snapped, and then swayed back and forth.

Goldmann peered through the hole in the floor and said that Eichmann was not moving. A doctor entered the second-floor chamber, inspected Eichmann, and formally declared that he was dead.

The witnesses all signed a statement confirming their presence at the hanging. Then Nir told the reluctant guards to cut the body down from the noose. Eichmann's face was white, and the rope had cut into his neck. As one of the guards, Shlomo Nagar, lifted Eichmann, he expelled some air caught in the dead man's lungs, producing a sound that almost made Nagar faint and that he would hear in his nightmares for years to come. He and several other guards placed Eichmann on a stretcher, covered him with gray wool blankets, and carried him out into the prison yard. Eitan stayed behind. He had seen enough.

Goldmann, whose parents and ten-year-old sister had been separated from him at Auschwitz, accompanied Nir and Hull in following the guards and the stretcher out into the yard.

There was a mist in the air, and with the prison lights shining through the barbed-wire fence, Goldmann was reminded of the extermination camp where his family had been killed. The guards brought the body out of the prison gates into a clearing in an orange grove. There a man who had once worked at an extermination camp crematorium attended a furnace. As the guards struggled to place the corpse into the smoldering fire with a long, two-pronged iron fork, one of them lost his balance, and the body tumbled to the ground. Everyone froze at the sight. Goldmann rolled up his sleeves and stepped forward to help place the corpse inside the furnace. In the fiery glow, Hull saw the Auschwitz tattoo on the Bureau 06 officer's arm.

Two hours later, the ashes were retrieved from the blackened reservoir. They filled half of a small nickel canister. Goldmann considered how many Jews must have made up the mountains of ashes outside the Auschwitz-Birkenau crematoriums. In the wintertime, the SS guards had forced him to spread these ashes on the paths to keep the Nazis from slipping on the ice.

With Hull joining them, Nir and Goldmann drove into the port of Jaffa. They arrived in the dark hours of the morning of June 1. Several other observers were waiting beside the police patrol boat *Yarden*, and together they motored out into the open sea. By casting Adolf Eichmann's ashes into the water, there would be no place to pay homage to his life or to build a monument honoring him. Six miles out, just outside Israeli territorial waters, the captain switched off the engines. The boat drifted in silence, rising and falling in the swells. A sliver of red light appeared on the horizon. As Hull said a prayer to himself, Nir walked to the back of the boat and emptied the canister into the swirling waves. The ashes drifted up on the crest of a wave, then disappeared. The engines were started, and the captain turned back to the coast. They reached the shore just as the sun slowly rose in the sky and Tel Aviv came back to life.

Epilogue

ELIE WIESEL, the Nobel Peace Prize winner, author, and Auschwitz survivor, attended the Eichmann trial as a reporter. Years later, he said that the capture and trial of the Nazi war criminal showed that

> Jewish history had a tremendous sense of imagination. A few Jews caught him and brought him to justice. They didn't kill him, which they could have in Buenos Aires. No, they brought him to the free and sovereign state of Israel where men could serve as his judges. The trial was almost more important in the field of education than in the field of justice. It was important for the Israeli youth to know what had happened, where we came from. And that's what the Eichmann trial really did. But not only in Israel, the real turning point was the awareness of the world towards the tragedy of the Jewish people.

David Ben-Gurion had achieved his ambition. The trial had a profound impact on Israel. It unified the country in a way it had not been unified since the 1948 war. It educated the Israeli public, particularly the young, on the true nature of the Holocaust. And, after sixteen years of silence, it allowed survivors to openly share their experiences. The trial also reinforced to Israelis that a sovereign state for Jews was essential for their survival.

As for the rest of the world, the Eichmann affair rooted the Holocaust in the collective cultural consciousness. The intensive coverage and the wave of Eichmann biographies and fantastic accounts of his capture contributed to the process. The debate stirred by the trial, particularly after the publication of *Eichmann in Jerusalem* by Hannah Arendt in 1963, nourished and strengthened those roots. Her comments on the banality of evil paled in comparison to the firestorm caused by her criticism of the trial and her indictment of many Jews as essentially having been complicit in their own extermination during the war. Hundreds of articles and books were published to counter or support her arguments, causing a thorough and passionate reexamination of the history of the genocide. The Holocaust was finally anchored in the world's consciousness — never to be forgotten — by the outpouring of survivor memoirs, scholarly works, plays, novels, documentaries, paintings, museum exhibits, and films that followed in the wake of the trial and that still continues today. This consciousness, in Israel and throughout the world, is the enduring legacy of the operation to capture Adolf Eichmann.

All those involved in the fifteen-year chase were marked by the experience.

Simon Wiesenthal and Tuviah Friedman won a tremendous amount of attention for their participation. Their roles were often inflated, largely because of the long absence of any statements by the Mossad. Encouraged by the renewed public interest in war crimes, both returned to hunting Nazis, although Wiesenthal pursued his cases with more vigor and more success than Friedman. Despite Wiesenthal telling his daughter that the Eichmann case would guarantee his name in history, it was his further forty-five years of relentless activity afterward, promoting "justice, not vengeance," that secured his legacy.

Fritz Bauer, whose involvement remained a secret for two decades, moved quickly on the cases of other war criminals already under investigation. In the weeks after Ben-Gurion's announcement, Bauer and his fellow West German prosecutors arrested a host of former Nazis implicated in the atrocities, including several of Eichmann's deputies. Right up to his death in 1968, the Hesse attorney general cracked down on German fascist groups and campaigned vigorously to unseat former Nazis from power, including Globke. He continued to prosecute war crimes, most famously in the 1963 Auschwitz trials.

For the Hermann family, whose contact with Bauer had been

pivotal in the hunt, their experience after the capture was disturbing. Somehow, whether it was because of the visit from Ephraim Hofstetter or because Jewish officials in Buenos Aires investigated his claim that he knew where Eichmann was, reporters got a tip in March 1961 that Hermann was actually Josef Mengele. After he was arrested, then quickly released by the police, an Argentine newspaper further exposed him by publishing reports that he was withholding information on Mengele and Eichmann. Before the operation to catch Eichmann unfolded, Sylvia Hermann left Argentina for the United States, where she remains today. In 1971, after Tuviah Friedman personally petitioned Prime Minister Golda Meir, Lothar Hermann received a reward for information leading to the arrest of Eichmann. Until then, his and his daughter's role in the capture had been kept a secret.

As for the Eichmann family, Vera and her youngest son, Ricardo, moved back and forth between Buenos Aires and West Germany for several years before settling in Osterburken, forty miles west of Heidelberg. Vera never accepted that her husband was guilty of his crimes, nor did she get over his execution. Ricardo scarcely remembers his father, and sharing his name is a weight that he continues to carry. Now a professor of archaeology in Germany, he recognizes the terrible deeds of Adolf Eichmann and is reluctant to speak about him. Of the three older sons, Horst continues to live in Buenos Aires and is reportedly a neo-Nazi leader. Dieter and Nick moved back to Germany, to Lake Constance, on the Rhine. They remain convinced that their father just obeyed orders and that most of what was said against him at the trial was false. Beyond that, they do not wish to discuss him.

Forty-seven years would pass before the Shin Bet and Mossad agents, as well as the El Al crew, were publicly recognized by the Israeli state for their role in the operation. For the crew, a simple but heartfelt note from the chief pilot, Zvi Tohar, thanking them for their "extraordinary devotion to duty" on this flight — "a landmark in the progress of Israeli aviation" — was the only reward they ever received. They all went back to their jobs and said nothing of the affair until very recently.

After returning to Israel, Zvi Aharoni was transferred to the Mos-

sad by Isser Harel and charged with heading a new group to hunt for
war criminals — most importantly Josef Mengele, Martin Bormann,
and Heinrich Müller. In 1962, on the day Eichmann was executed,
Aharoni was back in South America searching for Mengele. He received a tip from a former SS officer in Montevideo, Uruguay, that a
German in Brazil was helping the Auschwitz doctor to hide. A few
weeks later, Aharoni was in a jungle twenty-five miles south of São
Paolo when he spotted Mengele between two local bodyguards heading down a trail. All Aharoni had to do was keep following him until
an operation could be launched to take Mengele back to Ramleh
Prison. Aharoni was certain it could be done. But then he received
word from Isser Harel that he was to abandon the mission immediately. Earlier that spring, an eight-year-old boy named Yossele Schu-
macher had been kidnapped out of Israel by extreme Orthodox Jews
who were against the Zionist state. Harel marshaled many of his
agents, Aharoni included, to get him back. Yossele was eventually
found in New York, but Mengele escaped, eluding capture for the rest
of his life. The Auschwitz doctor drowned in Brazil in 1979. Aharoni
had retired from the Mossad long before then to become a businessman, settling in the southwest of England.

Avraham Shalom continued with the Shin Bet, rising to become
its director in 1981. He was forced to leave his post three years later
after two Palestinian youths, who had hijacked a bus with hand grenades and were then arrested by the army, were beaten to death on his
orders. It was an ignoble conclusion to an otherwise courageous and
remarkable career. Shalom entered the private security business and
now lives in Tel Aviv and London.

Peter Malkin became head of the Shin Bet operations department.
He left the world of espionage in 1976 to pursue his lifelong ambition
of becoming an artist. His best-known paintings are those he sketched
while in Buenos Aires. Malkin died in 2005.

Yaakov Gat also achieved further success within the Shin Bet. Later,
he joined a private security firm, where he worked until his retirement.

Moshe Tabor, who (among numerous others) had volunteered to
hang Eichmann when his sentence was declared, spent many more

years with the security services and retired on a pension. He died in 2006.

Shalom Dani died of a heart attack in 1963. His former colleagues still speak of him with reverence.

Rafi Eitan has enjoyed an illustrious career that is seemingly without end. He remained with the Israeli security services for fifteen years. Then he became a security and antiterror adviser to several Israeli prime ministers. Subsequently, Eitan ran the Defense Ministry's spy unit (where he recruited the American spy Jonathan Pollard), oversaw the Israeli state chemical industry, and in 2006 was elected to the Knesset.

Only three years after the Eichmann operation, at the height of his success and at just fifty years of age, Isser Harel resigned as chief of the Mossad and Shin Bet. Some within the Israeli halls of power feared that he was gaining too much influence within the government and grooming himself as a replacement for Ben-Gurion. After Harel launched a deadly, indiscreet campaign against German rocket scientists working for Egypt, his enemies maneuvered him out of the prime minister's favor. When Harel left Mossad headquarters for the last time, many of his staff were in tears. Aside from a brief stint in the Knesset, he spent his time writing books and advising on security issues. He died in 2003.

Harel and all of his operatives—no matter how long they remained in the security services or where their careers brought them—recounted their involvement in the mission to capture Eichmann and bring him to trial in Israel with unalloyed pride. In a profession known for its duplicitous acts, moral compromises, and often unforeseen and unwanted consequences, this is a rare state of affairs.

Rafi Eitan stated, with a level stare, not only that the operation had been executed almost flawlessly but also that its impact was clear: "All over world, and also in Israel, we started to understand the Holocaust."

For those like Peter Malkin, whose families had been devastated by the Nazis, their participation carried an even greater personal satisfaction. In 1967, while on a job in Athens, Malkin received a call from Avraham Shalom, who told him that his mother had been rushed to the hospital. Malkin returned to Tel Aviv immediately and went straight to her bedside. Her eyes were closed, her face drained of color. She did not react when he spoke to her.

"She can't talk," the old woman in the other bed said.

"Mama," Malkin whispered close by her ear, "I want to tell you something. What I promised, I have done. I got Eichmann."

His mother did not open her eyes, nor did she turn her head. It was seven years after he had grabbed Eichmann on Garibaldi Street. Malkin had kept the secret from her because of the oath he had sworn, but now he could not bear for her to die without knowing what he had done.

"Mama, Fruma was avenged. It was her own brother who captured Adolf Eichmann."

"She can't hear you," said the old woman, growing impatient with his visit.

Just as Malkin was losing hope, he felt a hand cover his own, and then his mother tightened her grip.

"Do you understand?" Malkin asked her eagerly.

Her eyes fluttered open. "Yes," she said. "I understand."

Acknowledgments

While writing this history, one based on research and interviews on four continents and involving an equal number of languages, I benefited from a range of generous assistance. Without the help of the individuals acknowledged here, *Hunting Eichmann* would likely still be an idea awaiting execution.

First, I would like to recognize my able team of research assistants, whose commitment to uncovering new material in archives, finding interview subjects, and working down my "to do" lists was unwavering. In Argentina: Valeria Galvan, Patricia Delmar, and Matias Delmar. In Israel: Nava Mizrahi and Franziska Ramson. In Germany, Ms. Ramson also proved indispensable. Thank you, thank you.

In the course of my research, numerous people steered me in the right direction and in many cases offered the fruits of their own labor. Ron Frank, the producer of *The Hunt for Adolf Eichmann,* and Peter Kessler, the producer of *I Met Adolf Eichmann,* provided me with the transcripts from their interviews, an essential resource, particularly since many of the people they questioned for their documentaries have since passed away. Uki Goñi, author of *The Real Odessa,* offered critical advice for my research in Argentina, as did Professor Daniel Lvovich, Professor Ignacio Klich, Jorge Camarasa, Kenneth Marty, and Richard Wald. Patricia Ambinder helped me understand Peter Malkin. Stan Lauryssens and Roelf van Til gave me insight into the Sassen-Eichmann relationship. In Israel, Professors Leonardo Senkman and Shlomo Shpiro were more than generous with their time and my many questions. Karen Broderick and Marvin Goldman were instrumental in collecting the pictures in the insert. Thank you also to Zvi Aharoni and Wilhelm Dietl for photographs of the operation.

This narrative would not have been possible without the firsthand recollections of those involved in the operation. Although I was not able to speak with Isser Harel, Peter Malkin, and Zvi Aharoni, their memoirs of the operation were essential in making this story come to life. I want to thank all those noted in the bibliography who spoke to me in the course of my research, but I would especially like to acknowledge Avraham Shalom and Shaul Shaul. They answered follow-up after follow-up with patience and exacting detail.

I would still be struggling with my pidgin German, and would be totally lost in Spanish and Hebrew, without my able translators: Tanja Gonzalez, Olga Cudnik, Dan Shorer, Milagros Simarro, Sari Cohen, and Judy Heiblum. Kudos also to Melissa Sarver, who transcribed many of my interviews.

I would have been sunk without my crack publishing team. First, Liz O'Donnell, my first line of defense, reworked what I too generously called a rough draft. I tremble to think what I would have done without her. Next, Susan Canavan, my editor at Houghton Mifflin, has been an invaluable treasure in bringing my work to the world with enthusiasm and skill. This is our third book together. My sincerest appreciation also goes to the whole team at Houghton Mifflin, especially Megan Wilson, Lori Glazer, Larry Cooper, and my manuscript editor, Barb Jatkola. I am also in debt to the great efforts of Scott Manning. A big thanks to Farley Chase, who ensured that this book would be published far and wide. And last but by no means least, kudos to my agent, Scott Waxman, who, as usual, was with this book from its gestation.

Finally, to my wife, Diane, and my baby girls, Charlotte and Julia: you are everything.

Notes

In citing works in the notes, short titles have generally been used. Works frequently cited have been identified by the following abbreviations.

AdsD   Archiv der Sozialen Demokratie der Friedrich Ebert Stiftung, Bonn
AGN   Archivo General de la Nación, Buenos Aires
AI   Author interview
BArch   Bundesarchiv, Koblenz
CZA   Central Zionist Archives, Jerusalem
HAE   *The Hunt for Adolf Eichmann*
HHStAW   Hessisches Hauptstaatsarchiv, Wiesbaden
IMAE   *I Met Adolf Eichmann*
ISA   Israel State Archives, Jerusalem
NA   National Archives, Washington, DC
OHD   Harman Institute of Contemporary Jewry, Oral History Division, Hebrew University, Jerusalem
YVS   Yad Vashem, Jerusalem

page CHAPTER 1

1 Outside Mauthausen, a concentration: "Eichmann Memoirs," p. 23; Aschenauer, pp. 332–33.
Dressed in his pale: Boyle, p. 5; NA, RG 319, IRR, Adolf Eichmann, "Interrogation of Dieter Wisliceny," December 2, 1946.

2 "Send down the Master": *The Trial of Adolf Eichmann,* p. 1768; "Eichmann Memoirs," p. 24; Hausner, p. 135.
Along the 250-mile route: "Eichmann Memoirs," p. 23.
Besides this stop: Cesarani, pp. 162–67.
Eichmann ran his office: Ibid., pp. 117–58.

3 The first stage: Zweig, pp. 49–59.
To prevent any escapes: Cesarani, pp. 162–69; Braham, *The Politics of Genocide,* pp. 434–37; Aschenauer, p. 336.

4   For all these plans: Cesarani, p. 166.

     When they reached: Braham, *The Politics of Genocide,* p. 386; Tschuy, p. 3.

     Gestapo agents fanned out: Höttl, p. 204; Lozowick, p. 246.

     Eichmann established: Tschuy, pp. 53–54.

     Fearing assassination: Wighton, *Eichmann,* pp. 154–55; NA, RG 319, IRR, Eich-
     mann, "Interrogation of Dieter Wisliceny."

     At the crack of dawn: YVS, O.3, File 6151, Testimony of Zeev Sapir, April 9, 1990;
     Z. Sapir interview, *IMAE;* Braham, *The Politics of Genocide,* pp. 590–94; Mermel-
     stein, pp. 2, 74.

6   "Jews: You have": YVS, Testimony of Zeev Sapir,; Z. Sapir interview, *IMAE.* In
     his account, Sapir also details how Eichmann executed several ghetto prisoners,
     but since there is no corroboration of this occurrence in any other historical re-
     cord, I have excluded the event. That said, it is clear from other histories that
     Eichmann was indeed touring Carpatho-Ruthenia at this time and that these vis-
     its were recorded in the press. See Braham, *The Politics of Genocide,* pp. 606–7;
     Hausner, p. 139.

     Soon after Eichmann's visit: YVS, Testimony of Zeev Sapir; Z. Sapir interview,
     IMAE; Levai, *Eichmann in Hungary,* pp. 104–7; Nagy-Talavera, p. 289; Lengyel,
     pp. 6–23.

7   Four days after: YVS, Testimony of Zeev Sapir; Levi, pp. 18–19.

     Six weeks later: Erez.

8   Five of the six: Braham, *The Politics of Genocide,* table 19.1. This figure is based on
     German statistics and includes some Jews already deported from Budapest.

     Every day, an average: Gutman and Berenbaum, pp. 88–89; Braham, *The Politics
     of Genocide,* p. 676.

9   Only the Jews: Hausner, pp. 139–40; Braham, *The Politics of Genocide,* p. 742.

     Still, there were forces: Erez.

     Incensed at the interruption: Ibid.

     A week later: Braham, *The Politics of Genocide,* pp. 771–75; Cesarani, pp. 184–85;
     Braham and Miller, pp. 138–40.

10   "Under no circumstances": Hausner, p. 143.

     With the war: For the sake of brevity, I have not included Eichmann's role in
     the famous "blood for trucks" deal with Joel Brand (see chapter 3). It is clear to
     me that Eichmann had little intention of fulfilling his end of the bargain. If you
     would like to know more about these events, there are a number of books devoted
     to the subject, including Brand's autobiography, *Desperate Mission: Joel Brand's
     Story* (New York: Criterion Books, 1958); Andre Biss's *A Million Jews to Save;* and
     Yehuda Bauer's *Jews for Sale.*

     Eichmann thought this was: *The Trial of Adolf Eichmann,* pp. 1518–19.

     He rode horses and took: Cesarani, pp. 186–88; NA, RG 319, IRR, Eichmann,
     "Interrogation of Dieter Wisliceny"; *The Trial of Adolf Eichmann,* pp. 1789, 1834,
     1855, 1971; Levai, *Black Book,* p. 109.

11   "You see, I'm back": Yahil, p. 517.

     The fact that: Ibid., pp. 152–53; Levai, *Eichmann in Hungary,* pp. 14, 164–66; Bra-
     ham, *The Politics of Genocide,* pp. 834–43.

     Before they met: Lauryssens, p. 76.

     "If until now": *The Trial of Adolf Eichmann,* p. 1530.

On a late December morning: *The Trial of Adolf Eichmann,* pp. 970–74; YVS, Testimony of Zeev Sapir; Z. Sapir interview, *IMAE;* Gutman and Berenbaum, pp. 50–57.

12 Once Sapir had arrived: YVS, Testimony of Zeev Sapir; Z. Sapir interview, *IMAE; The Trial of Adolf Eichmann,* pp. 970–74; Muller, pp. 135–38; Lengyel, pp. 16–20. Now, filing out: YVS, Testimony of Zeev Sapir; Z. Sapir interview, *IMAE; The Trial of Adolf Eichmann,* pp. 970–74.

CHAPTER 2

14 On April 12, 1945: Shirer, p. 1105; Gilbert, *The Day the War Ended,* pp. 8–9; Shephard, p. 7; Botting, p. 10.

While these forces: Shephard, pp. 7–8; Miller, p. 762.

As early as the summer: F. H. Hinsley, E. E. Thomas, C.F.G. Ransom, and R. C. Knight, *British Intelligence in the Second World War: Its Influence on Strategy and Operations,* vol. 2 (New York: Cambridge University Press, 1981), pp. 670–73.

15 "To the Hitlerites": Nizkor Project, "Holocaust Almanac—The Weczler-Vrba Report," http://www.nizkor.org/ftp.cgi/camps/auschwitz/ftp.py?camps/auschwitz //auschwitz.07.

Roosevelt had made: Conot, p. 9.

"shot to death": Overy, p. 6; Bower, p. 82.

"otherwise the world": Overy, p. 8.

Plans to capture: Botting, pp. 202–6; Bower, pp. 113–24.

"notorious offenses": Overy, p. 28.

16 In contrast: Ziemke, p. 219; Bower, pp. 111–13.

Guided by former inmates: Este, p. 687; Read and Fisher, p. 770; Read, pp. 762–63.

17 "The indignity of death": Reilly, p. 58.

"Why have we": Ibid.

By April 13: Read and Fisher, pp. 261, 317.

18 "Well, Eichmann": Aschenauer, pp. 415–16; Von Lang, *Eichmann Interrogated,* pp. 257–58; *The Trial of Adolf Eichmann,* p. 140.

Eichmann had romantic notions: Höttl, pp. 308–9; Von Lang, *Eichmann Interrogated,* p. 256; *The Trial of Adolf Eichmann,* p. 1520; Farago, p. 160. Eichmann was not averse to false bravado, but in this case his testimony after the war appears to be true, since it was confirmed by several of his SS colleagues, including Wilhelm Höttl and Dieter Wisliceny. See NA, RG 319, IRR, Adolf Eichmann, "Summary of Interrogation Reports from Counter Intelligence War Room, London," November 19, 1945, and NA, RG 319, IRR, Adolf Eichmann, "Interrogation of Dieter Wisliceny," December 2, 1946.

"I have never been": Eichmann, "Meine Gotzen—September 6, 1961," p. 536; Aschenauer, p. 416.

"For me": "Eichmann Memoirs," p. 46; *The Trial of Adolf Eichmann,* p. 1804.

19 From Prague: Eichmann, "Meine Gotzen—September 6, 1961," p. 538; "Eichmann Memoirs," pp. 48–49; Aschenauer, pp. 416–17; Von Lang, *Eichmann Interrogated,* pp. 258–61.

20 On April 30: Botting, pp. 46–47; Read and Fisher, pp. 385–86.

Fifty feet under: Gilbert, *The Day the War Ended,* pp. 41–42; Roper, p. 119; Read, p. 909.

21 Over the past month: Read and Fisher, pp. 257–58.

Of the top leadership: Shirer, p. 1135.

When Eichmann arrived: Höttl, pp. 301–2; Black, pp. 234–37.

"You: You belong": Cesarani, p. 31.

"Did everything turn out": Ibid., pp. 315–17; "Eichmann Memoirs," pp. 48–51; Aschenauer, pp. 416–20; Von Lang, *Eichmann Interrogated,* pp. 263–67; Lauryssens, p. 86.

CHAPTER 3

24 The following morning: "Eichmann Memoirs," p. 56; Lawson.

25 An innocent, uncomplicated: NA, RG 319, IRR, Adolf Eichmann, "Interrogation of Dieter Wisliceny," December 2, 1946; Pick, p. 114; Cesarani, pp. 23–29, 43–45.

Eichmann had bought: "Eichmann Memoirs," pp. 57–58; There have been any number of stories that Eichmann hid hundreds of pounds of gold in the mountains around Altaussee. Most of these stories originated with Wilhelm Höttl, an SS officer who knew Eichmann in Hungary and saw him before he escaped after the war. See Höttl, pp. 315–17, as well as ISA, 3017/8-a, Report of Höttl Adjunct, October 29, 1949. Unless this gold was stolen from Eichmann, he never had it in the first place, as he lived poorly from the moment he reached Altaussee in May 1945 until his capture fifteen years later.

"The war is over": Lawson.

Then he left instructions: I do not have a specific source for this statement, but the facts indicate that Eichmann and his wife had arrangements as to what she was to say and do after his escape. She was consistent over numerous investigations throughout the seven years she remained in Austria.

Then Eichmann went out: Lawson; Aschenauer, p. 423.

26 As he climbed: Matteson, pp. 3–39.

By dark, Eichmann: "Eichmann Memoirs," pp. 55–58; Cesarani, p. 202.

27 "Do you know": Weissberg, p. 121.

Once the peace: U.S. Department of Justice, exhibits, p. 95; Sayer and Botting, pp. 201–5; Ziemke, p. 320.

Since the liberation: Ziemke, p. 221; Sayer and Botting, p. 225.

28 "From Norway": Bar-Zohar, *The Avengers,* p. 108.

The day after Eichmann: Matteson, pp. 31–39; Black, pp. 258–59.

29 "Well, gentlemen": Bar-Zohar, *The Avengers,* p. 109.

Himmler followed: Gilbert, *The Day the War Ended,* pp. 390–91.

Other top Nazi leaders: Overy, pp. 33–35; Bloch, p. 44; Conot, pp. 31, 37, 70–72.

30 "The game is up": Bloch, p. 433.

Every day, more than: Ziemke, p. 380.

Although the Russians: Botting, p. 201; Wiesenthal, *The Murderers Among Us,* p. 56.

After the war: Briggs, p. 174; Cohen, pp. 188–213; Segev, pp. 140–49; Bar-Zohar, *The Avengers,* pp. 23–26.

31 With so many hell-bent: Overy, p. 37.

Eichmann and Jänisch: Eichmann, *Meine Flucht;* Aschenauer, p. 426.

Most wanted some food: Bischof and Ambrose, pp. 7–9.

As soon as night: Eichmann, *Meine Flucht.*

32   Born in an industrial: Cesarani, pp. 1–156. In this biographical summary of Adolf
     Eichmann before Hungary, I have drawn heavily on the thorough and balanced
     biography by David Cesarani, *Becoming Eichmann.* Much of the Eichmann histo-
     riography paints him as either a deluded madman who was bent on the destruc-
     tion of the Jews from cradle to grave or, thanks to Hannah Arendt, a sober, pas-
     sionless desk clerk. Cesarani revealed a more realistic portrait. I also referenced
     the following sources in completing this summary: "Eichmann Memoirs"; BArch,
     Sassen Transcripts, 6/110; *The Trial of Adolf Eichmann;* Lawson; Reynolds; Von
     Lang, *Eichmann Interrogated;* Bukey; Wighton, *Eichmann;* Clarke; Yahil; Mulisch;
     Arendt; Mendelsohn and Detweiler, vol. 8, pp. 71–93. Any quotes have separate
     notes.

     In Linz: Goldenhagen, pp. 28–29.

33   "the most dangerous enemy": Cesarani, p. 51.

     "They are in my hands": *The Trial of Adolf Eichmann,* p. 1589.

     "requisite hardness": Von Lang, *Eichmann Interrogated,* p. 157.

34   "The Führer has ordered": Ibid., p. 81.

     Eichmann was sent: Ibid., pp. 74–77.

     "political solution": Cesarani, p. 115; Hausner, p. 11.

     On January 20, 1942: Roseman, pp. 93–157.

35   "the Popes": *The Trial of Adolf Eichmann,* p. 1423.

     "They were stealing": "Eichmann Memoirs," p. 14.

     He was keen: Ibid., pp. 202–3; Eichmann, *Meine Flucht;* Aschenauer, p. 426.

36   While in the mountains: Cesarani, p. 202.

     "Otto Eckmann": Eichmann, *Meine Flucht;* Aschenauer, p. 426.

37   Wrecked tanks and cars: Spender, pp. 21–33, 77, 217; Ziemke, p. 242; Botting,
     pp. 94–115.

     "It is your own business": Adolf Eichmann, YVS, M.9, File 584a, Interrogation of
     Rudolf Scheide by Curt L. Ponger.

     In late June: Aschenauer, p. 426; Eichmann, *Meine Flucht.*

     A sea of soldiers: Bischof and Ambrose, pp. 219–37; Pearlman, p. 29.

CHAPTER 4

39   "Have you heard": Wiesenthal, *The Murderers Among Us,* p. 100.

     Only four weeks before: Ibid., pp. 10–14; Pick, pp. 31–98.

40   "SS Major-General Katzmann": Pick, p. 86.

     In late July: Wiesenthal, *The Murderers Among Us,* p. 100. According to Wiesen-
     thal, he met with Asher Ben-Natan (Arthur Pier), the head of the Haganah and
     Brichah in Austria in July. However, since Ben-Natan did not arrive in Austria
     until November—note Pearlman, p. 15—it is impossible that Wiesenthal met
     with him at this time. Nonetheless, it is clear that Wiesenthal had this informa-
     tion, so I have assumed that he met with one of Ben-Natan's compatriots, Ehud
     Avriel or Gideon Raphael.

     Raphael handed Wiesenthal: Pearlman, p. 14.

41 The name Eichmann: Wiesenthal, *The Murderers Among Us,* p. 100.

Unbeknownst to Wiesenthal: NA, RG 319, IRR, Adolf Eichmann, "Summary of Interrogation Reports from Counter Intelligence War Room, London," November 19, 1945. Specifically, the Allies had already interrogated SD agent Werner Goettsch and Wilhelm Höttl, both of whom knew Eichmann intimately, at this point in July.

"Eichmann!": Wiesenthal, *Justice Not Vengeance,* p. 67.

He could not bear: Wiesenthal, *The Murderers Among Us,* p. 25.

On July 28: NA, RG 319, IRR, Adolf Eichmann, "Summary of Interrogation Reports from Counter Intelligence War Room, London," November 19, 1945; Wiesenthal, *The Murderers Among Us,* p. 101.

42 Standing in a line: Eichmann, "Meine Gotzen — September 6, 1961," p. 541; Eichmann, *Meine Flucht;* Aschenauer, p. 426.

Contrary to the very: NA, RG 319, IRR, Adolf Eichmann, "Interrogation of Dieter Wisliceny," December 2, 1946.

In October: Pearlman, p. 30; Wighton, *Eichmann,* p. 227–28; Aschenauer, pp. 426–27.

43 He returned to Ober-Dachstetten: Aschenauer, pp. 426–27.

Two hours before dawn: Conot, pp. 100–105; Maser, p. 187.

44 After a brief introduction: *Trial of German Major War Criminals,* vol. 2, pp. 15–95.

45 "I suppose we'll": Conot, p. 105.

"I declare myself": *Trial of German Major War Criminals,* vol. 2, pp. 96–97; Taylor, p. 166.

"The privilege of opening": *Trial of German Major War Criminals,* vol. 2, pp. 97–98.

46 "Together with": *Trial of German Major War Criminals,* vol. 3, pp. 501–2.

"Yes, Eichmann handed me": *Trial of German Major War Criminals,* vol. 4, pp. 354–73.

47 The CIC had interviewed: Wiesenthal, *The Murderers Among Us,* p. 102.

By early September: NA, RG 319, IRR, Adolf Eichmann, SHAEF Headquarters, Military Intelligence, Adolf Eichmann, September 25, 1945; NA, RG 263, Adolf Eichmann Name File (CIA), The German SD and the Persecution of Jews 1933–44, August 27, 1945; NA, RG 319, IRR, Adolf Eichmann, CIC Report on Adolf Eichmann, October 21, 1945.

"urgently wanted at": NA, RG 319, IRR, Adolf Eichmann, SHAEF Headquarters, Military Intelligence, Adolf Eichmann, September 25, 1945.

"of the highest importance": NA, RG 319, IRR, Adolf Eichmann, "Summary of Interrogation Reports from Counter Intelligence War Room, London," November 19, 1945.

48 Yet at the start: U.S. Department of Justice, report, p. 41; Botting, pp. 202–6; Bower, pp. 113–24. For a more detailed analysis of the problems of the investigation of war criminals, see Tom Bower's *Blind Eye to Murder,* which provides an impressive, damning survey. As I note as well, individual investigators were eager to do their jobs, but political leaders lacked the commitment to pursue war criminals beyond the top echelon tried at Nuremberg.

They had been photographed: Overy, p. 32; Bischof and Ambrose, p. 218.

A few days after: NA, RG 319, IRR, Adolf Eichmann, CIC Report on Adolf Eichmann, January 10, 1946.

"a desperate type": NA, RG 263, Adolf Eichmann Name File (CIA), "SS Obersturmbannführer Adolf Eichmann," 1946.

At the Ober-Dachstetten camp: BArch, Sassen Transcripts, 6/96, pp. 57–58; Eichmann, *Meine Flucht;* Pearlman, pp. 31–33; NA, RG 65, Adolf Eichmann File (IWG FBI), "The Chase That Doomed Eichmann," article by Zwy Aldouby, no source.

49 "I have known": Aschenauer, p. 428.

They agreed to hold: BArch, Sassen Transcripts, 6/96, pp. 57–58; Eichmann, *Meine Flucht;* Pearlman, pp. 31–33; NA, RG 65, Adolf Eichmann File (IWG FBI), "The Chase That Doomed Eichmann."

CHAPTER 5

51 It was late May: Friedman, *The Hunter,* p. 117.
Near the end: Ibid., pp. 10–98.

52 He joined the Polish: Ibid., pp. 104–55.
"And we're anxious": Ibid., pp. 117–21.

53 Pier explained that: Ibid.; Pearlman, pp. 12–13; Diamant, Manuscript,; Bar-Zohar, *The Avengers,* p. 71.
"This is not": Friedman, *The Hunter,* pp. 117–24; Bar-Zohar, *The Avengers,* p. 76.

54 Five Jewish avengers: OHD, (130)4, Interview with Asher Ben-Natan; Bar-Zohar, *The Avengers,* pp. 59–62; Reynolds, pp. 27–32; ISA, 3017/8-a, Report of Dr. Nagel, n.d.

55 "We are Jews": Bar-Zohar, *The Avengers,* p. 61.
"I swear to you": Reynolds, p. 30.

56 Adolf Eichmann was still: R. Tramer, M. Eggers, and U. Schulze interviews, *IMAE;* O. Lindhorst interview, *IMAE;* Eichmann, *Meine Flucht;* BArch, Sassen Transcripts, 6/96.
After escaping: NA, RG 65, Adolf Eichmann File (IWG FBI), "A Woman Recalls a Friend Called Eichmann," article by Fern Eckman, no source; Pearlman, pp. 32–33.

57 At the end: R. Tramer, M. Eggers, and U. Schulze interviews, *IMAE;* Eichmann, *Meine Flucht.*
"Are you trying": Ben-Natan, pp. 72–74; Friedman, *The Hunter,* pp. 166–69; Diamant, Manuscript. As with much of the history of the capture of Adolf Eichmann, there are competing versions as to who exactly accomplished what. This is particularly true concerning the early postwar stage, when Friedman, Pier, Simon Wiesenthal, Manus Diamant, and others were operating together. In the case of this conversation with Weisl, Diamant and Friedman both claimed to have attended the interrogation. I studied a number of different accounts and found that Friedman's description of the episode was more convincing and was backed up by Arthur Pier (Asher Ben-Natan).

59 Friedman and Pier returned: NA, RG 319, IRR, Adolf Eichmann, "Interrogation of Dieter Wisliceny," December 2, 1946; Pearlman, pp. 16–18; Diamant, Manuscript.
Handsome and suave: Diamant, Manuscript; Ben-Natan, pp. 72–74.

60   "Thank you": Diamant, Manuscript; Briggs, p. 164.
61   Hundreds of copies: NA, RG 319, IRR, Adolf Eichmann, CIC Report on Adolf
     Eichmann, June 7, 1947.

CHAPTER 6

62   Eichmann wanted to: Eichmann, *Meine Flucht.*
     The capture and confession: Hoess, p. 174.
     One day Eichmann read: BArch, Sassen Transcripts, 6/96; Aschenauer,
     pp. 429–30; Aharoni and Dietl, p. 47.
63   He began to: Eichmann, *Meine Flucht.*
     In December 1947: Wiesenthal, *The Murderers Among Us,* pp. 109–10.
     This was a story: NA, RG 263, Adolf Eichmann Name File (CIA), SS Obersturm-
     bannführer SS Adolf Eichmann, Report from Berlin, June 17, 1946.
     He had also read: Adolf Eichmann, YVS, M.9, File 584a, Interrogation of Rudolf
     Scheide by Curt L. Ponger; NA, RG 319, IRR, Adolf Eichmann, CIC Report
     from Gerald Steiner, December 3, 1946.
     If Vera Eichmann succeeded: Wiesenthal, *The Murderers Among Us,* pp. 109–10.
64   Manus Diamant had told: Diamant, *Geheimauftrag,* pp. 228–29.
65   That December: Friedman, *The Hunter,* pp. 176–85.
     Follow-up trials: George Ginsburg, *The Nuremberg Trial and International Law*
     (Amsterdam: Martinus Nijhoff, 1990), p. 267.
     There was a scattering: Conot, pp. 516–19; Ashman and Wagman, p. 17.
66   One gloomy wintry: Wiesenthal, *The Murderers Among Us,* pp. 78–81.
     "If you don't hear": "Eichmann in Germany."
     The morning of his departure: Eichmann, *Meine Flucht;* Aschenauer, p. 429.
67   Eichmann's identification card: Goñi, p. 298.
     Before leaving: O. Lindhorst interview, *IMAE.*
     Then Eichmann picked up: Eichmann, *Meine Flucht;* Aharoni and Dietl, p. 147.
     The town was swarming: Aarons and Loftus, p. 40.
69   In February 1945: Meding, p. 50.
     "It was a mere": Newton, p. xv; Meding, p. 50.
     Perón came from: Goñi, pp. 1–3, 16–17; Rathkolb, p. 192.
     After Germany's defeat: Rathkolb, pp. 205–20.
70   "outrage that history": Meding, p. 158.
     "lodge like a cyst": Ibid., p. 40; Rein, p. 55.
     Led by the head: Meding, pp. 46–54; Goñi, pp. 101–15. No author can discuss the
     movement of war criminals to Argentina without referencing Uki Goñi's *The Real
     Odessa* and Holger Meding's *Flücht vor Nürnberg?* In particular when it comes to
     Adolf Eichmann, Goñi provides incredible insight into the machinations by
     which he entered Argentina.
     The network would never: Meding, pp. 76–83; Rathkolb, pp. 247–49; Klee,
     pp. 31–34; Lewy, p. xxiv; Goñi, pp. 229–31; Aarons and Loftus, pp. 30–31.
71   According to a confidential: NA, RG 59, 800.0128/5-1547, "La Vista Report";
     Simpson, pp. 185–87; Breitman, pp. 350–420.
     However, none of: Goñi, pp. 117, 231–35; Meding, pp. 67–88.
72   Traveling as Ricardo: Eichmann Immigration Card, Direccion Nacional de Mi-

graciones (DNM), Buenos Aires; *Giovanna C* Passenger List, July 1950, DNM; Goñi, pp. 292–317; Eichmann, *Meine Flucht.*

During his time: Eichmann, *Meine Flucht.*

73   Accompanying him: "Interview with Klaus Eichmann"; Goñi, pp. 299–300.

As the ship steamed: Eichmann, *Meine Flucht.*

The month-long journey: Angolina Bascelli, AI.

Eight times the size: Gunther, pp. 170–71; Prendle, pp. 1, 7; Scobie, p. 3.

"the distances": Gunther, p. 171.

74   "Listen": Eichmann, *Meine Flucht.*

Name? Ricardo Klement: *Giovanna C* Passenger List, July 1950, DNM.

CHAPTER 7

76   Carlos Fuldner: Eichmann, *Meine Flucht;* AGN, Martin Bormann File; AGN, Josef Mengele File.

Buenos Aires was awash: Goñi, p. 166.

Eichmann found that: Newton, pp. 65–69; Rein, p. 171.

The defeat of: Research Notes, *HAE.*

"Among all the capitals": Freiwald, p. 169.

77   Like Paris or Rome: "Buenos Aires: Argentina's Melting Pot," *National Geographic,* November 1967; Posner and Ware, pp. 96–97; Scobie, pp. 166–67; Prendle, pp. 168–70.

Eichmann had 485 pesos: Eichmann, *Meine Flucht;* AGN, Martin Bormann File; AGN, Josef Mengele File; Eichmann, "Meine Gotzen — September 6, 1961," pp. 452–53; Camarasa, pp. 152–53.

78   On June 30: H. Luehr interview, *IMAE; Clarin,* February 12, 1992; Scobie, p. 17; Meding, p. 217.

"German Company": Camarasa, pp. 152–57; Meding, pp. 215–16.

"gone through difficult": H. Luehr interview, *IMAE.*

79   "the uncle of": Aharoni and Dietl, p. 67.

So on the day: Eichmann, *Meine Flucht;* "Interview with Klaus Eichmann"; Lawson.

Flags were flown: Fraser and Navarro, pp. 163–65.

Two days after: "Interview with Klaus Eichmann"; Lawson; Lauryssens, p. 39.

80   "Veronika": Lawson.

As soon as the railways: "Interview with Klaus Eichmann"; Lauryssens, p. 39; Aharoni, *On Life and Death,* p. 118.

"Mrs. Eichmann and her sons": Wiesenthal, *The Murderers Among Us,* pp. 122–23; Israel State Archives, File 3017/8–9, Austrian Police Reports, 1950-54.

81   "The Nazis lost": Levy, p. 122.

"prolonging the concentration camp": Ibid., p. 123.

His compatriot: Friedman, *The Hunter,* pp. 185–209.

"You've sunk yourself": Ibid., p. 193.

82   "Tadek": Ibid., pp. 208–9; Levy, p. 122.

"There are some people": CZA, Z 6/842, Letter from Simon Wiesenthal to Nahum Goldmann, March 30, 1954; Wiesenthal, *The Murderers Among Us,* p. 123.

83 Upon his return: Pick, pp. 131–35; Wiesenthal, *The Murderers Among Us,* p. 124; Levy, pp. 123–24.
    "I have been dealing": CZA, Z 6/842, Letter from Simon Wiesenthal to Nahum Goldmann, March 30, 1954.

84 "This is of great": Pick, pp. 136, 137.
    "We are not": NA, RG 263, Adolf Eichmann Name File (CIA), Appeal to DCI by Mr. Adolph Berle and Rabbi Kalmanowitz, October 20, 1953. According to a secret CIC report in March 1952, the same lack of interest in pursuing Eichmann was stated as the policy of the CIC. At this time, however, the U.S. government was not nearly as blunt. The report states, "In view of the Subject's [Eichmann] reputation and the interest voiced by elements other than the US in his location and apprehension, it is felt that a disinterest in his arrest by U.S. authorities at this time might not be recommendable. Consequently, in reference to the inquiry submitted by Austrian police authorities, it may be advisable to confirm continued interest in [the] Subject's apprehension." See NA, RG 319, IRR, Adolf Eichmann, CIC Report from 430th CIC operations headquarters on Adolf Eichmann, March 31, 1952.
    "The time has come": Wighton, *Adenauer,* p. 310.

85 Kalmanowitz had passed: NA, RG 263, Adolf Eichmann Name File (CIA), Letter from Simon Wiesenthal to Dr. Goldmann, March 30, 1954.
    Dispirited by: CZA, Z 6/863, Letter from Simon Wiesenthal to Dr. Goldmann, September 21, 1954.
    Soon after: Wiesenthal, *The Murderers Among Us,* p. 124.
    "We've got other problems": Wiesenthal, *Justice Not Vengeance,* p. 74.

CHAPTER 8

86 Nick was tall: *Clarin,* May 27, 1960.
    Sylvia was also attractive: Friedman, *The Blind Man;* A. Kleinert, AI.
    "It would have been": Harel, p. 17.
    What his dinner guest: A. Hahn, AI; A. Kleinert, AI.

87 Even after six years: "Interview with Klaus Eichmann."
    As he had done: Lauryssens, p. 92.
    Willem Sassen: S. Sassen, AI.

88 "I would like": BArch, Sassen Transcripts, 6/110, pp. 9–10.
    Eichmann paused: Hausner, p. 83.

89 "real hot story": "Life and Eichmann."
    After the war: Groeneveld, pp. 358–66; Lauryssens, p. 48; Goñi, pp. 239–40.
    Sassen and Eichmann: P. Probierzym, AI; Hausner, p. 10; Rassinier, pp. 144–47; Lauryssens, p. 72.
    "Let us write": Hausner, p. 10.
    So began their sessions: S. Sassen, AI.

90 "I sat at my desk": Lauryssens, p. 77.
    "We used the Warsaw": Cesarani, p. 165.
    "I sent my": Lauryssens, p. 77.
    He continued with: BArch, Sassen Transcripts, 6/95.

91   He rented his modest: AGN, Martin Bormann File; "Eichmann in Germany"; Goñi, p. 303.

"Beware of Klement": "Interview with Klaus Eichmann."

When Eichmann lost: Ibid.; Harris, p. 216.

92   Eichmann was a quiet: R. Tonet interview, *IMAE*.

One night, he snatched: Hull, pp. 99–101.

Nor was he pleased: Von Lang, *Eichmann Interrogated*, pp. 286–90.

Klaus was more interested: Lauryssens, p. 101.

Eichmann's only wish: Lawson.

In Coronel Suárez: A. Hahn, AI; A. Kleinert, AI; Dr. E. Palenzola, AI; Harel, pp. 16–19; Friedman, *The Blind Man.*

93   Lothar knew that he: AdsD, Nachlass Fritz Bauer, Box 1, Letter from Lothar Hermann to Fritz Bauer, June 25, 1960.

Born in Stuttgart: Fröhlich, pp. 11–14; Perels and Wojak, pp. 9–17.

94   In December 1956: HHStAW, 461/32440/File 2, Arrest Warrant for Adolf Eichmann, December 12, 1956.

He charged his senior: HHStAW, 461/32440/File 2, Letter from Institute of Contemporary History, Munich, to Senior Public Prosecutor, Frankfurt on the Main, May 13, 1957; HHStAW, 461/32440/File 2, Letter from State Police, Buchen County, to Senior Public Prosecutor, Frankfurt on the Main, May 31, 1957; HHStAW, 461/32440/File 2, Letter from Federal Office of Criminal Investigations to Senior Public Prosecutor, Frankfurt on the Main, July 8, 1957; AdsD, Nachlass Fritz Bauer, Box 1, Letter from Lothar Hermann to Fritz Bauer, June 25, 1960.

95   Wearing a blue dress: A. Hahn, AI; A. Kleinert, AI; Friedman, *The Blind Man;* Harel, pp. 18–19. To recount the scene of Sylvia Hermann's visit to the Eichmann house, I drew on these four primary sources, which contradict one another on various levels. What is beyond doubt is that Hermann found the address of Adolf Eichmann and presented herself at the house to see if Nick's father was indeed the Nazi war criminal, an act of tremendous courage.

CHAPTER 9

98   On September 19: Vogel, pp. 55, 62.

"Eichmann has been": Harel, p. 4.

Bauer knew well: Perels and Wojak, p. 14; Shpiro, *Geheimdienste in der Weltgeschichte,* p. 306.

Although Chancellor: Schwarz, pp. 429–31; Fulbrook, pp. 60–61.

99   Bauer detested the fact: NA, RG 263, Adolf Eichmann Name File (CIA), The Eichmann Trial and Allegations Against Secretary State Globke, February 7, 1961. This is an extraordinary report from the American consul in Frankfurt. It reveals that Bauer, with the backing of Zinn, helped the Israelis capture Eichmann. It also reveals that Bauer hoped to use the capture of Eichmann to bring down Globke. Bauer hoped that Eichmann could corroborate testimony that Globke was involved in the deportation of Greek Jews.

Before making any move: Harel, pp. xviii–xix; Wojak, pp. 39–41; HHStAW,

461/32440/File 2, Letter to Senior Public Prosecutor, Frankfurt on the Main, from Federal Office of Criminal Investigations, July 8, 1957.

"I'll be perfectly frank": Producer's Notes, *HAE*.

100   Not far from: A. Shalom, AI; Y. Gat, AI; Bar-Zohar, *Spies in the Promised Land,* p. 156; Bar-Zohar, *The Avengers,* p. 161.

On a late September day: Harel, pp. 1–2.

101   The pursuit of war criminals: A. Shalom, AI; Fried, pp. 91–96; Bower, pp. 393–94.

The Mossad's lack: Fried, pp. 1–4; Douglas, pp. 154–56; Yablonka, p. 12.

Little mention: Zeev Eckstein, Kasztner's killer, was a paid informant of the Shin Bet, leading to accusations that the security services were behind the assassination, an unsubstantiated, unlikely scenario that Harel bitterly denied. Note Black and Benny, pp. 154–56.

Harel was the youngest: Bar-Zohar, *Spies in the Promised Land,* pp. 3–40; Black and Benny, pp. 25–47; Steven, pp. 36–46.

103   In 1947: Deacon, p. 56.

"Abdullah is going": Derogy and Carmel, pp. 84–85.

Two months later: Steven, pp. 15–16.

"You ought to resign": Bar-Zohar, *Spies in the Promised Land,* p. 98.

"The past is over": Thomas, p. 40.

Over the next: Black and Benny, pp. 131, 161–68.

104   With his successes: Steven, p. 63.

Harel was haunted: Harel, pp. 2–3.

He read transcripts: Diamant, Manuscript; Bower, p. 393.

Here was a man: Harel, pp. 2–3.

105   First, Isser Harel: Ibid., pp. 4–9.

He had made separate: HHStAW, 461/32440/File 2, Investigation of Maria Liebl, From State Police of Buchen to Frankfurt Senior Public Prosecutor, June 9, 1957.

106   Soon after: Harel, pp. 10–12; Aharoni, *On Life and Death,* p. 117.

107   When Shaul Darom: Harel, pp. 12–13.

The Mossad chief: ISA, 3037/2-a, Biography of Hofstetter, March 21, 1961.

At the end: Harel, pp. 14–15.

He was greeted: Documentary Interview Notes, *HAE;* Y. Gat, AI; L. Volk, AI.

108   Ilani inquired around: A. Kleinert, AI.

"My name is": Harel, pp. 16–22; AdsD, Nachlass Fritz Bauer, Box 1, Letter from Lothar Hermann to Fritz Bauer, June 25, 1960.

CHAPTER 10

111   On April 8: Harel, pp. 24–26; AdsD, Nachlass Fritz Bauer, Box 1, Letter from Lothar Hermann to Fritz Bauer, June 25, 1960; ISA, 6384/4-g, Letter from Lothar Hermann to Tuviah Friedman, June 5, 1960.

112   The letter from Lothar: Harel, pp. 26–27.

Harel had made: A. Shalom, AI.

"if you showed Isser": Bar-Zohar, *Spies in the Promised Land,* pp. 106–7.

113   If this proved: CZA, C 10/3702, Memo from Institute of Jewish Affairs, Report

8a; NA, RG 263, Adolf Eichmann Name File (CIA), Adolf Karl Eichmann, FBI Memorandum, September 15, 1948; ISA, 3017/8-a, Notice on June 7, 1951.

He uncovered: Derogy and Carmel, p. 155.

Given the Mossad's: Aharoni, *On Life and Death,* pp. 117–22; Y. Gat, AI. Although Isser Harel claimed in his autobiography that he never lost interest in the Bauer tip, it is clear from the evidence and the testimony of agents who later participated in the operation to capture Eichmann in 1960 that Harel did indeed shelve the dossier.

At the end of August: Harel, p. 27.

"Sometimes you put together": A. Shalom, AI.

114 Some months before: NA, RG 263, Adolf Eichmann Name File (CIA), Near Eastern Connections, March 19, 1958.

Both organizations: Breitman et al.; Simpson. These two books provide a comprehensive examination of the CIA and German recruitment of former Nazis and benefited greatly from the Nazi War Crimes Disclosure Act (1998), which declassified tens of thousands of U.S. intelligence records.

"born in Israel": NA, RG 263, Adolf Eichmann Name File (CIA), Near Eastern Connections, March 19, 1958.

Simultaneous with these: Wojak, pp. 30–31.

115 Neither of them: This conjecture that the BND and the CIA wanted to protect Globke is based on the fact that once Eichmann was captured, these organizations made strident attempts to excise any mention of Globke from Eichmann's memoirs, which were coming to light. See NA, RG 263, Adolf Eichmann File (CIA), CIA Cables, September 16–20, 1960.

In San Fernando: "Interview with Klaus Eichmann"; *La Razon,* April 24, 1961; *Ahora,* June 6, 1960; Aharoni and Dietl, pp. 100–102.

116 After a series: "Eichmann File," Tribunales Federales de Comodoro Py, Buenos Aires.

Jorge Antonio: Weber.

In *Hitler: The Last Ten Days:* Von Lang, *Eichmann Interrogated,* p. 287.

"The author should be": Ibid., p. 288.

117 "1. Every man": Ibid.

Eichmann was increasingly: P. Probierzym, AI.

"I am growing tired": Von Lang, *Eichmann Interrogated,* pp. 291–92.

CHAPTER 11

119 At dusk on Saturday: Friedman, *The Hunter,* pp. 13–15.

When Friedman had first: Ibid., pp. 208–20.

120 Schüle was the director: Fulbrook, p. 69.

Friedman had sent Schüle: ISA, 6384/4-g, Letter from Erwin Schüle to Tuviah Friedman, August 20, 1959; Friedman, *Die Korrespondenz,* Letter from Tuviah Friedman to Erwin Schüle, August 13, 1959; ISA, 3086/12-hz, Foreign Ministry Letter from Mr. T. Miron to Mr. Tzur, October 10, 1959.

He strode over: Friedman, *The Hunter,* pp. 236–50; ISA, 3086/12-hz, Letter from L. Savir to Dr. Shinar, October 23, 1959; Wojak, p. 33.

121 "issue the orders": Friedman, *The Hunter,* p. 251.

"completely incorrect": ISA, 6384/4-g, Letter from Lothar Hermann to Tuviah Friedman, October 17, 1959.

122   According to his source: Harel, p. 32.

Bauer had resolved: Z. Aharoni interview, *IMAE;* Aharoni, *On Life and Death,* pp. 123–26; Wojak, pp. 40–41.

Bauer could not reveal: Despite many efforts in Germany and Israel to uncover the identity of this source, I was unable to prove many of the abundant theories on his or her identity. Stan Lauryssens, the author of a biography on Sassen, presents the idea that Sassen was the informant (based largely on the confirmed fact that Sassen later worked with the Mossad on finding Mengele). See Lauryssens. Others state that the information came from captured Nazi smugglers in Austria or a fugitive Nazi who wanted to get back at Eichmann for past wrongs. See Derogy and Carmel; Hausner. I suspect that the information came from an agent in the German intelligence services (likely from a fugitive Nazi in Argentina), particularly given the continued silence on the subject.

123   In June: NA, RG 263, Adolf Eichmann Name File (CIA), Extradition Case of Nazi Josef Mengele, June 24, 1960; AGN, Josef Mengele File, Federal Police Report on Mengele, July 19, 1959; Posner and Ware, pp. 125–32; Astor, p. 169.

Since Werner Junkers: Goñi, p. 290.

Bauer had since: Friedman, *Die Korrespondenz,* Letter from Erwin Schüle to Tuviah Friedman, October 1959.

On the road: Z. Aharoni interview, *IMAE;* Aharoni, *On Life and Death,* pp. 121–25; Producer's Notes, *HAE.*

124   Both German Jews: Aharoni, *On Life and Death,* pp. 142–47; Segev, pp. 263–64.

"This is simply unbelievable": Aharoni, *On Life and Death,* p. 123.

125   "I want Zvi": Ibid., p. 125.

Harel agreed: Z. Aharoni interview, *IMAE;* Harel, pp. 32–37.

Though equal in height: Bar-Zohar, *Spies in the Promised Land,* p. 110.

126   Haim Cohen joined them: Harel, p. 37.

"Prevent Bauer": Derogy and Carmel, p. 177.

Harel had already: Shpiro, *Geheimdienste in der Weltgeschichte.*

Ben-Gurion was unequivocal: Wojak, p. 40; Yablonka, pp. 46–47; Harel, p. 38.

127   "Isser will deal": Bar-Zohar, *Ben Gurion,* p. 1374.

Three weeks later: NA, RG 263, Nazis/West Germany/Post WWII, Current Intelligence Weekly Summary, February 18, 1960; Williams, p. 478.

"evoked pictures": Tetens, p. 149.

Chancellor Adenauer promptly: NA, RG 263, Nazis/West Germany/Post WWII, Current Intelligence Weekly Summary, February 18, 1960; *Time,* January 20, 1960; Fulbrook, p. 63; Tetens, pp. 42–60; Prittie, pp. 278–81.

128   "almost nationwide": Tetens, p. 222; NA, RG 263, Nazis/West Germany/Post WWII, CIA Report, "Growth of Neo-Nazism," March 21, 1958.

Soon after the Cologne: Producer's Notes, *HAE.*

Already the Mossad chief: Y. Gat, AI.

"an influential middleman": ISA, 2354/8-hz, Announcement from Comité International d'Auschwitz, January 14, 1960.

"Please make sure": Friedman, *Die Korrespondenz,* Letter from Erwin Schüle to Tuviah Friedman, January 1960.

129   Third, the Mossad chief: OHD, (228)2, Interview with Joel Baromi; OHD, (228)3, Interview with Arye Levavi; Haim, "Jewish Leadership in Times of Crisis," pp. 122–23.

"take suitable measures": Ben-Gurion, p. 574.

"I am planning": Producer's Notes, *HAE.*

CHAPTER 12

130   His Israeli diplomatic papers: Documentary Transcript, *HAE.*
      Aharoni had the kind: Aharoni, *On Life and Death,* pp. 9–102.

131   "I am absolutely": Black and Benny, p. 138.

132   Waiting outside the airport: Z. Aharoni interview, *IMAE;* Aharoni and Dietl, pp. 88–91.
      In every country: Thomas, p. 68.
      Two days later: Z. Aharoni interview, *IMAE;* Harel, pp. 43–45.

133   Across the globe: Y. Gat, AI.
      Every attempt to speak: Harel, p. 40.

134   Forty years old: Y. Gat, AI.
      When Bloch returned: Ibid.
      The independent Nazi-hunter: Ibid.; Wiesenthal, *The Murderers Among Us,* pp. 126–29; Pick, pp. 143–46.

135   Like Tuviah Friedman: Pick, p. 144.
      "This must be how": Wiesenthal, *The Murderers Among Us,* p. 128.
      Wiesenthal gladly gave: Y. Gat, AI.
      Gat wanted to: Ibid.; Pick, pp. 144–45.

136   "For my friend": Z. Aharoni interview, *IMAE.*
      "Excuse me please": Aharoni and Dietl, pp. 92–96.

137   Listening to Juan's: Documentary Interview Notes, *HAE;* Harel, pp. 48–51.

138   That night: Aharoni and Dietl, pp. 88, 97.
      Aharoni and Juan: Ibid., p. 97.

139   Early that morning: Harel, p. 53.
      That was more: Ibid., pp. 98–103.

141   "Go back to": Research Notes, *HAE.*
      On March 11: Aharoni and Dietl, pp. 103–4.
      "And what do you": Ibid.; Harel, pp. 59–60.

142   At a café: Documentary Interview Notes, *HAE.*
      "What happened": Research Notes, *HAE.*
      "Ah. Never mind": Z. Aharoni interview, *IMAE.*

CHAPTER 13

143   Aharoni crawled along: Aharoni and Dietl, pp. 106–7.
      On this, Aharoni: *La Razon,* April 24, 1961; *Ahora,* June 7, 1960; Lauryssens, p. 117.
      The house looked: Donovan, p. 105; Pearlman, p. 2.
      Driving past: Z. Aharoni interview, *IMAE.*

144 Later that night: Aharoni and Dietl, pp. 106–7.
     In Tel Aviv: Harel, p. 61; Weber, pp. 40–41.
145 Two days later: Kurzman, pp. 410–11; Schwarz, pp. 441–44; Shpiro, "Intelligence Services and Foreign Policy."
     "I belong to a nation": Vogel, pp. 119–20.
146 No longer willing: NA, RG 263, Adolf Eichmann Name File (CIA), The Eichmann Trial and Allegations Against Secretary State Globke, February 7, 1961.
     On March 16: Z. Aharoni interview, *IMAE;* Aharoni and Dietl, pp. 106–12.
147 "It's possible there's been": Research Notes, *HAE.*
148 "They *looked* like": Eichmann, *Meine Flucht.*
149 Eichmann knew that: "Interview with Klaus Eichmann"; Ben-Gurion, p. 582; Von Lang, *Eichmann Interrogated,* p. 285.
     Those two men: Eichmann, *Meine Flucht;* "Interview with Klaus Eichmann."
150 His sons, however: Aharoni and Dietl, pp. 109–10.

CHAPTER 14

151 Once Aharoni learned: Aharoni and Dietl, pp. 112–13.
152 Over the past: Harel, p. 76; Demo Tape, *HAE;* Thomas, p. 75; Bar-Zohar, *Spies in the Promised Land,* pp. 108–9; Rein, pp. 143, 157–59.
153 Given what was: R. Eitan, AI.
     Rafi Eitan, the Shin Bet: Raviv and Melman, pp. 253–54; Black and Benny, pp. 418–19; Thomas, pp. 73–75; Harel, pp. 83–84.
154 The thirty-four-year-old: Harel, pp. 83–84; Malkin, *Eichmann in My Hands,* pp. 110–11; Black and Benny, p. 419.
     "What are the odds": Harel, pp. 83–84.
     "I'm putting you": R. Eitan, AI; Producer's Notes, *HAE.*
     "None of them": Harel, p. 84.
     On Sunday, March 20: Aharoni and Dietl, pp. 116–18.
156 Vardi was an Israeli: Ben Natan, pp. 84, 90.
     Vardi understood: Aharoni and Dietl, pp. 118–19.
157 Through a contact: Aharoni and Dietl, p. 120; "Interview with Klaus Eichmann"; AGN, Josef Mengele File.
     Through a clerk: J. Moskoviz, AI.
     On Sunday, April 3: Z. Aharoni interview, *IMAE;* Harel, pp. 73–77.
158 Yaakov Gat welcomed: Y. Gat, AI.
159 "Are you definitively sure": Research Notes, *HAE.*

CHAPTER 15

160 Avraham Shalom walked: A. Shalom, AI.
     The thirty-three-year-old: Ibid.
161 Logistics and operational: Malkin, *Eichmann in My Hands,* p. 122.
162 "Isser wants honest men": Steven, p. 39; Bar-Zohar, *Spies in the Promised Land,* pp. 66–67.
     "How would you feel": A. Shalom, AI.

Although the chief: Bar-Zohar, *Spies in the Promised Land,* p. 106.
The first choice: A. Shalom, AI; Y. Gat, AI; Demo Tape, *HAE.*
163 Aharoni entered: A. Shalom, AI; Harel, pp. 79–81.
164 The two top lawyers: Yablonka, p. 46; Papadatos, pp. 52–62; Robinson, pp. 103–6.
At Mossad headquarters: Steven, p. 111; A. Shalom, AI.
165 any equipment: A. Shalom, AI; Malkin, *Eichmann in My Hands,* p. 128.
166 "We're going to bring": Malkin, *Eichmann in My Hands,* p. 120.
What Eitan didn't: A. Shalom, AI.
Malkin entered: Malkin, *Eichmann in My Hands,* p. 124.
The two were: Ibid.; A. Shalom, AI.
167 "We'd just better hope": Malkin, *Eichmann in My Hands,* pp. 125–27.
There the thirty-seven-year-old: Documentary Interview Notes, *HAE.*
168 Over the next: Harel, p. 89; *New York Times,* March 16, 1960.
Aharoni showed them: R. Eitan, AI.
Each night: Malkin, *Eichmann in My Hands,* p. 127.
169 Malkin was eleven: Peter Malkin interview, Steven Spielberg Jewish Film Archive; McKechnie and Howell; Malkin, *Eichmann in My Hands,* pp. 19–72.
Malkin's first commissions: McKechnie and Howell.
Beyond focusing: A. Shalom, AI.
170 This mission was different: Malkin, *Eichmann in My Hands,* p. 54.
171 That left air travel: Harel, pp. 38–39.
This would not be: B. Tirosh, AI; D. Alon, AI; Goldman, pp. 23–29.
172 Once this was: Yaakov Medad interview, Massuah Institute; A. Shalom, AI; Harel, pp. 94–95.
A week before: Harel, p. 86.
173 On April 18: Ibid., p. 87; Y. Klein, AI.
"Okay, everyone": Malkin, *Eichmann in My Hands,* p. 140.
"I want to begin": Demo Tape, *HAE.*
174 He often instilled: A. Shalom, AI; Steven, p. 38.
"We will bring": Malkin, *Eichmann in My Hands,* pp. 140–41.

CHAPTER 16

175 On April 24: Y. Gat, AI; Harel, pp. 102–3.
176 Since arriving: Aharoni and Dietl, p. 126.
177 Entering the lobby: A. Shalom, AI; Davies, p. 111.
Like his colleagues: A. Shalom, AI.
"Compatriot": Ibid.
178 "What do you want": Ibid.; Y. Gat, AI.
179 Early the next morning: Y. Gat, AI.
180 Harel had already: Harel, pp. 86–89, 99–100.
There were scores: Y. Klein, AI; S. Shaul, AI; D. Alon, AI.
181 Harel knew El Al: B. Tirosh, AI.
A German Jew: Ibid.; S. Alony, AI; Goldman, pp. 44, 56, 61.
"Look, friends": B. Tirosh, AI.

182   Peleg was noticeably: Harel, p. 109.
       Before the meeting: B. Tirosh, AI.
       The captain understood: S. Shaul, AI.
       "It is a very": B. Tirosh, AI.
183   Lying flat: A. Shalom, AI; Y. Gat, AI; Aharoni and Dietl, pp. 128–29.
184   They had spent: Harel, pp. 116–19.
       In addition to Maoz: A. Shalom, AI; Documentary Interview Notes, *HAE*.
       In the best-case: A. Shalom, AI; J. Moskoviz, AI.
185   In New York: Y. Klein, AI.
       "You are hereby": L. Volk, AI.

       CHAPTER 17

187   "The initial team": Harel, p. 111.
       Top-level officers: Aharoni and Dietl, p. 7; Shpiro, *Geheimdienste in der Weltge-
       schichte,* p. 305; Malkin, *Eichmann in My Hands,* p. 129.
       Harel understood: Demo Tape, *HAE*.
188   "Dead or alive": Bar-Zohar, *Ben Gurion,* p. 1375; Derogy and Carmel, p. 176.
       There was nothing: Harel, pp. 94, 111–13; Bar-Zohar, *Spies in the Promised Land,*
       p. 65.
       Once they had Eichmann: Harel, pp. 210–11; NA, RG 263, Adolf Eichmann
       Name File (CIA), Extradition Case of Nazi Josef Mengele, June 24, 1960; U.S.
       Department of Justice, report, p. xx.
189   On Sunday, May 1: A. Shalom, AI.
       "worse than criminal": Malkin, *Eichmann in My Hands,* p. 122.
       Their house searches: Aharoni and Dietl, p. 131.
190   Another problem was: Yaakov Medad interview, Massuah Institute; Documen-
       tary Interview Notes, *HAE;* A. Shalom, AI.
       While Gat remained: Harel, p. 121.
       The Mossad chief: A. Shalom, AI.
191   "We can't be too": Harel, p. 122.
       "Look, this is not": Y. Klein, AI.
192   For a while: Ibid.; Harel, pp. 123–25.
       Klein thought vaguely: Y. Klein, AI.
193   "There is something": L. Volk, AI.
       "What your job": Y. Klein, AI.
194   On May 3: Harel, p. 135.
       The first was located: Malkin, *Eichmann in My Hands,* p. 168; A. Shalom, AI.
       Code-named Doron: Malkin, *The Argentina Journal,* p. 48; Harel, p. 132.
195   After the El Al: A. Shalom, AI; Harel, p. 130.
       On the evening: Malkin, *Eichmann in My Hands,* pp. 153–56.
196   In Vienna alone: Cesarani, pp. 68–72.
197   Reading about Eichmann's: Malkin, *Eichmann in My Hands,* pp. 132–38; Malkin,
       The Argentina Journal, p. 11; McKechnie and Howell.
       Now, his hands: Peter Malkin interview, Steven Spielberg Jewish Film Archive;
       Malkin, *Eichmann in My Hands,* pp. 155–56.

What neither Malkin: Aharoni and Dietl, pp. 130–31; Z. Aharoni interview, *IMAE;* Documentary Interview Notes, *HAE.*

CHAPTER 18

199   Since receiving word: Thomas, pp. 74–75.
It was clear: R. Eitan, AI.
Still, there were: A. Shalom, AI; Harel, pp. 147–48.

200   As for the operation's timing: Harel, pp. 131–32.
They were to practice: Y. Gat, AI.
At Ezeiza Airport: Y. Klein, AI; Harel, p. 138.

201   "Maybe it would": L. Volk, AI.
On the evening: Malkin, *Eichmann in My Hands,* pp. 163–64.

202   The forger had arrived: Harel, pp. 136–37.
None of the team: Steven, p. 112; Black and Benny, p. 177.
The team had relied: A. Shalom, AI; Y. Gat, AI; M. Tabor interview, *IMAE.*

203   He and Moshe Tabor: M. Tabor interview, *IMAE;* Malkin, *Eichmann in My Hands,* p. 210.
"When did you": Malkin, *Eichmann in My Hands,* pp. 163–64; Malkin, *The Argentina Journal,* p. 28.
Shalom scouted routes: A. Shalom, AI; Harel, p. 148.

204   He also assisted: Yaakov Medad interview, Massuah Institute; Aharoni and Dietl, p. 132.
The surveillance of: Peter Malkin interview, Steven Spielberg Jewish Film Archive; Malkin, *Eichmann in My Hands,* p. 132.
He also was learning: Malkin, *Eichmann in My Hands,* p. 158.

205   Many hours were: M. Tabor interview, *IMAE;* A. Shalom, AI.
Whenever all: A. Shalom, AI; Y. Gat, AI.

206   At the end: Malkin, *The Argentina Journal,* p. 31; Y. Gat, AI.
On a chilly Sunday: Harel, pp. 142–43.
In his early forties: A. Shalom, AI; Malkin, *Eichmann in My Hands,* p. 169.
For cover: D. Sasson, AI.
"We're glad you're here": Malkin, *Eichmann in My Hands,* pp. 169–70.
In the city: Harel, p. 160.

207   "The government has approved": A. Levavi, AI; OHD, (228)3, Interview with Arye Levavi.
Harel recommended: A. Levavi, AI.
A drawing of: Malkin, *Eichmann in My Hands,* p. 143.

208   "As soon as we": Ibid., pp. 175–77; Harel, p. 147.
In Malkin's view: P. Malkin interview, *HAE.*
One car would be: Harel, p. 147; Aharoni and Dietl, pp. 133–34; A. Shalom, AI; M. Tabor interview, *IMAE;* P. Malkin interview, *HAE.*

CHAPTER 19

210   On May 9: R. Eitan, AI.
Later that morning: Harel, pp. 147–49.

211 "What if he": Malkin, *Eichmann in My Hands,* pp. 179–80.
     Even with: M. Tabor interview, *IMAE;* A. Shalom, AI.
212 "I assure you": AdsD, Nachlass Fritz Bauer, Box 1, Letter from Haim Cohen to
     Fritz Bauer, May 10, 1960.
213 As Eichmann was: "Interview with Klaus Eichmann"; Eichmann, *Meine Flucht.*
     As soon as: Lawson.
     "We're planning": Y. Klein, AI.
     Once they had discussed: Ibid.
214 Klein told Harel: Ibid.; Harel, pp. 152–53.
215 At Tira: M. Tabor interview, *IMAE;* Producer's Notes, *HAE;* Malkin, *Eichmann
     in My Hands,* pp. 168–69.
     "Can you tell me": Aharoni and Dietl, p. 138.
     Meanwhile, in the garage: A. Shalom, AI.
     "You were chosen": Harel, p. 150.
216 What should they do: Aharoni and Dietl, p. 183.
     What would happen: Ibid., p. 136; A. Shalom, AI.
     What if they: Harel, p. 150.
     As many of the team: R. Eitan, AI.
217 "Are there any questions": Y. Gat, AI.
     Harel then told the men: Harel, p. 150.
218 Lying in his bed: A. Shalom, AI.
     In his room: P. Malkin interview, *HAE;* Malkin, *The Argentina Journal,* p. 77.
     "I'm going to": P. Malkin interview, *HAE.*

CHAPTER 20

219 When the Mossad team: Malkin, *Eichmann in My Hands,* pp. 181–83.
220 Adolf Eichmann started: Lawson; Pearlman, p. 1.
     This bus was usually: "Eichmann File," Tribunales Federales de Comodoro Py,
     Buenos Aires.
     Once at the plant: Ibid.; *Clarin,* May 27, 1960; Pearlman, p. 4.
221 Aharoni turned the Buick: Malkin, *Eichmann in My Hands,* p. 184; Peter Malkin
     interview, Steven Spielberg Jewish Film Archive.
     Gat was next to: Y. Gat, AI.
     In five minutes: A. Shalom, AI.
     Aharoni stopped: Aharoni and Dietl, pp. 136–37; M. Tabor interview, *IMAE.*
222 "Thank you": Aharoni and Dietl, p. 137; Malkin, *The Argentina Journal,* p. 102.
     Malkin prepared himself: P. Malkin interview, Spielberg Archive; P. Malkin inter-
     view, *HAE;* M. Tabor interview, *IMAE;* Pearlman, p. 53.
     They had no guns: A. Shalom, AI.
     The lights from the bus: Harel, p. 162; Z. Aharoni interview, *IMAE.*
223 Malkin looked toward: P. Malkin interview, Spielberg Archive; P. Malkin inter-
     view, *HAE;* McKechnie and Howell.
     Shalom and Gat: A. Shalom, AI; Y. Gat, AI.
     "Do we take off": R. Eitan, AI.
224 Standing side by side: M. Tabor interview, *IMAE.*
     Nursing a hot tea: Harel, pp. 160–61.

She would not go: Demo Tape, *HAE;* A. Shalom, AI.

225   He stared at: Harel, p. 161.
Bus 203 came: A. Shalom, AI; P. Malkin interview, *HAE;* P. Malkin interview, Spielberg Archive; Research Notes, *HAE;* M. Tabor interview, *IMAE;* Y. Gat, AI; R. Eitan, AI; Aharoni and Dietl, pp. 136–39; Harel, pp. 163–65; Malkin, *Eichmann in My Hands,* pp. 185–87.

229   *Never say:* R. Eitan, AI.

CHAPTER 21

230   Eichmann shuffled: M. Tabor interview, *IMAE;* Peter Malkin interview, Steven Spielberg Jewish Film Archive; Malkin, *The Argentina Journal,* p. 105.
For a moment: Malkin, *Eichmann in My Hands,* p. 188.
Aharoni wondered: Aharoni and Dietl, p. 140.
"No man can": NA, RG 263, Adolf Eichmann Name File (CIA), General Expansiveness of [excised], August 24, 1961.
At first Eichmann: Eichmann, *Meine Flucht.*

231   The doctor found: P. Malkin interview, Spielberg Archive.
Aharoni wanted to begin: Aharoni, *On Life and Death,* pp. 98–101.
"What's your name": Aharoni and Dietl, pp. 142–43; Harel, pp. 166–67; Z. Aharoni interview, *IMAE;* Research Notes, *HAE;* P. Malkin interview, Spielberg Archive; A. Shalom, AI; Friedman, *The Blind Man.* The exact transcript of the interrogation is not available. Aharoni and Harel recounted their versions as definitive. I have drawn from these two as well as the recollections of several others.

233   Joy swept over: A. Shalom, AI; Y. Gat, AI.

234   Shalom and Aharoni first: A. Shalom, AI; Aharoni and Dietl, pp. 143–44; Yaakov Medad interview, Massuah Institute.
When they reached: Harel, p. 161.
"The moment I saw": Producer's Notes, *HAE.*
Shalom recounted: A. Shalom, AI; Aharoni and Dietl, pp. 143–44.

235   "The typewriter": Documentary Interview Notes, *HAE.*
"That's all": Harel, pp. 169–70.
At the house: Lawson; Lauryssens, p. 125.

236   "I'm going back": Malkin, *Eichmann in My Hands,* p. 192.
A few hours later: Malkin, *The Argentina Journal,* p. 74.

237   It was unlikely: A. Shalom, AI; Y. Gat, AI; Aharoni and Dietl, p. 155.
If the police came: Harel, p. 199.
Tabor had already: M. Tabor interview, *IMAE.*

238   As he lay: Malkin, *Eichmann in My Hands,* p. 193.

CHAPTER 22

239   On the morning: Y. Gat, AI; A. Shalom, AI.
"I just have": Malkin, *Eichmann in My Hands,* p. 194.
"Why did you": Harel, p. 190.

240   "Why didn't your family": Z. Aharoni interview, *IMAE.*
"No, I don't know": Malkin, *Eichmann in My Hands,* p. 194.

241   "Are you prepared": Z. Aharoni interview, *IMAE*.
      "The old man is gone": "Interview with Klaus Eichmann."

242   Together they rushed: Ibid.; AGN, Martin Bormann File. In Klaus Eichmann's
      recollection of this day recounted to *Quick* magazine, he stated only that he went
      to his father's "best friend," not Carlos Fuldner. However, the Argentine archives
      reveal in a police report/interview with Fuldner that the Eichmann sons came to
      him, although he said that this occurred only after it was reported publicly that
      Eichmann had been taken by the Israelis. This later date seems suspect, and it is
      my conclusion that Fuldner and the "best friend" were the same individual.
      They also planned: S. Sassen, AI.
      Vera Eichmann went: "Eichmann File," Tribunales Federales de Comodoro Py,
      Buenos Aires; Weber, pp. 135–39.

243   A search around: Anderson, p. 98.
      News of the capture: Y. Klein, AI.
      "Let's do it": Ibid.
      The flow of ideas: Ibid.; M. Tabor interview, *IMAE;* Aharoni and Dietl,
      pp. 156–60.

244   "You are in charge": A. Shalom, AI.
      The El Al flight: Harel, p. 185.
      Meanwhile in Tel Aviv: B. Tirosh, AI.
      Every time a car: Malkin, *The Argentina Journal,* p. 57.

245   He was obedient: P. Malkin interview, Steven Spielberg Jewish Film Archive.
      Tabor was reminded: M. Tabor interview, *IMAE;* Z. Aharoni interview, *IMAE*.
      Nesiahu was an orthodox: *Intelligence and Terrorism Information Bulletin* (Israel),
      January 2004; Malkin, *Eichmann in My Hands,* pp. 96–97.

246   When one of Harel's: Ibid., p. 155.
      "The thought of cooking": Ibid., p. 198.
      In the early hours: Ibid., p. 199; Malkin, *The Argentina Journal,* pp. 13, 18, 19, 31,
      84.

247   They also scoured: Harel, pp. 209–10; *Clarin,* May 13, 1960.

248   "Adolf Eichmann has": Harel, pp. 170–71.
      "I've come": Bar-Zohar, *Ben Gurion,* pp. 1374–75.

249   "This morning I met": Yablonka, p. 30.

      CHAPTER 23

250   At the house: S. Sassen, AI; Lauryssens, pp. 125–26.
      Some of his associates: P. Probierzym, AI.
      Nick and Dieter had: "Interview with Klaus Eichmann."

251   Tacuara was a radical: Anonymous Tacuara members, AI; Gutman; Kenneth
      Marty, "Neo-Fascist Irrationality or Fantastic History? Tacuara, the Andinia Plan
      and Adolf Eichmann in Argentina" (PhD diss., Princeton University, 1996).
      Though not Tacuara: "Interview with Klaus Eichmann"; Anonymous Tacuara
      members, AI; Demo Tape, *HAE;* Gutman. In his interview with *Quick,* Klaus
      Eichmann referred to a "Peronist youth group" that came to their aid. It is clear
      from interviews with several Tacuara members, as well as from the research of
      Marty and Gutman, that this group was in fact Tacuara. Later, the fascist youth

movement took on a more prominent role in the Eichmann affair. Please see chapter 27 for more details.

Without her knowledge: L. Volk, AI.

252 Yosef Klein did not: Y. Klein, AI.

253 Now that he was: A. Shalom, AI.

254 "The search for": Aharoni and Dietl, pp. 149–50; A. Shalom, AI; R. Eitan, AI.

He had shuddered: Documentary Interview Notes, *HAE;* Malkin, *Eichmann in My Hands,* pp. 170–72; Posner and Ware, pp. 134–42.

Later that day: Aharoni and Dietl, pp. 150–51.

255 "Stop insulting me": Aharoni and Dietl, p. 152.

Earlier, when he: Harel, pp. 194–98; Z. Aharoni interview, *IMAE.*

256 On his arrival: Levai, *Eichmann in Hungary,* pp. 67–69; *The Trial of Adolf Eichmann,* p. 2014; Levai, *Black Book,* pp. 86–88, 108; Hausner, p. 137; Nagy-Talavera, p. 286.

"Once I've said no": Cesarani, p. 180.

"The sight of": Harel, p. 184.

257 "I know what": Malkin, *Eichmann in My Hands,* p. 236.

On May 16: Documentary Interview Notes, *HAE;* Harel, pp. 212–14.

258 "Dr. Menelle": Harel, p. 215.

Back at the safe house: A. Shalom, AI; Y. Gat, AI; Harel, pp. 194–98.

259 A few tasks: M. Tabor interview, *IMAE;* Aharoni and Dietl, pp. 157–58.

"To even be": Malkin, *Eichmann in My Hands,* p. 223.

260 "Are you the man": Peter Malkin interview, Steven Spielberg Jewish Film Archive; P. Malkin interview, *HAE;* Malkin, *Eichmann in My Hands,* pp. 201–4. There have been some arguments about whether it was possible for Malkin to carry on these conversations. In his memoir, Isser Harel related how Malkin spoke to Eichmann at length, but Aharoni discounted that possibility because of the lack of a common language. Other operatives on the mission have said that Malkin did speak to Eichmann. Further, Malkin's recollections of these conversations are pretty consistent, both in his memoir and in the interviews cited above. I have attempted to relate only those conversations that I have confirmed in both his book and the interviews, although they required some spare editing to make sense to readers.

CHAPTER 24

262 On a clear: Eban, pp. 306–13; Kurzman, p. 424.

After World War II: Bar-Zohar, *The Avengers,* pp. 24–25.

263 However, every effort: Harel, pp. 221–26; S. Alony, AI; D. Alon, AI; "Eichmann File," Tribunales Federales de Comodoro Py, Buenos Aires.

"Announcing the departure": Reynolds, p. 9.

At exactly: S. Shaul, AI.

264 May 20 was: Harel, pp. 216–17.

265 With international delegations: A. Shalom, AI.

Radio reports indicated: *La Nacion,* May 19, 1960; *La Razon,* May 19, 1960.

That night: "Interview with Klaus Eichmann"; Anonymous Tacuara members, AI; S. Sassen, AI; A. Levavi, AI.

"Don't do anything stupid": "Interview with Klaus Eichmann."

266   "Let me ask you this": Malkin, *Eichmann in My Hands,* p. 218.
        "You do realize": Ibid., p. 218.
        Eichmann was unfazed: Ibid., p. 220.

267   "I do like wine": Peter Malkin interview, Steven Spielberg Jewish Film Archive;
        Harel, pp. 208–9; Y. Gat, AI; Yaakov Medad interview, Massuah Institute; Aha-
        roni and Dietl, pp. 152–53. The signing of the statement by Eichmann is rife with
        conflicting stories. In Aharoni's memoir, he stated that he was the one who
        prompted Eichmann to sign, an assertion that has been supported by Avraham
        Shalom and Yaakov Gat. Meanwhile, Malkin, backed by Isser Harel's account,
        stated that he secured the signature. Given that Harel had access to all of the post-
        operation accounts, I chose to present the Malkin version, although I accept the
        possibility that it was a more collaborative process. In fact, this is how Rafi Eitan
        remembers the signing unfolding.

268   "I, the undersigned": ISA, 2150/4-hz, Letter from Michael Comay, Israeli UN
        representative, to President of UN Security Council, June 21, 1960.
        "What date should": Hausner, p. 275.
        "What the hell": Malkin, *Eichmann in My Hands,* p. 232; Yaacov Medad inter-
        view, Massuah Institute.

269   Captain Shmuel Wedeles: Collective testimony from El Al flight crew, AI.
        Ten minutes later: B. Tirosh, AI; S. Shaul, AI; D. Alon, AI.

271   On the way: A. Shalom, AI; Aharoni and Dietl, p. 161.
        A host of diplomats: L. Volk, AI.
        Klein ran about: Y. Klein, AI.
        At last, at 4:05: S. Shaul, AI.

272   Klein followed the plane's: Y. Klein, AI.
        "Who are those people": L. Volk, AI.

273   Arye Friedman and Mordechai Avivi: Harel, p. 228.
        Shalom and Aharoni watched: A. Shalom, AI; Aharoni and Dietl, pp. 161–62.
        In a café near: Harel, pp. 230–31.

274   He gathered: A. Shalom, AI; D. Alon, AI.
        In the dark hours: Y. Gat, AI; A. Shalom, AI.
        Everyone settled back: Harel, p. 235; Aharoni and Dietl, p. 162.

CHAPTER 25

276   On the cold: A. Shalom, AI; Malkin, *Eichmann in My Hands,* pp. 235–41.

277   At Maoz, Shalom Dani: Harel, pp. 243–44.
        Tabor spent most: M. Tabor interview, *IMAE;* R. Eitan, AI.
        Avraham Shalom also: A. Shalom, AI.
        He shared his: Harel, p. 240.

278   Harel had sent: Ibid., pp. 244–25; "Interview with Klaus Eichmann."

279   Back at Tira: Y. Gat, AI; Malkin, *Eichmann in My Hands,* pp. 240–41.
        "It isn't necessary": Malkin, *Eichmann in My Hands,* pp. 241–43; Aharoni and Di-
        etl, p. 163; A. Shalom, AI; Y. Gat, AI; R. Eitan, AI.

281   "We're advancing": S. Shabtai, AI; D. Alon, AI; D. Sasson, AI.
        "Are you going": L. Volk, AI.

At the airport: Harel, p. 249; A. Shalom, AI.

282   In the aeronautical: S. Shaul, AI.

Aharoni drove conservatively: Aharoni and Dietl, p. 164; Y. Gat, AI.

283   At a preappointed: Harel, pp. 250–51.

284   "Be absolutely silent": Y. Gat, AI.

"Do something with": R. Eitan, AI.

"Form a circle": D. Alon, AI.

Wedeles was right: Y. Gat, AI; Y. Klein, AI; Harel, pp. 251–52.

"Pretend to sleep": D. Alon, AI; S. Shabtai, AI; D. Sasson, AI.

285   As the Britannia: Harel, pp. 254–55.

Harel left his: A. Shalom, AI.

"You surprise me": Y. Klein, AI.

286   Minute after minute: Aharoni and Dietl, p. 165.

As Harel crossed: Harel, p. 255.

"El Al is ready": S. Shaul, AI; B. Tirosh, AI; O. Kabiri, AI.

287   Klein was standing: Y. Klein, AI.

288   "What is the problem": S. Shaul, AI.

At half past: "Interview with Klaus Eichmann."

CHAPTER 26

290   When the Britannia: S. Shabtai, AI.

"You've been accorded": Harel, p. 260.

291   The chief pilot: O. Kabiri, AI; S. Shaul, AI; D. Alon, AI.

Hour after hour: S. Shaul, AI; Harel, pp. 260–66.

292   Yosef Klein concluded: Y. Klein, AI.

"big exclusive": Ibid.

293   The last task: A. Shalom, AI; R. Eitan, AI.

Red lights flashed: D. Sasson, AI; D. Alon, AI; O. Kabiri, AI; S. Shaul, AI; Y. Gat, AI.

294   Harel congratulated: Harel, pp. 268–69.

So before the steward: Y. Gat, AI.

The rest of the stopover: A. Shalom, AI.

Before they took off: S. Shaul, AI.

295   Only five years: Goldman, p. 51.

Shaul and Hassin had: S. Shaul, AI.

It flew up: Ibid.; D. Alon, AI.

With the plane: Harel, p. 269.

At 6:55 A.M.: Aharoni and Dietl, p. 116.

There was no celebration: S. Shabtai, AI.

296   The captain also praised: S. Shaul, AI.

Customs officials attempted: M. Tabor interview, *IMAE;* Y. Gat, AI; B. Tirosh, AI.

"I have been waiting": Aharoni and Dietl, p. 166.

"The monster is": B. Tirosh, AI.

Tabor and Gat escorted: Y. Gat, AI; Reynolds, pp. 10–11.

"I brought you": Harel, p. 271; Bar-Zohar, *Ben Gurion,* pp. 1374–77.

297   Only a few hours: ISA, 3039/1-a, Hofstetter Memo; Harel, p. 274.
      "How many people": R. Eitan, AI.
      "I am Adolf Eichmann": Yablonka, p. 31. Curiously, Halevi issued the warrant
      under the International Treaty for the Convention on the Prevention and Punish-
      ment of the Crime of Genocide (under the UN charter), which applied only to
      crimes committed after 1949. The correct law would have been Israel's Nazi and
      Nazi Collaborators Law (1950).
      Harel then cabled: AdsD, Nachlass Fritz Bauer, Box 1, Letter from Haim Cohen
      to Dr. Fritz Bauer, May 22, 1960; Harel, pp. 274–75.
298   "I have to inform": "The Beast in Chains," *Time*, June 6, 1960; Robinson, p. 105.
      "When they had": Robinson, p. 106.

      CHAPTER 27

300   On May 25: A. Shalom, AI.
      When Shalom returned: Ibid.; Y. Gat, AI.
301   "You were in": M. Tabor interview, *IMAE*.
      "Look, didn't you": Malkin, *Eichmann in My Hands*, p. 250.
      "I'm not naive": Aharoni and Dietl, p. 167.
      Eichmann was being: Von Lang, *Eichmann Interrogated*, pp. xix–xx; S. Nagar in-
      terview, *IMAE*.
302   On the afternoon: Yablonka, pp. 66–67.
      The two men: ISA, 3039/1-a, Hofstetter Memo.
      "You recognize me": Von Lang, *Eichmann Interrogated*, pp. 4–5.
303   "But, Captain": Ibid., p. viii.
      In Israel, the shock: Yablonka, p. 36.
304   "The Jewish state": Cesarani, p. 239.
      As for the half: Yablonka, pp. 36–37.
      "Israeli agents": *Time*, June 1, 1960.
      Arturo Frondizi had: A. Levavi, AI.
      Frondizi was also: Rein, pp. 177–79; Cesarani, p. 238.
      "I don't think": A. Levavi, AI.
      "Jewish volunteers": ISA, 2150/4-hz, Letter from the Permanent Representative of
      Israel to the President of the Security Council, June 21, 1960.
      "supreme moral justification": Ibid.
      The Argentines clearly: Rein, pp. 179–81.
305   Unable to strike: Ibid., pp. 206–7; Haim, "Jewish Leadership in Times of Crisis."
      On July 12: "Eichmann File," Tribunales Federales de Comodoro Py, Buenos Ai-
      res.
      One afternoon: L. Volk, AI.
306   By the fall: "Eichmann File."
      Chancellor Konrad Adenauer: Wolffsohn, p. 25.
      Still, as the trial: Gardner-Feldman, pp. 134–35; Lavy, pp. 87–88; Vogel, pp. 125–26.
      Although there was no overt agreement, officials on both sides have alluded to
      this understanding.
307   "General Heydrich ordered": Eichmann, "Memoirs."

Within days of: Lauryssens, p. 128.

The chief of: NA, RG 263, Adolf Eichmann Name File (CIA), Existence of Eichmann Memoirs, September 13, 1960; NA, RG 263, Adolf Eichmann Name File
(CIA), *Life* and Eichmann Memoirs, September 16–20, 1960.

The Mossad had: NA, RG 263, Adolf Eichmann Name File (CIA), Adolf Eichmann Case, August 15, 1960; ISA, 3039/1-a, Hofstetter Memo.

308   While Eichmann's shocking: M. Gilead interview, *IMAE;* Cesarani, p. 243.

These documents: Yablonka, p. 73.

"Congratulations on your": Levy, p. 89.

"You never saw": Ibid.

In the months: ISA, 3039/1-a, Hofstetter Memo.

On the evening: Friedman, *The Hunter,* pp. 255–56.

309   On November 1: YVS, TR.3, File 1052, Testimony of Zeev Sapir, January 11, 1960.

An Israeli association: Yablonka, p. 95.

After being rescued: YVS, TR.3, File 1052, Testimony of Zeev Sapir, January 11,
1960; Zeev Sapir Testimony at Eichmann Trial, Steven Spielberg Jewish Film Archive; Z. Sapir interview, *IMAE;* YVS, O.3, File 6151, Testimony of Zeev Sapir,
April 9, 1990.

CHAPTER 28

311   In the valley: Musmanno, pp. 11–13; Arendt, p. 3.

312   "Adolf Eichmann, rise": Guri, p. 2.

"First count": *The Trial of Adolf Eichmann,* pp. 3–10.

313   "When I stand": Ibid., p. 62.

"In moments like these": Mulisch, p. 37.

On May 28: Z. Sapir interview, *IMAE.*

314   "How many Jews": *The Trial of Adolf Eichmann,* pp. 970–74; Zeev Sapir Testimony at Eichmann Trial, Steven Spielberg Jewish Film Archive; Z. Sapir interview, *IMAE.*

315   Once Hausner finished: Cesarani, pp. 272–74.

Given his clipped: Mulisch, p. 127.

"From the point": *The Trial of Adolf Eichmann,* p. 1575.

316   Throughout the cross-examination: Cesarani, pp. 272, 282–305. The Israeli court
allowed only a small portion of the Sassen documents to be entered into evidence—just those pages that Eichmann had handwritten or to which he had
added comments while editing his memoirs in Argentina.

"For the dispatch": *The Trial of Adolf Eichmann,* p. 2218.

317   Eichmann was motionless: Guri, p. 299.

While he waited: Eichmann, "Meine Gotzen—September 6, 1961"; Eichmann,
"Meine Memoiren—June 16, 1960"; BArch, Sassen Transcripts, 6/95, folder 1.

Eichmann began: Hull, xi–xiv.

318   "search for peace": Ibid., p. 35.

"There is no Hell": Ibid., p. 24.

"I have not sinned": Ibid., p. 83.

Two days after: M. Gilead interview, *IMAE.*

"Why are you sad": Hull, p. 155.

319   Accompanied by Hull: Ibid., pp. 155–60; R. Eitan, AI; M. Gilead interview, *IMAE;* S. Nagar interview, *IMAE.*

"I hope, very much": Malkin, *Eichmann in My Hands,* p. 173.

"Long live Germany": Hull, p. 159; Arye Wallenstein, "Eichmann Dies on the Gallows," Reuters, June 1, 1962.

The two guards hit: Hull, pp. 160–69; M. Gilead interview, *IMAE;* Hausner, p. 446.

EPILOGUE

322   "Jewish history had": E. Wiesel interview, *HAE.*

The trial had: Yablonka, pp. 250–51.

As for the rest: Cesarani, pp. 324–57.

323   Simon Wiesenthal and Tuviah Friedman: "The Eichmann Chase"; Pick, pp. 151–327.

In the weeks after: NA, RG 263, Nazis/West Germany/Post WWII, Current Intelligence Weekly Summary, July 7, 1960; Cesarani, p. 335.

324   For the Hermann family: OHD, (228)4, Interview with Nathan Lerner; CZA, Z 6/2412; A. Kleinert, AI; *Clarin,* March 25, 1961; Goñi, p. 318; Friedman, *The Blind Man.*

Now a professor: Ricardo Eichmann, Letter to author, December 2006.

Of the three: Aharoni and Dietl, pp. 176–77.

"extraordinary devotion": Letter from Zvi Tohar to Daniel Sasson, May 24, 1960.

325   After returning to Israel: Aharoni and Dietl, pp. 179–81; letter to author from Wilhelm Dietl, September 14, 2008. Contrary to news reports in September 2008 based on an interview with Rafi Eitan, the author received no confirmation from other agents that the Mossad actually located the doctor during the operation to capture Eichmann. Avraham Shalom told the author quite firmly that they did not locate Mengele at that time.

326   Rafi Eitan has enjoyed: Thomas, pp. 86–91; Aharoni and Dietl, p. 181.

Only three years: Thomas, pp. 42–46; *Guardian,* February 20, 1993.

"All over the world": R. Eitan; AI.

327   "She can't talk": Malkin, *Eichmann in My Hands,* p. 258; Peter Malkin interview, Steven Spielberg Jewish Film Archive.

Bibliography

ARCHIVES AND LIBRARIES

Archiv der Sozialen Demokratie der Friedrich Ebert Stiftung, Bonn.
Archivo General de la Nación, Buenos Aires.
Biblioteca National, Buenos Aires.
Bundesarchiv, Koblenz.
Central Zionist Archives, Jerusalem.
Columbia University Library, New York.
Direción Nacional de Migraciones, Buenos Aires.
Harman Institute of Contemporary Jewry, Oral History Division, Hebrew University, Jerusalem.
Hessisches Hauptstaatsarchiv, Wiesbaden.
Israel State Archives, Jerusalem.
Massuah Institute for the Study of the Holocaust, Kibbutz Tel Itzhak, Israel.
National Archives and Records Administration, Washington, DC.
New York Public Library, New York.
New York University Library, New York.
Steven Spielberg Jewish Film Archive, Hebrew University, Jerusalem.
Tribunales Federales de Comodoro Py, Buenos Aires.
United States Holocaust Museum, Washington, DC.
Yad Vashem, Jerusalem.
YIVO Institute for Jewish Research, New York.

DOCUMENTARY INTERVIEWS AND MATERIALS

The Hunt for Adolf Eichmann, directed by Dan Setton, 1998. Interview transcripts of Zvi Aharoni, Manus Diamant, Michael Gilead, Isser Harel, Peter Malkin, Moshe Tabor, and Elie Wiesel.
I Met Adolf Eichmann, directed by Clara Glynn, 2003. Interview transcripts of Zvi Aharoni, Martha Eggers, Michael Gilead, Otto Lindhorst, Heinz Lühr, Shlomo

Nagar, Zeev Sapir, Ursula Schulze, Moshe Tabor, Roberto Tonet, and Ruth Tramer.

AUTHOR INTERVIEWS (AI)

Roberto Alemann, Dan Alon, Shmuel Alony, anonymous Tacuara members, Angolina Bascelli, Rafi Eitan, Yaakov Gat, Amelia Hahn, Oved Kabiri, Yosef Klein, Anthony Kleinert, Dr. Leonhardt, Arye Levavi, Jose Moskoviz, Dr. Ernesto Palenzola, Pedro Probierzym, Saskia Sassen, Daniel Sasson, Shamri Shabtai, Avraham Shalom, Shaul Shaul, Baruch Tirosh, and Luba Volk.

EICHMANN PRIMARY SOURCES

Eichmann, Adolf. *Meine Flucht.* Hessisches Hauptstaatsarchiv, Alliierte Prozesse, 6/247, folder 1.

Eichmann, Adolf. "Meine Gotzen—September 6, 1961." Israel State Archives, Jerusalem. Also available at http://www.mazal.org/various/eichmann.htm.

Eichmann, Adolf. "Meine Memoiren—June 16, 1960." In *The Trial of Adolf Eichmann: Record of Proceedings in the District Court of Jerusalem.* Vol. 9. Jerusalem: Trust for the Publication of the Proceedings of the Eichmann Trial, 1992. Microfiche.

Sassen Transcripts. Collection of Robert Servatius. Hessisches Hauptstaatsarchiv, Alliierte Prozesse, 6/95–III.

DERIVATIVE WORKS

    a. Aschenauer, Rudolf. *Ich, Adolf Eichmann: Ein historischer Zeugenbericht.* Augsburg: Druffel-Verlag, 1980. A distilled version of the Sassen transcripts.

    b. "Eichmann Memoirs." National Archives and Records Administration, CIA Records Search Tool.

    c. Eichmann, Adolf. "Memoirs." *Life,* November 28 and December 5, 1960.

"Interrogation of Adolf Eichmann by Avner Less, Bureau 06." In *The Trial of Adolf Eichmann: Record of Proceedings in the District Court of Jerusalem.* Vols. 7 and 8. Jerusalem: Trust for the Publication of the Proceedings of the Eichmann Trial, 1992.

DERIVATIVE WORK

    Von Lang, Jochen, ed. *Eichmann Interrogated.* New York: Farrar, Straus & Giroux, 1983.

BOOKS AND ARTICLES

Aarons, Mark, and John Loftus. *Unholy Trinity: How the Vatican's Nazi Networks Betrayed Western Intelligence to the Soviets.* New York: St. Martin's Press, 1991.

Aharoni, Zvi. *On Life and Death: The Tale of a Lucky Man.* London: Minerva, 1998.

Aharoni, Zvi, and Wilhelm Dietl. *Operation Eichmann: The Truth About the Pursuit, Capture and Trial of Adolf Eichmann.* London: Orion, 1998.

Ambrose, Stephen. *The Supreme Commander: The War Years of D. D. Eisenhower.* New York: Doubleday, 1970.

Anderson, Jack. *Peace, War, Politics: An Eyewitness Account.* New York: Forge, 2000.

Andrus, Burton. *The Infamous of Nuremberg.* London: Leslie Frewin, 1969.

Arendt, Hannah. *Eichmann in Jerusalem: A Report on the Banality of Evil.* New York: Penguin Books, 1987.

Aronson, Shlomo. *Hitler, Allies, and the Jews.* New York: Cambridge University Press, 2004.

Ashman, Charles, and Robert Wagman. *Nazi Hunters.* New York: Pharos Books, 1988.

Astor, Gerald. *The Last Nazi: The Life and Times of Dr. Joseph Mengele.* New York: Donald I. Fine, 1985.

Bar-Zohar, Michael. *The Avengers.* New York: Hawthorn Books, 1968.

———. *Ben Gurion: A Biography.* Tel Aviv: Biblioteka-Aliia, 1987.

———. *Spies in the Promised Land: Iser Harel and the Israeli Secret Service.* Boston: Houghton Mifflin, 1972.

Bauer, Yehuda. *Jews for Sale: Nazi-Jewish Negotiations, 1933–1945.* New Haven, CT: Yale University Press, 1994.

Ben-Gurion, David. *A Personal History.* New York: Funk & Wagnalls, 1971.

Ben-Natan, Asher. *The Audacity to Live: An Autobiography.* Tel Aviv: Mazo, 2007.

Bernstein, Victor. *Final Judgment: The Story of Nuremberg.* New York: Boni & Gaer, 1947.

Bischof, Gunter, and Stephen Ambrose. *Eisenhower and the German POWs.* Baton Rouge: Louisiana State University Press, 1992.

Biss, Andre. *A Million Jews to Save: Check to the Final Solution.* London: A. S. Barnes, 1975.

Black, Ian, and Morris Benny. *Israel's Secret Wars: A History of Israel Intelligence.* London: Hamish Hamilton, 1991.

Black, Peter. *Ernst Kaltenbrunner: Ideological Soldier of the Third Reich.* Princeton, NJ: Princeton University Press, 1984.

Bloch, Michael. *Ribbentrop.* New York: Crown, 1993.

Botting, Douglas. *In the Ruins of the Reich.* London: George Allen & Unwin, 1985.

Bower, Tom. *Blind Eye to Murder: Britain, America and the Purging of Nazi Germany—A Pledge Betrayed.* London: Andre Deutsch, 1981.

Boyle, Kay. *Breaking the Silence: Why a Mother Tells Her Son About the Nazi Era.* New York: Institute of Human Relations Press, 1962.

Braham, Randolph. *Eichmann and the Destruction of Hungarian Jewry.* New York: Twayne, 1961.

———. *The Politics of Genocide: The Holocaust in Hungary.* New York: Columbia University Press, 2000.

Braham, Randolph, and Scott Miller, eds. *The Nazis' Last Victims: The Holocaust in Hungary.* Washington, DC: United States Holocaust Memorial Museum, 1998.

Breitman, Richard, et al. *U.S. Intelligence and the Nazis.* New York: Cambridge University Press, 2005.

Briggs, Emil. *Stand Up and Fight.* London: George G. Harrap, 1972.

Bukey, Evan Burr. *Hitler's Hometown: Linz, Austria 1908–1945.* Bloomington: Indiana University Press, 1986.

Camarasa, Jorge. *Odessa al Sur: La Argentina Como Refugio de Nazis y Criminales de Guerra.* Buenos Aires: Planeta, 1995.

Cesarani, David. *Becoming Eichmann: Rethinking the Life, Crimes, and Trial of a "Desk Murderer."* New York: Da Capo Press, 2006.

Clarke, Comer. *Eichmann: The Man and His Crime.* New York: Ballantine Books, 1960.

Cohen, Rich. *The Avengers.* New York: Alfred A. Knopf, 2000.

Conot, Robert E. *Justice at Nuremberg.* New York: Harper & Row, 1983.

Cookridge, E. H. *Gehlen: Spy of the Century.* New York: Random House, 1972.

Crassweller, Robert. *Peron and the Enigmas of Argentina.* New York: W. W. Norton, 1987.

Davies, Howell, ed. *The South American Handbook 1960.* Bath, England: Trade and Travel Publications, 1960.

Dawidowicz, Lucy S. *The War Against the Jews, 1933–1945.* New York: Bantam Books, 1986.

Deacon, Richard. *The Israeli Secret Service.* London: Hamish Hamilton, 1977.

Derogy, Jacques, and Hesi Carmel. *The Untold History of Israel.* New York: Grove Press, 1979.

Diamant, Manus. *Geheimauftrag: Mission Eichmann.* Vienna, 1995.

———. Manuscript. Massuah Archives, Israel.

Donovan, John. *Eichmann: Man of Slaughter.* New York: Avon, 1960.

Douglas, Lawrence. *The Memory of Judgment: Making Law and History in the Holocaust.* New Haven, CT: Yale University Press, 2001.

Dwork, Deborah, and Robert Jan van Pelt. *Auschwitz, 1270 to the Present.* New York: W. W. Norton, 1996.

Eban, Abba. *Personal Witness.* New York: G. P. Putnam's Sons, 1993.

"The Eichmann Chase." *Newsweek,* July 25, 1960.

"Eichmann in Germany." *Der Stern* 13, nos. 25–27, 1960.

Eichmann in the World Press. Jerusalem: Israel Ministry of Foreign Affairs, 1960.

Eisenhower, David. *Eisenhower at War.* New York: Random House, 1986.

Elkins, Michael. *Forged in Fury.* New York: Ballantine Books, 1971.

Erez, Tsvi. "Hungary—Six Days in July." *Holocaust and Genocide Studies* 3, no. 1 (1988): 37–53.

Eshed, Haggai. *Reuven Shiloah: The Man Behind the Mossad.* London: Frank Cass, 1997.

Este, Carlo. *Eisenhower: A Soldier's Life.* New York: Henry Holt, 2002.

Farago, Ladislas. *The Aftermath: Martin Bormann and the Fourth Reich.* New York: Simon & Schuster, 1974.

Fitzgibbon, Constantine. *Denazification.* New York: W. W. Norton, 1969.

Fraser, Nicholas, and Marysa Navarro. *Eva Peron.* New York: W. W. Norton, 1985.

Freiwald, Aaron. *The Last Nazi: Josef Schwammberger and the Nazi Past.* New York: W. W. Norton, 1994.

Fried, Tal. "Official Israeli Institutions in Pursuit of Nazi War Criminals, 1945–60." PhD diss., University of Haifa, 2002.

Friedlander, Henry. *The Origins of Nazi Genocide: From Euthanasia to the Final Solution.* Chapel Hill: University of North Carolina Press, 1995.

Friedman, Tuviah. *The Blind Man Who Discovered Adolf Eichmann in Argentina.* Haifa: Institute of Documentation in Israel, 1987.

———. *Die Korrespondenz.* Haifa: Institute of Documentation in Israel, 1993.

———. *Die Korrespondenz der zwei Nazi-Forscher Tuwiah Friedman und Simon Wiesenthal in den Jahren 1946–1950, Part I.* Haifa: Institute of Documentation in Israel, 2005.

———. *The Hunter.* Edited and translated by David C. Gross. Haifa: Institute of Documentation in Israel, 1961.

Fritzsche, Hans. *Sword in the Scales.* London: Allan Wingate, 1953.

Fröhlich, Claudia. *Wider die Tabuisierung des Ungehorsams — Fritz Bauers Widerstandsbegriff und die Aufarbeitung von NS-Verbrechen.* Frankfurt: Campus Verlag, 2006.

Fulbrook, Mary. *German National Identity After the Holocaust.* Cambridge, England: Polity Press, 1999.

Gardner-Feldman, Lily. *The Special Relationship Between West Germany and Israel.* London: George Allen & Unwin, 1984.

Gilbert, G. M. *Nuremberg Diary.* New York: Da Capo Press, 1995.

Gilbert, Martin. *The Day the War Ended: May 8, 1945; Victory in Europe.* New York: Henry Holt, 1995.

———. *The Holocaust: A History of the Jews of Europe During the Second World War.* New York: Holt, Rinehart & Winston, 1985.

Goldenhagen, Daniel. *Hitler's Willing Executioners: Ordinary Germans and the Holocaust.* New York: Alfred A. Knopf, 1996.

Goldman, Marvin. *El Al: Star in the Sky.* Miami, FL: World Transport Press, 1990.

Goñi, Uki. *The Real Odessa: How Perón Brought the Nazi War Criminals to Argentina.* London: Granta, 2003.

Groeneveld, Gerard. *Kriegsberichter: Nederlandse ss-oorlogsverslaggevers 1941–45.* Nijmegen, Netherlands: Vantilt, 2004.

Gunther, John. *Inside South America.* New York: Harper & Row, 1966.

Guri, Haim. *Facing the Glass Booth: The Jerusalem Trial of Adolf Eichmann.* Detroit: Wayne State University Press, 2004.

Gutman, Daniel. *Tacuara: Historia de la Primera Guerrilla Urbana Argentina.* Buenos Aires: Vergara Grupo Zeta, 2003.

Gutman, Yisrael, and Michael Berenbaum, eds. *Anatomy of the Auschwitz Death Camp.* Bloomington: Indiana University Press, 1994.

Haim, Avni. *Argentina and the Jews: A History of Jewish Immigration.* Tuscaloosa: University of Alabama Press, 1991.

———. "Jewish Leadership in Times of Crisis: Argentina During the Eichmann Affair." In *Studies in Contemporary Jewry,* ed. Peter Medding, vol. 11, *Values, Interests and Identity,* 117–23. New York: Oxford University Press, 1995.

Harel, Isser. *House on Garibaldi Street.* London: Frank Cass, 1997.

Harris, Whitney. *Tyranny on Trial: The Trial of the Major German War Criminals.* Dallas: Southern Methodist University Press, 1999.

Hausner, Gideon. *Justice in Jerusalem.* New York: Harper & Row, 1966.

Hoess, Rudolf. *Commandant of Auschwitz.* London: Pan Books, 1959.

Hohne, Heinz, and Hermann Zolling. *Network: The Truth About General Gehlen and His Spy Ring.* London: Secker & Warburg, 1972.

Höttl, Wilhelm. *The Secret Front: The Story of Nazi Political Espionage.* London: Weidenfeld & Nicolson, 1953.

Hull, William. *The Struggle for a Soul.* New York: Doubleday, 1963.

"Interview with Klaus Eichmann." *Quick,* January 1966.

Klee, Ernest. *Persilscheine and Falsche Passe.* Frankfurt: Fischer Taschenbuch Verlag, 1996.

Korey, William. "Reporting the Eichmann Case." *Survey,* no. 39 (December 1961).

Kurzman, Dan. *Ben-Gurion: Prophet of Fire.* New York: Simon & Schuster, 1983.

Lauryssens, Stan. *The Eichmann Diaries.* Unpublished English-language version provided by author.

Lavy, George. *Germany and Israel: Moral Debt and National Interest.* London: Frank Cass, 1996.

Lawson, Colin. "Eichmann's Wife Speaks." *Daily Express,* December 12, 1961.

Lengyel, Olga. *Five Chimneys: The Story of Auschwitz.* New York: Howard Fertig, 1995.

Levai, Eugene. *Black Book on the Martyrdom of Hungarian Jewry.* Zurich: Central European Times, 1948.

Levai, Jeno, ed. *Eichmann in Hungary: Documents.* New York: Howard Fertig, 1987.

Levi, Primo. *Survival in Auschwitz: The Nazi Assault on Humanity.* New York: Collier Books, 1961.

Levy, Alan. *The Wiesenthal File.* London: Constable, 1993.

Lewy, Gunter. *The Catholic Church and Nazi Germany.* New York: Da Capo Press, 1964.

"*Life* and Eichmann." *Newsweek,* December 5, 1960.

Lozowick, Yaacov. *Hitler's Bureaucrats: The Nazi Security Police and the Banality of Evil.* New York: Continuum, 2002.

Malkin, Peter. *The Argentina Journal.* New York: VWF Publishing, 2002.

———. *Eichmann in My Hands.* New York: Warner Books, 1990.

Marwick, Arthur. *The Sixties: Cultural Transformation in Britain, France, Italy, and the United States.* New York: Oxford University Press, 1999.

Maser, Werner. *Nuremberg: A Nation on Trial.* New York: Charles Scribner's Sons, 1979.

Matteson, Robert. *The Capture and the Last Days of SS General Ernst Kaltenbrunner.* N.p.: R. E. Matteson, 1993.

McKechnie, Gary, and Nancy Howell. "Double Exposure." *Orlando,* December 1988.

Meding, Holger. *Flücht vor Nürnberg? Deutsche und Österreichische Einwanderung in Argentinien, 1945–1955.* Köln: Böhlau Verlag, 1992.

Mendelsohn, John, and Donald Detweiler. *The Holocaust.* New York: Garland, 1982.

Mermelstein, Mel. *By Bread Alone: The Story of A-4685.* Los Angeles: Crescent Publications, 1979.

Miller, Merle. *Ike the Soldier: As I Knew Him.* New York: Putnam, 1987.

Mulisch, Harry. *Criminal Case 40/61: The Trial of Adolf Eichmann.* Philadelphia: University of Philadelphia Press, 2005.

Muller, Filip. *Eyewitness Auschwitz: Three Years in the Gas Chambers.* New York: Stein & Day, 1979.

Musmanno, Michael. *The Eichmann Kommandos.* Philadelphia: Macrae Smith, 1961.

Naftali, Timothy. "New Information on Cold War CIA Stay-Behind Operations in Germany and on the Adolf Eichmann Case." Nazi War Crimes Interagency Working Group, Washington, DC, 2006.

Nagy-Talavera, Nicholas. *The Green Shirts and the Others: A History of Fascism in Hungary and Romania.* Oxford: Center for Romanian Studies, 2001.

Newton, Ronald. *Nazi Menace in Argentina, 1931–47.* Stanford, CA: Stanford University Press, 1992.

Overy, R. J. *Interrogations: The Nazi Elite in Allied Hands.* New York: Viking Press, 2001.

Padfield, Peter. *Donitz: The Last Fuehrer.* New York: Harper & Row, 1984.

Page, Joseph. *Peron: A Biography.* New York: Random House, 1983.

Papadatos, Peter. *The Eichmann Trial.* New York: Praeger, 1964.

Pearlman, Moshe. *The Capture of Adolf Eichmann.* London: Weidenfeld & Nicolson, 1961.

Perels, Joachim, and Irmtrud Wojak, eds. *Fritz Bauer: Die Humanität der Rechtsordnung.* Frankfurt: Campus Verlag, 1998.

Pick, Hella. *Simon Wiesenthal: A Life in Search of Justice.* Boston: Northeastern University Press, 1996.

Posner, Gerald, and John Ware. *Mengele: The Complete Story.* New York: McGraw-Hill, 1986.

Potash, Robert. *The Army and Politics in Argentina, 1945–1962.* Stanford, CA: Stanford University Press, 1980.

Prendle, George. *Argentina.* Oxford: Oxford University Press, 1963.

Prittie, Terence. *Konrad Adenauer, 1876–1967.* Ann Arbor, MI: Tom Stacey, 1972.

———. *Willy Brandt: Portrait of a Statesman.* New York: Schocken Books, 1974.

Rassinier, Paul. *The Real Eichmann Trial, or, The Incorrigible Victors.* Torrance, CA: Steppingstones Publications, 1979.

Rathkolb, Oliver. *Revisiting the National Socialist Legacy.* Innsbruck: Studien Verlag, 2004.

Raviv, Dan, and Yossi Melman. *Every Spy a Prince: The Complete History of Israel's Intelligence Community.* Boston: Houghton Mifflin, 1990.

Read, Anthony. *The Devil's Disciples: Hitler's Inner Circle.* New York: W. W. Norton, 2003.

Read, Anthony, and David Fisher. *The Fall of Berlin.* New York: Da Capo Press, 1992.

Reilly, Joanne. *Belsen: The Liberation of a Concentration Camp.* New York: Routledge, 1998.

Rein, Raanan. *Argentina, Israel, and the Jews: Peron, the Eichmann Capture and After.* Bethesda: University Press of Maryland, 2003.

Reynolds, Quentin, with Zwy Aldouby and Ephraim Katz. *Minister of Death: The Adolph Eichmann Story.* New York: Viking Press, 1961.

Robinson, Jacob. *And the Crooked Shall Be Made Straight: The Eichmann Trial, the Jewish Catastrophe, and Hannah Arendt's Narrative.* New York: Macmillan, 1965.

Rojer, Olga. *Exile in Argentina, 1933–45: A Historical and Literary Introduction.* New York: Peter Lang, 1989.

Roper, Hugh Trevor. *The Last Days of Hitler.* New York: Macmillan, 1947.

Roseman, Mark. *The Wannasee Conference and the Final Solution.* New York: Metropolitan Books, 2003.

Sayer, Ian, and Douglas Botting. *America's Secret Army: The Untold Story of the Counter Intelligence Corps.* London: Grafton, 1989.

Schwarz, Hans-Peter. *Konrad Adenauer: A German Politician and Statesman in a Period of War.* Oxford: Berghahn Books, 1991.

Scobie, James. *Argentina: A City and a Nation.* Oxford: Oxford University Press, 1964.

Segev, Tom. *The Seventh Million: The Israelis and the Holocaust.* New York: Hill & Wang, 1993.

Shephard, Ben. *After Daybreak: The Liberation of Belsen, 1945.* London: Jonathan Cape, 2005.

Shields, Stephen. "Triumph and Tragedy." *American Heritage,* December 1989, 82–93.

Shirer, William. *The Rise and Fall of the Third Reich: A History of Nazi Germany.* New York: Simon & Schuster, 1990.

Shpiro, Shlomo. *Geheimdienste in der Weltgeschichte: Spionage und verdeckte Aktionen von der Antike bis zur Gegenwart.* Munich: Verlag C. H. Beck, 2003.

———. "Intelligence Services and Foreign Policy." *German Politics* 11 (April 2002): 23-42.

Silverstein, Ken. *Private Warriors.* New York: Verso, 2000.

Simpson, Christopher. *Blowback: America's Recruitment of Nazis and Its Effect on the Cold War.* London: Weidenfeld & Nicolson, 1988.

Skorzeny, Otto. *Skorzeny's Secret Mission: War Memoirs of the Most Dangerous Man in Europe.* New York: E. P. Dutton, 1959.

Smith, John. *The Plot to Save Eichmann.* Chicago: Domino Publications, 1961.

Spender, Stephen. *European Witness.* London: Hamish Hamilton, 1946.

Steven, Stewart. *The Spymasters of Israel.* New York: Macmillan, 1980.

Szita, Szabolcs. *Trading in Lives? Operations of the Jewish Relief and Rescue Committee in Budapest, 1944–45.* New York: Central European University Press, 2005.

"Tale of Epic Capture." *Life,* June 20, 1960.

Taylor, Telford. *The Anatomy of the Nuremberg Trials.* New York: Alfred A. Knopf, 1992.

Teicholz, Tom. *The Trial of Ivan the Terrible: State of Israel vs. John Demjanjuk.* New York: St. Martin's Press, 1991.

Tetens, T. H. *The New Germany and the Old Nazis.* London: Secker & Warburg, 1961.

Thomas, Gordon. *Gideon's Spies: The Secret History of the Mossad.* New York: St. Martin's Press, 2000.

Toland, John. *The Last 100 Days: The Tumultuous and Controversial Final Days of World War II in Europe.* New York: Random House, 1966.

The Trial of Adolf Eichmann: Record of Proceedings in the District Court of Jerusalem. 9 vols. Jerusalem: Trust for the Publication of the Proceedings of the Eichmann Trial, 1992.

Trial of German Major War Criminals: Proceedings of the International Military Tribunal, Nuremberg, November 14, 1945–October 1, 1946. London: Published Under Authority of Her Majesty's Attorney, 1946.

Tschuy, Theo. *Dangerous Diplomacy: The Story of Carl Lutz, Rescuer of 62,000 Hungarian Jews.* Grand Rapids, MI: William B. Eerdmans, 2000.

U.S. Department of Justice. Office of Special Investigations. "In the Matter of Josef Mengele: A Report to the Attorney General of the United States, October 1992." Report and exhibits, 1992.

Van der Vat, Dan. *The Good Nazi: The Life and Lies of Albert Speer.* New York: Weidenfeld & Nicolson, 1997.

Vogel, Rolf. *The German Path to Israel.* London: Oswald Wolff, 1969.

Von Lang, Jochen. *The Secretary: Martin Bormann, the Man Who Manipulated Hitler.* New York: Random House, 1979.

Wald, Richard. "The Tolerated Kidnapping: The Impact of the Eichmann Affair on Argentina." PhD diss., University of Edinburgh, 1993.

Weber, Gaby. *La Conexion Alemana: El Lavado del Dinero Nazi en Argentina.* Buenos Aires: Edhasa, 2005.

Weissberg, Alex. *Advocate for the Dead: The Story of Joel Brand.* London: A. Deutsch, 1958.

Wiesenthal, Simon. *Justice Not Vengeance.* New York: Grove-Weidenfeld, 1989.

———. *The Murderers Among Us: The Simon Wiesenthal Memoirs.* New York: McGraw-Hill, 1967.

Wighton, Charles. *Adenauer: A Critical Biography.* New York: Coward-McCann, 1963.

———. *Eichmann: His Career and Crimes.* London: Odhams Press, 1961.

Williams, Charles. *Adenauer: The Father of the New Germany.* Boston: Little, Brown, 2000.

Wojak, Irmtrud. *Eichmann Memoiren: Ein Kritisches Essay.* Frankfurt: Campus Verlag, 2001.

Wolffsohn, Michael. *Eternal Guilt? Forty Years of German-Jewish-Israeli Relations.* New York: Columbia University Press, 1993.

Yablonka, Hanna. *The State of Israel vs. Adolf Eichmann.* New York: Schocken Books, 2004.

Yahil, Leni. *The Holocaust: The Fate of European Jewry, 1932–1945.* New York: Oxford University Press, 1990.

Ziemke, Earl. *The U.S. Army in the Occupation of Germany, 1944–46.* Washington, DC: Center of Military History, 1975.

Zweig, Ronald W. *The Gold Train: The Destruction of the Jews and the Looting of Hungary.* New York: HarperCollins, 2002.

Index

Adenauer, Konrad, 84–85, 98–99, 127, 145, 306–7, 316

Aerolineas Argentinas, 200, 214, 252, 273, 292

Agami, Moshe, 297, 302

Aharoni, Zvi
  meets with Bauer in Israel, 123–25, 128, 146
  background of, 130
  arrives in Argentina, 130–31, 176, 178–79
  learns that Eichmann has moved from Chacabuco Street, 132–33, 138, 141–42
  locates Eichmann's San Fernando house, 136–45
  identifies Eichmann visually, 151–52, 154, 179
  takes photos of Eichmann, 154–59
  returns to Israel to discuss Eichmann's capture, 158–59, 163–64
  on capture team, 159, 162, 163, 167–68, 173, 176, 183–85, 196, 207–10, 215, 219
  surveillance of Eichmann by, 197–98, 204
  in capture operation, 216, 221–29
  interrogates Eichmann, 230–34, 239–41, 254–56, 279–80, 353n
  efforts of, to get Eichmann to sign agreement to stand trial in Israel, 241, 255, 267–68, 356n
  at El Al's arrival in Buenos Aires, 271, 273
  chauffeurs Eichmann to airplane, 277, 279, 282–86
  hears Ben-Gurion's announcement about Eichmann's capture, 298–99
  after Eichmann's death, 325
  spots Mengele in Brazil, 325

Allies
  approach Hungary, 2, 9
  bomb Budapest, 7–9
  draw up war criminal lists, 10, 15–16, 24, 28, 31, 48, 63–64
  liberate concentration camps, 14–17, 39
  Eichmann's escapes from, 19, 24–27, 31–32, 35–37, 48–50, 56, 62–63, 71–75, 84, 239
  search for ex-Nazis, 25–31, 41–43, 48
  occupy Germany, 27–31
  hold war crimes trials, 43–48, 57, 63, 65, 70, 240, 303, 312
  smuggle Nazi war criminals out of Germany, 71, 114, 345n
  See also France; Great Britain; Soviet Union; United States

Alps, viii, 22–27, 31–32
  See also specific places in

Altaussee (Austria)
  Eichmann family members in, 19–22, 24–26, 31, 47, 54–55, 60, 63, 80, 336n

Amadeo, Mario, 305

Anti-Semitism
  in Europe, 5, 30, 32, 102
  Eichmann's, 25, 32–35, 62, 88, 196–97,
    260, 318
  in Argentina, 70, 76, 83, 86–87, 93, 152,
    251, 305
  Klaus Eichmann's, 86, 92–93, 157, 207,
    305
  Eichmann denies his, 90, 260–61
  West German outbreaks of, 127–29, 145
  See also Final Solution; Jews; Nazis
Antonio, Jorge, 116
Arendt, Hannah, 323, 337n
Argentina
  diplomatic issues with Mossad capture
    operation in, viii, 152, 164, 207,
    304–6
  Eichmann is smuggled into, 66–69,
    71–75, 91, 122, 340n
  government officials' support for
    ex-Nazis in, 69, 83, 93, 123, 152, 157
  anti-Semitism in, 70, 76, 83, 86–87, 93,
    152, 251, 305
  Jewish community in, 70, 107, 186, 272,
    305
  description of, 73–74, 77
  150th anniversary independence
    celebration in, 172, 173, 180, 181–82,
    185, 186, 244, 247
  heightened security in, during
    anniversary celebrations and period
    of Eichmann's capture, 180, 189,
    196, 201, 203–4, 264–65, 271, 276
  Ministry of Aviation of, 201, 252, 272,
    281
  See also Buenos Aires; Coronel Suárez;
    Tucumán
Argentinisches Tageblatt, 92, 149
Assassination (Mossad considers, as a
    possibility for Eichmann), 126,
    167–68, 199, 237
Auschwitz-Birkenau concentration camp
  Sapir in, 7, 11–12, 314
  extermination of Jews at, 8–9, 256, 302,
    312–14, 320
  news from, 15, 16–17
  Eichmann at, 19

  survivors of, 52, 59, 170, 192, 309–10,
    322
  Mengele's role at, 65, 122, 188, 240, 254,
    257
  trials of war criminals from, 323
  See also Höss, Rudolf
Austria
  deportation operations in, 3, 39
  forced march of Hungarian Jews to, 11
  as Eichmann's native country, 19, 35
  Germany's occupation of, 33
  former Nazis in, 81
  Jewish avenger groups in, 168
  See also specific places in
Avivi, Mordechai, 273

Bach, Gabriel, 313–14
Baky, László, 9
Baromi, Joel, 306
"Barth, Adolf," 31, 36, 74
Bauer, Fritz
  background of, 93–95, 128
  learns that Eichmann is in Argentina,
    93–95, 113
  launches search for Eichmann, 95, 109,
    343n
  prods Israelis to search for Eichmann,
    98–100, 105–7, 121–25, 146, 212
  learns of Israel's halt in search for
    Eichmann, 113–14
  new source of Eichmann information
    for, 121–23, 125, 126, 132, 139, 346n
  learns that Eichmann has been
    captured, 297–98
  capture operation's impact on, 323
Bauer, Kurt, 49, 56
Belgium, 3, 70, 96
Belzec concentration camp, 66, 312
Ben-Ari, Mordechai, 172–73, 296
Ben-Gurion, David
  on hunting war criminals, 53, 145, 304
  as Israeli prime minister, 83, 262, 326
  Middle East concerns of, 113
  Harel as reporting to, 116, 124, 125–27,
    235, 248–49, 296–97
  Friedman beseeches, to search for
    Eichmann, 121

Ben-Gurion, David (*cont.*)
  authorizes search, capture, and
      transport of Eichmann to Israel,
      126, 128, 129, 187–88, 207
  offers legal justification for capture of
      German on foreign soil, 144–45, 304
  learns of Eichmann's capture, 248–49
  learns of Eichmann's arrival in Israel,
      296–97
  announces Eichmann's capture and
      detention, 298–301, 303–8, 323
  on significance of Eichmann trial, 313
Ben-Natan, Asher. *See* Pier, Arthur
Bergen-Belsen concentration camp, 14,
    16–17, 66, 90, 202
Berlin (Germany), 14, 17–21, 33, 71
Blaa-Alm (Austria), 22–24, 26
Blanc, Shimon, 274, 291
Bloch, Michael, 133–35
Bohne, Gerhard, 71
Boldt, Gerhard, 116–17
Bormann, Martin, 21, 44, 240, 325
Bower, Tom, 338n
Bradley, Omar, 16
Brand, Joel, 27, 334n
Brandt, Willy, 94
Brazil, 81, 216
  El Al landing in, 182, 263, 269–71, 273,
      282, 286, 288–89
Brichah (Jewish underground group), 40,
    51–54, 309
Britannia airplanes
  El Al's, 173, 182, 186, 214, 244, 273–74,
      277, 282, 288, 289
  other airlines flying, 200–201
  El Al's, on flight to Argentina, 262–64,
      269–73
  El Al's, on flight to Israel, 290–95
Buchenwald concentration camp, 16
Budapest (Hungary), 1, 3–4, 7–10, 37–38,
    46, 71, 256, 309
Buenos Aires (Argentina)
  Eichmann capture operation in, vi,
      vii–viii, 221–29
  as Eichmann's destination, 69, 71–75
  German community in, 69, 76–77,
      86–87, 117, 152, 224, 242

ex-Nazi network and supporters in,
      69–72, 75, 76, 87–93, 116, 125, 152,
      157, 224, 237, 240–41, 250–51,
      265–66, 276, 285, 288–89
  Jewish community in, 70, 107, 186, 272,
      305
  description of, 74, 77
  Eichmann living in, 89, 91–92
  Mossad agents look for Eichmann on
      Chacabuco Street in, 106–7, 111–13,
      115, 132–33, 136–39
  Friedman learns that Eichmann lives in,
      121
  anniversary flight as El Al's first to, 171,
      180, 200, 264, 271
  capture team starts to gather in, 175–79
  heightened security in, during period of
      Eichmann capture, 180, 189, 196,
      201, 203–4, 264–65, 271, 276
  harbor of, 184, 244, 253
  See also Capture operation; Ezeiza
      Airport; Olivos neighborhood; San
      Fernando neighborhood
Bureau 06 (Israel), 302, 308–10, 319
Burger, Anton, 22, 23, 26, 59
Bus 203, vi, vii–ix, 183, 207, 220, 222–29

Camp Iyar, 301–3, 317, 319
Capital punishment, 317
CAPRI (company), 78, 89, 122, 157
Capture operation (in Buenos Aires)
  map of, vi
  description of, vii–ix, 221–29
  difficulties associated with, 152–53
  importance of keeping Eichmann alive
      during, 153, 174, 188, 222, 228
  agents involved in, 153–54, 159, 160–63
  plans for team's Argentina journey and
      stay during, 164–66
  team for, meets for first time, 166–71
  three different possibilities for, 168
  team for, starts to gather in Buenos
      Aires, 175–209
  date for, 191, 195, 200, 210–11, 213
  finalizing of plans for, 206–12
  contingencies outlined for, 216–18
  team waits for appointed time in, 219–20

Eichmann's glasses lost during, 236, 243, 250

team's silence about, in later years, 300–301

See also Cars; Garibaldi Street; Safe houses; Transporting (of Eichmann from Argentina to Israel)

Caroz, Yaakov, 248

Cars
in capture operation, vi, vii–viii, 189, 206–9, 216, 221–29
rental of, 166, 172, 190, 191, 204, 234
trapdoor in, 203, 215, 234
repairing and polishing of, 212, 215, 219
for taking Eichmann to plane, 277, 282–83
return of, 285, 293
See also License plates

Catholic Church and officials, 9, 68–72, 75, 91, 122, 305

Central Registry of War Criminals and Security Suspects (CROWCASS), 28, 48

Cesarani, David, 337n

Chacabuco Street (Olivos neighborhood)
Eichmann's former residence on, 95, 106–7, 111–13, 115, 122, 132–33, 136–38, 141, 144, 279

Chelmno concentration camp, 312

Choter-Ischai (Jewish Brigade captain), 39, 40

Churchill, Winston, 15, 30

CIA, 39, 84–85, 104, 114–15, 231, 307, 345n
See also Office of Strategic Services

CIC (Counter Intelligence Corps, U.S. Army), 26, 28–31, 42–43, 47–49, 63–66, 342n

Cohen, Benno, 297, 302

Cohen, Haim, 122, 124–26, 212, 297–98, 346n
on legal justification for capture of German on foreign soil, 144–45, 164
on getting signed statement from Eichmann agreeing to stand trial in Israel, 241

Cold war, 65, 66, 85, 114

Communists, 32, 34, 70–71, 104, 114

Concentration camps
conditions in, 2, 7, 11–13, 16–17, 34, 38
tattoos in, 12, 315, 320
liberation of, 14–17, 39
survivors of, 39–40, 51–52, 59, 85, 93–94, 98–99, 170, 192, 206, 274, 292, 296, 309
Eichmann's low visibility in, 42, 266
Eichmann's involvement with, 62, 167, 307
doctors associated with, 65, 122, 188, 240, 254, 257
forgers in, 162, 202
See also Final Solution; *specific concentration camps, victims, and survivors*

Coronel Suárez (Argentina), 92–94, 108, 121

Czechoslovakia, 3, 10, 19, 31, 33, 39, 63, 64, 70, 171
See also Theresienstadt concentration camp

Dachau concentration camp, 86, 274

Dachsgrube coal mines, 11–12, 310, 314

Dakar (Senegal), 182, 183, 263, 273–74, 282, 289, 291, 293–95

Damascus (Syria), 84, 113

Dani, Shalom
on capture team, 162, 173, 177, 195, 201–3, 215, 234, 259–60, 293
background of, 202
after Eichmann's death, 326

Darom, Shaul, 105–7

Denmark, 2, 3, 94

Department IVB$_4$ (Third Reich Security), viii, 2, 31, 47, 90

Deportation (of Jews to concentration camps)
Eichmann's deception concerning, 3–4, 6, 9, 13, 90, 256, 310
as Eichmann's specialty, 3–4, 6, 8–10, 13, 15, 18, 19, 33–35, 90, 104–5, 118, 192, 256, 266, 310, 312, 315–17

Deportation (of Poles), 34

Diamant, Manus, 59–61, 64–65, 104

Diplomatic pouches, 131–32, 155, 165–66

Disguises
  capture team's use of, 219
  for Eichmann and kidnappers as they
      board plane, 243–44, 253, 259, 273,
      276–77, 279, 280, 284
Dömöter, Edoardo, 72
Dönitz, Karl, 24, 29, 44
Doppl (Austria), 58, 60–61
Doron (safe house), 194–95, 203, 205–9,
  211
Drori, Moshe, 296
Dulles, Allen, 114, 307

Eban, Abba, 262, 272
"Eckmann, Otto," 36–38, 42–43, 62, 63, 74
Eden, Anthony, 15, 28
Egypt, 49
  Israel's tensions with, 83, 167, 294–95,
    326
  Suez War with, 104, 113
Eichmann, Adolf
  capture of, vii–ix, 225–29
  real identity hidden by, in Argentina,
    viii, 69, 72, 78–79, 87, 91, 96, 122,
    132, 224, 251
  role of, in Nazi genocide of Jews, viii,
    1–4, 6–11, 35, 41, 45–48, 62, 90, 92,
    100–101, 104–5, 121, 168, 218, 245,
    256, 298, 308, 312–13
  deportation as Nazi specialty of, 3–4, 6,
    8–10, 13, 15, 18, 19, 33–35, 90, 104–5,
    118, 192, 256, 266, 310, 312, 315–17
  in Munkács, 6, 13, 309–10
  concern of, about being identified as a
    war criminal, 10, 24, 42–43, 48–49,
    56–57
  mistresses of, 10, 25, 58–61, 256
  postwar plans of, 18–19, 27
  destruction of files of, 19
  escapes from Allies, 19, 24–27, 31–32,
    35–37, 48–50, 56, 62–63, 66–69,
    71–75, 84, 239
  establishes Nazi resistance group in
    Austria, 21–23, 26–27
  background and marriage of, 24–26,
    32–35

  anti-Semitism of, 25, 32–35, 62, 88,
    196–97, 260, 318
  musical interests of, 25, 57, 213
  postwar poverty of, 25, 78, 91–92, 106,
    112–13, 115–16, 144, 183–84, 230,
    336n
  lack of guilt experienced by, 32, 88,
    117–18, 197, 239, 241, 261, 266, 307,
    315–16, 318
  spiritual views of, 32, 75, 317–19
  SS tattoo of, 36, 49, 231
  as German POW, 36–38, 49, 59, 239
  as having kept a low profile among
    Jewish victims, 42
  personal characteristics of, 43, 47, 58,
    78, 88–89, 96, 109, 117
  Jewish avengers' search for, 54–56
  smuggled out of Europe, 66–69, 71–75,
    91, 122, 340n
  Argentine jobs held by, 77–78, 89,
    91–92, 109, 116, 122, 149, 157, 220,
    242–43
  as brooding over Germany's loss, 78, 88,
    89, 116–18, 149, 221
  appearance of, in postwar years, 79, 92,
    96, 151–52, 155, 167, 197, 203, 225,
    256
  posing of, as sons' uncle, 79, 87, 96
  autobiographies of, 87–91, 117–18, 149,
    307–9, 316, 317, 345n
  West German arrest warrant for, 94
  Sylvia Hermann meets, 95–97, 343n
  plastic surgery rumors about, 109, 112
  rumors about, not followed up on,
    114–15
  Nazi-hunters as learning alias of, 122,
    124, 126
  Mossad considers assassinating, 126,
    167–68, 199, 237
  learns he's being sought in Argentina,
    148–50
  Mossad's concerns about ability of, to
    defend himself or escape, 152–53,
    205, 237–38
  capture team recognizes, 178–79
  on day of capture, 220–21

as resigned to his fate once caught,
228–30, 245, 255, 280, 292, 302–3
as captive in Buenos Aires safe house,
230–34, 236–41, 244–48, 255–57,
260–61, 266–69, 274–75
Mossad's interrogation of, in Buenos
Aires, 230–34, 239–41, 254–56, 353n
Mossad's efforts to obtain signed
agreement from, to stand trial, 241,
255, 267–68, 304, 356n
Israeli charges against, 297, 312
interrogations of, in Israel, 302–3, 308
international reaction to capture and
forthcoming trial of, 304–6
trial and execution of, 311–17
ashes of, 320–21
See also Capture operation; Deportation; Final Solution; Garibaldi
Street; Identity(ies); Photographs;
Transporting; Trial; names of
relatives, associates, and specific
people searching for
Eichmann, Adolf Karl (Eichmann's
father), 19, 32, 41–42, 312
Eichmann, Dieter ("Dito," Eichmann's
son)
during World War II, 24–26, 42
names of, 48, 80, 232
Nazi-hunters' involvement with,
64–65
in Argentina, 78–82, 95, 115, 121, 138–41,
149, 150, 155, 158, 305
search for Eichmann by, 224, 236, 237,
240, 241–43, 250–51, 265–66
Eichmann writes final letter to, 318
after Eichmann's death, 324
Eichmann, Horst (Eichmann's son)
during World War II, 24–26, 42
Nazi-hunters' involvement with, 64–65
in Argentina, 78–82, 115, 121
and merchant marine, 92, 149, 242
political views of, 157, 207, 324
Eichmann writes final letter to, 318
Eichmann, Klaus ("Nick," Eichmann's
son)
during World War II, 24–26, 42

Nazi-hunters' involvement with, 64–65
with father in Argentina, 78–82, 92, 115,
121
keeps original surname, 80, 240
anti-Semitism of, 86, 92–93, 157, 207,
305
description of, 86
Mossad's use of, to learn Eichmann's
identity and location, 86–87,
92–93, 95–97, 108, 141–42, 150
wife of, 147–49, 213
search for Eichmann by, 224, 236, 237,
240, 241–43, 250–51, 265–66, 354n
learns Eichmann was taken to Israel,
288–89
Eichmann writes final letter to, 318
after Eichmann's death, 324
Eichmann, Margarita (Nick's wife),
147–49, 213
Eichmann, Nick. See Eichmann, Klaus
("Nick")
Eichmann, Otto (Adolf's brother), 54–55,
135, 164
Eichmann, Ricardo Francisco (Eichmann's
youngest son), vii, 95, 121, 318, 324
birth of, in Argentina, 91, 144, 149
Nazi-hunters observe, in San Fernando,
143–44, 155, 203, 260
Eichmann, Vera (Veronika) Liebl
efforts of, to declare husband legally
dead, vii, 63–64
with husband in Argentina, vii, 78–80,
121, 213
Eichmann leaves behind, after the war,
10, 24–26, 73
locations of, during World War II, 10,
21, 24
marriage of, 24–25, 40, 42, 80, 92
declines to join Nazi Party, 25
denies having contact with husband
after war, 47, 60
Nazi-hunters knowledge of location of,
54–55, 59
Nazi-hunters' involvement with, 60,
64–65
Nazi-hunters lose trail of, 80–84

Eichmann, Vera (Veronika) Liebl (*cont.*)
  remarriage claims about, 92–93, 105,
    109, 134–35, 148
  Nazi-hunters renew search for, 95, 105,
    134–35, 139, 143–44
  Nazi-hunters find, in San Fernando,
    143–44, 146–48, 151
  Mossad's surveillance of, 196
  nightmare of, 213, 220
  and Eichmann's capture, 224–25,
    235–37, 240, 242–43, 305, 306
  grants permission for sale of rights to
    Eichmann's memories, 307
  Eichmann writes final letter to, 318
  after Eichmann's death, 324
Eichmann in Jerusalem (Arendt), 323
Einsatzgruppen, 34, 55, 65
Eisenhower, Dwight, 14, 16, 17, 29
Eitan, Rafi
  background of, 153–54
  as part of Mossad capture team, 153–54,
    173, 174, 199–200, 204–6, 216–17,
    219–20
  and Shalom, 161, 162–63
  in charge of tactical plans for Eich-
    mann's capture, 165–66, 172, 179,
    205, 208, 264
  and Malkin, 166–68
  arrives in Buenos Aires, 195–97
  heads team meeting at Maoz, 199–200
  and finalization of capture plans,
    209–12
  in capture operation, 221–25, 227–29
  with Eichmann in Tira, 234, 237–38,
    246, 255, 257, 260, 268–69, 274–75,
    277
  and Mengele plan, 254
  on trip to airport with Eichmann, 280,
    283–85
  leaves Buenos Aires, 293, 300
  witnesses Eichmann's execution, 319,
    320
  after Eichmann's death, 326
El Al
  first flight of, to Buenos Aires, 171, 180,
    200, 264, 271
    choosing, for transporting Eichmann to
      Israel, 171–73
    Argentine anniversary celebration as
      cover for transporting Eichmann
      on, 172, 173, 180, 181–82, 244
    "monkey business crews" on, 172, 263
    crew selection for, 173, 180–82, 244
    employees of, summoned to Buenos
      Aires, 185–86
    dates for flights of, 191, 195, 200, 237,
      264, 273–74
    finding parking place for plane at
      airport, 201, 214, 252, 273
    contingency plans for, 204
    Eichmann dressed in uniform of, 243,
      253, 259, 273, 279, 280, 284
    private passengers booked for special
      flight on, 251–52, 272, 273
    flight from Israel to Argentina by,
      262–64, 269–73
    arrival of, in Argentina, 271–73
    return crew for, 274, 279, 280–81,
      283–86, 295–96
    flight plans of, for trip from Buenos
      Aires to Israel, 282, 286–88, 294
    return flight of, to Israel, 285–88,
      290–95
    recognition of role of, in capture
      operation, 324
    See also Britannia airplanes
England. *See* Great Britain
Eshel, Arie, 83
Eytan, Walter, 100
Ezeiza Airport (near Buenos Aires)
  Aharoni arrives at, 130–31
  Gat arrives at, 175–76, 179
  Klein arranges for Eichmann's
    departure from, 200–201, 213–15,
    243–44, 252–53, 259, 271–72, 279,
    281, 284–88
  El Al flight arrives at, 271–73
  capture team prepares for flight from,
    277–78, 280–82, 300
  El Al's departure from, 285–88, 290–95
  See also El Al; Klein, Yosef; Volk,
    Luba

Feiersleben, Hans, 49, 57, 67
Final Solution (Holocaust)
    Eichmann's role in, viii, 1–4, 7–11, 35,
        41, 45–48, 62, 90, 92, 100–101,
        104–5, 121, 168, 218, 245, 256, 298,
        308, 312–13
    Jewish Mossad agents and officials
        having lost families to, viii, 65, 107,
        131, 134, 162, 170, 173, 182, 192, 197,
        202, 206, 245, 259, 263, 268, 302,
        320
    Himmler's order to begin, 2, 10, 46
    deportation as Eichmann's specialty in,
        3–4, 6, 8–10, 13, 15, 18, 19, 33–35, 90,
        104–5, 118, 192, 256, 266, 310, 312,
        315–17
    Sapir as survivor of, 4–7, 11–14, 309–10,
        314–15, 334n
    revelation of, to world, 14–17, 44–45,
        128, 153, 174, 216, 304, 313–16,
        322–23, 326
    Eichmann's estimate of number of Jews
        killed in, 19
    Eichmann's role in, not immediately
        recognized by Allies, 31, 45–49
    survivors of, 39–40, 51–52, 59, 85,
        93–94, 98–99, 170, 192, 206, 274,
        292, 296, 309
    meaning of term, 46, 312
    Eichmann as wanting to set the record
        straight on, 89, 267
    West Germany's compensation to
        Jewish survivors of, 98–99, 145
    number of survivors of, in Israel, 101
    survivors' early silence about, 101, 304,
        309, 322
    Israel's existence as linked to, 104
    as causing Jews to lose their faith,
        124
    West Germany's silence about, 128
    and selection of Eichmann's Israeli
        guards, 302
    See also Concentration camps;
        Deportation; Yad Vashem
"Following orders"
    as Eichmann's defense, 32, 74, 90, 105,
        117–18, 241, 260–61, 266, 303,
        315–16, 319, 324
    Catholic officials on, 70–71
    Eichmann denies, 80
    Malkin enlists Eichmann's cooperation
        by urging, 280
France, 3, 8, 39, 44, 45, 70, 96
Frank, Hans, 30, 44
Frankfurt (Germany), 92, 93, 105, 128, 146
Freemasons, 32, 71
Freude, Rodolfo, 70
Frick, Wilhelm, 44
Friedman, Anna (Tuviah's wife), 81–82,
    118, 120
Friedman, Arye, 273, 292
Friedman, Bella, 51, 52
Friedman, Tuviah ("Tadek")
    Holocaust experiences of, 51–52
    enlistment of, in effort to find
        Eichmann, 51–54
    search for Eichmann by, 57–61, 65–66,
        81–82, 85, 118–21, 123, 212
    Eichmann file kept by, 82, 104, 120, 308
    on Eichmann's whereabouts, 118–21,
        128–29, 149
    urges reward for locating Eichmann,
        120, 135
    impact of capture operation on, 323,
        324
Fritzsche, Hans, 44
Frondizi, Arturo, 152, 304–5
Fuldner, Carlos, 70, 76–78, 242, 251, 354n
Fuldner Company, 122, 139, 146
Funk, Walter, 44

Garibaldi Street (San Fernando neighbor-
    hood)
    Eichmann's capture on, vii–ix, 221–29
    Mossad surveillance of Eichmann's
        house on, 151–52, 154–59, 178–79,
        183–84, 190–91, 194–200, 203–6,
        219
    routes to and from, 172, 189–91, 194–95,
        203–4, 207–8, 212
    team plans for capture on, 199–200,
        207–8, 216

Garibaldi Street (*cont.*)
    Eichmann asked for directions on, 213
    Eichmann's lost glasses on, 236, 243, 250
Gas chambers
    in Auschwitz, 8–9, 12, 15, 62, 90
    in other concentration camps, 90, 105,
        121, 292, 307, 320
Gat, Yaakov
    interviews Eichmann and Liebl families
        in Germany, 133–36, 144
    background of, 134
    on capture team, 158–59, 163, 173, 175,
        178–79, 184, 189–90, 194, 215, 217,
        219, 300–301
    in capture operation, 216, 221, 223, 225,
        227, 228
    with Eichmann in Tira, 233, 237, 239,
        268
    with Eichmann en route to Buenos
        Aires airport, 282–84
    with Eichmann on flight to Israel, 294
    with Eichmann in Israel, 296
    after Eichmann's death, 325
Gehlen, Reinhard, 114, 307
Germany
    deportation operations in, 3
    Allies as driving toward, 8, 14
    scientists from, 16, 69, 345n
    surrender of, 24
    Allied occupation of, 27–31
    POWs from, 31
    Eichmann born in, 32, 42, 233
    Eichmann returns to, after World War
        II, 35–36, 49, 56–57, 62–63, 239
    war crimes trials held in, 43–48, 57, 63,
        65, 70, 92–95, 120, 128, 303, 312, 323
    Eichmann leaves, for last time, 68
    rumors that Vera Eichmann moved to,
        81
    Kristallnacht in, 87, 130, 160–61
    interviews with Vera Eichmann's family
        in, 105, 128, 133–34, 144
    Jewish avenger groups in, 168
    See also Hitler, Adolf; Nazis; War
        criminals; West Germany
Giovanna C (ship), 73–74, 78

Glasses (Eichmann's), 236, 243, 250
Gleiwitz concentration camp, 13
Globke, Hans, 99, 115, 127–28, 145, 306–7,
    316, 323, 343n, 345n
Globocnik, Odilo, 34
Goebbels, Joseph, 21, 114
Goettsch, Werner, 338n
Goggles (for Eichmann), 227, 231, 237–38,
    255–56, 267, 268, 292
Goldmann, Michael, 319, 320
Goldmann, Nahum, 83–85
Goñi, Uki, 340n
Goren, Yoel, 106–7, 112–13, 279, 280,
    284
Göring, Hermann, 20, 29, 44, 45, 312
Great Britain, viii
    on Holocaust, 15
    concentration camp liberation by, 16
    search for ex-Nazi war criminals by, 28,
        30, 48, 67
    and Palestine, 30, 40, 102, 103, 130–31,
        153–54, 169
    at Nuremberg trials, 44, 45
    See also Allies
Greece, 39, 295, 343n

Haganah
    killing of ex-Nazis by, 30–31
    search for Eichmann by, 51–54, 57–61
    disbanding of, 65
    members of, 102–4, 120, 153–54, 161,
        169, 263
    airplanes used for, 171
Halevi, Emanuel, 297, 358n
Harel, Isser (head of Mossad)
    learns about Eichmann, 100–105
    as Mossad and Shin Bet chief, 100–105,
        131, 134, 185, 187, 300
    background of, 101–4
    and Bauer, 105–6, 124–25, 345n
    calls off early Eichmann search in
        Argentina, 112–14, 122
    Ben-Gurion as boss of, 116, 124, 125–27,
        235, 248–49, 296–97
    renews search for Eichmann in
        Argentina, 125–29, 132

learns that Klement is likely Eichmann, 138, 144, 152, 155, 159, 164

learns where Eichmann is living, 144

capture mission concerns of, 152–54, 164–66, 170

goes to Buenos Aires to oversee capture, 153, 166, 177, 180, 186–87, 190–91, 245–46

orders Aharoni to return to Tel Aviv for debriefing, 158

puts capture team together, 160–63, 169, 202

in charge of transporting Eichmann to Israel, 168, 171–73, 191, 193–95, 213–15, 234–35, 243–44, 273–74, 277–79, 282, 283, 285–88, 290, 292, 294, 295–98

motivational talks by, 173–74, 215–16, 252

"go" order for capture operation from, 178–79

receives Ben-Gurion's blessing for mission, 187–88, 207

Mengele search by, while in Buenos Aires, 188–89, 240, 254–55, 257–58, 264–65, 274, 278–79

meets with team members in Buenos Aires, 190–91, 206, 207–12, 215–16

illness of, during capture operation, 206–7, 224–25

learns of capture operation's success, 234–35

sees Eichmann at Tira, 255–57

and date for announcement of Eichmann's capture, 293, 297

hears Ben-Gurion's announcement about Eichmann's capture, 298–99

after Eichmann's death, 325, 326

Hassin, Gady, 270, 274, 282, 294–95

Hausner, Gideon, 312–13, 315, 316

Hebrew language, 33, 40, 41, 58, 130, 233, 312

Helmut, Gregor, 264
    See also Mengele, Josef

"Heninger, Otto," 49, 56–57, 67, 74, 232, 239

Hermann, Lothar
    learns of Eichmann's presence in Argentina, 86–87, 115
    reports from, on Eichmann's location, 92–95, 98, 121–23, 129, 133, 212
    searches for Eichmann in Argentina, 95, 97, 111–14
    Israelis' interest in identity of, 105–7
    Hofstetter's interview with, 108–10, 302, 324
    Israeli dismissal of reports from, 112–14, 124–25
    after Eichmann's trial, 323–24

Hermann, Sylvia
    and search for Eichmann's true identity, 86–87, 92–93, 95–97, 111–12, 122, 133, 240, 343n
    after Eichmann's trial, 324

Heydrich, Reinhard, 19, 32, 34–35, 205, 307

Himmler, Heinrich
    order from, to begin Final Solution, 2, 10, 46
    other orders from, 11, 18–20, 22, 23, 29
    death of, 29
    associates of, 70

Hitler, Adolf
    Hungary's occupation by forces under, 1–4, 9, 10
    Eichmann's responsibilities under, 2–3, 266
    genocidal aims of, 15, 32–34, 46
    death of, 20–22
    supporters of, 27, 70, 73, 76, 87, 93, 94, 102, 116–17, 251
    West German textbooks on, 128
    See also Final Solution; Nazis

Hitler: The Last Ten Days (Boldt), 116–17

Hitler Youth, 26, 27, 45, 73

Hofer, Franz, 19

Hofstetter, Ephraim ("Karl Huppert"), 107–10, 112, 302–3, 308, 324

Holocaust. See Final Solution

Horthy, Miklós, 9–11, 15

Höss, Rudolf, 8–9, 11, 44, 45, 62, 313

Höttl, Wilhelm, 335n, 336n, 338n

Hudal, Alois, 70–71

Hull, William, 317–21

Hungary

Eichmann's determination to remove
  Jews from, 1–11, 35, 39, 54, 256,
  314–16

Nazi support in, 4, 5, 8, 9

Eichmann's visibility in, 42, 192,
  309–10, 314

Jewish sabotage in, 59

See also Budapest; Munkács

Hünsche, Otto, 26

"Huppert, Karl." See Hofstetter, Ephraim

ICRC, 72, 122

Identity(ies)

Eichmann's use of false, in Argentina,
  viii, 69, 72, 78–79, 87, 91, 96, 122,
  132, 224, 251

other former Nazis' use of false, 17–18,
  57–58

Eichmann's use of false, in Europe,
  31–32, 36–38, 42, 48, 49, 62–63,
  67–69, 74

Nazi-hunters' use of false, 52, 135, 152

Eichmann's use of false, with women, 56

Jews' use of false, under Nazis, 59

exposure of some of Eichmann's false,
  62–63, 231–32, 239

prevalence of false, in postwar Europe,
  71

Israelis' interest in Lothar Hermann's,
  105–7

Mossad agents' use of false, 108, 130,
  135, 160, 162, 165, 172, 202, 206, 276

Mossad agents' efforts to discover
  Eichmann's Argentine, 109–10,
  132–33, 135–44, 146–48, 151–52,
  154–59, 163–64, 216

rumors about Eichmann's possible,
  113–15

of Bauer's source on Eichmann, 122,
  123, 125, 346n

establishing true, of Nick Eichmann,
  136–38, 141–42, 150

witnesses on Eichmann's true, 164, 297,
  302, 308–10, 314

Eichmann admits to true, 228, 231–32,
  268, 297

Eichmann's false, for flight to Israel,
  259, 277

Mengele's false, in Argentina, 264

See also Disguises; Passports

Ilani, Ephraim (Mossad agent), 107–8,
  110, 113

on capture team, 163, 168, 173

as Buenos Aires expert, 168

in Buenos Aires, 175, 176, 179, 184, 193,
  194, 215, 234–35, 257, 293

Inbau, Fred, 231

Innsbruck (Austria), 19, 68, 82

International Committee of the Red Cross
  (ICRC), 72, 122

International Military Tribunal (Nuremberg). See Nuremberg trials

Interpol, 95, 99, 149

Irgun (Jewish extremist group), 102, 103,
  131

Iron Guard (Romania), 22, 76

Israel

rumors about Eichmann being in
  postwar, viii, 63, 114

War of Independence in, 65, 131, 153,
  161, 169, 173, 181, 245, 263, 309

Jews resettling in, 81–82, 118–20

significance of trying Eichmann in, 82,
  126, 128, 153, 173–74, 188, 194,
  252–53, 267, 304, 313–16, 322,
  326–27

Nazi-hunters prod, to search for
  Eichmann, 82–85, 98–100, 105–7,
  121–25, 135, 146, 212

West Germany's reparations treaty with,
  98–99, 145

legal justification for prosecuting Nazis
  in, 101, 126, 144–45, 164, 303–4,
  358n

Nazi-hunting as not primary activity of,
  101, 113, 170, 187

war crimes trials in, 101, 107, 311–23

existence of, linked to Holocaust, 104

West Germany's first diplomatic
  meeting with, 145

invited to attend Argentina's 150th

anniversary celebration, 172,
    184–86, 195, 244
ambassador to Argentina from, 206–7,
    213, 265, 304–5
Eichmann knows he's been captured by,
    233
Mossad's efforts to get Eichmann to
    sign agreement to stand trial in,
    241, 255, 267–68, 304, 356n
Eichmann agrees to go to, to stand trial,
    268
Eichmann's arrival in, 295–97
number of Holocaust survivors in,
    304
Eichmann's trial and sentencing in,
    311–19
capital punishment in, 317
See also Ben-Gurion, David; Capture
    operation; Knesset; Mossad;
    Palestine; Transporting; Trial
Israel Mission, 98–100
Italy, 3, 8
Eichmanns smuggled to Argentina via,
    68, 72–73, 79, 91, 122
El Al refueling in, 182, 263, 294, 295

Jackson, Robert, 45
Jänisch, Rudolf, 22, 27, 31, 36–37, 42, 48,
    62
Jaworzno concentration camp, 11–13, 40
Jerusalem. See Israel
Jewish Agency for Palestine, 40, 53, 297
Jewish Brigade, 30, 39, 167
Jewish Settlement Police, 130
Jews
    avengers against ex-Nazis among, viii,
        30–31, 54–56, 62–63, 85, 167–68,
        262–63
    Eichmann's determination to eliminate,
        1–11, 17–20, 34–35
    numbers of, in Hungary before World
        War II, 2
    confiscation of wealth of, by Nazis, 3, 6,
        25, 106, 256, 312
    deportation of, to concentration camps,
        3–9, 13, 15, 18, 19, 33–35, 90, 104–5,
        118, 192, 206, 266, 310, 312, 315–17

ghettoization of, by Nazis, 3, 4–5, 9, 34,
    51, 192, 202, 256, 309–10, 312, 314
strictures on, in Nazi-controlled areas,
    3, 5, 9, 33, 35, 93–94, 99, 161, 256,
    312
numbers of Hungarian, deported by
    Eichmann, 8, 46
extermination of, by Nazis, 8–9, 12–13,
    15–17, 34, 45, 46, 64, 85, 86, 88, 197,
    302, 312–14, 320
as bargaining chips for Germany late in
    war, 10, 18–20
number of, exterminated in Holocaust,
    19, 48, 256, 313
Eichmann denies killing any, 32, 80, 90,
    117–18
number of, targeted for extermination,
    35, 88
number of, in Argentina, 76
as responsible for their fate under
    Nazis, 90
war crimes compensation for, 98–99,
    145
immigration of Moroccan, to Israel,
    104, 202, 245
Holocaust as causing loss of faith of,
    124
as Mossad volunteers, 132–33, 135–43,
    146–48, 155–58, 234–35, 257–58,
    264, 277, 278, 304
See also Anti-Semitism; Concentration
    camps; Deportation; Final
    Solution; Palestine
Jodl, Alfred, 29, 44
"Juan" (sayan), 136–43
Junkers, Werner, 123
Jurmann (German landlady), 255, 257

Kabiri, Oved, 274
Kalmanowitz, Abraham, 84–85
Kaltenbrunner, Ernst, 19–23, 26, 28–29,
    31, 44, 239
"Kaplan, Maurice" (Dr.)
    on capture team, 163, 195, 220, 246, 282
    arrives in Buenos Aires, 206
    in capture operation, 216, 221, 227
    examines Eichmann, 230–31, 279

"Kaplan, Maurice" (Dr.) (*cont.*)
  sedates Eichmann, 253, 276, 279–80,
    292, 294
  on airplane with Eichmann, 284
Kasztner, Rezsö, 101, 107, 256, 344n
Keitel, Wilhelm, 29, 44
Khrushchev, Nikita, 104
Kibbutzim
  Polish, 52, 53
  Latvian, 101–2
  in Palestine, 102, 130, 131, 153, 161, 309
Kistarcsa internment camp (Hungary), 9
Klein, Yosef, 173
  summoning of, to Buenos Aires, 185–86
  learns of Buenos Aires duties, 191–95
  background of, 192
  makes airport arrangements for
    transporting Eichmann, 200–201,
    213–15, 243–44, 252–53, 259, 271–72,
    279, 281, 284–88
  returns to New York, 292–93
"Klement, Nikolas," 136–38, 141–42, 150
  See also Eichmann, Klaus ("Nick")
"Klement, Ricardo"
  as Eichmann's Argentine identity, 69,
    72, 74–75, 78–79, 231, 232, 242
  identified as former Chacabuco Street
    resident, 111, 122
  rumors about, as Eichmann's Argentine
    identity, 115
  Bauer learns true identity of, 122, 124,
    126
  Mossad's attempts to confirm real
    identity of, 132–42, 144
  moves away from Chacabuco Street,
    133, 138
  Mossad tries to discover new address
    for, 136–38
  Mossad considers possibility that
    Eichmann is not, 216
  admits true identity under interroga-
    tion, 230–34
  See also Eichmann, Adolf; Identity(ies)
Knesset, 128, 129, 298–99, 308, 325, 326
Kops, Reinhard, 71, 72
Krawietz, Nellie, 49, 56–57, 62, 66, 67
Kristallnacht, 87, 130, 160–61

Krupp, Gustav, 44
Kuhlmann, Herbert, 73, 78, 91
Kuwait, viii, 120, 121, 123, 128, 149

Landau, Moshe, 312, 315, 316–17
Latvia, 101–2, 312
"Lavi, Meir" (*sayan*), 235, 278
Leers, Johannes von, 114
Less, Avner, 302–3, 308, 313, 317
Levavi, Arye, 207, 265, 304–5
Ley, Robert, 30, 44
License plates, 203, 205, 215, 228, 234
Lidice (Poland), 312
Liebl, Vera (Vera Eichmann's maiden
    name)
  Vera's use of, to travel, 79, 81, 139
  See also Eichmann, Vera (Veronika)
    Liebl
Liebl family, 64, 105, 128, 133–34, 144
Life magazine, 88, 307
Lindhorst, Anna, 66, 67
Linz (Austria)
  Eichmann raised in, 19, 21, 24–25, 32,
    41–42
  Wiesenthal in, 39, 60, 64, 80, 83
  Diamant in, 59–61
  rumors of Eichmann's death in, 85
Lithuania, 312
Lodz (Poland), 34
"Lorenzo" (*sayan*), 138
Lühr, Heinz, 78
Lukas, Karl, 63, 64
Lüneburg Heath (Germany), 54–55,
    62–63, 66, 71
Lvov (Poland), 85

Madagascar, 34, 261
Majdanek concentration camp, 307, 312
Malkin, Fruma, 170, 197, 247, 327
Malkin, Peter
  on capture team, 163, 166–71, 173,
    199–200, 203–6, 210–11, 285
  reads Eichmann file, 168, 170, 196
  fears Eichmann, 168–69, 218
  background of, 169–70
  and capture plans, 194, 208–10, 215, 216,
    219–20

arrives in Buenos Aires, 195–97
mother of, 197, 301, 326–27
in capture operation, 221–28
with Eichmann in Tira, 231, 237,
    246–47, 260–61, 266–69, 274, 276,
    279–80, 355n
searches for Eichmann's missing glasses,
    236
sketches Eichmann, 246–47, 266, 325
leaves Buenos Aires, 293
returns to Israel, 300
after Eichmann's trial, 325, 326–27
Manor, Amos, 164, 170, 254
Maoz (safe house), 184–85, 190–91, 201–3,
    259, 273, 274, 277
Map (of capture operation), vi
Margaret (princess), 292–93
Mast, Baron, 82–83
Matteson, Robert, 28–29, 31
Mauthausen concentration camp, 1, 2,
    39–40
Medad, Yaakov, 172, 177, 184, 203, 285
searches for safe houses, 189–91, 194,
    204
searches for cars, 204
with Eichmann at Tira, 229, 237, 267,
    268, 274
"wife" of, 245–47
Meding, Holger, 340n
Meir, Golda, 173, 235, 248, 299, 305, 324
Mengele, Josef
Nazi deeds of, 65, 123, 188, 240, 254, 257
smuggling of, out of Europe, 71
in Argentina, 91
West German arrest warrant for, 123
Harel hopes to seize, 188–89, 240,
    254–55, 257–59, 264–65, 274,
    278–79, 325
Eichmann denies knowing whereabouts
    of, 240, 254–55
speculation about location of, 263, 272
alias of, 264
rumor that Hermann was, 324
spotted in Brazil, 325
Mercedes-Benz factory (Buenos Aires),
    116, 149, 220, 242–43
"Michael" (sayan), 146–48

Mildenstein, Edler von, 32–33
Minsk (Soviet Union), 34
Mohnke, Wilhelm, 73
Momm, Eberhard, 114
Mösenbacher, Maria, 58, 60–61, 64
Mossad
in Eichmann's capture, vii–ix, 221–29
agents who lost families to Holocaust,
    viii, 131, 134, 170, 173, 182, 197, 202,
    245, 259
Harel as chief of, 100–105, 134
early search for Eichmann in Argentina
    by, 100–114
Nazi-hunting as not primary activity of,
    101, 113, 170, 187
false identities used by, 108, 130, 135,
    160, 162, 165, 172, 202, 206, 276
Ben-Gurion as authorizing, to search
    for, capture, and transport
    Eichmann, 126, 128, 129, 187–88,
    207
considers assassinating Eichmann, 126,
    167–68, 199, 237
Eichmann files of, 131–32
sayanim use by, 132–33, 135–42, 146–48,
    155–58, 234–35, 257–58, 264, 277,
    278, 304
tries to interview Eichmann and Liebl
    families in West Germany, 133–36
surveillance of Garibaldi Street house
    by, 151–52, 154–59, 178–79, 183–84,
    190–91, 194, 195–200, 203–6, 219
consequences for, if Eichmann capture
    fails, 152, 187, 217
significance of Eichmann's capture to,
    153
holds Eichmann in Buenos Aires safe
    house, 230–34, 236–41, 244–48,
    255–57, 260–61, 266–69, 274–75
efforts of, to get Eichmann to sign
    agreement to stand trial, 241, 255,
    267–68, 304, 356n
transports Eichmann to Israel, 282–95
as not revealing role in Eichmann's
    capture, 300–301
and publication of Eichmann's
    memoirs, 307

Mossad (*cont.*)
  recognition of role of, in capture,
      324–26
  See also Capture operation; Harel, Isser;
      Safe houses; Transporting; *names of
      specific agents*
Müller, Heinrich, 18, 33, 35, 65, 325
Munkács (Hungary), 4–8, 13, 309, 310, 314
Mussolini, Benito, 69, 251, 305

Nagar, Shlomo, 320
Nazis
  Eichmann's role among, viii, 1–4, 6–11,
      35, 41, 45–48, 62, 90, 92, 100–101,
      104–5, 121, 168, 218, 245, 256, 298,
      308, 312–13
  occupation and removal of Jews from
      Hungary by, 1–11, 35, 39, 54, 256,
      314–16
  confiscation of Jewish wealth by, 3, 6,
      25, 106, 256, 312
  Roosevelt's call to punish, 8, 15
  scientists among, 16, 69, 345n
  postwar life plans of, 17–18
  SD unit of, 21, 27, 32–34, 205, 338n
  Allied search for former, 25–31, 41–43,
      48
  branches of, 27
  Eichmann's rise among, 32–35
  Einsatzgruppen and, 34, 55, 65
  Friedman's search for former, 51–54,
      57–61, 65–66
  number of, involved in war crimes, 65
  smuggling of former, out of Europe,
      66–69, 91, 111, 191
  Buenos Aires network of supporters
      and former, 69–72, 75–78, 87–93,
      116, 125, 152, 157, 224, 237, 240–41,
      250–51, 265–66, 276, 285, 288–89
  Eichmann's ID number among, 232, 233
  See also Concentration camps;
      Deportation; Final Solution;
      Kristallnacht; Neo-Nazis; War
      criminals; *names of specific Nazis*
Neo-Nazis, 127–29, 157, 324
Nesiahu, Judith, 245–46, 268, 280, 293

Netherlands, 3, 70, 90
Neurath, Konstantin von, 44
New Zealand, 121
Nir, Arye, 318–21
NKVD (Soviet secret service), 30
Nordhausen concentration camp, 16
Nuremberg Laws, 33, 99
Nuremberg trials, 43–48, 57, 63, 65, 70,
      240, 303, 312

Ober-Dachstetten (Germany), 42, 43,
      48–50, 56, 62, 63, 84
Oberländer, Theodore, 127–28
Office of Strategic Services (OSS), 39–41,
      53
  See also CIA
Ohrdurf concentration camp, 14, 16, 17
Olivos neighborhood (Buenos Aires), 86,
      87, 91–92, 109, 122
  Eichmann's house in, 95, 106–7, 111–13,
      115, 122, 132–33, 136–38, 141, 144,
      279
OSS. *See* Office of Strategic Services

Palestine
  Jewish emigration to, as answer to
      "Jewish problem," 10, 33, 90, 261,
      315
  Great Britain and, 30, 40, 102, 103,
      130–31, 153–54, 169
  Eichmann travels to, 33, 261
  rumors of Eichmann's birth in, 39, 41,
      58, 104, 114
  Jews emigrating to, after World War II,
      40, 51–53, 134, 173, 202, 309
  Jews emigrating to, before World War
      II, 102, 130–31, 160, 170
  kibbutzim in, 102, 130, 131, 153, 161,
      309
  killing of youths from, 325
  See also Brichah; Haganah; Israel;
      Jewish Brigade
Palmach (Haganah strike force), 153–54
Papen, Franz von, 44
"Paperclip" capture operation, 16
"Partisan's Song," 229

Passports
  Eichmann's, from Red Cross, 72, 122
  Vera Eichmann's, 79, 81, 135
  for capture team, 165, 202, 277
  forging of, in Buenos Aires, 201–3, 259,
    277
Patton, George, 16
Peleg, Adi, 181–82, 252, 253, 273, 281, 283,
    290
Perón, Eva, 79, 80
Perón, Juan
  and ex-Nazis, 69–72, 76, 89, 91, 152
  terrorist groups linked to, 168, 189, 201,
    247, 265, 354n
Photographs (of Eichmann), 4, 42
  difficulty of finding, 4, 42, 47, 57–61
  distribution of, 61, 64
  Mösenbacher's, 61, 64, 104, 135, 164, 167
  on his Red Cross passport, 72
  Wiesenthal's copy of, 83, 135
  Bauer's copy of, 95, 96
  as a Nazi officer, 104–5
  Mossad's interest in obtaining new, 109,
    112, 154–59
  older, as basis of comparison with
    current Eichmann, 135, 151, 164, 167
  Aharoni takes new, 154–59, 164, 167
  Mossad's taking of, for passport, 259
Photographs (of Klaus "Nick" Eichmann),
    112
Photographs (of Vera Eichmann), 146–47
Pier, Arthur (Ben-Natan, Asher), 51–54,
    57–59, 61, 65, 104, 120, 337n
Pilecki, Witold, 15
Pius XII (pope), 9, 71
Plaszow concentration camp, 40
Poland
  Jewish uprisings in, 2, 90
  Jewish genocide in, 3, 34, 197, 313
  Red Army advancing to, 12
  resistance movement in, 15, 59
  Germany's occupation of, 33–34, 39, 170
  See also Auschwitz-Birkenau concentra-
    tion camp
Pollard, Jonathan, 325
"Pooch, Hilel" (sayan), 257–58, 264, 278

"Pooch, Neomi" (sayan), 257–58
POWs
  German, 31, 65, 245
  Eichmann as, 36–38, 49, 59, 239
  Polish, 52
Prague, 10, 19, 63, 64
  See also Theresienstadt concentration
    camp
Press
  on concentration camps, 16–17
  on Eichmann's deeds, 56, 79–80, 92,
    149, 235
  on war crimes trials, 62, 92, 120, 128,
    315, 322–23
  rumors about Eichmann's location in,
    62–63, 120–21, 128, 149
  on anti-Semitism in Buenos Aires, 76
  on flight for Israel's anniversary visit to
    Argentina, 180
  on fresh search for Eichmann, 241
  capture team looking for news that
    Eichmann's capture was revealed in,
    247, 258, 276, 293
  on Eichmann's capture and presence in
    Israel, 300
  on who should try Eichmann, 303–4,
    306
  on Hermann, 324
Priebke, Erich, 71

Rademacher, Franz, 114
Radom (Poland), 51–53
Raeder, Erich, 44
Ramim (safe house), 215–18
Raphael, Gideon, 40, 337n
Recife (Brazil), 182, 263, 269–71, 273, 282,
    286, 288–89
Red Army
  approaches Hungary, 2, 5, 8, 10–11
  approaches Poland, 12
  rescues Sapir, 13, 309
  approaches Germany, 14, 19
  liberates Auschwitz, 17
  seizes Budapest, 17–18
  seizes Berlin, 20
  Nazi war criminals' treatment by, 30–31

Reich Security Main Office (RSHA), 19–23, 35, 46–47, 49, 117
    See also Department IVB$_4$
Reid, John, 231
Remer, Otto, 94
"Rendi" (*sayan*), 157–58
Reparations treaty (between West Germany and Israel), 98–99, 145
Rettenbach-Alm (Austria), 23–24, 26–27
Ribbentrop, Joachim von, 30, 44, 45, 123
"Roberto" (*sayan*), 132–33, 157
Romania, 3, 8, 10, 22, 76
Rome (Italy), 182, 263, 294, 295
Ronen, Azriel, 274
Roosevelt, Franklin, 8, 9, 15
Roschmann, Eduard, 71
Rosen, Pinhas, 164
Rosenberg, Alfred, 44
RSHA. *See* Reich Security Main Office
Rudel, Hans-Ulrich, 89
Russians. *See* Red Army; Soviet Union

Safe houses
    for Eichmann and Mossad agents, 153, 212, 217
    renting, 166, 172
    capture team gathers at, 176, 215–16
    heightened security when moving Eichmann to and from, 180, 189
    search for, 184–85, 189–91, 194–95
    need to switch, 209, 210
    getting ready to leave, 277, 293
    See also Doron; Maoz; Ramim; Tira
Salta (ship), 79
San Fernando neighborhood (Buenos Aires)
    Eichmann builds new house in, 115–16
    identification of, as Eichmann's new neighborhood, 137, 138
    Aharoni locates Eichmann's house in, 141–45
    land records for Eichmann's house in, 146–48
    See also Garibaldi Street
Sapir, Zeev, 4–7, 11–14, 309–10, 313–15, 334n

Sassen, Saskia, 90, 250
Sassen, Willem
    as recorder of Eichmann's memories, 87–91, 117, 149, 316, 317, 359n
    background of, 88
    Eichmann's sons visit, 242, 250–51
    sells rights to Eichmann's autobiography, 307
    as possible informant, 346n
Sauckel, Fritz, 29–30, 44
Sayanim, 132–33, 135–43, 146–48, 155–58, 234–35, 257–58, 264, 277, 278, 304
Schacht, Hjalmar, 44
Scheide, Rudolf, 37, 63
Schirach, Baldur von, 44, 45
Schmidt, Francisco, 111–13
Schoegl, Richard, 53
Schröder, Gerhard, 128
Schüle, Erwin, 119, 123, 128–29, 212
Schwammberger, Josef, 71
Scientists (Nazi), 16, 69, 345n
SD unit (Nazi Party), 21, 27, 32–34, 205, 338n
Servatius, Robert, 308, 315
Seyss-Inquart, Arthur, 44
Shalom, Avraham
    background of, 160–61
    on capture team, 160–63, 165, 167, 173, 183–85, 195–96, 208, 215, 218, 237, 264
    on Malkin, 169–70
    in charge of safe houses and routes in Buenos Aires, 172, 189–90, 195–96, 203–4, 219, 234, 244, 265, 271, 273, 277–79
    in Buenos Aires, 176–79, 183–85, 189–91, 195–96, 206
    in capture operation, 216, 221, 223, 225, 227–29
    with Eichmann in Tira, 230–32
    in charge of getting Eichmann from safe house to airplane, 244, 252–53
    and Mengele plan, 254
    waits for Eichmann's arrival at airport, 281–83, 285
    leaves Buenos Aires, 293

hears announcement of Eichmann's arrival in Israel, 300–301
after Eichmann's death, 325, 327
Shaul, Shaul, 263, 270, 274, 282, 286–88, 291–95
Shimoni, Yehuda, 171, 181, 185, 186, 195, 201
  background of, 173
  briefs Klein on his Buenos Aires duties, 191–93
  coordinates El Al's departure from Israel, 214, 263, 272
Shin Bet (Israeli internal security service)
  Harel as head of, 103, 104, 134, 187
  Aharoni as chief interrogator for, 124, 131, 231, 301
  Gat as agent of, 134
  Eitan as administrator in, 153
  Shalom as agent of, 160–63
  capture team's connections with, 163
  legal advice sought by, for capture operation, 164
  Malkin as agent of, 166–71
  Eichmann detained by, in Israel, 296
  recognition of role of, in capture operation, 324–26
  informers for, 344n
Shinar, Felix, 98–100, 105
Ships (to transport Eichmann from Argentina to Israel), 171, 184, 244, 253
Sima, Horia, 22, 26
Slavic people, 128
Sobibor concentration camp, 90, 312
Socialists, 86, 94, 99
Solingen (Germany), 32, 233
Soviet Union
  and extermination of Jews, 15, 34, 312
  interest of, in German scientists, 16
  Nazi war criminals sent to, 30, 71
  at Nuremberg trials, 44, 45
  Eichmann tells friend he's leaving for, 66
  and cold war, 67, 85, 161
  softening of Stalin's policies in, 104
  See also Allies; Red Army

Spain, 172, 251
Speer, Albert, 29, 44
Stalin, Joseph, 15, 30, 104
Der Stern, 307
Stern Gang (Jewish extremist group), 102, 103
Streicher, Julius, 30, 44
Suez War, 104, 113
Sweden, 9, 94
Syria, 84, 113

Taboada, Diógenes, 304–5
Tabor, Moshe
  on capture team, 162–63, 167–69, 173, 194, 199, 203, 219–20
  background of, 167–68
  at first meeting of capture team, 167–69
  as capture team's handyman, 203–6, 215, 234, 259, 277
  in capture operation, 208–9, 216, 221–25, 227, 228
  with Eichmann in Tira, 237, 245, 274
  in trip to airport with Eichmann, 280, 285
  with Eichmann in Israel, 296
  does not tell about role in capture, 301
  after Eichmann's death, 325–326
Tacuara (organization), 251, 265, 305, 354n
Tattoos
  for concentration camp inmates, 12, 315, 320
  for SS members, 36, 49, 231
Theresienstadt concentration camp, 18–20
Tira (safe house), 194, 203, 211–12, 217, 218, 224
  room for hiding Eichmann in, 211–12, 215, 219
  Eichmann taken to, 228–29
  Eichmann's stay in, 230–34, 236–41, 244–48, 255–57, 260–61, 266–69, 274–75
  contingency plans for police attack on or Eichmann's escape from, 237–38
  emotional difficulty of team's caring for Eichmann at, 244–48, 255–60, 266
  Harel visits Eichmann at, 255–57

Tira (safe house) (*cont.*)
  preparations at, to get Eichmann to
    plane, 258–60, 276–77, 279–80
  cleaning and leaving of, 293
Tirosh, Baruch, 181, 182
Tohar, Zvi (El Al pilot)
  and flight from Israel to Argentina,
    181–82, 244, 263–64, 269–74
  on flight from Argentina to Israel,
    281–82, 284–88, 290–96, 324
Trains. *See* Deportation (of Jews to
    concentration camps)
TransAer, 200, 214
Transporting (of Eichmann from
    Argentina to Israel)
  plans for, 128, 153, 171–73, 180–83,
    193–95, 243–44, 273–74
  Harel in charge of, 168, 171–73, 191,
    193–95, 213–15, 234–35, 243–44,
    273–74, 277–79, 282, 283, 285–88,
    290, 292, 294, 295–98
  dates for, 191, 195, 200, 237, 264,
    273–74
  sedating of Eichmann for, 253, 271, 276,
    279–80, 292, 294
  description of, 282–85, 290–95
  See also El Al
Treblinka concentration camp, 312, 313
Trial (Eichmann's)
  "following orders" as defense in, 32, 74,
    90, 105, 117–18, 241, 260–61, 266,
    303, 315–16, 319, 324
  as opportunity to educate the world
    about the Holocaust, 128, 153,
    173–74, 216, 267, 304, 313–16,
    322–23, 326
  in Israel, 311–17
  verdict, sentencing, appeals, and
    execution related to, 317–19
  international impact of, 322–23
  sons' view of, 324
Tucumán (Argentina)
  Eichmann's work in, 78, 80, 89, 91, 122,
    142
  Dieter Eichmann says father is in, 139,
    144, 146, 148, 151, 157

Ulm (West Germany), 120
United Arab Republic, 113
United Jewish Appeal, 156
United Nations, 28, 305, 358n
United States
  rumors about Eichmann being in
    postwar, viii
  on calls for punishment of war
    criminals, 8, 15
  postwar interest of, in former Nazis, 16,
    71, 114
  at Nuremberg trials, 44, 45
  and cold war, 67, 85
  Jews resettling in, 81, 324n
  Bauer asks for assistance from, in
    extraditing Nazi war criminals, 146
  civilian airlines of, 263
  war archives in, 308
  See also Allies; CIA; CIC
United States Army, 14–17, 26
  See also Allies; CIC
University of Buenos Aires, 305

"Vardi, Yitzhak" (financier), 156–57
Vatican. *See* Catholic Church and officials
Vicente López district (Buenos Aires), 86,
    136, 255, 264, 278
Vienna (Austria)
  Eichmann in, 33, 42, 54, 58, 196–97, 297
  Friedman in, 51, 52, 57–61, 65–66, 81, 82
  Diamant in, 59–60
Volk, Luba
  as El Al representative in Buenos Aires,
    185–86, 193, 251–52, 272, 281
  as ignorant of flight's purpose, 201
  flees Buenos Aires, 305–6

War Crimes Unit, 40
War criminals
  Allies' call to punish, 8, 15
  Eichmann's concern about being
    identified among, 10, 24, 42–43,
    48–49, 56–57
  lists of, 10, 15–16, 24, 28, 31, 40, 48,
    63–64
  trials called for, 15, 53, 126, 298

Kaltenbrunner's efforts to dissociate
   himself from, 22
Allies' search for, 27–31
Jews searching for Nazi, 30–31, 51–56,
   60, 62–66, 80–85, 134–36, 167–68,
   262–63
trials for, in Germany, 43–48, 57, 63, 65,
   70, 92–95, 120, 128, 303, 312, 323
cold war's impact on hunt for, 65, 66,
   85, 114
estimate of numbers of Nazi, 65
Catholic officials not accepting term of,
   70–71
smuggling of, by United States, 71, 114
number of, in Buenos Aires, 76
West Germany's claim of jurisdiction
   over, 84, 126, 144, 164, 303–4
West Germany's lack of interest in
   pursuing, 84–85, 98–99, 115, 122–23,
   164
hunting, as not Israel's main priority,
   101, 113, 170, 187
trials for, in Israel, 101, 107, 311–23
Israel's interest in bringing Eichmann
   to trial as, 126, 166, 173–74, 216,
   298–99, 358n
United States asked for help in
   extraditing, 146
Eichmann tried as, in Israel, 311–17
continuing search for, after Eichmann's
   death, 323, 325
See also names of specific war criminals
Warsaw (Poland), 2, 59, 90
Wedeles, Shmuel, 263, 269, 274, 280–81,
   284, 290
Der Weg (Nazi newspaper), 89, 115
Weiden (Germany), 37–38
Weisl, Joseph, 57–59, 339n
Weiss, Kurt, 114
Weizmann, Chaim, 171
West German Office for the Prosecution
   of National Socialist Criminals, 120
West Germany (Federal Republic of
   Germany)
   rumors about Eichmann being in
      postwar, viii, 113

as having jurisdiction over war
   criminals, 84, 126, 144, 164, 303–4
lack of interest in pursuing war
   criminals by, 84–85, 98–99, 115,
   122–23, 127–28, 164, 345n
war crimes trials in, 92–95, 120, 128, 323
constitution of, 93, 94
reparations treaty of, with Israel, 98–99,
   145
former Nazis in government of, 99, 115,
   127–28, 145, 157, 306–7, 316, 323,
   343n, 345n
as not following up on rumors about
   Eichmann's location, 114–15
Eichmann prefers to be tried in, 117, 241
Bauer seeks Eichmann's extradition to,
   125, 126
neo-Nazi outbreaks in, 127–29, 145
silence about Holocaust in, 128
Mossad tries to interview Eichmann
   and Liebl families in, 133–36
Israel's first diplomatic meeting with,
   145
reaction in, to news of Eichmann's
   capture and forthcoming trial,
   306–7
war archives in, 308, 313
Vera Eichmann returns to, after
   Eichmann's death, 324
See also specific places and people in
Wiesel, Elie, 322
Wiesenthal, Pauline, 308
Wiesenthal, Simon
   search for Eichmann by, viii, 63–66,
      80–85, 115, 212–13
   background of, 39–40, 85
   learns about Eichmann, 39–41, 61
   works with other Nazi-hunters, 60,
      134–36
   stamp collecting by, 81, 82
   learns that Eichmann is in Argentina,
      82–83
   Eichmann file of, 85, 104, 164, 308
   urges Israel to offer reward for locating
      Eichmann, 135
   impact of capture operation on, 323

Wisliceny, Dieter, 46–48, 58, 335n
World Jewish Congress, 83, 121, 212
World War I, 32

Yad Vashem, 82, 85, 104, 118, 308
Yarden (boat), 320–21
Yemen, 171
Yiddish, 40, 41

Yitzhaki, Haim, 297–98
"Yossef," 132, 139, 155, 277

"Zichroni," 259, 277
Zinn, Georg-August, 99, 343n
Zionism, 33, 101–2
    See also Israel; Palestine
Zorea, Meir, 262